Debates on Civilization in the Muslim World

Debates on Civilization in the Muslim World

Critical Perspectives on Islam and Modernity

edited by
Lutfi Sunar

OXFORD
UNIVERSITY PRESS

OXFORD
UNIVERSITY PRESS

Oxford University Press is a department of the University of Oxford.
It furthers the University's objective of excellence in research, scholarship,
and education by publishing worldwide. Oxford is a registered trademark of
Oxford University Press in the UK and in certain other countries.

Published in India by
Oxford University Press
YMCA Library Building, 1 Jai Singh Road, New Delhi 110 001, India

ISBN-13: 978-0-19-946688-7
ISBN-10: 0-19-946688-2

Typeset in ScalaPro 10/13
by The Graphics Solution, New Delhi 110092
Printed in India by Replika Press Pvt. Ltd

Contents

PART III   MODERNIZATION, GLOBALIZATION, AND THE FUTURE OF THE CIVILIZATION DEBATE

Preface

The term 'civilization' plays a significant role in today's world. Through the ages the term has been discussed by those who considered themselves civilized and also by those who rejected the term. The discussion still continues. The word is used today in a broad context and on many different levels: from social sciences to international politics, from interreligious issues to cultural research, and from history to social identities. Most of the time, the concept of civilization is understood to have a positive connotation. Among these connotations it is used (*a*) to describe the entirety of collective human values, (*b*) as an expression of a humanitarian–legal–moral attitude and consequential behaviours against barbarianism and therefore as a world view which results from the idea of being civilized, and (*c*) as a vision of existence and order. On the other hand, the concept of civilization is also viewed as being an abstraction of modernity and secularism. In any case, it has become an obscure historical term used in national, cultural, and political contexts.

In the social sciences, however, civilization is one of the most oft-debated concepts. But the debates around civilization are still framed by Western assumptions and concerns—as with the very idea of civilization itself. Nevertheless, civilization remains a central theme for non-Western theorists, especially in the Muslim world. Since its birth as a concept, civilization has been defined and brought into existence by an encounter with the 'other'. Similarly, Muslim communities have also attempted, in various forms, to place themselves somewhere related to what they saw as civilization. This encounter with civilization as a fact is comprised of a series of investigations that include multi-dimensional analyses of frameworks of evaluation, methods of interpretation, and, eventually, attempts to go beyond the concept itself. All of these developments contribute to the formation of the very concept.

The authors in this volume challenge the embedded prejudices within social theory and offer alternative viewpoints emerging from the different ways in which the Muslim world has perceived the issue. There are various civilizations within the so-called Western and non-Western worlds—neither civilization nor culture is homogenous. Relations between societies do not necessarily imply superiority and triumph of one civilization over another, but involve a give-and-take approach. Even resistances to Western modernization are not homogenous, but involve rejection as well as envy. This book offers a complex assessment of key ideas in the modernist discourse from non-ethnocentric perspectives and offers a new understanding of civilization.

Around this aim, the book is divided into three parts dedicated to the following: (*a*) defining and discussing civilization; (*b*) debates on the civilization in the contemporary Muslim world; and (*c*) modernization, globalization, and the future of the civilization debate. The first part reviews, analyses, and discusses definitions of civilization and modernity, and the Eurocentric understanding of these notions. The second part examines non-Western civilizations' efforts of resistance against assimilation by Western perspectives and dominance. The third part focuses on the future of the debate in a broader context. The overall objective of this volume is to expose complex issues for further discussion pertaining to modernization, globalization, (de) colonization, and multiculturalism.

In a time period in which shortcomings and problems of change are deeply felt within the Islamic world, this book has been prepared with the hope that it will contribute to build a better and more just world order with its specific civilizational analysis. The overall belief in the book is that when they are able to overcome their civilizational crises, Muslim societies have a lot to contribute to our world and our future.

Lutfi Sunar
Istanbul, September 2016

Acknowledgements

This project has a huge amount of work, research, and dedication in its background. It would not have been possible to realize this project if I did not have the support of many individuals and organizations. Therefore I would like to extend my sincere gratitude to all of them.

The idea of this book emerged as an outcome of an international conference, 'The Civilization Debate', hosted by ILKE (Ilim Kültür Eğitim Derneği, Association for Science Culture and Education) and supported by Uskudar Municipality in February 2013 in Istanbul. The book has been formulated with some of the papers presented at the conference and with new chapters that have been added later on in order to deal with all encounters with civilization in the Muslim world. I would like to thank our supporters from ILKE and the Uskudar Municipality for their support.

I am also grateful to Scientific Studies Association (ILEM) for providing their expertise and technical support. Without their superior knowledge and experience, this book could not have been edited.

I would also like to thank the contributors, who hail from different countries and academic institutions. Their ideas and the discussions paved the way and prepared the framework into which this volume fits. I am grateful to all of them for their meticulous work, collaboration, and patience through the publication process. One of them, Farid Alatas, deserves special mention. He encouraged me to engage with this project and present it to Oxford University Press. I am thankful to him for this and other kinds of support that I have received from him throughout my academic life.

Of course, this book would not have been realized without the help and support of Oxford University Press and its very kind staff. From the first moment that we contacted them and shared the idea of this edited volume, they encouraged us to work together on this project. For that reason, I specifically thank the editorial team for their supportive attitude and availability whenever I needed help. I would also like to thank the two 'anonymous' reviewers for their invaluable insights.

Lastly, I would like to thank my colleagues Firdevs Bulut and Senanur Avcı Tosun for their invaluable contribution to the entire process of bringing the volume together. This book would not have been completed without their efforts on every aspect of the articles and the volume as a whole.

Lutfi Sunar
Istanbul, October 2016

Introduction

Debates on Civilization, Islam,
and Modernity
Some Critical Perspectives on the Current Agenda

Lutfi Sunar

Today it is possible to talk about a growing set of research focused on the developmental journey of civilization. Sigmund Freud's *Civilization and Its Discontents* (1962), Theodor Adorno and Max Horkheimer's *Dialectic of Enlightenment* (1972), Herbert Marcuse's *One-Dimensional Man* (1968), Michel Foucault's *The Birth of the Prison* (1995), Norbert Elias' *Civilizing Process* (1978), Edward Said's *Orientalism* (1977) and *Culture and Imperialism* (1994) are a few examples. In the social sciences, the concept of civilization has been a highly debated one (see Árnason 2003).

In order to introduce the debate on civilization, first we need to critically take stock of the approach towards the roots and formation of the concept and its definition as it stands today. In order to do this, we will start with an elaborate analysis of the formation of civilization, as a definitive category, in Enlightenment thought. In this way, we can delineate the necessary ground for understanding the historical context of the debates occurring around the concept of civilization in the Islamic world. Then it would be necessary to evaluate the problem of civilization with different approaches in various Muslim geographies.

A very wide spectrum of ideas and approaches is emerging: from a fundamental rejectionist–traditionalist approach to a conformist one. At the same time, changes in the meaning of civilization in the West, with the emergence of progressivism and positivism, along with critiques of its meaning have had a tremendous effect on the meaning of civilization in the Muslim world. Today, debates around civilization have evolved from an ontological to epistemological, and even a political, position. In Muslim countries, civilization as a concept may not have been developed and used in order to constitute an identity. However, the persistence of global inequality, violence and terror, globalization and multiculturalism, all have reinforced the need to define the idea of civilization and its future prospects.

BROKEN MIRRORS, DISTORTED REFLECTIONS

In the non-Western world, encounters with civilization are shaped by a tragic sense of defeat and loss (see Scott 2004). Dostoevsky's Underground Man had strange feelings before the Crystal Palace. A stupendous officer in uniform stimulated a complex of civilization inside him. He approached his own people with this complex, and tried to get rid of this complex by crushing them. *Notes from the Underground* is without a doubt among one of the masterpieces describing the tragic encounter of a non-Western man with civilization. We find a similar encounter in nineteenth-century Istanbul, in Ahmet Mithat's novel *Felatun Bey ile Rakım Efendi* (2005). Felatun Bey is a cheeky spendthrift whose hilarious attempt to be a civilized gentleman presents a tragicomical case. This snobbish man actually knows that everything he does to be civilized has nothing to do with civilization, but he can only come this far in civilizing himself by imitating everything. His so-called modern actions remind us of characters in Charlie Chaplin movies where they pit themselves against machinery. Octavio Paz's Pachuco (1962) also came in contact with civilization through a Yankee who disdained him in New York. He had strange feelings about him and he did everything in order to be like him. However, in the end, he is reminded of the fact that he is a pachuco, regardless of what he does, and that he cannot be a real son of civilization. For this reason, Paz (1962, p. 11), in his monumental work, *The Labyrinth of Solitude*, notes that 'the history

of Mexico is the history of man seeking his parentage, his origins....
He wants to go back beyond the catastrophe he suffered; he wants
to be a son again, to return to the center of that life from which he
was separated'. Frantz Fanon (1967) himself goes through a similar
experience in Paris. When he decides to live in Paris as any other
Parisian, he discovers the bleak reality of 'our good negro' attitude.
Fanon realizes that Western civilization has certain doubts about
black-skinned people like him, and he is constantly reminded of the
fact that he can never be a civilized person like the white men. The
most he can obtain from such a civilization is to be a submissive-
silent man who adopts Western values. However, when he demands
civilization as a whole, he is restricted by impassable borders. Thus
Fanon, as Robert Bernasconi (2001) has aptly expressed, sees the racist nature of civilization. He then turns his imperious master's own
jargon upside down and starts to question them.

In fact, similar encounters with civilization are also present in the
homeland of civilization. One of these encounters happens in Franz
Kafka's (2009) escort in Wien. His metamorphosed cockroach man
is desperate against civilization that totally captures him, his family,
and society. Even his cockroach-ness cannot enable him to get rid of
the desperate hopes of belonging in the civilized world. His attitude
is actually a way of resisting the covert violence that surrounds him.
Albert Camus' (1989) civilized stranger understands the real meaning of civilization in other lands. His version of civilization is that
of a white one taken to a colony. However, this civilization is useless
both for the 'taker' and the 'taken'. Its violence affects everyone and
makes them a stranger to themselves. In any case, civilization comes
with a cost. But this cost, as Jean P. Sartre (2004) puts it, is paid by
the other.

'Civilization' is probably the most tragic subject of the last two
centuries. With its emergence, implications, what it covers and leaves
out, civilization has become an indispensable part of the debates
about modern society. Once modernity is defined in terms of what
is civilized during the Enlightenment, it remains impossible to talk
about civilization as a distinct social phenomenon. On the other
hand, civilization bears the heavy burden of the violence exerted upon
other societies for the sake of civilizing them. Similarly, civilization
in non-Western societies is one of the first names of the white and

magnificent master; it is a mirror reflecting shiny dreams and lost hopes that can never be reached. Then it reflects a focal point of fury, and lastly the localness at hand, which in other words, is the attachment, the feeling of belonging to the defined idea of civilization. And this mirror, as Darius Shayegan (1997) clearly expresses, is broken and does nothing but create a wounded consciousness.

CIVILIZATION AS A UNIT OF ANALYSIS

At the beginning of the twentieth century, Max Weber transformed civilization into a macro-level analysis unit in social sciences (see Kalberg 2015). His civilizations, which he defines on the axis of religions, show an integrative existence against a unified and unique West (Weber 2009). While dealing with connections that tie social phenomena to each other in history, he also transforms this into an effort to view the larger picture of the historical integrity of the West. According to him, the West is an integrative civilization comprised of separate societies. In the contemporary world, there are some other civilizations such as the Chinese, Indian, and Islamic civilizations that are also defined on a religious axis. Weber says that every civilization has a unique frame of mind and this framework largely affects the way they think. His purpose, in contrast to what Oswald Spengler (1926) claims, is to show that the uniqueness of Western civilization is not in decline, but rather it will be the one and only civilization still preserving its own vitality.

In *A Study of History*, philosopher of history Arnold Toynbee (1935) carried this analysis forward and described civilizations as main actors in history. Toynbee sees civilization as the foundational unit of historical analysis and he defines it by combining religious characteristics with geographical and political aspects. Toynbee has a cyclical historical approach in principle and his real purpose is to find out the lines of rise and fall of history and to understand the historical cycle. Similar to him, in *Social and Cultural Dynamics*, Pitirim A. Sorokin (1937) is interested in the essential outline of social change, and especially tries to reveal the characteristics which keep a civilization alive. Toynbee (1948) and Sorokin (1941) follow Spengler with a specific pessimism pertaining to the period between the two wars, and they believe that Western civilization, having lost its vitality, was headed for the last round-up and thus started to be destructive.[1] Another historian coming after them, Fernand Braudel (1995) finds the middle ground between Weber and Toynbee. According to him, civilizations that are identified with certain geographies have preserved their status as a historical subject/actor. Although they defeat each other from time to time, especially each one of the three ancient Mediterranean civilizations, Rome (Christian West), Slavic (Byzantine, Russian), and Mesopotamian (Islamic), they preserved their own geography and thus survived (Braudel 2001). Civilization, just like geography, is a destiny and there is no way of escaping from it. In the end, according to him, there is nothing in civilizational histories but long-term repetitions.

After World War II, there is a consensus among modernization theorists that the modern West civilized and modernized all others because of a nineteenth-century global optimism. This idea started to decline in the 1970s; however, it re-emerged in a different form with the collapse of the Eastern bloc and with the end of the Cold War. Francis Fukuyama's enlightened prophecy that history has come to an end ushered in a new global optimism since the 1990s. In *The End of the History and the Last Man*, Fukuyama (1992) claims that history really has come to an end and Western civilization remains the one and only true civilization, eliminating all its alternative rivals from the ground. Despite the fact that the two sides in the Cold War—one socialist and the other liberal—are actually just different sides of the same Western civilization, what Fukuyama points out is that debates will henceforth revolve around civilization. His groundbreaking idea was carried to a different dimension by Samuel P. Huntington. Leaning on the Weberian religion–civilizational identity, Huntington in *The Clash of Civilizations* (1993) mentioned that from now on the clash would be between civilizations and not ideologies. Debates thriving around these two works have transformed the period in which we live into a 'time of civilizational debate'. These two theses regarding the clash of civilizations have brought forward many alternative and critical theses regarding cooperation and coexistence between civilizations.

With the impact of the postcolonial legacy and globalization, civilizations are not separated from each other by geographical borders; rather, different civilizations live in the same place, sometimes in the same city. Although some are less eager to acknowledge, we now live in a world in which civilizations are merged into one another—from culinary culture to ways of worship, and from family relations to home designs. So when we talk about the other civilizations, we could be talking about a phenomenon relating to our neighbour, or any person we meet around the corner or in the subway. Thus, in the context of current problems related to migration, citizenship, and multiculturalism, debates on civilization are still a fertile ground for social scientific research.

Within this framework, from the nineteenth century, civilization has increasingly become a lively ground of debate in the Muslim world. Analysing these debates is beneficial not only to see the intellectual and political answers to Western civilization, but also to make new conceptual contributions to the global debates about the issue. When the current literature is examined, it is possible to see that in the Muslim world, only the reactionary oppositions towards civilization have dealt with these debates. This prevalent understanding may be true to a great extent, but it leaves out the systematic philosophical and conceptual debates. However, as different voices from the Muslim world such as Jamal al-Din al-Afghani, Muhammad Iqbal, Malek ben Nabi, Alija Izetbegovic, Sayyid Qutb, Hassan Hanafi, Ali Shariati, and Abdallah Laroui, or those from the non-Western world such as Frantz Fanon, Octavio Paz, Pitirim A. Sorokin, or Mahatma Gandhi did, it is of utmost importance to discuss the problem within different conceptual frameworks to open up new horizons about contemporary problems.

THE CIVILIZED WEST AND THE POSSIBILITY OF AN ISLAMIC CIVILIZATION

Before beginning a debate on civilization, we should discuss its meaning, nature, and history. The roots of the concept of civilization can be traced back to its Latin root *ki*—which means to be situated, to be in a place. There are many words in the Western political lexicons such as *civitas* (city, city-state, state containing cities; also, citizenship), *civis* (citizen; townsman), *civicus* (of a town or city; of a citizen), *civilis* (political, of a state; as becomes a citizen), and *civilitas* (politics; politeness) which have been derived from this root. As Wilkinson

(2007) states, 'the common elements of these concepts are *place, city* and *state politics*'. Among the words coming from this root as a noun, 'civilization' is newly formulated, in the era of enlightenment.

When we watch a documentary on TV, it may mention the Roman civilization; when we go to a museum, we see a number of ancient civilizations; when we open a history book, it can talk about the birth of the Japanese civilization. However, when we look at the genealogy and development of the concept of civilization, we clearly see that it was developed with the rise of modern society. Civilization is, therefore, a new concept that emerged during the Enlightenment era to define modern social formation. It was only after this that the concept was applied to the study of history. Thus, civilization came to be at the centre of all debates on modern society, albeit hoisted on to history.

Until the end of the nineteenth century, civilization was mostly used in the singular form and regarded as something pertaining only to the West. According to Enlightenment thought, civilization was the last station on the progressivist historical line, and the West had arrived by walking on this line properly and progressing enough to reach the end of history (Pagden 1988; see also Springborg 1992). Others could not walk this path and thus failed to become civilized. Therefore, civilization as defined by the West has an agentive function because it enables progress and development. Especially in their polemics against the clergy, Enlightenment thinkers stressed that a new society was emerging and that that society by its very existence was superior to all others, even the West's own immediate past.

Enlightenment thinkers defined civilization as an opponent of nature. According to this, humanity's victory over nature with the developments in science and technology is one of the basic indicators of civilization. Thus, an unbroken tie is formed between civilization and science. In this context, as Anthony Pagden discusses in this book, there were some special links between civilization and 'civitas' or urban living. Civilization was seen as the result of developments in conditions of the human being. The founding fathers of the Enlightenment, such as Condorcet and Montesquieu through to Lamarck, have a specific description of civilization based upon the progressivist understanding of historical development. Progressivism is constructed upon the thesis that humanity at the very beginning was in a primitive situation and it improved with its own experience and findings. This view was named as conjectural or natural history for the first time by Hume, and it then nearly became the official world view and the source-bed of all other theories of the Enlightenment. However, it is impossible to have anthropological or biological proofs of the primitive eras of humanity and the primitive society. Conjectural history emerged as a speculative philosophical idea of history for this very reason. According to this, history has an internal meaningful progressivist mechanism. As nature has its own law, history and society also have theirs. Just as with natural laws, these laws can be discovered through scientific examinations. Consequently, when laws of history and society were displayed, civil society, as a new form of society, emerged.

Thus, in understanding and explaining the world, Hazard (1963) defines two rival systems of thought that have incessantly competed with each other since the mid-seventeenth century and which constitute the very basics of this approach. The Enlightenment way of explaining society and history that was based on natural law emerged as an opponent to the church's explanation of history and society based on divine law. In a way, civilization emerged as a part of the historical struggle between feudalism and capitalism. Scottish Enlightenment thinkers, who contributed a great deal to the progressivist theory of history and civilization, explain progress as economic growth and domination of trade in society. According to them, civil society is a bourgeoisie society and civilization is a process in which bourgeoisie values and ethics dominate society (Oz-Salzberger 1995). Despite this, at the beginning of the eighteenth century, societal theory of the church, founded on over a thousand years of experience of the church, was more integrative and strong. This could be because it offered an explanation of the society that was not only based on human conditions, but also on moral norms. For this reason, its rival civilizational theories had to nourish themselves with a moral theory as well. Enlightenment–progressivist moral theories, which founded themselves upon natural rights and natural law debates, developed since the beginning of the seventeenth century and associated civilization with social contract. According to this, civilization is a social form that emerged as a result of a process in which humans came together within their rational decision to escape from the state of nature and form a political entity. So, this new form represented a break from the primitive state of nature and also a historical progress.

As Lutfi Sunar so elaborately references Hume, Montesquieu, and Smith in his article in the book *Rethinking the Conception of Civilization and Its Others: A Critical Evaluation,* the definition reifies the dichotomy between the primitive and the civilized, thus of the other; at the centre of this new civilized form is self-legitimization. 'Being civilized' was defined as getting rid of the state of barbarism with reference to the concept of the barbarian, which European thought has known very intimately since antiquity. Civil society was placed at the very opposite end of despotism which was seen as the political form of barbarism. In these ways a new subtle ground was discovered for the study of history which it itself could not provide.

Progressivist narration of history, which provided the background in placing civilization and barbarism within a historical framework, manifests itself in the periodization of history into specific eras and thus, in the classification of societies into various different types corresponding to this periodization (Bury 1920; Nisbet 1980). Periodization, as in all ancient systems of thought, is based on religious ideals in the medieval Christian world. History is divided into three main periods corresponding to the Holy Trinity. With a 'regressionist' approach nurtured by the idea of expulsion from heaven, it is believed that progress has been happening from the golden ages to the end of time.[2] Enlightenment thinkers reversed this idea and claimed that humanity moves into better times. At the core of these materialist–progressivist ideas, there was a quest of defining the newly emerging European modern society as a natural outcome of the historical process. According to this, history of humanity in general is comprised of three periods: Ancient, Middle, and Modern times. The social forms corresponding to each of these periods are savage, barbarian, and civil societies. According to these ideas, there is an indispensable and systematic course of historical progress that is based on the change of knowledge, scientific studies, and trade (way of earning a living). Enlightenment thinkers named this last phase as civilization, and its society as civilized society. In this way, civilization became one of the final purposes of historical development. In the establishment of these wholly conceptual categorization and definitions, barbarism, as the second concept which always comes together with civilization, has a specific importance. If it was not for barbarism, civilization would remain a speculative concept (Todorov

2010). The fact that civilization is the final phase of history and that civilized society is superior to others was proven through comparative analyses done with other social forms. Thus, evaluations and comparisons about the 'other' became obligatory in order for civilization to define itself. One can follow and see in great astonishment that in debates about civil society in Enlightenment thought, civilization is nearly always defined in terms of its opposites.

As previously stated, periodization prepared the necessary ground for world history to be written from a modern perspective. The basic factor that lies at the centre in periodization made it possible to depict the factors that enabled progress at the same time. However, another purpose of periodization is to show the former phases of societies apart from the modern ones and, thus, to show that at the end of the day modern society is the one and only existing form. In this way, it is proved that in the course of progress of world history, non-Western societies have not reached the final stage, that is, civilization. Because other societies have historical backgrounds that do not render a European-style of progress possible, they are always being narrated as a negative side of the European history of civilization. This was also mostly true about the histories of Muslim societies. According to Orientalist theories following the Enlightenment–progressivist discourse, Muslims have remained at the medieval stage in the course of history. Rationalist developments in Muslim societies, which may represent progressivist dynamics (and which of course are borrowed from ancient Greece and Rome), were hindered and thus, Muslim societies could not become civilized. Viewed from this perspective, histories of Muslim societies are seen as a historical regression or stagnation. The idea that Muslim societies could never be civilized because of their internal dynamics was reaffirmed more and more. For this, Islam as a religion was seen as one against progress and one whose political system nourishes despotism that destroys rationality. Reactions against these ideas and accusations are mostly of an apologetic–reactionist nature,[3] however, as critiques of historical progress developed in time, this problem began to be approached from different perspectives.

In fact, as Mustafa Demirci states in his chapter, 'The Question of Ages in Islamic Civilization: A Different Periodization', every civilization has its own phases of development, historical paths, different rhythms, and typology, depending on its specific internal dynamics and interactions. Every civilization has its own periods. This is because of the fact that since all of these occur within a specific time, they have their own different series of cultures, value sets, and typology, which reflect their character types. As such, dividing a civilization into different periods helps one to observe a piece of the changing culture models and values, as well as the types of humans that represent them, within a specific culture and civilization. With these judgements in mind, Demirci starts with the reality that every civilization has its own historical adventure and holds that it is, therefore, absolutely necessary for every civilization to use its own perception of time. He also emphasized that Islamic civilization is in need of a healthy perception of time that systematically reflects its own historical experiences.

As emphasized here, debates about civilization are closely related to the birth of modern society. In order to guarantee their existence against the church's idea of a normative society, moderns offered a normative historical progress as an alternative. At least like the church's idea of history and society, progressivism was a moral framework. Progressivism concretized itself by dividing history into periods and determining specific types of society indigenous to some specific periods. However, in order to reiterate this it was necessary to show that non-Western societies with whom a Western social form was still in rivalry were backward at the time when modern civilization was born. Thus, by frequently applying the concepts of barbarism and despotism, Enlightenment thinkers were rendering progress and civilization indigenous only to the West. Emergence of civilization as an exclusionist category thus caused ideas and reactions against it to be formed in this framework.

RECEPTION AND REFLECTION ON CIVILIZATION IN THE MUSLIM WORLD

This theoretical context of the concept of civilization also largely affects its conception and reception in the non-Western world. Once civilization was allocated to Europe in the Enlightenment period, hegemony of the Western subject over non-Western societies gained a moral character (Bowden 2009, pp. 227–8). Nineteenth-century imperialism was grounding, legitimizing, and rendering its expansionist policies ethical by using the concept of a 'civilizing mission'. Thus, encounters with Western 'civilization' were shaped in the framework of struggle against imperialism and political pressure, and economic and technological backwardness. For that reason, reactions against it have a complex nature.

In the Islamic world, there have been various kinds of reactions against the category of civilization as proposed by the Enlightenment. One of the most interesting reactions is the initiation of efforts to interpret Islamic thought from new perspectives. At the starting point of these initiations, there is a search for modern concepts and categories in the corpus of different classical thinkers. In the framework of the debates on civilization, today, the most cited name is Ibn Khaldun (Alatas 2014). His theory of 'umrân on social formations has long been accepted as an early interpretation of civilization (see Sunar and Yaslıçimen 2008). According to him, there are cycles of history with certain God-given rules to these historical changes. In the framework of medieval thinking, he thought that all societies rise and fall in a time limit. It is interesting that popularization of Ibn Khaldun's theory of 'umrân in the Ottoman thought and the idea of civilization in the Enlightenment coincide to the same time. However, there is a difference between them: the first emerged as a concept in questioning the reasons of decline, while the second emerged as a concept to make sense of the advance.

In all circumstances, Ibn Khaldun still stands at the focal point of debates on a different social order and societal formation. It is becoming more and more popular to refer to his theory while searching for an alternative meaning-cluster for civilization. It is possible to observe this even in the change of the number of publications about Ibn Khaldun. However, these researches are mostly part of an anachronistic approach that searches for some modern concepts and interpretations in Ibn Khaldun's thought. Thus, Ibn Khaldun as a classical thinker is being made ordinary with this reductionist approach. In order to go beyond this, as Vahdettin Işık mentions in his chapter in this volume, 'The Vision of Order and Al-'Umrân as an Explanatory Concept in the Debates on Civilization', Ibn Khaldun should be dealt with in his own intellectual world and conceptual framework. With such a reading, it will be possible to see that not only Ibn Khaldun, but also other pioneering representatives of classical Islamic thought have different epistemological and methodological frameworks. Therefore, Ibn Khaldun's concept of 'umrân is not an alternative to civilizational debates as it has been shown until now; rather it is an initiation of a totally different evaluation of social being.

In fact, the example of Ibn Khaldun, along with questioning possibilities of a theoretical start, has a specific importance for he is identified with civilizational debate in Islamic thought and his ideas are eligible to be dealt with in a different critical framework. Thus, a subtle framework about civilizational debate in the Islamic world was created. In a spectrum stretching from an apologetic and implementing edge to a reductionist one, in order to gain a meaningful systematic explanation in these debates it is necessary to make use of classical thought while abiding by one's own epistemological framework. The theoretical perspective that Işık proposes in his chapter is thus important in order for other thinkers' ideas to be evaluated contextually.

After civilization was defined as the driving force behind the Western expansionism, there were some reactions towards it. The first and most visible of the reactions against the Western idea of one progressivist civilization is mostly characterized by an idea of forming a unity around ethnic and religious identities, and then transforming this unity into a line of struggle. A united European civilization emerging with an identity that is formed at a very later phase resulted in the fact that in other parts of the world, other united identities started to emerge. Especially identities in geographies threatened by European expansionism started to be placed at the centre of new definitions of civilization against Western civilization. In this context, the pan movements like Pan-Asianism and Pan-Islamism were against the idea of a single universal Western civilization, and they challenged the idea of the 'civilizing mission'. In his chapter, 'Beyond Civilization: Pan-Islamism, Pan-Asianism and the Revolt against the West', Cemil Aydın particularly analyses the pan-Islamist ideology of the Ottoman Empire and the pan-Asian ideology of twentieth-century Japan as efforts to both resist as well as assimilate some aspects of Western civilization. These alternative civilizationist ideas forming around long-term identities of geography were accompanied by others forming around ethnic identities: pan-Slavism, pan-Turkism, pan-Africanism, and pan-Iranianism. However, for the time being, it is hard to say if these pan-isms became successful. What remains from these pan-ist ideas is a belief that European civilization is not the only one and that other civilizations are also possible.

It has been stated earlier that conceptual and factual encounters with civilizations did not occur under normal circumstances, and civilizations expanded to the non-Western world via wars and weapons (Keddie 1983). Compared to other parts of the world, because of the political unity at the time when imperialist expansion started, the Islamic world encountered the hegemony of the Western world later and resisted imperialism in a stronger and more resolute way. In the first era of expansion of imperialism, the Muslim world still kept its intellectual tradition alive and struggled to produce answers to new societal forms using their own internal conceptual and intellectual system. For this reason, civilization and civilizing forces faced a strong resistance, traces of which can still be seen today. As Yenigün discusses in his chapter, 'The Rise and Demise of Civilizational Thinking in Contemporary Muslim Political Thought', one of the founders of contemporary Islamist thought, Afghani, offered the concept of civilization as a political theory of Muslim resistance against the unitary conceptions of civilization of the West. Afghani saw that the Islamic *ummah* would live under different nation states and, therefore, he defined civilization in a way that it surpassed this fragmentation; it is also a definition that has been harshly debated until now. And, as Aydın states in his chapter, Afghani sees pan-Islamism as a possible basis for such kind of a unity. According to him, European nation-states and societies were tied to each other with a strong bond of civilization; Muslim states could also do the same within a superior and overarching idea of civilization.

According to Afghani and some other contemporary Islamist thinkers, the idea to have a shared civilization would also effectively be useful in struggling with imperialism and the destructive expansionism of Western civilization. It is possible to see this kind of a resistance in the Ottoman Empire. During Ottoman modernization, attitudes against Europe had a complicated nature. In contrast to China, India, or Japan, Europe is both a rival and a neighbour to the Ottomans, with whom they have lived. Sometimes they even included parts of each other in different periods of history. Thus, the Ottoman Empire was closely influenced by developments in Europe. One natural outcome of European modern society was its effects on the Ottoman Empire. Against the developments of its closest and oldest neighbour and enemy, reactions from the Ottoman elite were two-dimensional. On the one hand, with loss of power and superiority, Ottomans had a rejectionist attitude towards all products of civilization, and their intellectual mindset shaped for hundreds of years did not accept the new relations of sovereignty. On the other, new European systems, ideas, and behaviours were rapidly spreading with the effect of the imperial pragmatist behaviour that dominated social and political life. Thus, as Necmettin Doğan states in his chapter, 'Interaction of Concepts of Progress and Civilization (in) Turkish Thought', according to the Turkish elite these two concepts are both an enemy to be fought off and a novelty that should benefit from the outcomes.

At this point, especially Islamist thinkers' positions in the face of this problem have very interesting internal contradictions. They had to accept the Ottomans' backwardness and Europe's superiority in technology, but at the same time they had to seek and find solutions for salvaging their roots and history; this is one of the basic dilemmas in this debate (Mardin 1962). Turkish Islamists regarded civilization in a positive way as 'Western mansions', but at the same time they saw it as an outdated phenomenon. In these definitions, it is seen that technology is viewed as the main factor defining civilization. Islamist thought relates Muslim societies' backwardness to technological reasons and sees technology as the defining factor of Western civilization. Therefore, if Muslim societies want to get rid of their current situation, they have to adopt this modern technology. However, if they happen to adopt it, there will emerge the problem of Westernization. This is probably the most difficult line of the problem of civilization. Although Islamists came forward with some solution to this problem, they could never make peace with Ziya Gokalp's modern Turkish definition, 'I am from the Turkish nation, Islamic *ummah*, and western civilization!'[4] This was quite an unacceptable eclectic and pragmatic solution for Islamist thinkers and they searched for different authentic conceptions.

Therefore, throughout the twentieth century, civilization and civilizing (in other words, the West and Westernization) constituted one of the main dilemmas of Muslim thought. While these debates were going on, the birth of the concept of Islamic civilization was a very important development. The idea of Islamic civilization emerged within the Western redefinition of civilization around world religions at the end of the nineteenth century; and this idea was extensively acknowledged by the Islamists. In this way, Islamic civilization against Western civilization became a favourable idea: their civilization for them, our civilization for us. From this point on, what has been lost and should be rescued and reformulated was not a political regime or a religious construction, but a civilization. In creating this intellectual 'possibility', debates in Western thought played a significant role.[5] When Enlightenment's linear understanding of history started to be questioned from the last quarter of the nineteenth century, its civilization was portrayed as a pluralist phenomenon. Thus, civilization was defined not as a specific type of society emerging in Europe at the end of a certain historical progress, but as a general name given to a set of socio-cultural and physical–intellectual values and behaviours in a specific geography. From this time on, it was possible to talk about a Japanese civilization, or an indigenous civilization, and so on. Thus criticisms about civilization were directed at contemporary Western civilization and civilization was no longer conceived as a queer category.

Without a doubt, modern society and thus civilizational criticisms in Europe played a significant role in this. Especially criticisms by Nietzsche, Freud, Spengler, Heidegger, and the members of the Frankfurt School had very serious adherents in the Islamic world. In different geographies at the same time and sometimes unaware of each other, Afghani, Iqbal, ben Nabi, Qutb, Izetbegovic, and Shariati expanded the boundaries of these criticisms against the idea and ideology of contemporary civilization and its crises and contributed to these debates. These thinkers also thought that Islamic civilization could produce solutions to the social ontological problems of today's world.

Qutb is one of the earliest and foremost influential thinkers in that respect. Although today he is read and interpreted quite differently, Qutb is an important thinker who has made many contributions not only to contemporary Islamic thought, but also to contemporary political thought and social theory. According to him, modern civilization corrupts man's relationship with nature and God, and that creates an unjust world. For him, Islam has an integrative proposition of order in reconstructing this corrupted harmony. In order to reconstruct a just world in which everything would be in an order, the values and norms of Islamic civilization are needed. Halil Ibrahim Yenigun in his chapter, 'The Rise and Demise of Civilizational Thinking in Contemporary Muslim Political Thought', is of the opinion that Qutb may be one of the possible starting points in constructing a universal critical political thought. However, the current extremist usage of his ideas is the most significant hindrance to the founding and acceptance of this kind of a theory.

Similar to Qutb, a contemporary of his and an important thinker in modern Muslim thought, Shariati's critique of civilization is also based on the tension line between the individual and the society. According to him, a societal form atomizing the individual alienates him and renders him vulnerable and unsupported against many contemporary problems. As S. Javad Miri discusses in the chapter, 'Revisiting Shariati: Probing into Issues of Society and Religion', Shariati offers new content and context to the debates, stating that this detachment between the individual and society is because modern civilization breaks the ties between humans and the divine. Similar to Shariati, Izetbegovic, as a political and philosophical actor of our times, thinks that the main problem of the contemporary civilization is that it is detaching humans from the holy. According to him, this detachment does not only happen on a materialistic basis, but also on a religious one. And for him, throughout history there are two extreme approaches about human reality: at one end there is pure religion (spirituality-based) and at the other there is materialism (material-based). Both of these extreme understandings make people unhappy and societies unbalanced. While Christianity of Middle Ages or Brahmanism of India represents pure religion, ancient Greek and Rome and the modern civilization of Europe represent materialist way of living. According to Izetbegovic, Islamic civilization was the middle point of these extreme edges. As a moderate way of life, Islam converges religion and worldly desires with each other, merging the other world into this world. Izetbegovic criticizes contemporary Western materialist civilization and considers Islam as an alternative against this falsely developed civilization. With reference to his most important work, *Islam between East and West*, Mahmut Hakkı Akın makes the assertion that even as a Muslim thinker, Izetbegovic belonged to both the West and the East.

Similar evaluations about civilization can be found in the different lines of the contemporary Arab thought. Starting from Malek ben Nabi, thinkers such as Hassan Hanafi and Abdallah Laroui evaluated civilization in their debates intensifying around the idea of tradition (*turath*) and dealt with a different understanding of civilization from a critical point of view. Possibly they were not as radical as Shariati, Qutb, and Izetbegovic; however, these thinkers also had a critical conceptualization of civilization. As the two major sources of contemporary Arab-Islamic thought, since the late nineteenth century, Arab-Islamic culture and Western thought have dealt with the question of tradition (turath) in relation to modernity in the context of the socio-political changes in Arab societies. According to the Orientalist paradigm and modernization theories, Arabic societies should change their traditional social formation in order to modernize. This approach rebuilds the dichotomy between tradition and modernity in the case of Arabic societies under the cover of turath and modernity, continuity and change, religiosity and secularity. As in the other non-Western societies, a couple of new perspectives on the adoption of the European civilization emerged in contemporary Arab thought. However, as Driss Habti discusses in the chapter, 'Debating Islam, Tradition, and Modernity in Contemporary Arab-Islamic Thought', as important representatives of the contemporary Arab thought, Hanafi and Laroui reject the dichotomy between tradition and modernity and assert that the Arabic turath can be a foundational element in reinstating a new and different civilization against Western civilization. Hanafi and Laroui made great use of and benefited from the criticisms in the contemporary Western thought against civilization and they claimed that today non-Western societies should reinterpret their own traditions in a rational manner. As seen in the cases of Qutb, Shariati, Iqbal, and Izetbegovic, these and similar ideas that present holistic critiques and suggestions became more and more popular in the Muslim world, especially from the 1990s onwards.

Consequently, the concept of civilization in the Islamic world emerged not as a phenomenon happening far outside of its realm, but as a part, reflection, and vision of the resistance that tries to transform itself. In the Muslim world, civilization is a synonym for modernization. The oppressive nature of the efforts to modernize transformed civilization into a lifestyle that was mostly imposed by the colonialists and their local counterparts. As a result, most of the time what civilization meant for Muslim societies was to give up on their own identities and traditions, and at the same time changing and becoming lost. It is because of this, which Syed Farid Alatas names 'erring modernization', that the Muslim world neither achieved total modernization, nor remained loyal to its own identity. Because of this process that was both oppressive and alienating, contemporary Muslim societies have a hybrid and eclectic social, political, and intellectual structure. This hybridity and eclecticism restrain the formation of a civilization in which mindsets and values are in harmony with its material reality. In order for this structure to gain a meaningful integrity, top-down modernization programmes should be revised and outdated traditions should be overcome. It is possible to say that the thinkers mentioned previously struggled to draw this kind of an intellectual framework. It is obvious that at the end of the day, the aim to redefine civilization cannot be detached from the Muslim experience and from the necessities of the time. So, debates about civilization should get rid of fundamentalist–traditional and oppressive–modernist aspects.

WHAT ABOUT THE FUTURE OF CIVILIZATION IN THE NON-WESTERN WORLD?

It has been twenty-five years since a new phase came within the rearousal of the debates on civilization at the beginning of 1990s. In this period, the world has not become a more democratic, global, equal, and prosperous place as was expected. In contrast, we have witnessed that inequalities and socio-economical polarizations have deepened. Along with full-scale wars, serious economic, political, and social tensions have been rapidly increasing. Under these circumstances it is necessary to question whether civilization as an explanatory concept will survive, and also whether modern Western civilization as the main form determining the course of these debates will preserve its status. This questioning should also include various different criticisms and quests in the Islamic world to produce a universalistic way of thinking.

At the beginning of the 1990s as ideas about clash of civilizations were put forth, it was also believed that civilizations would be brought closer to each other, together with all the debates on globalization and multiculturalism. It is widely accepted that globalization emerged as a significant force connecting societies, economies, and cultures to each other, and the effects were most visible in recent decades.[6] And in the civilization debate, civilizations are defined as cultural blocs whose boundaries are usually drawn based on dominant religions in societies around the world. To better understand the nature and future of the inter-civilizational relations, the impact of globalization needs to be addressed. In globalization literature, one can discern two contradictory approaches regarding the impact of globalization on the intercultural and inter-societal relations. On the one hand there is the 'civilizing/integrative globalization' approach, which builds on the idea that the increasing exposure to democratic ideas, foreign people, and cultures through globalization will make societies and cultures more open and tolerant towards each other. On the other, the 'destructive globalization/globalization as a threat' approach argues that globalization sharpens and threatens identities, and creates reactionary backlash all around the world. According to this approach, while globalization demands the integration of national economies, it pits culture against culture and people against people. Yunus Kaya, in his chapter, 'Civilizations in an Era of Globalization', touches upon these concepts and analyses this debate on globalization literature as well as the debate on global culture, compares opposing views, weighs empirical evidence, and discusses the implications for the civilization debate.

Like globalization, multiculturalism was another concept that had a positive connotation about the future of the relations between civilizations. The classical concept of civilization expressed unity, singleness, and even particularness, with each civilization accusing the other past and contemporary civilizations of barbarianism even towards the very parameters that each civilization used. As such, even while every civilization considered itself as 'the civilization', it is a point which may neither be questioned nor criticized, and is instead something to which one may simply belong. Being very popular through globalization with the effect of postmodern thought, multiculturalism was expected to go beyond these limits and define a new façade of the relationship between those identities. Just as Edward Said argues in his book *Orientalism*, Orientalist works deal with how Western civilizations make other civilizations/'barbarians' into a research topic and then crystallize their authority to distort them. As an identity, civilization carries an inherent quality of otherization due to its drawing such a sharp line between 'us' and 'them'. Within the structure of the national identity of a nation state lies political authority, and due to this authority other identities are able to exist as sociological and hierarchal sub-identities under this overarching identity. However, just as it is possible for one to simultaneously hold multiple identities depending on the different roles he/she plays, even during times when these identities may clash with each other, it may also be possible for one to claim membership to more than one civilization at the same time. This is not 'a cheap eclecticism' in and of itself, it is seen that every civilization has taken from others in order to form and sustain itself. In this respect and according to Murat Çemrek, in order to conceptualize civilization, one must be able to understand the concept of 'otherness', and as much as one understands this, he/she must also understand the idea of 'pluralism'. He recommends that a new and critical reading of the concept of 'civilization' is the remedy against the illness of making civilization into a taboo.

As a consequence of modern conceptions, today civilizations are approached as static beings unrelated to each other. Against the Western civilization that was defined as a closed being in the course of the debates going on for two hundred years, other civilizations were defined but again within closed characteristics. Today we still debate with a wrong definition of civilization produced by the Enlightenment understanding of a monistic progressivism. Modern discourse that is shaped around the fact that civilizations reject the existence of one another, in fact, ignores the interwoven parts of the history of humanity. Not only in the pre-modern history, even in modern history interactions between the experiences of humanity continued. For this reason, it is today quite difficult to talk about a possibility of dealing with civilizations as purely different and detached categories from one another. Efforts to produce a homogenous history can only be vitalized through otherization as modernity did with itself. And it is inevitable that every effort of definition in this direction will produce a similar history of power relations, violence, and reactions. Khosrow Bagheri Noaparast's 'An Epistemological Base for a Dynamic Conception of Civilizations and Intercultural Relations' in this volume discusses that in order to go beyond the static and closed to reach out to other civilizations, it is necessary to firstly find an intellectual ground in which it will be possible to reach a dynamic conceptualization of civilization. According to this, contributions to the developmental course of knowledge came together and constructed a world history in which all civilizations benefited from each other. A redefinition of civilization, not as a closed category but as an open category that includes and exists with the other can change the direction of the tragic encounters that have been experienced up to today.

As Swiss thinker Johan Galtung (1994) puts it, looking out of the window can take us very far away. Perhaps we can even see a rainbow there and conceive that all colours give meaning to each other.

NOTES

1. For a comparison of Toynbee's and Sorokin's analysis of civilization see David Wilkinson (1996) and for Sorokin's critique see also Lawrence T. Nichols (1997).
2. See Necmettin Alkan (2009) for the details of periodization of history in the medieval age.
3. See Ducane Cündioğlu (1996) for a bibliographic record of the wide-ranged studies on Islam and science.
4. See Ureil Heyd (1950) for a discussion on the life and teachings of Ziya Gökalp.
5. See Hourani (1983), for a discussion on the influence of François M. Guizot's term 'Islamic civilization' on the formation of the civilizational outlook in the Muslim world through Afgani's writings.
6. For a critical discussion on this issue see Aijaz Ahmad (2007) and Mehdi Mozaffari (2002).

BIBLIOGRAPHY

Ahmad, A. 2007. *In Our Time: Empire, Politics, Culture*. London: Verso.
Ahmet Mithat. 2005. *Felâtun Bey ile Râkım Efendi*. Ankara: Akçağ.
Alatas, S. F. 2014. *Applying Ibn Khaldun: The Recovery of a Lost Tradition in Sociology*. Routledge.
Alkan, N. 2009. 'Tarihin çağlara ayrılmasında "Üç"lü sistem ve "Avrupa merkezci" tarih kurgusu'. *Uluslararası Sosyal Araştırmalar Dergisi* 2(9): 23–42.
Árnason, J. P. 2003. *Civilizations in Dispute Historical Questions and Theoretical Traditions*. Leiden, Boston: Brill.

Bernasconi, R. 2001. *Concepts of Race in the Eighteenth Century*. Bristol: Thoemmes.

Bowden, B. 2009. *The Empire of Civilization: The Evolution of an Imperial Idea*. Chicago, Illinois; London: University of Chicago Press.

Braudel, F. 1995. *A History of Civilizations*. New York: Penguin Books.

———. 2001. *Memory and the Mediterranean*, translated by S. Reynolds. New York: A.A. Knopf.

Bury, J. B. 1920. *The Idea of Progress: An Inquiry into Its Origin and Growth*. London: Macmillan and Co.

Camus, A. 1989. *The Stranger*, translated by M. Ward. New York: Vintage International.

Cündioğlu, D. 1996. Ernest Renan ve reddiyeler bağlamında İslâm-bilim tartışmalarına bibliyografik bir katkı. *Divan* 1(2): 1–94.

Dostoevsky, F. 2006. *Notes from the Underground*. London: Hesperus.

Elias, N. 1978. *The Civilizing Process: The History of Manners*. New York: Urizen Books.

Fanon, F. 1967. *Black Skin, White Masks*. New York: Grove Press.

Foucault, M. 1995. *Discipline and Punish: The Birth of the Prison*. New York: Vintage Books.

Freud, S. 1962. *Civilization and Its Discontents*. New York: W.W. Norton.

Fukuyama, F. 1992. *The End of History and the Last Man*. New York: Free Press.

Galtung, J. 1994. *Human Rights in Another Key*. Cambridge, UK; Oxford; Cambridge, MA: Polity Press; Blackwell Publishers.

Hazard, P. 1963. *The Crises of the European Mind, 1680–1715*. Cleveland: World Pub. Co.

Heyd, U. 1950. *Foundation of Turkish Nationalism: The Life and Teachings of Ziya Gökalp*. London: Luzac.

Horkheimer, M. and T. W. Adorno. 1972. *Dialectic of Enlightenment*. New York: Herder and Herder.

Hourani, A. 1983. *Arabic Thought in the Liberal Age, 1798–1939*. Cambridge [Cambridgeshire]; New York: Cambridge University Press.

Huntington, S. P. 1993. 'The Clash of Civilizations?' *Foreign Affairs* 72(3): 22–49.

Kafka, F. 2009. *The Metamorphosis and Other Stories*, translated by J. Crick. Oxford, UK: Oxford University Press.

Kalberg, S. 2015. 'Max Weber's Sociology of Civilizations: A Preliminary Investigation into Its Major Methodological Concepts'. In *Max Weber*, edited by A. Sica, pp. 48–66. London: Anthem Press.

Keddie, N. R. 1983. *An Islamic Response to Imperialism: Political and Religious Writings of Sayyid Jamal ad-Din al-Afghani*. Berkeley: University of California Press.

Marcuse, H. 1968. *One-Dimensional Man*. London: Sphere Books.

Mardin, S. 1962. *The Genesis of Young Ottoman Thought: A Study in the Modernization of Turkish Political Ideas.* Princeton, NJ: Princeton University Press.

Mozaffari, M. 2002. *Globalization and Civilizations.* New York: Routledge.

Nichols, L. T. 1997. 'Sociological Paradigms and Civilizational Studies: Complementary Contributions of E. A. Ross and P. A. Sorokin'. *The Comparative Civilizations Review* 36: 16–37.

Nisbet, R. A. 1980. *History of the Idea of Progress.* New York: Basic Books.

Oz-Salzberger, F. 1995. *Translating the Enlightenment: Scottish Civic Discourse in Eighteenth-Century Germany.* Oxford; New York: Clarendon Press; Oxford University Press.

Pagden, A. 1988. 'The Defence of Civilization in Eighteenth-Century Social Theory'. *History of the Human Sciences* 1(1): 33–45.

Paz, O. 1962. *The Labyrinth of Solitude: Life and Thought in Mexico.* New York: Grove Press.

Said, E. W. 1977. *Orientalism.* London: Penguin.

———. 1994. *Culture and Imperialism.* New York: Knopf.

Sartre, J. P. 2004. Preface. In *The Wretched of the Earth,* edited by F. Fanon, C. Farrington and H. K. Bhabha, pp. xliii–lxii. New York: Grove Press.

Scott, D. 2004. *Conscripts of Modernity: The Tragedy of Colonial Enlightenment.* Durham: Duke University Press.

Shayegan, D. 1997. *Cultural Schizophrenia: Islamic Societies Confronting the West.* Syracuse, NY: Syracuse University Press.

Sorokin, P. A. 1937. *Social and Cultural Dynamics.* New York, Cincinnati: American Book Company.

———. 1941. *The Crisis of Our Age: The Social and Cultural Outlook.* New York: Dutton.

Spengler, O. 1926. *The Decline of the West: Perspectives of World-history,* translated by C. F. Atkinson. London: G. Allen and Unwin.

Springborg, P. 1992. *Western Republicanism and the Oriental Prince.* Cambridge: Polity Press.

Sunar, L. and F. Yaslıçimen. 2008. 'The Possibilities of New Perspectives for Social Sciences: An Analysis Based on Ibn Khaldun's Theory of Umrân'. *Asian Journal of Social Science* 36(3): 408–33.

Todorov, T. 2010. *The Fear of Barbarians: Beyond the Clash of Civilizations.* Chicago: University of Chicago Press.

Toynbee, A. 1935. *A Study of History.* London: Oxford University Press.

———. 1948. *Civilization on Trial: Essays.* New York: Oxford University Press.

Weber, M. 2009. 'Prefatory Remarks to Collected Essays in the Sociology of Religion' [Vorbemerkung]. In *The Protestant Ethic and the Spirit of Capitalism with Other Writings on the Rise of the West* (4th ed.), edited and translated by S. Kalberg, pp. 205–20. New York: Oxford University Press.

Wilkinson, D. 1996. 'Sorokin versus Toynbee on Civilization'. In *Sorokin and Civilization: A Centennial Assessment*, edited by J. B. Ford, P. Talbutt, and Michel P. Richard, pp. 141–58. New Brunswick, NJ: Transaction Publishers.

———. 2007. Global Civilization: Yesterday, Today and Tomorrow. In *Encyclopedia of Life Support Systems (EOLSS)*, edited by R. Holton, pp. 96–111. Oxford, UK: Eolss Publishers.

Part I

Defining and Discussing Civilization

1 The Idea of Civilization in Eighteenth-Century Social Theory

Anthony Pagden

L'expansion de l'activité civilisée est constamment doublée par ses risques d'échec: et ce qui lui fait obstacle n'est pas seulement ce qui demeure indomptable dans la nature, mais la puissance de destruction que la civilisation porte en elle même.
— Jean Starobinski, *Diderot dans l'espace des peintres*

Today we all live in cultures. Some of these are highly local; most are discrete. We speak freely of political cultures and popular cultures in very much the same way as we speak of the culture of Bali or the culture of the Hopi. We speak far less often of 'civilizations', and even less often of *civilization*. The word has become at best problematical. It is widely associated by many with an implied triumph of 'Western' values over all others or, as in Samuel P. Huntington's now notorious *Clash of Civilizations*, with the irreconcilable antagonism of human groups towards one another.[1] One of the reasons for the objection to this word—and not to the supposedly more neutral 'culture'—is that unlike culture, 'civilization' describes both a process (that of civilizing) and comparative evaluation (that of being 'civilized'). And if today we speak only cautiously of civilization (and then almost always in the plural) that is because the word has a history which ties it not only to late eighteenth-century conceptions of human progress but also to early nineteenth-century claims of biological determinism.

A civilization is generally taken to be the state, social, political, cultural, aesthetic—even moral and physical—which is the optimum condition for all mankind, and this involves the implicit claim that some peoples are civilized, some are not, and only the civilized are in a position to know what it is to be 'civilized'. As John Stuart Mill observed in 1836, the term 'civilization' like most terms of what he called 'the philosophy of human nature' had more than one meaning. It could be used to describe 'the best characteristics of Man and Society; further advanced in the road to perfection, happier, nobler, wiser'. Or it could imply merely a distinction between a 'wealthy and powerful nation' and 'savages and barbarians'. Disaggregating the two, however, as he admitted, was difficult. His own day was, he believed, 'pre-eminently the era of civilization' (Mill 1977, p. 119). But it was not universally so, and, furthermore, civilization was, in Mill's opinion, by no means an unmixed blessing.

Mill had inherited a word which, in 1836, was less than a century old. It seems to have been first used in its modern sense by the economist and physiocrat Victor de Riqueti, Marquis de Mirabeau, in 1756, in an immensely popular book tellingly entitled *L'Ami des Hommes, ou Traité de la population*[2] (Mirabeau 1756, p. 136; Starobinski 1989). Its origin, however, as with all words, was far older. 'Civil', 'civility', and 'to civilize' are all terms which were already in wide general use by the mid-sixteenth century. They all derive (as, of course, does 'citizen') from the Latin *civitas*. Originally the word referred to the community, or what would later come to be called 'the state', rather than the urban space itself (Brett 2011, pp. 2–3). (For that there was another Latin term *urbs* from which we derive such related notions as *urban*, *urbane*, and *urbanity*.) But the community could never easily be separated from the physical location in which civil existence was carried out, so that in all the modern vernacular languages that emerged out of Latin, they eventually became if not synonymous, then certainly interdependent. They all referred to those values associated with the life lived in cities, in ordered communities with recognized social structures and fixed locations, lives which, to use the corresponding set of Greek derivatives, were also 'politic', and thus also 'polite'. By the mid-eighteenth century these terms had become, largely if not exclusively, attached to a set of formal behavioural characteristics broadly described as 'manners'. 'Polite' and 'civil' had thus come to acquire much the same range of references as they possess today. By the mid-eighteenth century, they still described the qualities which separated social man from the 'savage', but they were now far more heavily freighted with the sense of what criteria might be used to distinguish between individuals *within* civil society. That 'civility' had already begun to lose its former antithetical clarity is suggested by the fact that when Samuel Johnson refused to include the word 'civilization' in his dictionary, James Boswell protested, 'with great deference to him', that he thought '*civilization* from *to civilize* better in the sense opposed to *barbarity* than *civility*' (quoted in Dampierre 1960). The rapid acceptance of the term was also part of the transformation and extension of a conceptual vocabulary for social theory, which is characteristic of the human sciences in the Enlightenment.

By the early part of the eighteenth century there already existed a distinction, as Montesquieu characterized it, between 'barbarians' and 'savages'—a term that, in common with many eighteenth-century authors, he understood primarily in the botanical sense, as something as yet uncultivated. The latter he described as 'small nations' who had 'been unable to unite together' (*ne peuvent pas se reunir*). They are, for the most part, hunter-gatherers, and as an example he mentions the Tupi people of Brazil. The reason given for the failure of the savages to 'unite together' is some accident of terrain or climate, or what Edward Gibbon called their 'supine indolence' and, significantly, their 'carelessness of futurity'. It was never from choice or from some vaguely intuitive understanding of the perils of any larger existence.[3] The 'barbarians' have entered some kind of society, but they remain semi-nomadic pastoralists who have not yet developed the capacity for civil association (Montesquieu's example is, somewhat puzzlingly, the Manchu). However, they are at that stage when 'civilization' has become a future possibility (Montesquieu 1951, p. 11). Over time, this tripartite distinction became more rigid and in the nineteenth century it was even written into the new code books of international law (Mazower 2012, pp. 70–1).

What Montesquieu had described was what John Stuart Mill would later identify as something akin to a law of human progress: the shift from the individual to the society. Civilization was essentially a process of aggregation and cooperation—the working out in time of the 'sympathy' which bound all human beings inexorably to one another. It was cooperation, in Mill's understanding, that had allowed mankind to flourish and had prevented 'lions and tigers from long

ago extirpating the race of men'. And it was their underdeveloped ability to cooperate that 'makes all savage communities poor and feeble'
(Mill 1977, p. 122).

'Civilization' thus became an important concept in the language
of those whose social theory constituted a refutation of the claims
of a countervailing tradition in Western thought, which like most
such traditions had its roots in antiquity but whose best-known
eighteenth-century exponent was Jean-Jacques Rousseau. This
maintained that men had become morally corrupted by society and
that the ideal human community must approximate, as far as it was
able, to the state of nature. Mirabeau's usage varies hardly at all
from the common sense of 'civility'. It was, he said, the 'softening of
customs, urbanity, politeness, and the spread of understanding so
that the niceties are observed' (Mirabeau 1756, p. 136). Such a definition made it possible for him, in his attempt to establish religion
as the only lasting check on man's naturally destructive passions,
to speak of 'the barbarity of our civilization' and of civilization as
masking the true moral and political virtues. But as the structural
linguist and semiotician Émile Benveniste pointed out, 'civilization'
differs crucially from 'civility' in that its *–ation* ending indicates the
presence of an agent—an agent who is purely human. This last
point, together with the fact that the term had for long had a legal
significance (the transfer of a case from a criminal to a civil court)
located it immediately in a discourse which, as Benveniste says, was
resolument non theologique (resolutely non-theological; Benveniste
1966, p. 307). The word was, therefore, as Mill had seen, far better
suited than 'civility' to describe a continuous process, the outcome
of cooperative action, to which men are committed by the nature of
their intelligence (Constant 1815, p. 146). Men in the state of nature,
because the demands of their physical environment are so great,
are capable only of very low levels of cooperation. Montesquieu's
savages were savage precisely because the degree of sociability
attained by the primitive warrior horde was insufficient to allow
for the development of the arts and sciences. As Boswell had seen,
'civilization' described the antithesis to this condition far better than
'civility' would have done. Why these terms—'civilization', 'civility', 'barbarism', 'savage'—should have come to acquire during the
Enlightenment, and beyond, the pre-eminence they did within this

particular set of socio-anthropological concerns, requires, however, some preliminary historical explanation.

At the most fundamental level, the rejection of a Rousseauian moral vision involved the claims of a simple evolutionary psychology. In *Esquissse d'un tableau historique des progrès de l'esprit humain* of 1792—perhaps the most widely influential of the eighteenth-century histories of human progress—the Marquis de Condorcet argued that the human species *must* be subject to a process of constant and irreversible improvement through 'the steady growth of the intellectual and physical faculties' simply because that is its innate disposition (Condorcet 1793, p. 330). As with the child, so with the race as a whole. The pursuit of knowledge is, argued Adam Ferguson (1792 p. 206), 'no less an exigency of the mind than the means of subsistence and accommodation are an exigency of mere animal life'.

Humankind's true end was civilization, and because all humans are the products of reflective action, civilizations are inevitably plural, dynamic, and complex. They are also inescapable. Even Rousseau knew that. As an individual, you could return to the state of nature— or at least something close to it—to those uncomfortable places Rousseau professed to prefer to Paris: the Swiss Alpine villages, Canadian forests, modern-day fantasies of ancient Greece or Rome. Humanity as a species, however, had no such option. But then, as Kant, an acutely critical reader of Rousseau, pointed out: 'Rousseau did not ultimately wish that the human being *go* back to the state of nature, but rather that it should *look* back upon the state of nature' (Kant 2007, p. 422).

'Among animals,' observed Kant, 'the individual attains [its ends] immediately; among men only the species over the passage of generations, but in the end, through the species, the individual does so also.' Mankind went through three stages: the cultivated, the civilized, and what he called the 'moralized'. 'And where are we now?' he asked. To which the answer was: '(A) in the highest degree cultivated; (B) only half civilized; (C) hardly moral at all.... We are refined and polite, but without civic spirit'. We have no grounds for complacency. True progress was a never-ending struggle for improvement. Humans were never intended to remain still, satisfied, complacent, and happy with what they had and what they could do. That was what was wrong with those 'noble' savages Rousseau professed to admire. Any people which has seemingly 'arrived at its goal and lives in simple joyfulness', wrote Kant, was merely 'superfluous', which is why the poor Tahitians would never be able to give an answer to the question of 'why they exist at all and whether it would not have been just as good to have this island populated with happy sheep and cattle as with human beings who are happy merely enjoying themselves'. Some might even say that 'the world would lose nothing if Tahiti were simply swallowed up'. Luckily for the Tahitians, however, their island had been visited by more 'cultured nations', who might, much as Kant (2007, p. 65) despised their rapacious ways, have the unintended merit of return-ing them to their true purpose as human beings.

Intellectual progress, what Condorcet called 'this need of ideas or new sensations, the first mover of the progress of the human spirit', generated increasingly complex sets of human needs (Condorcet 1793, p. 57). These, as the conjectural historians understood, increased exponentially as they were satisfied, and as they grew, so, of course, they changed. Civilization, as the Neapolitan Francesantonio Grimaldi observed in his *Reflessioni sopra l'ineguaglianza tra gli uomini* of 1799, was the process by which the 'natural and sympathetic senti-ments' and even the physiognomy of the human animal were radi-cally altered by the increased satisfaction, and thus the ever-shifting nature of their needs. Since it allows for the proliferation of satisfiable needs, civilization also produces a great variety among its members. The Milanese Gianrinaldo Carli, whose *Lettere americane* of 1780 offered one of the most compelling analyses of an actual 'primitive' society, claimed that there was no discernible continuity over time within even a single individual, let alone an entire community. The English astronomer Edmond Halley, he said, was not the same man when he fell in love with Mary Tooke in 1682 (with whom he subse-quently enjoyed a famously long and happy marriage) as he was when he observed his comet in 1680. In the same way, he claimed, the Isaac Newton who wrote commentaries on the book of the Apocalypse was not the same man who discovered the laws of gravity (Carli 1794a, p. 169). The numbing sameness which Grimaldi perceived among savages and their apparent oneness with nature, which he scorned Diderot for supposedly admiring, were merely the consequences of their willingness to accept the immediate impulse to survival as sufficient. Thus, they all became alike, each one adopting 'a mask which makes him like his fellow'. The *varietas rerum* (variety of things) which previous commentators had struggled so hard to explain away and which, in the eyes of men like Carli and Grimaldi, the savage world had eliminated in the interests of survival, was simply the substance of the human condition.

Grimaldi's image of the mask of sameness haunted the champions of the civilized world. For they were all acutely aware that the continual process of amelioration, and hence of liberation, and enlightenment could always be blocked and as rapidly reversed. As Benjamin Constant in his unfinished *De la perfectibilité de l'espèce humaine*[4] of about 1805, bitterly observed, 'A physical calamity, a new religion, the invasion by barbarians or a few centuries of oppression could carry away all that has raised up, all that has ennobled our species.... In vain then would one speak of enlightenment, or liberty or philosophy' (Constant 1967, pp. 41–2; see Hofman 2009, pp. 248–71). Constant, of course, had seen the pluralistic vision of the Enlightenment overrun first by the Terror and then by the rise of Napoleon (Fontana 1991, pp. 29–47). But even so optimistic a pre-Revolutionary writer as Condorcet (to whose *Esquisse* Constant's own treatise is heavily indebted) could construe the history of human societies as, at one level, the history of persistent attempts, sometimes by false beliefs, more often by the will of those who seek power over others—Condorcet's 'tyrants, priests, and hypocrites'—to obstruct the natural flow of knowledge (Condorcet 1793, p. 336). 'All nations,' wrote the abbé Guillaume Thomas Raynal (1781, p. 27), the author of one of the eighteenth century's bestsellers, the *Histoire philosophique et politique ... des deux Indes*, 'swing from barbarism to civility [*l'état policé*] and from civility back to barbarism.'[5] But, however strong these forces might be, and the champions of civilizations were not inclined to underestimate them, they must eventually crumble before the far stronger natural forces of 'enlightenment'.

The process which Constant called the *egale repartition des lumieres* was, he believed, ultimately inescapable (Constant 1815, p. 95). Sooner or later the cultures of the uncivilized will vanish just as the barbarisms of the European 'Gothic Ages' had vanished in their turn. Once the European colonists have shed their own shackles of unreason they will, proclaimed Condorcet, 'civilize the savage races which have hitherto occupied such vast countries, or make them disappear even without conquest' for they, the peoples of America, Africa, and Asia, 'seem to be waiting only to be civilized and to receive from us the means to be so, and find brothers among the Europeans to become their friends and disciples' (Condorcet 1793, pp. 335–7).

This insistence on illumination, on man's innate drive for an understanding which must inevitably lead to an ever-increasing sociability, demanded a radical revision of many current accounts— Rousseau's in particular—of the origins of human society. In the first place, it greatly reduced the role assigned to individual legislators and to moments of sudden and irreversible transformation. For, Constant argued, the kind of societies where it was possible for individual legislators and founding fathers to have had any measurable impact must have been ones in which the sum total of knowledge was very small, too small, indeed, to be regarded as significantly different from the 'barbarian' communities which had preceded them. Nostalgia and the inherent instability of even the most civilized community meant that the primitive yearnings for a single man to represent the age, around whom 'all the forces will group themselves', were hard to resist (Constant 1815, pp. 90–4). But no matter how deep our potential for barbarism may be, the civilizations we actually inhabit are, he claimed, too complex to have been anything other than exercises in cooperation. No one, protested the jurist and one of Rousseau's most excitable critics, Simon Linguet, could be expected to accept as a plausible historical account, the Ciceronian claim that the origin of human society was to be found in the acts of supremely gifted first legislators (Linguet 1767, p. 221). To have been capable of such deeds they would have had to have been 'celestial intelligences rather than men'. Then they would have needed to be in possession of an instrument—language—which must itself be a social artefact. And it is clearly absurd to suppose that these early men would be in a position to respond to the rhetorical claims of a Solon or a Lycurgus unless they already possessed the sentiments necessary for understanding them. 'One cannot claim,' he concluded, 'that society is the effect of a sentiment of which it itself is the cause' (Linguet 1767, pp. 208–9). Men, in short, must have been capable of a high degree of sociability from the moment they first appeared on the planet. As Carli observed in his eulogy of Inca society, there was no evidence from anywhere in the world to show that man had ever lived a solitary language-less existence. Even the most primitive of peoples lived in bands held together by speech. To claim that language was an invention was to deny to man the power of communication which even animals possess, for language is to man only what barking is to dogs, the 'signs by which they communicate their thoughts', and without which he would not have been able to survive at all (Carli 1794b, p. 143).

The philosophical history of civilization was, then, a history of progressive complexity and progressive refinement which followed from the free expression of those faculties which men possess only as members of a community. For the political economists, the insistence on a continuous historical past together with the refusal to engage in vain conjecture not only eliminated founding fathers and first legislators, but also did away with any real or useful distinction between nature and culture. 'Art itself,' said Ferguson 'is natural to man.' He is 'destined from the first age of his being to invent and to contrive'. The psychological model for the history of irreversible human progress had always been the life of the human individual (Ferguson 1996, p. 6). 'Not only the individual,' wrote Ferguson, 'advances from infancy to manhood, but the species itself from rudeness to civilization.' But it was difficult to align this with the idea that the pre-social condition of men had been one in which they were, in Ferguson's words, 'possessed of mere animal sensibility, without any exercise of the faculties that render them superior to brutes, without any political union, without any means of explaining their sentiments' (Ferguson 1996, p. 2).

For Ferguson and Smith, as for such men as Linguet, Gaetano, Filangieri, Grimaldi, Constant, and Carli, the classical 'state of nature' could, therefore, only be a simple fiction composed of 'wild suppositions' and 'fruitless inquiries', which, as Ferguson noted, were generally devised *ex post facto* to satisfy 'the desire of laying the foundation of a favourite system, or a fond expectation, perhaps, that we may be able to penetrate the secrets of nature'. Humans, real humans, had always been distinct, superior, and endowed with the capacity for natural improvement. What Ferguson listed as man's 'disposition to friendship or enmity, his reason, his use of language and articulate sounds' are attributes of the self; they 'are to be retained in his description, as the wing and the paw are in the eagle and the lion' (Ferguson 1996, p. 3).

As Linguet pointed out, the advocates of the state of nature, from Pufendorf to Rousseau, had persistently dodged the issue of whether they thought it to have had a real existence or not. The American political philosopher Judith Shklar (1969, p. 2) once remarked that the purpose of the state of nature was only to 'induce moral recognition in the reader'. If indeed this was true, if the state of nature was nothing more than instructive fantasy, then it could be of no conceptual value for the theorist of civilization. The theorist, who according to Ferguson was a natural historian obliged 'to collect facts' and not 'offer conjectures', could not simply 'put the facts aside', as Rousseau (1959, pp. 132–3) had claimed he could. If the state of nature had indeed never had any existence in real historical time, then it could never be of any use even as a thought-experiment (Hont 2005, pp. 163–4). No man, claimed Carli (1794a, pp. 104–6), could be compelled to any kind of moral understanding through the contemplation of a 'romance' about a condition which was wholly alien to our nature as men. Man, as Adam Smith (1976, p. 85) said bluntly, 'who can subsist only in society was fitted by nature to that situation for which he was made'.

If the state of nature could be shown, both theoretically and empirically, to be a simple fiction, if human societies were the consequence of a natural uninterrupted growth of which the final product was something termed 'civilization', then it must also be the case that the inequalities present in all civil societies must, *pace* Rousseau, be natural ones. The seeming equality of savage society, or even of Rousseau's Alpine villages, was an illusion. Equality in ignorance, sloth, and abject poverty was mere bestiality. The only true equality was the equality of enlightened cooperation that could be achieved only through civilization. All men might indeed be born equal, but the moral and intellectual status of the child was hardly relevant. It was what he or she became that mattered. The skills of the inventor and the artist, said Ferguson, depended on the toil of the mechanic. As European travellers tirelessly remarked, in savage societies such distinctions do not exist. The savage possesses an undivided personality and, in Ferguson's words, 'acts from his talents in the highest station which human society can offer' (Ferguson 1996, p. 186). Only in barbarous societies, as Smith insisted, could the same man be a producer, a statesman, a judge, and a warrior (Hont and Ignatieff 1983,

p. 7). Such equality could survive only at a very low level of technical development. In any civilized society, there must be a marked difference between the arts and the professions, between, in Ferguson's terms, the statesman and 'the tools he employs' (Ferguson 1996, p. 183). For Smith, the loss of the undivided personality, the creation of the division of labour, and, with it, of property and of social inequality was an inescapable feature of the commercial society. Inequality was not, of course, desirable in itself; but, as his famous analogy between the condition of the African chieftain and the European pauper made clear, the only possible society of equals was not the community of semi-angelic beings of Rousseau's imagination, but merely one in which all men lived equally miserably.

***

All the attempts to describe and account for civilization that I have mentioned so far were based upon one or another kind of conjectural history. They were remarkably persuasive, partly, at least, because they were grounded in a large measure of sociological and ethnographical data, which dispensed with any natural law argument based upon 'innate ideas'. But the history, despite the insistence of its authors upon the certainty of their data, remained conjectural. No one could *know* what the origins of society had been, and no sociology based on historical projection could escape the charge levelled at it by biologists that it might itself be proved false at any moment by the discovery of new data or by future events. There was, of course, another set of explanations for the human *diversitas rerum* (diversity of things) which the philosophical histories had largely obscured. There had always been those who were prepared to argue that the differences between the various races of the world at any one point could only be ascribed to a set of responses to environmental conditions. The climate argument although it clearly persuaded Jean d'Alembert that it had a sound empirical basis, offered at best an incomplete account of human difference, since it could only ever determine disposition (Shklar 1998, p. 301). If, asked Claude-Adrien Helvétius, climate determined personal disposition, why were the Romans, 'so magnanimous, so audacious under a Republican government[,] ... today so soft and effeminate'? And why had the Persians and 'those Asiatics who were so brave under the name of Elamites, become so cowardly and base by the time of Alexander' (Constant 1988, p. 319)? David Hume took much the same view. Soil and climate, after all, have remained unchanged throughout time, so far as we know. If human nature was determined by climate, then it should be unaffected by history, but, in fact, the 'character of nation' is never the 'same for a century together' (Hume 1978, pp. 316–17). 'I believe no-one,' he remarked caustically, 'attributes the difference of manners in Wapping and St. James's [poor and rich districts of London] to a difference of air or climate' (Hume 1985, p. 204). As even its most convinced advocate, Montesquieu was ready to admit that under certain circumstances 'the moral cause will destroy the physical'. Thus, 'slavery debases, weakens and destroys the spirit, while liberty shapes, elevates and fortifies it' (Montesquieu 1949, pp. 61–2).

But if climate and situation would not do, not all were convinced that some kind of biological explanation was entirely unavailable. Even Carli (1794a, pp. 175–85) had been prepared to argue that the habit of leadership, the unequal distribution of property, even the aesthetic inequalities displayed by the art of Asia, Africa, America, and Europe might all correspond at some level to man's status *qua* animal. The significant *rupture* with the more firmly sociological modes of explanation came, however, at the beginning of the nineteenth century. The growth of physical anthropology and the continuing debates over the nature of the great apes made it intellectually respectable to raise, in another and radically more deterministic language, doubts as to whether the genus 'humanity' might not prove on examination to contain more than one species (see, for example, Prichard 1814). In addition to this, and as is evident in most of the French writings on the subject, there was a need to find an irrefutable, hence scientific, argument with which to oppose the abolitionists. There was also a need, during the Restoration, to undermine all claims that a social revolution could bring an immediate change in the distribution of status within human societies, and all of these eventually led to the revival of biological explanations for the rise and distribution of 'civilization'. For Jean-Baptiste Lamarck for whom there was a relationship amounting to interdependence between the 'moral' and the 'physical', and whose psychology was almost simplistically Lockean, civilization could simply be described as a condition of advanced sensational complexity (Lamarck, 1809, p. 4). In the state of nature all men must be equal because all are equally brutish. There is simply nothing for their intelligences to operate on, and reason, like any other faculty, will develop only if it is used. The degree of an individual's intelligence will very much depend on what he or she does. But what he or she does will, in the first instance, be the consequence of a natural disposition. There then comes into being, he wrote, 'the real existence of a scale relative to the intelligence of the individuals of the human species' (Lamarck 1830, p. 320). It was this scale, he claimed, which was the first cause of the division of labour and not, as both Smith and Rousseau, with different ends in view, had supposed, the other way about. Only those who have extended leisure will be able to develop their mental capacities to the full. Those who labour will, of necessity, be made or will remain brutish, and, in a pre-industrial society, it was clear that there had to be a helot class so that the others should be free to enjoy their *otium*. By grounding this distinction, not, as all social theorists from Aristotle to Smith had done, in education but in what he called an 'organic phenomenon', Lamarck (1830, pp. 291–2) had effectively made the process irreversible. For man, there could be no condition other than that of civilization, of a world divided between those who consumed and those who produced.

Lamarck's argument for a biology of civilization exists only in outline. But one of his successors, Jules Joseph Virey, best known perhaps for his involvement with the case of the wild boy of Aveyron, attempted, in his *Histoire naturelle du genre humain* of 1824 and a lecture delivered to the Académie de médecine in 1841 on the physiological causes of civilization, to provide a more thoroughgoing account of the biological mechanism of civilization and a legitimation of the inequalities it necessarily involved. Arguments for a natural equality of the kind put forward by Rousseau must, he claimed, lead directly to the collapse of the civilized world. Since for Virey (1824, p. 69) man ruling over his fellow was merely a special case of his domination over other species, Rousseau's 'natural equality' between men would logically require that man abandon his domination over animals. The natural inequality between the races derives from the obvious and observable facts that the species was divided into two distinct groups: the 'blacks', which meant all Africans, Americans, and Asians, and the 'whites', which included all Caucasians (Virey 1824, pp. 436–8). The latter have already attained 'a more or less perfect level of civilization'. The others, however, never arrive at anything other than a 'constantly imperfect civilization'. The reason for this may be found in the fact, which, so he believed, few had previously noted (although it is, of course, a feature of Rousseau's account of the deleterious effects of the social process), that sociability in men is the same process as domesticity in animals—the dogs of savages were, he claimed, less docile than the dogs of civil men—for like domesticity sociability is a process of 'interior contraction'. The results are physiologically evident (Virey 1841, pp. 402–5).

Both domestic animals and civilized men have white flesh; untamed animals and uncivilized men have dark flesh. The implication of this was that refinement, the civilities which Mirabeau had seen as masking the true virtues of civil society, were, in fact, constitutive of it. We must, said Virey, overthrow the old and pernicious notion that delicacy leads to decay. The reverse is true. 'Even among those savages in South America,' he wrote, repeating much older stereotypes of the 'Patagonians', 'where the sexes mingle without distinction of parentage and where fathers delight in corrupting their own children' all are valiant and robust. What they clearly are not is 'civilized'. True, his concept of 'delicacy' is ambiguous since it precludes sensuality and '*les peuples donnés aux plaisirs*' (peoples given over to pleasure) and is typified by '*les hommes austères des pays froids*' (austere men from cold climates) (Virey 1824, pp. xii–xvi). But it is equally clear that the older virtues of the Roman republic—and of Revolutionary France—translate out not as the civic virtues which for an earlier generation seem to have made commercial society, and hence 'civilization', possible but as the signs of inescapably savage communities. Virey's socio-biology, deterministic and anti–historical, led him to revise arguments for natural inequality which had lain dormant for over a hundred years. He even attempted to inject new life into a modified version of Aristotle's theory of natural slavery, and many of his conclusions were not unlike those which some of the apologists for the Spanish domination of America had come up with two hundred years ago, although theirs were more generally psychological than directly biological. It might, he said, seem unjust to some that there are races—the 'blacks'—who had been singled out to serve others, 'but is it any more unjust for the lion to devour the gazelle?' (Virey 1824, pp. 67–70). Without an abundant supply of labour—without slavery—European civilization would not have been possible. The sceptical challenge which had dominated the human sciences for so long had been swept away. The answer to the question 'What is right?' was now being given in terms of neither a natural law theory nor historical empiricism but in the supposed biological, and hence 'scientific' and unchallengeable, composition of the species.

Virey's biological racism was not an isolated case, and, for the Romantics and their heirs, it came to constitute a significant if not dominant feature of a social theory of civilization: an insistence on the immutability of the inherited order, the claim to be a science of human conduct, and, above all, an unfailing belief in progress and the superiority of technology over all the other 'arts'. What emerged from the Romantic critique of this image of the optimal state for man was, of course, the divide which is now associated most strikingly with the German antimony between *Zivilisation* and *Kultur*. For Nietzsche, civilization was indeed precisely what Virey had declared it to be— 'the ages of the domestication of man'. But it was, as it had been for Rousseau, a domestication which had been forced upon him, which was 'intolerant of the most audacious and brilliant minds' and had atrophied his better self. Civilization, Nietzsche concluded, 'means something else than culture, something which is perhaps the reverse of culture' (quoted by Starobinski, 1989, p. 43).

NOTES

1. Huntington is not, however, concerned with 'civilization' as a concept in the singular but with 'civilizations' in the plural, nor does he offer any account of 'civilization' that would distinguish it in any significant way from 'culture' (Huntington, 1996, pp. 40–1).
2. Émile Benveniste (1966, p. 343) claimed the possibility of a prior usage in the unpublished manuscripts of Adam Ferguson.
3. On savage indolence, see Pocock (1999, pp. 79–96).
4. Published as the seventeenth chapter to the *Mélanges de littérature et de politique* in 1829.
5. Raynal uses *l'état policé* and *civilization* as synonyms.

BIBLIOGRAPHY

Barsanti, G. 1983. *La mappa della vita*. Naples: Guida Editori.
Benveniste, E. 1966. 'Civilisation: Contribution à l'histoire du mot'. In *Problemes de linguistique générale*, pp. 336–45. Paris: Gallimard.

Brett, A. S. 2011. *Changes of State, Nature and the Limits of the City in Early Modern Natural Law.* Princeton, NJ: Princeton University Press.

Carli, G. R. 1794a. *Delle lettere americane* [1780]. *Opere* (Vol. XI). Milan.

——. 1794b. *Della diseguaglianza fra gli uomini* [1792]. *Opere* (Vol. XIX), Milan.

Condorcet, Marquis de (Marie Jean Antoine Nicolas de Caritat). 1793. *Esquisse d'un tableau historique des progrès de l'esprit humain.* Paris: Agasse.

Constant, B. 1815. *De l'esprit de conquête et de l'usurpation: dans leurs rapports avec la civilisation européenne.* Paris: Le Normand.

——. [1829] 1967. *De la perfectibilité de l'espèce humaine,* edited by P. Deguise. Lausanne: Éd. l'Age d'homme.

——. 1988. *Political Writings,* edited by Biancamaria Fontana. Cambridge: Cambridge University Press.

Dampierre, E. 1960. 'Note on "Culture" and "Civilisation"'. *Comparative Studies in Society and History* 3: 328–40.

Ferguson, A. 1792. *Principles of Moral and Political Science: Being Chiefly a Retrospect of Lectures Delivered in the College of Edinburgh,* 2 vols. Edinburgh: W. Creech.

——. 1966. *An Essay on the History of Civil Society,* edited by D. Forbes. Edinburgh: Edinburgh University Press.

Fontana, B. 1991. *Benjamin Constant and the Post-revolutionary Mind.* New Haven and London: Yale University Press.

Grimaldi, F. 1958. 'Riflessioni sopra l'ineguaglianza tra gli uommi [1779–1780]'. In *Illuministi Italiane,* vol. V, edited by F. Venturi. Milan-Naples: Riccardo Riccardi.

Hofman, E. 2009. 'The Theory of the Perfectibility of the Human Race'. In *The Cambridge Companion to Constant,* edited by H. Rosenblatt, pp. 248–71. Cambridge: Cambridge University Press.

Hont, I. 2005. *The Jealousy of Trade: International Competition and the Nation-state in Historical Perspective.* Cambridge Mass.: Harvard University Press.

Hont, I. and M. Ignatieff. 1983. 'Needs and Justice in the Wealth of Nations: An Introductory Essay'. In *Wealth and Virtue: The Shaping of Political Economy in the Scottish Enlightenment,* edited by I. Hont and M. Ignatieff, pp. 1–44. Cambridge: Cambridge University Press.

Hume, D. 1978. *A Treatise of Human Nature,* edited by L. A. Selby-Bigge and P. H. Nidditch. Oxford: Oxford University Press.

——. 1985. 'Of National Characters'. In *Essays Moral, Political, and Literary,* edited by E. F. Miller, pp. 197–215. Indianapolis: Liberty Classics.

Huntington, S. P. 1996. *The Clash of Civilizations and the Remaking the World Order.* New York: Penguin Books.

Kant, I. 2007. 'Review of J. G. Herder's *Ideas for the Philosophy of the History of Humanity*'. In *Anthropology, History, and Education*, edited and translated by G. Zöller and R. B. Louden, pp. 121–42. Cambridge, UK; New York: Cambridge University Press.

Lamarck, J. 1809. *Philosophie zoologique, ou exposition des considérations relatives à l'histoire naturelle des animaux*. Paris: Dentu.

———. 1830. *Systeme analytique des connaissances positives de l'homme*. Paris: B. Baillière.

Linguet, S. 1767. *Théorie des loix civiles, ou principes fondamentaux de la société*. London.

Mazower, M. 2012. *Governing the World: The History of an Idea*. New York: Penguin.

Mill, J. S. 1977. 'Civilization'. In *Essays on Politics and Society*, vol. 18, edited by J. M. Robson, pp. 117–48. Toronto: University of Toronto Press.

Mirabeau, H. G. R. 1756. *L'Ami des Hommes, ou Traité de la population*. Paris: Avignon.

Montesquieu, C. S. 1949. *Œuvres complètes*, edited by Roger Caillois. Paris: Bibliothèque de la Pléiade.

———1951. *De l'esprit des lois*, edited by R. Caillois. Paris: Bibliothéque de la Pléiade.

Pocock, J. G. A. 1999. *Barbarism and Religion*. Cambridge: Cambridge University Press.

Prichard, J. 1814. *Researches into the Physical History of Man*. London: J. and A. Arch.

Raynal, G. T. F. 1781. *Histoire philosophique et politique des établissements et du commerce des Européens dans les deux Indes*. A Genève: chez Jean-Leonard Pellet.

Rousseau, J. J. 1959. *Discours sur l'origine et les fondements de l'inégalité (Œuvres complètes, Tome 3)*, edited by B. Gagnebin and M. Raymond. Paris: Gallimard.

Shklar, J. N. 1969. *Men and Citizens: A Study of Rousseau's Social Theory*. Cambridge: Cambridge University Press.

———. 1998. 'Jean d'Alembert and the Rehabilitation of History'. In *Political Thought and Political Thinkers*, edited by S. Hoffmann, pp. 294–316. Chicago: University of Chicago Press.

Smith, A. [1759] 1976. *The Theory of Moral Sentiments*, edited by D. D. Raphael and A. L. Macfie. Oxford: Clarendon.

Starobinski, J. 1989. *Le Mot civilisation*. Paris: Gallimard.

Virey, J. J. 1824. *Histoire naturelle du genre humain*. Paris: Crochard.

———. 1841. 'Des causes physiologiques de la sociabilité chez les animaux et de la civilisation dans les hommes'. *Bulletin de l'académie de médecine* 6: 402–5.

2 Rethinking Civilization and Its Others

Historical Stages and Social Taxonomies

Lutfi Sunar

CIVILIZATION DEBATE: DEFINING CIVILIZATION AS A PRINCIPAL CATEGORY

One of the philosophers who framed the contemporary discussions around the concept of civilization, Arnold Toynbee (1935, p. 455), defines civilizations as 'institutions of the highest order—institutions, that is, which comprehend without being comprehended'. Following him, today a civilization is mostly defined as a complex state of society. Societies reach this state after passing through some specific stages. The birth of civilization is mainly defined through the separation from and domination over natural environment. According to some anthropologists, civilization is achieved through domination that extinguishes equality and creates social hierarchy within society. Some historians date civilization back to the invention of symbolic forms of communication, especially those such as writing systems. On the one hand, civilization is often described as urbanization, centralization, specialization, and division of labour. On the other, civilization has also been linked to the rise of the arts, especially great architectural monuments. However, these neutral definitions of civilization are somewhat deceptive. According to these definitions, all societies throughout world history have had a kind of civilization. But I believe this is only one side of the story. The other side is related to the birth and definition of modernity. A civilized society is defined in opposition to an uncivilized one; in other words, it is precisely the presence of this 'other' society that creates what we understand to be civilization.

Another historian who centralizes the concept of civilization is Fernand Braudel, who states that although we now use this word in the plural form, it was used in the singular form for a long time. According to Braudel (1995, pp. 6–7), who highlights that the word 'civilization' was first used in the plural form in 1819, when the word is used in singular form with an additional descriptive word before it (like Western civilization, Hindu civilization, Ancient civilization, and so forth), its former ethical and intellectual superiority disappears. However, using this concept in the plural form is not enough; because the hierarchy between civilizations is exactly where the story begins. Braudel (1995, p. 8) recognizes this and asserts that Western civilization was in a position to inspire and 'lend' to others during the nineteenth century. How the concept of civilization is considered and discussed in other parts of the world is not the subject of this chapter. However, it should be noted that though using the word 'civilization' in its plural form is a step forward, the fact that the roots of the 'concept of civilization' are obtained from Western civilizations maintains the one-sided nature of the relationship between the East and the West.

That Europe is described as a civilization and gradually identified with the concept of civilization is closely related to the transformation that took place during the century of Enlightenment. Therefore, in this chapter I will focus on this period in order to explore the nature of the concept of civilization. During Enlightenment, Europe reshaped itself and placed modern society within world history. In order to understand this transformation, we need to analyse two issues. The first is the intensification of the debates on society, especially after the second half of the seventeenth century. The identification of Europe as a civilization that was a result of these discussions, which were framed around an intensive clash with the church, relates to the change of the social structure that was formerly represented by the church and feudalism or, as denoted later, the traditional world and the dark forces. Describing Europe as a civilization was considered identical to reshaping it. Emphasizing a social structure that resulted from human endeavour was a political attitude adopted with the aim of creating a distance from the church and the aristocracy. However, the concept of civilization found its real meaning in the second half of the eighteenth century. In this period, we see that Europe was increasingly in contact with other societies and its structure was changing. From the 1770s onwards, European powers, led by England, began to gain advantage over the settled civilizations of China, India, and the Near East using their experiences of colonizing the unsettled civilizations of America, Oceania, and Africa. Thus, the concept of civilization that was originally developed against the feudal society began to come into play as a distinctive reaction against other societies. Within this framework, the story of civilization has two dimensions; one is descriptive and the other is exclusionary. In this study, my central hypothesis is that if the second dimension of this concept had not been developed, the first would not be sufficient to sustain itself and the system that we recognize as modernity today would not have adequate grounds to identify itself.

Today we know that the conception of civilization has taken its shape as a consequence of conjectural history that was devised by Scottish Enlightenment thinkers to construct a more secular society. This progressive perception of history depends precisely on the hypothesis that history goes forward in accordance with the experiences of humanity. Hence, progressive thinkers teleologically envisage civilization as an ultimate point in the historical process and a fertile new crop for their theoretical and conjectural historical model. Enlightenment thinkers commonly considered the idea of progress as an integral characteristic of European civilization. Civilization, therefore, as a sociological concept could only be actualized in Europe.

Yet, civilization has been invigorated by negations. European thinkers have constantly fortified the limits of civilization by defining its outsiders and distinguishing them from its insiders. Within this framework, the concept of the 'barbarian', which had been in circulation for a long while in the West since Ancient Greece, has functioned as a determinant to identify the 'civilized'. Modern European social theory has been decisively shaped by this 'barbarian–civilized' dichotomy, and the notion of the 'other' has a central place in it. This chapter will consider the problem of defining Western civilization through the notion of the 'other' with reference to ideas from the founding thinkers of the Enlightenment such as Vico, Montesquieu, Hume, Smith, Ferguson, and Hegel about the historical development of social formations. Historical periodization theories and taxonomies of societies have a significant place in how we conceptualize modern society in a progressive way and lead to the exclusion of non-Western societies from the civilization basin by describing them as 'barbarians' and 'savages'. Therefore, this chapter will focus on a discussion of civil society theories and will examine the classifications of societies by outstanding thinkers from the Enlightenment. In this way, it will be revealed how 'othering' is a natural extension of the concept of modern society, something necessary in order for it to identify itself.

FROM *SOCIETAS* TO *CIVITAS*: TRANSFORMATION OF CIVIL SOCIETY

The most important discussions held during the Enlightenment were about the new social order to be established in Europe. This conflict that is reflected as a fight between the old and the new was integral to the establishment of a new societal model in the wake of the feudal society. Out of this environment emerged the conceptualization of society, which was widely used to express a new unity. With the development of the concept of civil society, the relationship between society as a concept and modern social order crystallized, and the concept of society became integrated into civilization within the framework of progressive historical philosophy. It also began to play a primary role in the identification of Europe that was distinguished from 'the other'.

Keith Michael Baker, in his study, discussing the rapid entrance of the words 'social', 'society', and 'sociable' into the dictionaries and how they were brought into usage, states that 'society' includes an inherent voluntary meaning. Though the word 'society' and its derivatives did not first appear in the eighteenth century, as it can be seen in the table prepared by Daniel Gordon based on his review of books written in French in the seventeenth and eighteenth centuries, there was a noticeable increase in the frequency of the usage of these words (Baker 2001, p. 85). In this framework, the meaning of the word 'society' revolved around two points: coming together for a common purpose to form associations and friendship, companionship, and camaraderie (Baker 2001, p. 86). At the end of the eighteenth century, while the former gradually stayed in the background, new definitions developed to broaden the latter. Baker states that in the eighteenth century, after the definition appeared in *Dictionnaire universal* written by Antonie Furetières in 1690, the concept expanded in three ways. The first expansion was about social needs; people meet their needs with mutual support and collective action. The second expansion referred to the gathering of individuals based on their similar natures. The third expansion asserted that society is potentially dangerous and problematic. Diderot and d'Alambert handled each of these themes in two items in the *Encyclopédie*. In the first scenario, society is considered as a legal notion and two types of societies are mentioned: societies that include most of humanity (*sociétés généreles*) and societies located in a specific place, that is, a town, city, or state (*sociétés particuliéres*). In the second case society is considered as an ethical term. The most interesting feature of this is that it counts society as natural and a necessity for humanity (Baker 2001, pp. 87–90).

Thereby, it is possible to observe a critical transformation of the meaning of the concept of society at the end of the seventeenth century. This concept representing small groups like professional associations, guilds, and saloon communities at the beginning of the 1700s became associated with a group of abstract and general meanings like ethnical societies, nations, and countries. The former meanings of the concept like cooperation and friendship did not fade away but evolved into a more general meaning as a fundamental form of collective human existence. The institutionalized existence of human society began to be understood as a result of human nature (Baker 2001, p. 96). According to Baker, the concept of society during the Enlightenment provided a good answer to the value crisis in the seventeenth century that can be called Augustism. This value crisis was brought about by Christian individualism or the sinner's disconnection from God, renouncement of friends, and condemnation to faulty morals. From this perspective, the concept of society at the time of the Enlightenment was less about the discovery of individualism than acting as a veil to it. The invention of society provided a middle way between certainty and doubt, religion and relativism, compassion and despair, and absolute power and anarchy. It was considered as a tolerable, imperfect but reformable institution of human beings (Baker 2001, p. 95).

The concept of society that was used in relation to freedom, with the progress of time, began to be used by thinkers of the Enlightenment to express a unity that is politically organized in a specific land. It can be claimed that society became possible as a solution to the tension between the newly developing concepts of liberty and that need is developed based on the idea of mutual contract. Accordingly, people need to coexist without giving up on their freedom. Therefore, social contract, which is the father of sociological theory, allows for both. Baker states that the main concepts of the Enlightenment, 'progress' and 'civilization', do not count for much without 'society' (Baker 2001, p. 84). This is because these ideas, in the pursuit of describing a new order, function as descriptors of the newly emerging society. Features of this new order began to be identified with the concept of civil society and were historically contextualized with progressivism. Ultimately, with the help of these two descriptor concepts, society was no longer a philosophical abstraction; it turned into a concrete entity in the nineteenth century. This can be most clearly explained by the evolution of the concept of civil society from Locke to Hegel.

In the formation and transformation of the concept of civil society in the modern context, Locke, Scottish ethics philosophers (like Hume, Ferguson, and Smith), and Hegel have a special place (Khilani 2001, p. 18). Enlightenment thinkers generally considered civil society as one of the important constituents of social formation and gave it a special place. This is because civil society represents the space of bourgeoisie against the feudal authority.

The concept of civil society, which was used first in Aristotle's famous book *Politics* in Ancient Greece, once again became an important part of the political and philosophical language along with discussions about the nature of modern society (Aristotle 2013). The concept of *koinonia politike* (κοινωνια πολιτικη) has no distinctive definition other than phenomena like 'political order', 'society', and 'public space'. That is to say, Aristotle does not attribute a central role to the concept of civil society. What Aristotle means by this idea is that people are brought together by the social contracts they create and their coexistence is guaranteed by liberty and equal relationships. This is because 'koinonia' implies values like coexistence, solidarity, association, and sharing. The word also signified all kinds of human communities in Ancient Greece. Considering that was civil society's social dimension, Aristotle did not make a society–state (*polis*) distinction in its political dimension. According to Aristotle, a person had the opportunity to gain existence and value only if s/he was a citizen of a polis, whereas being within the boundaries of a polis as a foreigner or slave did not give him/her the right to be a part of the decision-making mechanism of the political society. In other words, the precondition of civil society according to Aristotle's political philosophy is that independent individuals have a voice regarding the state apparatus (Springborg 1986, p. 202).

The concept of civil society was not used frequently as there was no clear distinction between the state and society, and we see it return to the literature again with the re-emergence of cities. Especially with the newly emerged bourgeoisie demand for some political rights, the concept of civil society was reshaped. Thereby, the phenomenon of civil society that survived until today obtained its position on the stage of history again as a conceptualization grounded and structured by the bourgeoisie and with the emergence of the modern capitalist state; the concept of civil society continued its existence until today as a concept describing the dominant class of bourgeoisie.

Thomas Hobbes brought the concept of civil society to the centre of the political discussions of the new era and was the most prominent thinker and political philosopher of the seventeenth century. Hobbes handled the concept of civil society based on the 'social contract' and brought a new dimension to this notion. According to Hobbes, individuals live in a 'state of nature' before the contract. In this state, war, disorder, and chaos are predominant both between the state and individuals and among the individuals themselves. Hobbes emphasizes that the selfish, aggressive, competitive, and combative nature of individuals will be controlled only by the formation of a social contract under a strong state authority. Accordingly, as an outcome of this contract, individuals give up the idea of self-protection and willingly form a 'mutual' contract to be assigned to someone or a council who will protect the group's safety and peace; in this way, the state is created. Hobbes names the society that appears in this process as civil society, but he does not clearly distinguish it from the concepts of political society, political order, or state.

John Locke was the philosopher who distinguished these concepts from each other. Locke, who gave its modern meaning to the concept of civil society, considers the state of nature as a state in which mutual cooperation and protection are in effect. Evidence of Locke's theories regarding human nature can be found in his reflections on the state of nature. According to Locke, individuals who exist in a state of nature, where there is no official governing body or state, have God-given, non-transferable, and inalienable rights. Locke outlines these inherent rights as life, liberty, property, and pursuit to happiness, and gathers them all under the rights of property. He accepts that these rights are a human being's birthright. Individuals who possess these natural rights in the state of nature live an equal and free life. According to Locke, civil society is established when individuals form a contract in order to preserve their basic rights in the state of nature at optimal level. Civil society, which is the opposite of the state of nature, is not a temporary and unfavourable condition, but is where individual rights themselves reside and where the centre of civilization is created. In a sense, Locke prescribes limitation of the power of the government or the state institution for the benefit of the society. Therefore, Locke asserts that a civilized society appears as a consequence of the social contract.

The concept of civil society gained its actual context with the theories of Scottish moral philosophers. These theoreticians developed the idea of gradual historical change that was later termed as 'conjectural history'. In the scope of this idea of society's conjectural and gradual development, these thinkers went beyond using the term 'civil' as an adjective and began to use it as a noun in the form of the word 'civilization'. Hume, Ferguson, and Smith, prominent Scottish Enlightenment thinkers, picture the history of social development in a progressive manner and mention commercial society, which corresponds to the last stage as civil society or civilization. According to Hume (1959, pp. 97–101), the purpose of the social contract is not an abstract ideal, but the protection of human rights. Like Locke, Hume also believes that society emerged in order to prevent injustices— especially those against the right of property—in accordance with the universal tendencies of human nature. According to Hume, the main source of injustice is the violation of property rights. This is because the institution of property that serves to satisfy human needs in the best way emerged in the course of historical experiences by itself, just as the state did, and has been preserved because it is beneficial. In the absence of these two, the satisfaction of human needs becomes problematic.

The prominent figures of the Scottish Enlightenment granted a special place to trade in this gradual historical change. According to them, among all types of livelihood, trade is the most advanced economic activity that serves to construct a civilized society. Thus, the civil society is in a position to be a commercial society at the same time. According to Smith, who brought these commercial society theories to their furthest point, only commercial societies have been able to distinguish the market from personal relationships. Furthermore, Smith asserts that once the foundation to meet the needs in the market is established in the commercial society, a natural sympathy for non-instrumental ethical interactions is also formed. Accordingly, Smith states that commercial societies that neither depend on compulsory relationships like family and kinship bonds or master–slave systems nor on involuntary relationships constitute the highest level of humanity. Consequently, Smith further elaborates that bonds like kinship are an attribute of pre-commercial societies. Therefore, commercial societies are an ethical order as much as they are an economic and social order (Khilani 2001, pp. 20–1).

Smith explains that the emergence of civilized society has led to the development of a better way to satisfy human needs. This way way does not come into being as a result of the conscious preferences of individuals but is an unintended collective outcome of personal activities that humans realized while meeting their needs. In order to understand this mechanism, we need to understand Smith's theory of human nature. According to Smith, humans instinctively strive after their interests in order to perpetuate their existence. Smith casts away all former negative comments on the self-interested human type and declares that these interest-seeking efforts are the primary dynamics of a civilized society. This is because, as Smith maintains, while individuals strive to satisfy their own needs and maximize their interests, they contribute to the formation of a balance without even noticing it and, therefore, this serves to maximize the interests of the entire society as well. Smith explains this with his division-of-labour theory. Consequently, there is a division of labour that serves as the foundation for human beings to come together and create society. Individuals have to share tasks with others in order to better meet their needs. This leads to specialization in professions, and a more productive economic life spontaneously comes into being. Had individuals wanted to satisfy their needs by themselves, it would have led to unproductive economic activity. Division of labour and specialization increase productivity and efficiency and provide the means for the development of a civilized society. As is seen, Smith's analysis regarding civil society has an economic component. Perhaps what makes Smith a classic is that he comprehended at a very early stage that economic activities constitute the foundations of modern society. His division-of-labour theory has become a foundation for all theories developed to explain modern society in sociology.

Patricia Springborg states that a considerable part of Western thought regarding politics at the beginning of the nineteenth century emanated from a three-stage schematization, which reflected a general consensus on the subject. The evolution of Western forms and institutions was considered as a transition from a primitive society that is ruled primarily by family, clan, or tribe (stage 1) to a political society that is signified by the emergence of the city-state (stage 2), and finally to an industrial society that is based on the modern nation state (stage 3) (Springborg 1986, p. 185). This schematization can be seen in its clearest form in the work of Hegel, the German philosopher. Hegel, who formalized the new and in many ways the ultimate form of the concept of civil society that is developed by the Scottish Enlightenment thinkers in the frame of commercial society and ethics theories, saved political authority from being perceived as a negative factor in the scope of civil society. In his book *The Philosophy of Right*, which he wrote in 1821, Hegel suggests that civil society and the state have separate domains. In this way, he tries to overcome the tension between civil society and the state. According to Hegel, civil society does not assure freedom nor is it formed through contracts; civil society serves as a mediator between the family and the state, and undertakes a transformative role. The main factor is love-based trust in the family, need-based conflict in civil society, and harmony-based association with the state. Need- and ambition-based conflicts in civil society have resulted in the emergence of the state as a regulatory authority. Therefore, the state and civil society represent two distinct

territories. At the same time, Hegel asserts that civil society constituted one aspect of the modern nation state that was developed in
eighteenth-century Europe, especially in the period after the French
Revolution in 1789. In this way, Hegel signifies that civil society is
not an alternative political domain, but a functional element of the
modern nation state.

As will be seen in the discussions later, these debates that were
held around the concept of 'civil' are closely related to European
political environment when viewed from a certain perspective. That
Locke considered the right to property and its assurances as the
foundation of civil society and of Hume's, Smith's, and Ferguson's
efforts to provide a foundation for new social relations in the scope of
the theories of social contract and commercial society constitute an
article of the debates on new social structure that continued during
the Enlightenment period. An outstanding aspect of these debates is
the effort to create a new political order in the wake of the former
feudal society, in which commerce and property are the main factors.
However, if we consider this effort only within the domestic political context of Europe, we cannot understand the transition from the
concept of civil society to the concept of civilization. Therefore, as
discussed at the beginning of this study, we need to consider this in
the scope of the issue of positioning the new form of the modern society within other world societies. The fields to display this issue most
clearly are historical staging and social taxonomies that developed in
parallel with the debates on civil society.

A ROAD TO A HIERARCHIZED WORLD: STAGING
HISTORY AND CLASSIFYING SOCIETIES

While introducing the newly emergent social order, the Enlightenment
thinkers ascribed two main fields. One of these was the staging of history within the context of philosophy of history, and the other was the
taxonomy of social types in parallel to this historical staging. In this
way, a main framework was developed to explain, make sense of, and
rationalize the emergent social order. It would not be an exaggera-
tion to claim that the historical development theories of each one of
the Enlightenment thinkers are correspondingly a description of the
social types. Perhaps one of the most important aspects of modern

social theory that distinguishes it from former social theories is this particular attribute.

The taxonomy of types of societies based on particular characteristics has a long history. Developing a new social order generally means developing a new social taxonomy.[1] As Gerhard Lenski (1994, p. 2) explains, 'taxonomies are theories of order'. After the sixteenth century, European thinkers were in a position to make more extended analyses on social taxonomies as an outcome of their confrontation with different societies. However, classification of societies based on various points of view became a common occupation in the Enlightenment period. This was because a new social order was established in this period, and there was an effort to place this emergent order among the existing social orders.

Within the scope of already existing Western and Oriental traditional classifications, societies were classified based on various factors. Ibn Khaldun classified societies as nomad and urban with regard to their lifestyles and situatedness (see Sunar and Yaslıçimen, 2008). In a similar way, in his work on Indian religions, Biruni classified societies according to their beliefs (for a detailed discussion, see Ataman, 2008). In Middle Age Europe, it was common for societal classifications to be made according to religion. Classifications based on geography or climate are also common in all traditional thoughts. Though all these classifications were used throughout the Enlightenment period, in contrast to former ones, social types were based on a historical staging. Within the scope of progressive historical thinking, it was believed that different social types emerged in a progressive pattern from underdeveloped to developed societies. In this framework, the three-stage historical classification that has a firmly established place in Western thought mingled with the deep-rooted terms 'savage', 'barbarian',[2] and 'civilized', and evolved to form a new framework from which to understand the history and society.

Necmettin Alkan (2009) states that the three-stage historical approach that substantially spread during the Enlightenment period was a legacy of Christianity. According to him, the foundation of the ternary system that is used today, which divides history into ages (Ancient Age, Middle Age, and New Age) is a historical categorization developed by the father of Catholic Church, Aurelius Augustinus (354–430), based on the Bible. Alkan indicates that German theologian and historian Christoph Cellarius (1638–1707) put this system into its final form with reference to the tradition and legacy of Augustinus. This ternary classification transferred from Cellarius to the Enlightenment thinkers became one of the most important foundations they used in establishing modern society. This is because the Enlightenment thinkers considered the time period between Ancient Rome and Greece and their own modern period as the Dark Middle Age and stigmatized it as an underdeveloped period in the natural course of historical development. Alkan notes that this is one of the most important foundations of Eurocentric historical approach.

Three Worlds of Vico: The Birth of Humankind

Giambattista Vico (1668–1744), who was a professor of Latin Rhetoric at Napoli University, significantly contributed to the development of this three-stage historical approach. Perhaps he was 'the first modern writer to develop a broadly comprehensive and secular or humanistic taxonomy' (Lenski 1994, p. 3). In his *Principles of a New Science*, based on the knowledge of Egyptians, Vico stages history into three ages that each nation experiences in time: (*a*) the age of gods, (*b*) the age of the heroes, and (*c*) the age of men [or humanity] (Vico 1948, p. 18). In the first age, society has a theocratic feature, and social and judicial laws have divine origins. In the second, societies are aristocratic, and laws are imposed. In the third age, there are popular political alliances, and laws are based on human mind and reason (Vico 1948, p. 5). In the opening of the book, Vico (1948, p. 3) talks of *three worlds*: (a) world of nature (globe, or the order of natural institutions), (b) world of human minds (metaphysical world), and (c) world of human spirits (civil world or world of nations). However, no order, hierarchical or chronological, is assigned to these worlds, except that he says metaphysics (or the world of human minds) stands 'above' the natural world. Also at the closing paragraph of the 'idea of the work' Vico discusses three worlds, which seem to be the same as these three worlds. But in this case, they are assigned explicit orders, representing the historical order 'in which the human minds of the gentiles have been raised from earth to heaven' (Vico 1948, p. 23). This time, the order is both chronological and hierarchical. But what is chronologically first, is hierarchically the simplest, and what is chronologically last, is hierarchically the most complex. According to the chronological order in which men have raised their head from earth to heaven, first comes (*a*) the world of nations, then (*b*) the world of nature, and finally (*c*) the world of minds and of God. Does Vico take these three successive worlds to correspond to the three ages as well? It seems so, as is also suggested by the systematic series of trilogies he uses throughout his work, such as three kinds of natures, three kinds of governments, three kinds of languages, and three kinds of jurisprudence, which are all in harmony with one another (Vico 1948, p. 18).

As Lenski (1994) states, 'Vico's developmental, or proto-evolutionary, view of human societies and their history became a central element in most of the taxonomies that followed in the next two hundred years.' However, the way Vico stages history into ages is developed to explain the roles of people in each stage of history. That this staging is essentially based on the Egyptian tradition and does not centralize the historical progression of humanity distinguishes him from subsequent Enlightenment thinkers in this regard.

Montesquieu: A Taxonomy Based on Climate and Geography

One of the others who follow the old classification methods like Vico is Montesquieu,[3] who has an important place in analysis of society. Considering his contributions to the systematic analysis of society with his views that the social sphere is shaped within the framework of certain laws, it can be asserted that he deserves to be called the founder of sociological science. Furthermore, Montesquieu can be seen as the pioneer of sociological thinking with regard to social taxonomies (Zeitlin 1968, p. 16). On the other hand, he also has provided remarkable contributions to the definition of modern society. However, none of these contributions are comparable to the fact that he revived the theory of Oriental despotism. Even though he has no official titles, being the modern godfather of the Oriental despotism renders him immortal. The concept of despotism, which has been used since the time of Aristotle (2004, p. 207) and returned to the European modern political dictionary with Bodin (1967, pp. 48–52), is turned into a tool that defines non-European societies by Montesquieu, and this was an important contribution to the definition of the modern society (Rubiés, 2005). As Rubies (2005, p. 174) states:

In a traditional history-of-ideas analysis such as that conducted by Melvin Richter, the fundamental similarity between the Aristotelian formulation of despotism as a legitimate form of monarchical government which applies to oriental peoples due to their servile nature, and Montesquieu's latter elaboration of despotism as a basic type of government which also excludes an element of political liberty, is interrupted by the shift of emphasis towards the idea of conquest, dispossession, and slavery in Bodin, influencing subsequent discussions in Grotius, Hobbes, Pufendorf, and Locke.

We already noted that Montesquieu follows the old taxonomy methods. The effects of climate and geography on the characteristic of human societies are especially important to him. In this framework, Montesquieu spared a considerable part of his magnum opus, *The Spirit of the Laws*, which he wrote in 1748. He laid these foundations in his polemical book, *Persian Letters*, which he wrote in 1721 to explain the behavioural and institutional influences of climate on human communities (Montesquieu, 2008). In this framework, Montesquieu (1989, pp. 231–4) divided the world into three geographical and climatic zones: north (cold), middle (moderate), and south (hot). He suggests that there are three different political systems (republic, aristocratic or democratic, monarchy or despotism) and, accordingly, three different social types that appear in these three zones (Montesquieu 1989, p. 10). The ruling principle of the republic that is suitable for the cold climate and small states of the north is *virtue*. On the other hand, despotism appears in regions of hot climates like the South and Asia, in big states, and in vast lands of the East where it reaches its natural and perfect form and is dependent on *fear*. According to Montesquieu (1989, pp. 21–9), in Europe where the moderate climate is dominant, the reign relies on *honour* and appears in the middle-sized states. Montesquieu finds it problematic to maintain the republic. This is because if the population increases, it is not possible for the republican administration to keep functioning. However, he does not categorically reject the republic. He considers despotism, which he places in opposition to the social and political form of Europe that is moderate in every aspect, as a system that is completely incompatible with human nature. Montesquieu left a remarkable influence on his descendants' ideas regarding non-Western societies because he considered and handled despotism as a holistic social system. This contradiction is due to the very paradoxical nature of the concept (despotism).

According to Montesquieu, despotism represents a political form from which Europe stands clear due to natural reasons based on geography and climate. Accordingly, despotism is a system peculiar to Asia where a single individual enforces the laws, and the population is at the mercy of the ruler. As the weather gets warmer towards the south, ethics become more and more limited: 'In Asia there reigns a spirit of servitude that has never left it, and in all the histories of this country it is not possible to find a single trait marking a free soul; one will never see there anything but the heroism of servitude' (Montesquieu 1989, p. 284). This system, whose main principle is fear and terror, is the highest level of political evil. Montesquieu (1989, p. 119) is aware of that when he says, 'the principle of despotic government is endlessly corrupted because it is corrupt by its nature'—a principle that is inherently paradoxical. According to this statement, despotism is both natural and unnatural. It has its source in nature, but, on the other hand, it is against human nature. It evokes limitless rebellions and is rebuilt just after it is demolished; but, on the other hand, there is a non-reformable chaotic administration. When he reviews the existing samples of despotism, Montesquieu sees reform in Russia, and there is an almost-perfect administration in China. He tries to show how unmanageable despotism is in his *Persian Letters* (Montesquieu 2008). Here, Montesquieu draws attention to problems that would appear as the lands that are governed get broader, and the rulers become distant from the ones they rule. According to Montesquieu, sovereigns who rule vast geographies are compatible with nature, but they are not natural.

Zeitlin (1968, p. 12), who views Montesquieu as a genuine son of the age, states that what distinguish his views from former Aristotelian climatic explanations is that he mentions not only political forms but also social structures. According to him, Montesquieu does not derive these social types from pre-observation principles, but bases them on observations (Zeitlin 1968, pp. 17–18). His concept of social law, which was derived from historical knowledge, statements by travellers, and his own personal journeys, and social typologies he developed with reference to climatic and geographic conditions, and the comparative analysis he conducted on society, legal order, and governmental regimes formed an important foundation for the successor scientists, especially the social evolutionists. However, his idea of European superiority due to its convenient and moderate climate became clear in *The Spirit of the Laws* (see Bernal 1987, p. 28 for a discussion). Montesquieu is the one who brought into play the concept of Oriental despotism that forms the foundation of his analyses regarding Eastern societies. On the other hand, it is frequently indicated that he utilized Oriental societies to criticize the situation of Europe at that time in his book. According to this perspective, the ideas regarding the Orient that Montesquieu used in domestic politics corresponded to the way the Orient was frequently viewed by Enlightenment thought.

Though he bases his ideas on empirical foundations as much as possible, that Montesquieu keeps connecting his ideas to climatic theories makes him related to Middle Age thinking in a way. This is because his naturalist analysis reveals that nature has an inevitable influence on society. Therefore, because society is described by a field that is not designated directly by human beings, beginning from his own time, Montesquieu's social taxonomies were criticized by Anquetil-Duperron (1876) and Voltaire (1994); and for that reason they were no longer used later on.

Law of Progression and Temporalization of Social Classifications

Progressivism, which developed in the age of Enlightenment, prepared a new ground for the taxonomy of societies. Various forms of progressivism that grant a central place to humankind within historical development created a huge literature with regard to the forms that societies obtained over time. Turgot, who is the founder of progressivism, in his unpublished manuscript on universal history written in 1750, does not develop a clear social taxonomy, but in the opening pages provides 'a presumed sequence of societal development beginning with societies dependent on hunting, followed by pastoral societies, and then by agricultural societies' (Lenski, 1994). This progressive taxonomy line was maintained in various forms during the French Enlightenment and eventually expanded into a decimal taxonomy, developed by Condorcet, a close friend of

Turgot, within the framework of the development of sciences at the end of the century. Furthermore, those who succeeded in explaining the development of societies using the law of progression and, as a consequence of this, presented modern social structure as a natural outcome of human activities were the Scottish Enlightenment thinkers. Therefore, social taxonomies became time dependent based on the concept of historical stages.

In *The Origin of Distinction of Ranks* written in 1711 by John Millar, one of the significant members of the Scottish Enlightenment, it is stated that 'among the several circumstances which may affect the gradual improvements of society, the difference of climate is one of the most remarkable' (Millar 2006, p. 87). In this book, Millar shows that societies are at various ranks depending on their position in settled life, political structure, inequality levels, marriage patterns, family life models, and other aspects. While grouping societies together, Millar (2006) uses the conceptual cluster of savages, barbarians, and civilized societies on the one hand, and hunters, shepherds, and farmers on the other.

Taxonomy of societies obtained a new form in Scottish Enlightenment within the framework of progressive history, which is called 'natural history' by Hume and 'conjectural history' by Dugald Stewart. Stewart asserts that the theoretical history that is also defined as 'the natural history' of society is also the most suitable way to think about Europe. According to this perspective, what will enable us to understand the daily events in a historical respect is 'natural history' that is a theoretical framework in which the natural factors behind the events are considered. In this way, progressivism performed two things at the same time: positioned modernity against tradition and, with reference to chosen historical cases, formed a theoretical framework for the knowledge-in-pieces regarding 'the other'. Stewart (1854, p. 30) says:

> When in such a period of Society as that in which we live, we compare our intellectual acquirements, our opinions, manners, and institutions, with those which prevail among rude tribes, it cannot fail to occur to us as an interesting question, by what gradual steps the transition has been made from the first simple efforts of uncultivated nature, to a state of things so wonderfully artificial and complicated.

Therefore, the way to explain the meaning of theoretical history is by making comparisons in order to show how developed Europe is.

Unlike the previous comparisons, these are unrealistic comparisons used to fill the blanks in the theoretical world of history and help to define the stages of progression.

Hirschman references the study of Scottish historian William Robertson, which he wrote in 1769, *A Review on the Social Development in Europe*, as an important study that shaped the historical view of the Scottish Enlightenment:

> The expression 'the polished nations', in contradistinction to the 'rude and barbarous' ones, came to be commonly used in England and Scotland toward the second half of the eighteenth century. It designated the countries of Western Europe whose increasing wealth was clearly perceived to have much to do with the expansion of commerce. The term 'polished' may well have been selected because of its affinity with *adouci* [softened]: in this manner the *douceur* [gentleness] of commerce could have been indirectly responsible for the first attempt at express-ing a dichotomy that reappeared later under such labels as 'advanced–backward', 'developed–underdeveloped', and so on. (Hirschman 1997, p. 61)

We see that in the studies written in this period, the expressions 'hunter', 'gatherer', and 'agricultural societies' emerged in parallel to the attributions 'savage', 'barbarian', and 'civilized', which are in turn used in parallel to the three stages of historical progression. 'In the next several decades, this early and more or less implicit taxonomy based on the means of subsistence became increasingly explicit and was, with various modifications, used as the basis for increasingly sophisticated analyses by a growing number of Enlightenment intel-lectuals' (Lenski 1994, p. 4).

David Hume: Social Types through Natural History

The most significant contributions Hume made to the analysis of modern society were the theories of property, religion, and civil society. Within these theories, there are important arguments regarding non-Western societies within the framework of positioning modern soci-ety. David Hume was the first one who handled the social taxonomy table within the scope of the progression of humanity and applied it to the past. Hume explains the historical stages with the development of property and determines deep-rooted distinctions between modern commercial society, which he calls civil society, and barbarian societies. Accordingly, humankind moved from hunting and fishing to agriculture, and from there to a structure predominated by commerce. That Europe was the only continent that had reached this last stage was substantially an outcome of its expeditions. A specific social pattern and cultural equipment corresponded to each stage, according to the primary occupations and available opportunities of the people (Fontana 1995: 147). Hume's thoughts regarding commercial society and its superiorities were shaped by his observations of the English commercial empire. In *Of Commerce*, he purports that the prosperity of the English turned to both military and political power and, therefore, created a social system that dominated the entire world (Hume 1994a). The historical and social analyses of the subsequent Scottish Enlightenment thinkers like Smith, Ferguson, Millar, and Kames owe many things to Hume, the father of theoretical history (Whelan 2009, pp. 8–19).

The natural history of Hume considers contemporary non-Western societies as a vivid sample of the previous primitive stages of Europe. This thought will find its representation in the discipline of anthropology later on, and the correspondence of this idea to the concept of Enlightenment is a sign of Europe's apparent superiority and gives it the 'legitimate' right to rule others. This idea which found its roots in the diaries of travellers and provoked the imperial desires of Europeans also led to the courage to judge non-European societies. Clearly, living in the same World as 'barbarians' further empowers the image of threat. As Hume often state, the fact that Rome was destroyed by barbarian Germans should be kept in mind. Hume (1993, p. 56) thinks that civil Europe has not yet reached its maturity and there is the possibility of decline as the example of Rome showed. Barbarians could neither understand the value of a civilization nor could they truly respect it (Hume 1994b). A civilization must control 'barbarians' with all its capabilities. This control would also contribute significantly to their process of civilization. Like other Scottish philosophers, Hume considered that the Scottish and Germans who once revolted against the Roman Empire walked the road from barbarism to civilization; and in order for this to happen for all barbarians, a long time must pass. Until that time, the more civilized must rule and control the less civilized. In this respect, with references to Roman history, the roots of the idea to control the non-Western regions for the sake of 'civilizing' them were produced.

By attributing a theoretical feature to history, Hume contributed to the conceptualization, rationalization, and legitimization of modernity significantly by removing the necessity of providing concrete evidence to understand modern society. In this way, the necessity to use examples from non-Western societies in order to legitimize modern ones has also been removed. Around the idea of a natural law of progress in history, modern society naturally gained a moral superiority over others and paved the way for the old and the non-Western to become the 'Other'.

Adam Smith: Division of Labour and Social Types

Adam Smith (1723–1790) follows Hume and develops his own stages and social types. According to Smith, the primary factor determining a social type is the manner of livelihood. Smith, who tries to create a new social philosophy by combining politics with ethics and economics, theorizes that how people earn their livelihood shapes their perception of the concept of property, and, therefore, determines their thoughts regarding justice and government.

Smith arrived at the idea of social stages by questioning the relationship between the legitimacy of government and justice. According to this approach, the history of humanity has developed through four consecutive stages, namely hunting, stockbreeding, agriculture, and commerce. The most primitive society in the stages of social development is the hunter society, ignorant of property and government. The second stage is shepherding, where property corresponds to herds. In this social type, the first forms of the concepts of justice and government begin to appear. The third and fourth stages are the agricultural stage and commercial stage (Smith 2007, pp. 712–15, 737–8).[4] In these stages, the property relations become complex and a need arises for powerful governmental systems to secure justice. According to this concept, Smith considers Black African and North American 'savage' hunter and gatherer tribes to be in the first stage, nomad tribes of Central Asia in the second stage, the rest of the East in the third stage, and European countries in the fourth stage, which is the highest level.

In the frame of this taxonomy, Smith developed analyses to serve as the foundation of nineteenth-century social sciences by explaining 'Oriental despotism' in economic terms. As an eighteenth-century thinker, Smith was still using Eastern societies as evidence for domestic political issues. In this framework, as he did in the case of physiocrats, he used Oriental despotism as a horrific example to show how the involvement of the sovereign in domestic commercial activities would result in negative consequences. Smith, who was influenced by the thoughts of travellers, but, like many contemporary Europeans writing on the East, especially by Bernier (2007, pp. 35–6, 683, 729–31, 837–40), discussed the role of the government in building roads and channels and the advantage it received from this with an economic analysis. He further analysed how irrigation and prosperity services increased the government's income. Smith claimed that the land tax and land rent was the same thing in China, India, Egypt, and other countries of Asia, in contrast to Europe. He claimed that, therefore, the governors in the East had both public and private relationships with the land (Smith 2007, pp. 730, 838). From this, Smith derived that the public and private spheres were not separated from each other in the East.

According to Jennifer Pitts (2005, p. 34), who wrote a detailed study about Adam Smith, he is unlike other conjectural historians who view the members of primitive hunter societies as ignorant and unenlightened. However, Ronald Meek (2011) considers him and other Scottish and French historians as similar in this regard. According to Meek, these historians claim that European society is superior to hunter and shepherd societies. According to Pitts, though Smith considers the development of commercial society as a success story, it would be unfair to say that he saw hunter and shepherd societies as ignorant and 'corrupted'. This is because Smith mentions these societies with respect and does not show disdain for them. Though he sometimes uses words like 'savage' and 'barbarian', he uses them in the context of his historical theory. In other words, he uses these words not in a judgmental manner with an intention of evaluating, but in an analytical manner to express the first stages of humanity. On the other hand, Pitts (2005, p. 37) states that unlike many other Scottish historical philosophers, Smith never compares primitive people with children. In these assessments, Pitts ignores the general mindset lying behind the historical staging and taxonomy of social types—the ones that we try to exhibit in this study. Even though he does not use degrading expressions, Smith presents non-Western societies as outmoded archaic forms with the historical staging he employs. The division of labour theory developed by Smith became one of sociology's core themes and was used to distinguish modern society from other societies for a long time. As discussed in greater detail later, in my opinion, Smith represents an important voice connecting Hume and Hegel, and providing empirical validation to conjectural history through an economic analysis.

Adam Ferguson: Social Stages in the Transition to Civil Society

The Enlightenment thinkers maintain that the process of humanity's thinking evolves from a primitive mental structure to a more rational and civilized one. Therefore, they formulize the progression as the progression of the mind and intelligence. This can be seen clearest in the views of ethics theoretician Adam Ferguson (1723–1816), who was the successor of Hume,[5] a contemporary of Smith and one of the important figures of the Scottish Enlightenment. Despite the fact that Ferguson kept an opposing position to Hume's social contract theory, he stayed loyal to his progressive natural history approach. In his work, *An Essay on the History of Civil Society*, written in 1767, he considered the progression of humanity as an intellectual development within the context of natural history (Heath and Merolle, 2008). He was influenced by Montesquieu and attempted to analyse the functioning mechanism of modern society which he called civil society (Ferguson 1819, p. 120). With reference to Montesquieu, Ferguson (1819, pp. 189, 211, 288, 433, 487–92, 504) considered despotism as the biggest danger that modern society had encountered and believed that modern society could be achieved by some kind of evolution. Ferguson (1819, pp. 149, 472), who developed a taxonomy of social types according to this progressive approach, reshaped the taxonomy developed according to livelihood manners by Smith with his own anthropological point of view of 'savage', 'barbarian', and 'polished' (civilized). He claimed that by studying the conditions that various contemporary societies lived in, the former societies of Europe could be understood, and therefore he attributed a function to the stage theory in understanding European society (Ferguson 1819, pp. 146–7).

According to Ferguson, all non-European societies are savages or barbarians.

> From one to the other extremity of America; from Kamtlilchatka westward to the river Oby; and from the Northern Sea, over that length of country, to the confines of China, of India, and Persia; from the Caspian to the Red Sea, with little exception, and from thence over the inland continent and the western shores of Africa; we everywhere meet with nations on whom we bestow the appellations of barbarous or savage. (Ferguson 1819, p. 149)

According to him, this distinction between barbarous and savage people must create a material difference of character, and may furnish two separate headings under which to consider the history of mankind in their rudest state: that of the savage, who is not yet acquainted with property; and that of the barbarian, to whom it is, although not ascertained by laws, a principal object of care and desire. It is very evident, according to Ferguson, that property is the matter of progress (Ferguson 1819, p. 149). Besides, liberty is another sign of the difference between civil and uncivil people.

> Liberty, in one sense, appears to be the portion of polished nations alone. The savage is personally free, because he lives unrestrained, and acts with the members of his tribe on terms of equality. The barbarian is frequently independent, from a continuance of the same circumstances, or because he has courage and a sword. (Ferguson 1819, p. 472)

Ferguson remains loyal to the commercial society theories and indicates that in despotic societies where there is no property or freedom, commerce would not develop and these societies would consequently remain poor (Ferguson 1819, p. 504).

Hegel: Freedom of Spirit through Migrating from Orient to Occident

Hegel has an important place in European thinking and his position is the result of the historical interpretation he developed, and on which modernity is often based. As he systemized the intellectual and philosophical legacy of the Enlightenment thinkers, Hegel also, for the first time, placed the former knowledge about Eastern societies within a holistic historical philosophy. While developing his own ideas, Hegel was deeply influenced by and utilized the Scottish Enlightenment. Starting from the 1770s, he rapidly translated the studies of commercial society theoreticians like Smith, Ferguson, and Steuart into German and began to influence German thinkers (Jones 2001, p. 111). With reference to Karl Rosenkranz, who wrote Hegel's biography in an early stage in 1844, Jones says that Hegel read the book of Sir James Steuart, *Principles of Political Economy*, for three months in 1799, and systematically drew analysis from it (Jones 2001, p. 109). Between all these economic politicians, the one who impressed Hegel the most was Adam Smith.[6] He acknowledges that his theory of mechanization in society, in particular, is based on the division of labour. Hegel, who obtained the idea of progressive history from Scottish Enlightenment thinkers, uses this theory on an abstract logical platform to distinguish the modern West from others. When we compare him with those who lived before him, the first thing that arises is the confidence he has in the historical verity of modern society. With this confidence, Hegel believes that the Spirit of the modern West actualized all of its purposes and, therefore, represents the final stage of history.

> There is also no doubt that Hegel was typical of his age. He loved Europe or, as he put it, the temperate zone; he respected the Asian mountains and India; he hated Islam and had complete contempt for Africa. (Bernal 1987, p. 294)

When we arrive at the beginning of nineteenth century, with the rise of Orientalism, the Orient was of interest to the West only as a chapter, long since ended, of the universal history into which it had become integrated. Hegel was an outstanding theoretician of this understanding. He formulated the stages of humanities like a human's life and saw the Orient as the childhood of mankind. As Hentsch states:

> His Universal History placed the West in the vanguard of the march of Reason.... In the age of the steam engine, Hegel perfected the motor of History which was to propel the world toward a predetermined objective consciousness of self, and the liberty which such consciousness implied. (Hentsch 1992, p. 140)

We can find his thoughts on modernity and others most clearly in his *Introduction to the Philosophy of History*. On 22 December 1782, he wrote to Duboc, 'It is quite an interesting and nice job to assess the world nations passing by me' (Hegel 1984, p. 494). In those days, he was preparing his lectures on the philosophy of world history and was interested in India and China. According to Hegel (1902, pp. 63–4), who systemizes the idea of Enlightenment thinkers, the stabilized East cannot participate in the development of history, world history that is, which is nothing but the 'progression of the consciousness of freedom', Geist revealing itself from the East to the West (Hegel 1902, pp. 158, 167). In Hegel's historical schema, history begins from the contemporary stage of the East. However, the East cannot leave this state due to the stability created by the giant empire. In Hegel's (1902, p. 166) own words, these empires 'belong not to the time, but to the space'. As Henstch suggests, though the West is considered as an exception in the Hegelian scheme, 'it is the one who will grant its entire meaning to history and there is no civilization but the West' (Henstch 1996, p. 186).

According to Hegel, who remains loyal to the Enlightenment trilogy tradition, Geist follows a three-stage historical course in this process: subjective spirit, objective spirit, and world spirit. In this regard, Hegel counts three stages for the absolute spirit to reach freedom.[7] The stage where only one person, the despot, is free corresponds to the Eastern world. Here, the spirit directly realizes itself. The stage where only some people are free corresponds to the Roman and Greek worlds. In Greece, the spirit gains knowledge and begins to realize itself. In the case of Rome, the spirit deepens within itself and reaches an abstract universality and, by breaking away from the objectivity contradiction, becomes an entity within itself. The German world in which everyone is free constitutes the third stage. In this stage, the spirit turns towards itself. Therefore, it finds its own reality and concrete nature in itself within the apparent contradiction and turns back to its substantiality again (Hegel 1902, pp. 62–3, 164).[8] According to Hegel, corresponding to these characteristics, the political governmental regime is despotism in the first stage, democracy and aristocracy in the second stage, and monarchy in the third stage (Hegel 1902, p. 164).

Hegel evaluates the liberation of the spirit according to its connection to nature. So, as the spirit gets closer to nature or gets embedded within, the domain of freedom shrinks. Otherwise, freedom brings itself to the light and the spirit realizes itself. In other words, as the human controls nature, the spirit realizes and liberates itself.

In this framework, Hegel thinks that the spirit and nature are embedded in the East, which he places in the first stage within his explanation of despotism. The East corresponds to childhood; there is mental freedom, but no subjective freedom. Therefore, freedom belongs to only one person—the despot. There is no rationalist state and the state is formulated around the family relationships. There is no individual freedom in the East, no intermediary institutions between the state and the society, and equality paves the way for despotism. There is togetherness of the spirit and nature. The East has not yet gained independence from nature; it continues its existence by relying on nature. According to Hegel, in the second stage of the spirit's manifestation, in Greece, the spirit is under nature's dominance. For the individual at this stage, there is a consciousness of freedom. However, though the ideas of beauty, freedom, and morality appear in this stage, the state does not yet emerge. In Rome, which also reflects this stage, the state is apparent. This stage is the maturation stage of the spirit. In the third stage where everybody is free, the spirit breaks away from nature and even controls it. In this stage where the spirit realizes itself, objective truth and freedom are allies. This alliance that shapes the last stage of history represents the unity of the Nordic Germans and Christianity. Hegel calls this stage the 'German' stage.

In this framework, in Hegel's thinking, the East represents nature, whereas the West represents the human mind; the East corresponds to the childhood of humanity (Hegel 1902, p. 165), whereas Greece corresponds to its adolescence. (Hegel 1902, p. 167), and the West corresponds to its maturity (Hegel 1902, p. 170). As humanity progresses by struggling against nature and by dominating it, Hegel sees the domination of the West over the East as the progression of the humanity.

PROGRESS, SOCIETY, AND CIVILIZATION

Progress, society, and civilization were the significant concepts constituting the main categories of the Enlightenment period. Among these three, civilization has a special place in the identification of new Europe. The description of the emergent modern society as civilization reveals the exclusive and inclusive characteristics of its identity. In this framework, in the description of the modern society as a civilization, periodization of world history by staging it into ages and the taxonomy of social forms along with these stages played important roles. The concept of civilization that springs from the point where these two fields meet has two dimensions: one is descriptive (self), and the other is distinctive (other). While historical staging constitutes the descriptive dimension, social taxonomy forms the distinctive dimension by creating a ground for the comparison. In this study, it is claimed that if it were not for the latter, the former would not be able to continue its existence.

The usage of civilization as a descriptive concept appeared to be a means towards the secular development that is shaped by human experiences against the church and the feudal social order. From this perspective, the idea that history of humankind has a continuous progressive line shaped by human acts was presented as an attractive alternative to the ancient societal model of the church. Within the scope of this alternative theory, the idea of progressive history that becomes concrete with the staging of world history takes an important place. The first Enlightenment thinker who conducted this kind of staging was Italian historian Vico. However, Vico's classification of the history of humankind is more like a scheme of the formation of humanity depending on classical ideals, rather than a discussion on the history of mankind. Montesquieu's taxonomy, which left deep marks within the scope of social law, is more geographical rather than historical. In this aspect, Montesquieu still depends on the old thinking. The ones who transferred the idea of progressive history to social analysis were two important figures of the French Enlightenment, Turgot and Condorcet. They formulized the concept of progressive history and developed the idea that social structures are in a continuous progress from ancient to modern times and correspondingly different social types appear. However, a combination of progressive historical stages with societal developments and the emergence of social types were succeeded by Scottish Enlightenment. In this framework, Hume was the first to present the various structures obtained by societies time-dependently along with the idea of natural history. Hume, who explained the historical stages with the development of property, believes that humanity moved from hunting and fishing to agriculture and from there to civil society where commerce predominates. Following him, it became common to explain the development of societies with economic factors in the Scottish Enlightenment period and, soon after, it became an important element in the explanation of modern society. In this context, the transition to civilization is realized by the division of labour and the transformation of economic livelihood depending on the changes in the specialization in Smith's thinking. In this framework, the humanity has a development course of four consecutive stages: hunting, stockbreeding, agriculture, and commerce. Ferguson, another important figure of the Scottish Enlightenment, develops his historical staging within the scope of intellectual progression and determines three social types: the savage, the barbarian, and the polished (civilized). These historical staging and social taxonomies of the Enlightenment age provide a substantial foundation for the description of modern society. On this ground, the relationship between the historical development and social taxonomies are repeatedly interpreted in the nineteenth century. The three-world theory of Hegel that corresponds to the progress of the spirit; Comte's law of three stages, depending on the development of the scientific thinking; and Marx's dialectic materialism, depending on the modes of productions, are the most important of these interpretations. Especially Hegel clearly grounded his own theory on the idea that modern society should be completely defined through means of 'the other'. As modern society becomes entrenched starting from the 1850s, the old multi-stage historical development concept is gradually replaced by a two-stage historical approach: that of the modern and pre-modern stages. Eventually, the social formations that correspond to these stages are expressed as modern and traditional societies. The social taxonomy of Morgan based on kinship–field distinction; of Maine, based on status–contract distinction; of Durkheim, based on organic–mechanical social labour division; of Tönnies' community–society distinction; of Spencer, based on simple–complex distinction; and of Mauss, based on potlatch–meta distinction reveals this kind of duality. Though pre-modern societies may present variety and differences among themselves, when they are considered in comparison to the modern world, they seem to be one.

It can be clearly seen that the underlying motivation behind all these different descriptions and classifications is the effort to show the uniqueness of modern society. These historical staging and social taxonomies try to explain the structure of modern society and place it into a historical schema. Even though different themes are developed within each theory, two common aspects unite these social taxonomies. The first of these aspects is that they are all developed with a progressive perspective. In this context, the modern social structure constitutes the final stage of development. The other common aspect of these taxonomies is the approach to Oriental societies. The Orient is always placed at the beginning, in an early stage. Therefore, the idea of civilization, which sounds perfectly concrete and natural when used today, is actually developed artificially in order to establish the modern identity of Europe around the idea of the 'other'.

NOTES

1. According to Johannes Fabian, there are some ideological parts of tax-onomies: 'It may then turn out that the axiom of arbitrary imposition was not a universally valid epistemological principle but an expression of a world view, if not of social and political schemes of power and repression' (Fabian 1975, p. 195).
2. For a detailed analysis on the birth, development, and transformation into a fundamental element for the Western identity of the term 'barbarian', see Parker (2010).
3. For an assessment on Montesquieu's influence in the eighteenth century and the position of Rousseau against his theories, see Muthu (2003, p. 37).
4. Here, Smith considers pre-commercial societies as the societies at different levels of barbarism. For other discussions, see also Smith (2007, pp. 117–18, 206–8).
5. Ferguson took over Hume's duty as the librarian in Faculty of Advocates in January 1757 and became his successor in this manner as well.
6. For the relationship of Hegel's *cunning of reason* and Adam Smith's *invisible hand*, see Hirschman (1997, p. 17).
7. Hegel (1902, p. 61) says that if the essence of matter is gravity, the essence of the spirit is freedom. According to him, freedom is the only truth of the spirit (Hegel 1902, p. 62).
8. As Fabian puts into words, symbolization serves as a tool of time-dependency in Hegel's thinking and it is also used as an important tool to otherize the East. See Fabian (1999, pp. 161–3).

BIBLIOGRAPHY

Alkan, N. 2009. 'Tarihin çağlara ayrılmasında "üç"lü sistem ve "Avrupa merkezci" tarih kurgusu'. *Uluslararası Sosyal Araştırmalar Dergisi* 2(9): 23–42.

Anquetil-Duperron, A. H. 1876. *Extracts from the Narrative of Mons. Anquetil du Perron's Travels in India*, translated by K. E. Kanga. Bombay: The Commercial Press.

Aristotle. 2004. *Politika*, translated by M. Tunçay. İstanbul: Remzi Kitabevi.

———. 2013. *Aristotle's Politics*, second edition, translated and an introduction, notes, and glossary by Carnes Lord. Chicago and London: University of Chicago Press.

Ataman, K. 2008. *Understanding Other Religions: Al-Biruni's and Gadamer's 'Fusion of Horizons'*. Washington, D.C.: Council for Research in Values and Philosophy.

Baker, K. M. 2001. 'Enlightenment and the Institution of Society: Notes for a Conceptual History'. In *Civil Society: History and Possibilities*, edited by S. Kavira and S. Khilnani, pp. 84–104. Cambridge: Cambridge University Press.

Bernal, M. 1987. *Black Athena: The Afroasiatic Roots of Classical Civilization, Vol. 1: The Fabrication of Ancient Greece, 1785–1985*. New Brunswick, NJ: Rutgers University Press.

Bodin, J. 1967. *Six Books of the Commonwealth*. Oxford: B. Blackwell.

Braudel, F. 1995. *A History of Civilizations*. New York: Penguin Books.

Fabian, J. 1975. 'Taxonomy and Ideology: On the Boundaries of Concept Classification'. In *Linguistics and Anthropology: In Honor of C. F. Voegelin*, edited by M. D. Kinkade, K. L. Hale, and O. Werner, pp. 183–98. Lisse: The Peter de Ridder Press.

Fabian, J. 1999. *Zaman ve öteki: Antropoloji nesnesini nasıl oluşturur*, translated by S. Budak. Ankara: Bilim ve Sanat Yayınları.

Ferguson, A. 1819. *An Essay on the History of Civil Society*, eighth edition. Philadelphia: A. Finley.

Heath, E. and V. Merolle, eds. 2008. *Adam Ferguson: History, Progress and Human Nature*. London: Pickering and Chatto.

Hegel, G. W. F. 1902. *The Philosophy of History*, translated by J. Sibree. New York: P. F. Collier.

———. 1984. *Hegel, the Letters*, translated by C. Butler and C. Seiler. Bloomington: Indiana University Press.

Hentsch, T. 1992. *Imagining the Middle East*. Montréal; New York: Black Rose Books.

Hirschman, A. O. 1997. *The Passions and the Interests: Political Arguments for Capitalism before Its Triumph*. Princeton, NJ: Princeton University Press.

Hume, D. 1959. *A Treatise of Human Nature*. London; New York: Dent; Dutton.

———. 1993. 'Of Civil Liberty'. In *Selected Essays*, edited by S. Copley and A. Edgar, pp. 49–56. Oxford: Oxford University Press.

———. 1994a. 'Of Commerce'. In *Hume: Political Essays*, edited by K. Haakonssen, pp. 93–104. Cambridge: Cambridge University Press.

———. 1994b. 'Of the Rise and Progress of the Arts and Sciences'. In *Hume: Political Essays*, edited by K. Haakonssen, pp. 58–77. Cambridge: Cambridge University Press.

Jones, D. M. 2001. *The Image of China in Western Social and Political Thought*. New York: Palgrave.

Khilani, S. 2001. 'The Development of Civil Society'. In *Civil Society: History and Possibilities*, edited by S. Khilani and S. Kaviraj, pp. 11–32. Cambridge: Cambridge University Press.

Lenski, G. 1994. 'Societal Taxonomies: Mapping the Social Universe'. *Annual Review of Sociology* 20: 1–26.

Meek, R. L. 2011. *Social Science and the Ignoble Savage*. Cambridge; New York: Cambridge University Press.

Millar, J. 2006. *The Origin of the Distinction of Ranks*, edited by A. Garrett. Indianapolis: Liberty Fund.

Montesquieu. 1989. *Montesquieu: The Spirit of the Laws*, translated B. C. Miller, H. S. Stone, and A. M. Cohler. Cambridge: Cambridge University Press.

———. 2008. *Persian Letters*, translated by M. Mauldon. Oxford, New York: Oxford University Press.

Muthu, S. 2003. *Enlightenment against Empire*. Princeton, NJ: Princeton University Press.

Pitts, J. 2005. *A Turn to Empire: The Rise of Imperial Liberalism in Britain and France*. Princeton: Princeton University Press.

Rubiés, J. P. 2005. 'Oriental Despotism and European Orientalism: Botero to Montesquieu'. *Journal of Early Modern History* 9(1–2): 109–80.

Smith, A. 2007. *An Inquiry into the Nature and Causes of the Wealth of Nations*, edited by S. M. Soares. Lausanne: MetaLibri Digital Library.

Springborg, P. 1986. 'Politics, Primordialism, and Orientalism: Marx, Aristotle, and the Myth of the Gemeinschaft'. *The American Political Science Review* 80(1): 185–211.

Stewart, D. 1854. 'Account of the Life and Writings of Adam Smith'. In *The Collected Works of Dugald Stewart*, Vol. X, edited by W. Hamilton, pp. 5–100. Edinburgh: T. Constable and Co.

Sunar, L. and F. Yaslıçimen. 2008. 'The Possibilities of New Perspectives for Social Sciences: An Analysis Based on Ibn Khaldun's Theory of Umrân'. *Asian Journal of Social Science* 36(3): 408–33.

Toynbee, A. 1935. *A Study of History*, vol. I, second edition. Oxford: Oxford University Press.

Vico, G. 1948. *The New Science of Giambattista Vico*, translated by M. H. Fisch and T. G. Bergin. Ithaca, New York: Cornell University Press.

Voltaire. 1994. *Voltaire: Political Writings*. Cambridge, New York: Cambridge University Press.

Whelan, F. G. 2009. *Enlightenment Political Thought and Non-Western Societies: Sultans and Savages*. New York: Routledge.

Zeitlin, I. M. 1968. *Ideology and the Development of Sociological Theory*. New Jersey: Prentice-Hall.

3 The Question of Ages in Islamic Civilization

A Different Periodization

Mustafa Demirci

When civilizations step into the stage of history, they make new definitions in the realm of existence, knowledge, and values. A historical consciousness is formed by establishing a 'sense of self' in which the human defines his/her own existence in a new world of perception, transforming the current geography into a new form within the frame of this sense and forming a new 'space perception'. This consciousness is also formed by re-interpreting this civilization in order to position itself in a meaningful space in the course of the history of humanity and forming a new 'historical consciousness'. In this way, each civilization that steps on to the stage of history, places itself at the centre of the historical adventure of humanity and develops a historical perception and an apprehension for the future. This new historical perception is formed by creating an impression that the entire human history was experienced along the axis of this particular civilization, in order to create it, and the faith of the entire humanity depends on this civilization (Davutoğlu 2007, p. 21). In this respect, discussions on time perceptions in studies on civilizations are not mere calendar work. On the contrary, it reflects the existing senses of belonging and self, along with brand new perceptions of historical existence, the particular and independent position of that civilization in history, and the awareness of the historical course. In this chapter, I will draw attention towards the time perceptions and historical consciousness of civilizations and address the time perception of Islamic civilization and how it places itself within the history of humanity compared to Euro-centralist time perception. The main subject of this chapter is the time perceptions that civilizations have developed about the periods and ages they have lived through their long lifetimes.

Algerian thinker Malek ben Nabi, one of the outstanding Islamic scholars who contemplated on the relation between civilization and time, claims that a civilization can be built on the values developed about 'land, human, and time'.

> Every civilization has a beginning date; it uses the rise of a divine inspiration or a mythology as the basis of its initiation. The history of Islam begins with the divine inspiration. This event became the inception of the developments that will change the faith of this world and the beginning of a new civilization. These people, who were stuck in Arabia subcontinent and had perception of 24 hours only, stepped into the stage of history with the revelation of divine inspiration and played the most active role in the history of earth through the next fourteen centuries. (bin Nabi 1992, pp. 47–8)

Ben Nabi points out that in the times we live in, one of the most fundamental problems of Muslims is time perception and historical consciousness. According to him, each phenomenon reflects the ideas, actions, and feelings that are accordant with the spirit of the time. Therefore, Islamic civilization needs to identify its position in its own history and interpret the phenomena accordingly. He says that 'every plagiarism about the history and time by civilizations is both a suicide and a murder' (1992, pp. 41–2).

In their establishment phase, civilizations classify time into two sorts: *daily time* and *historical time*. The daily time of humans refer to those who live in the universe of a civilization from their birth to their death. The latter, which can also be called empirical time, forms the historical memory of the civilizations and determines their positioning in history. We see that each civilization periodizes history in this sense and makes its own past somehow meaningful. In this chapter, Islamic civilization's periodization of its history beyond the historical proposal suggested by European civilization is discussed.

THE DRAWBACKS OF THE EUROCENTRIC HISTORICAL PARADIGM

Through the historical model it developed, the Western civilization succeeded to procure acceptance of the assumption that it is the only civilization embracing the whole past and the future. The paradigms universalized through the textbooks led to the adoption of this European-centred historical draft that identifies the history of humanity with the Western civilization as an absolute reality. According to this understanding, history begins with Ancient Greece, continues with the Roman Empire and the feudal Middle Age, progresses towards the Renaissance, Reformation, Enlightenment, and the Industrial Revolution, and, at the end of this phase, extends to the modern times. This understanding has not only affected historiography, but has also resulted in academic areas like philosophy, reasoning, economics, and politics being understood and interpreted according to this European-centred time perception. In this situation, members of non-Western civilizations who have different historical approaches and experiences, like Hindu, Chinese, and Islamic civilizations, are brought up in this Western-centred perception of time and history. They look at history with the belief that no contribution has been made by their own civilizations. This historical draft that is based on a linear, progressive, and monopolistic model is nothing but a one-sided historical fiction presented through the eyes of victors (Davutoğlu 1997, p. 25).

The categories of Old Age, Middle Age, and New Age developed by Western historians and adopted in many corners of the world, including the Turkish–Islamic world, are actually fabricated by Enlightenment thinkers through researches on European history completely based on the Jewish–Christian philosophy. There are many drawbacks of the use of this historical draft, which is useful only for the consideration of issues related solely to Europe, when studying the histories of other civilizations.

The archaeological and geological researches since the end of the eighteenth century till date and the expansion of knowledge on prehistoric ages raised many questions about the classification of the ancient history of humanity and also resulted in the emergence of various approaches. How efficient could the use of these categories be in the interpretation of some other geography's history that proceeds within a different culture, with a different rhythm, and under different conditions and motivations? For example, the collapse of the Western Roman empire in AD 476 is considered as the break point between the Old Age and the Middle Age. How deeply did this collapse affect the Chinese, Hindu, and non-Western world? Did they stand to gain from this in any way? On the contrary, they were not affected by this event at all.

It is now becoming common practice to take some events in the European history as the criteria for the entire human history. However, using the categories prioritized by European civilization for the evaluation of other civilizations that have been proceeding along a different line and have experienced different interactions with different actors is always dangerous, generally suspicious, and mostly deceptive. As Spengler (1997) emphasizes rightfully, this plan was totally meaningless and meagre. It both limited the field of the history and occasionally turned it into nonsense. Does this not seem correct considering the fact that the ancient times, including thousands of years, are compared to the European-centred history of a few centuries and the still unstudied pre-Hellenism histories are all considered as one? For instance, what does 'Middle Age' mean to the Islamic world or the Chinese and Hindu civilizations? Or does this so-called Middle Age start and end at the same dates in all civilizations? (Lewis 1996, pp. 126–7).

Even these questions are based on the false assumptions and suggestions that the European or the Roman–German civilization coincides with the universal human civilization. European historians make this assumption based on the theory that the European continent has improved in a continuous and linear progression since the time of the ancient Greeks, while other civilizations have maintained a static structure resisting the change. Therefore, if one adopts this approach when looking at other civilizations, they will necessarily be seen as underdeveloped and unprogressive, stuck in the first ages of the historical process (Sorokin 1997, p. 74). The approach considers Islamic history and civilization as a single unchanging unity, except for some minor changes, from Prophet Mohammed until today—this is the biased European attitude based on the assumption of the 'static East' explained earlier. However, due to various reasons, Muslim historians also consider the history of Islam as a routinized history under the control of various dynasties, which ironically coincides with the European attitude.

Considering this issue logically, evaluating the whole world according to the criteria developed by Europeans makes as little sense as attempting to describe all human lives based on one person's birth date, youth, old age, and death. The history of humanity is too enormous to be reduced only to the developments in European history. There is no evidence that the incidents representing the break points in European history resulted in similar radical changes in the history of the Chinese, Hindu, and Islamic worlds or in other societies in other parts of the world. Besides, there is no consensus even between European historians about when the Middle Age began and ended. While this 'Middle Age' was slowly coming to an end in the West, empires like that of the Ottomans, the Mughals, the Safavids, the Golden Horde in the East, or the Ming dynasty in China were experiencing one of their brightest eras (Ülgener 1991, pp. 23–4). Similarly, Europeans accept the exploration of America or the conquest of Istanbul by Ottomans as milestones separating the Middle Age from the New Age. They later served as milestones for Europe after it initiated the Western Renaissance; however, there was no development in other parts of the world related to these events, and it was perhaps considered as a significant period only in Ottoman history. Even according to the most optimistic interpretations, the impacts of these incidents were brought to light many years later (Sorokin 1997, p. 75). Therefore, these events cannot be considered as milestones for the geographies that are not in direct relation with them—it is meaningless to attempt that.

Unless an alternative approach is developed against the public opinion building up an attraction towards the European history created by Orientalists, there is an absolute danger that this public opinion will become permanent in people's minds (Darling 2006, p. 181). And that will bring along disturbance in our peace of mind and confusion in the way we perceive our history. This is because these identifications of Europeans are essentially based on the Enlightenment philosophy and some historical hypotheses related to Christian theology and generally reflect the mindset behind them. In this respect, the reflections of the histories of other societies on these identifications are like the distorted lights passing through a broken lens. Trying to understand the history of Islam by depending on these European-centred historical classifications is almost no different from 'straightjacketing our brains' (Genc 2006, pp. 331–7).

One of the biggest obstacles in the way to understand the history and the civilization of Islam in a healthy and holistic manner is the European-centred conception of history (Hodgson 2001, p. 174). This is because this perception somehow distorts the image of the history of Islam to its foundations. For example, two of the major conquest movements of Islam (the conquest in the first period of Islam and Seljuk–Ottoman conquests) are considered as threats and negative developments. More importantly, European-centred approaches found it worthy to mention the history of Islam only through the points that somehow affected the history of Europe (like events in Andalusia and in the Ottoman Empire). At the same time, these approaches identify the Islamic world only with Muslims in the Mediterranean geography and the Arabs. However, the central regions of the Islamic world are the non-Arabian geographies of the Iranian and Turan people, between the Nile and Amu Darya.

Because the European-centred perspective addresses this issue based on the dynamics, institutions, and structures that constitute the past and present of Europe, it assesses other civilizations only through the lack of these factors. This kind of an anachronistic approach will always reveal a distorted historical view. It can be claimed that the declinist historical approach towards the Ottoman Empire that evaluated only what it could not achieve instead of analysing the stages it went through is the most recognized example of this kind of a historiography. In this frame, as Said states (1979, p. 202), the West has been interested in how Eastern societies, particularly the Ottoman Empire, are supposed to act as parallels to the demands of the West, instead of how they really are, and has pictured the non-Western world not as the subject, but the object of the history.

One of the misperceptions established by the progressive European perspective is that Muslims are perpetually in regression. The history of Islam is always considered as the history of a regression, without even questioning if such a regression existed in reality. This belief is so rooted that this regression is accepted to start from a point and to contain even the greatest and brightest ages of Islam, and the history of Islam is presented without any successes or growth; at least it has never had success that could compete with the history of the West. From a European-centred point of view, Islam and its civilization is the history of failures, collapses, and regressions. The reasons for the worldwide successes of Muslims in science, art, and politics during more than one thousand years (eighth to eighteenth centuries) and the key motivations of the great civilization they established are only rarely studied. Hence, the assumption of 'static East/Islam' is a compulsory consequence of the Eurocentrism.

THE NEED FOR A SPECIAL PERIODIZATION OF THE HISTORY AND CIVILIZATION OF ISLAM

All civilizations have developmental stages, historical periods, different rhythms, and civilization types of their own depending on their internal dynamics and the interactions they have faced. Therefore, the periodization of the civilization enables us to see the diversifying cultural models, values, and types of people representing these models and values within the civilization. Studying the differences and changes between ages, we can determine the line between two consecutive periods. With reference to this theory, Shelomo Dov Goitein remarked that in periodization of the history of Islam, the 'ideal human models' in different periods can be used as the base. According to this claim, the 'conqueror' human model represented by *sahaba, tabi'un,* and *tabi' al-tabi'in*[1] in the first period of Islam is a model with pure religious passion and mostly characterized by the Arabic temperament. The 'scholar–philosopher' model in the succeeding classical era that corresponds to the Abbasid and Seljuk peoples is a human model more likely to be identified with cultural tendencies and interest in abstract issues. After the classical era, there comes the 'devotee, sufi' human type who is respectful towards the legacy of the past and the traditions, is self-enclosed, experiences his/her religious passion within himself/herself, and is mostly represented by the Iranians and the Turkish (Goitein 1968, p. 225).

Surely, each civilization has a history that developed in accordance with its own streamline and is composed of multifaceted movements that propound various values in different periods as the results of its experiences, accumulations, and break-ups. We do not mean to claim that civilizations are developed within their isolated world; on the contrary, the history of any community cannot develop without any interaction with the outside world. Every great civilization is shaped by strong interactions with others. However, each civilization process maintains its life according to its morphological characteristics and its own values while progressing in its own historical line. In this process, every civilization experiences its own ages of childhood, maturity, and elderliness, and these ages undoubtedly differ from the ages of other civilizations (Sorokin 1997, p. 78). Identifying the periods of historical unity and categorizing it accordingly reveal the different stages and types of civilizations experienced by this unity. Goitein (1968, p. 224) emphasizes that periodization is not only a must for categorizing disorganized information with pedagogical purposes, but a *scientific precondition*. A history without periodization is like a book with no chapter, no plan at all.

Though the history of Islam is a history of long-rooted traditions and great powers, this situation does not indicate uniformity in any way. If one does not take into consideration the different processes through which Islam has evolved over thirteen centuries, one will picture an abstract Islam that is not consistent with historical realities. In addition, attributions of Islamic culture and its contributions to humanity will be neglected. For instance, if the difference between the cultural lives in the eighth and ninth centuries and the eleventh and twelfth centuries of the Islamic civilization is not well understood, there will be a misunderstanding that Islamic culture and thinking is only the repetition of Hellenistic legacy. However, there started an individualization movement in the Islamic world from the tenth century and a new era began for Islam, one unlike any of the previous centuries. Therefore, just for the sake of finding the truth, it is required to divide the long-term processes of Islamic history into its own organic sections. Otherwise, the history of Islam will be considered and interpreted within European-centred categories. A study that is developed depending on the internal dynamics of the civilization will also form the foundations of paradigms that give meaning to, frame, and explain everything that takes place in any period. In this respect, periodization can be regarded as a sort of traffic sign that integrates parts that seem independent of each other and gives the historians studying a certain period an idea of the band s/he is working on. However, periodization should be based on a certain social or cultural change and should be unbiased; it should not be stuck in the progression–regression frame. Drawing a detailed graph of the history of Islam based on these paradigms is a kind of precondition for further studies in this area.

Unless periodization is conducted, the historical and time perception in hand will remain obscure and unclear, and historians will have to wander like a ship that has lost its route in the sea not knowing which port they were headed towards. In order to compare each stage that the history of Islam has come through with other stages within the history of Islam and with other civilizations of the same age, the periodization must be conducted in a way to highlight the differences. For instance, in order to be able to make a comparison between the Ottoman Empire and Abbasids in the areas of science and thinking or about the institutions of economics and politics, we can determine which parameters to use to interpret the differences between these two areas and states based on a periodization developed with a well-established perspective. Especially in the case of the distinct differentiation between Ottomans and Abbasids in science and intellectual tradition, it can be described within the frame of two different types of civilization developed by the Islamic civilization. Is the culture of *sharh* (explanation) and *hashiyah* (annotation) in the Ottoman period a 'second classical era' within the Islamic civilization or is it mainly the repetition of the previous one? An answer can be given to this question only with a well-developed point of view that identifies and describes the dominant culture and characteristics of these periods. Otherwise, we will end up interpreting the differentiation between the Abbasid period and the Ottoman period in science and intellectual life as a regression just like how it has been done until today.

The periodization of the history of Islam in Turkey until today has not been sufficiently dwelled on. Zeki Velidî Togan (1985, p. 26), Nihal Atsız (1977, p. 19), Ibrahim Saricam with Seyfettin Erşahin (2005, pp. 184–97), İsmail Özçelik (2001, p. 27), Mehmed Niyazi (2008, pp. 184–97), and Mehmet Genc (2006) have drawn attention to the necessity of such a periodization. On the other hand, Ibrahim Kafesoglu points out that the division of history into three ages cannot be employed in the consideration of Turkish history and suggests the production of a new categorization (Kafesoglu 1964, pp. 1–13;

see also Kafesoglu 1984, pp. 254, 343–53, and Kafesoglu and Donuk 1990). Islamic historians have not brought this issue forward staidly as a problematic subject until now. Generally, a periodization based on the sequence of dynasties like the Era of Bliss, Rashidun Caliphs, Umayyads (Arabian Kingdom), Abbasids (Islamic Empire), Seljuks, and Ottomans is preferred. This kind of periodization differs from region to region and from nation to nation. The approaches developed are within the limits of the perspectives of the historians of a certain nation, for instance, Arab, Turkish, Russian, or European historians periodize history based on their own premises. For example, the perspective of Arab historians is quite unclear: the history of Islam starts with Rashidun Caliphs, is followed by the Umayyads and Abbasids, then comes a long gap and a period of uncertainty, and then it starts again in the nineteenth century. This perspective tends to consider the history of Islam as an unproductive period after a few centuries of glorious Arab reign. The political domination of the Turkish and the Barbary empires is historically meaningless and invalid for them; in this way, they deprive themselves of their own history unwittingly. In the case of the European-centred approach, historians separate the history of Islam into two major eras considering two major periods of military attacks towards them (first conquests of Islam and the spread of Islam and the attacks by the Ottomans). The historical perspectives of Arabs, Turks, Iranians, Muslims of the Indian subcontinent, Africans, and all other nations, which have been informed by the imperialist mentalities and have been under the impact of the West for too long, are divided and even full of hostile images to a point where they are prevented from seeing the unity they had once in the history. Due to these kinds of perspectives, the historical perception of different regions and nations of the Islamic world should be reconsidered in a systematic way. The classification of the history of Islam that is acceptable in all parts of the words related to Islam could be effective in correcting all these limited points of view and in uniting them (Hodgson 2001, p. 266).

However, adopting an approach centralizing one of these dynasties or nations means neglecting the continuities that flow deeper in the history and exceed all the political structures in the history of Islam. Besides, it is not sufficiently emphasized that Islam has not only produced political structures, but also has its own intellectual tradition, social structure, culture, art, and civilization in the broadest sense. However, historical unity essentially exists as a civilization; this civilization contains a number of nations, and hundreds of states are established and collapsed within it. No matter how strong and active these states are, they are no more than a part of a unity. Therefore, an attempt of periodization requires us to highlight the civilization dimension of the history of Islam and look at history through the framework of civilization. Hence, Islamic civilization, as a history that covers the history of many nations, should be used as a base for such a periodization.

There are a series of difficulties when it comes to the periodization of the Islamic civilization. These difficulties do not arise for the first centuries of the Islamic civilization. This is because it is easier to study this period as a unity for there was only one political authority, and the impact of the regional powers was relatively limited. However, as time passed, the domain of the Islamic world expanded and the geographical and political differences made it harder to study the history of Islam politically as a unity. On the other hand, a common cultural legacy in the area of general knowledge, the common attitudes that are shaped around the religion of these societies, and interregional interactions have resulted in the minimization of the differences and the manifestation of continuity. There can be seen the extensions of a single structure integrating a broad geography from Timbuktu to Kashgar, from Jakarta to Kazan: a single civilization with a single history that contains all localities and diversities. In this respect, in order to be able to develop a periodization that not only transcends nations and regions but also contains them without externalizing even one, it is necessary to study the history at the level of the civilizations. Also, the changes within the developmental process of civilization should be taken into consideration in these kinds of studies.

As it is known, science cannot be done with singular phenomenon. It is necessary to know and analyse the systematics of the subject and to recognize the positions of the singular phenomenon in the unity. After all, the human mind seeks a meaningful system in the area it explores. With reference to that, it can be said that there must be an interrelation between historical studies that focus on a particular subject and the higher historical perspectives/theories. In that case, it can be seen that any singular phenomenon does not just happen out of nothing, but is part of a historical unity and is determined by a meaningful system. Therefore, a historian must handle historical phenomena from the broader perspective, keeping in mind the historical context they take place in, while s/he deepens her/his historical studies. S/he can broaden her/his perspective step by step: first based on decades or generations, and later one or more centuries. However, only if a perspective broad enough to consider a few centuries is preferred, the independent courses and continuities of the various traditions forming a whole culture, fault lines, and simultaneous expansions and depressions, growths and declines can be recognized (Hodgson 1993, I, p. 18).

An alternative perspective that integrates and frames all narrow-scale studies needs to be developed against the disintegrator historical approach, which is also called tunneling historiography. It studies history in a different manner, deprived it of its political, economic, cultural, and social dimensions and confining it only within a certain period. The powerful traditions on which historical phenomena developed and the chain of causation that maintains continuity between the events cannot be recognized; and therefore, historical realities cannot be settled within a theoretical and conceptual framework and a holistic idea of history cannot be derived from these specific studies in question. In this respect, picturing a panoramic view of the history of Islam emphasizing the milestones and long-term processes becomes a precondition for historical studies.

A PROPOSAL FOR THE PERIODIZATION OF THE HISTORY AND CIVILIZATION OF ISLAM

Though there have been various developments in the periodization proposals regarding Ottoman history (see Armagan 2006), there is no systematic periodization of the history of Islam developed in the Islamic world yet. This is because this kind of an attempt requires a historian to have much more than mere historic knowledge and the history of Islam is a history that develops on strong traditions and does not display the sharp break points like Western history does. Therefore, in the subsequent section of this chapter, the existing periodization models will be assessed and a new periodization proposal will be presented.

Three significant studies have been conducted on the systematic periodization of the history of Islamic civilization by Goitein, André Miquel, and Marshal Hodgson. Goitein (1968), in his article 'A Plea for Periodization of Islamic History', divides the history of Islam into four ages: (a) The Age of Arabism or Arabic Islam (500–850), (b) Interim Civilization Age (850–1250), (c) Institutionalized, Territorial, non-Arabic Age (1250–1800), (d) Transition to National Cultures: Inspiration by Origins rather than Islam (1800–). Goitein developed his periodization mainly based on the Arabic nation. Therefore, the ages he proposes are developed according to the significant transitions experienced by Arabs in time. Another characteristic of his study is that monetary economy and the development of the bourgeoisie have been determinative on his categorization for he generally concentrates on trade history, the bourgeoisie, and Mediterranean trade.

French historian Miquel (1990), in his two-volume work *Islam and Its Civilization*, divides the history of Islam into four ages: (a) the Age of Expansion and Spread (610–750), (b) the Age of Baghdad Caliphates (750–1050), (c) Turkish–Mongolian Domination and the New Face of Islam (from eleventh century till the end of eighteenth century), (d) Imperialism and the Arabic Renaissance (from the nineteenth century to the twentieth century). Because the perspective of French academic tradition has been profound on the categorization of Miquel; nations, especially the transitions experienced by the Arabs, have been determinative on his categorization.

M. G. S. Hodgson (1993), in his three-volume work *The Venture of Islam*, discusses the 'main topics of Islamic history' in six ages: (a) the Islamic infusion: genesis of a new social order (...–692), (b) the classical civilization of the high caliphate (692–945), (c) the establishment of an international civilization (945–1258), (d) crisis and renewal: the age of Mongol prestige (1258–1503), (e) second flowering: the empires of gunpowder times (1503–1789), (f) the Islamic heritage in the modern world (1789–).

In these three works of periodization just mentioned, there are both coinciding parts and significant differences. I will try to develop a new periodization by both comparing these three studies and pointing out their deficiencies. The main topics of the periodization that I favour by comparing the above studies will be discussed in detail in the following pages. The periodization is the following: (a) the age of

conquests and the foundation (610–750), (*b*) the classical age of the
Islamic civilization (750–1258), (*c*) the zenith of the financial power of
Islam and the age of empires (*d*) colonization by the West and the age
of depression (1800–...).

The First Period: The Age of Conquests and Formation (610–750)

Let us begin discussing the issue of the starting date of the Islamic history. Goitein considers the history of Islam as the history of the Arabs;
therefore, he begins Islamic history with the rise of the Quraysh tribe
as they established a commercial alliance (*ilaf*) in Mecca in AD 500.
Hodgson does not state an exact date; however, he predicates on
the spread of Islam out of the Arabian Peninsula (Iranian–Semitic
region). Miquel considers the first revelation to Prophet Mohammed
in AD 610 as the starting date of the history of Islam.

Miquel describes the first age of Islamic history as the age of expansion and spread, from its origin (AD 610) until the middle of the eighth
century (around AD 750). During this period, the history of Islam was
monopolized by the Arabs and the Arabic tradition was dominant in
all areas. Due to extraordinarily rapid conquests in this period, the
centre of the Old World from Spain to China came under the domination of Islam within a short span of time. As a consequence of these
conquests, important trade routes came under the control of Muslims.
Most significantly, the foundations of Eastern and Mediterranean
civilizations were laid as a result of these conquests. This situation
is embodied by the adoption of Arabic as the official language and
the minting of coins. On the other hand, this century is distressed
by the rebellions and lawlessness of the Shias and the Kharijites, and
an internal disintegration is experienced. In the last few years of this
period, national movements started to emerge. Despite the chaos
due to all these acts of violence, fights between brothers, factionalism, and disputes, Islam, still young, used the time in its favour and
established its system of religion and also procured acceptance of its
essential principles and beliefs. While concluding his views on this
period, Miquel says: 'Here we are on the edge of a new history: history
of Baghdad.' After the collapse of the Umayyads, shifting the centre
of the civilization closer to the great trade routes of the world was

necessary for the Islam of eighth to the thirteenth centuries to meet the classical cultures of the ancient ages, and for the birth of a new civilization (Miquel 1990, p. 79).

Hodgson defines the first period of the Islamic history as the 'Age of Last Sassanians and First Caliphates' (...–692). According to him, in the residential areas between the Nile and Amu Darya (*oikoumen*), great names and traditions of humanity emerged between 800 BC and AD 600. Hodgson names this period as the 'Axis Age', a concept he borrowed from Karl Jasper. Islam stepped into this world during the last few years of this age. According to him, the ways for a new order were being paved in Iran, the Fertile Crescent, and Arabia in this period. Therefore, Hodgson starts his discussions by studying three great civilizations that were developed in these regions before the emergence of Islam. In this period, the political order of Sassanians was shaken, and Muslims, led by the close friends of Prophet Muhammad, dominated the land from the Nile to Amu Darya, and even areas lying further away. Hodgson ends this first period in AH 73/ AD 693. That year Abdullah ibn Zubayr led a rebellion against the Umayyad Caliphate but was defeated and killed in Mecca after a six-month siege by General Al-Hajjaj ibn Yusuf. According to Hodgson, The Age of High Caliphates' (AD 692–5) starts from this date on.

As it can be seen in the periodizations summarized previously, the involvement of Turks in the history of Islam is accepted as the milestone for the end of the first period. Indeed, the involvement of Turks in the political life of Islam had significant impacts in the long term. As is stated by Goitein, the beginning of this was with the establishment of Samarra. However, their influence in Samarra was not enough to initiate the radical transitions in the Islamic history. Though the centralized management of Abbasids passed on to the Turks in the political–military area with the establishment of Samarra, Baghdad remained the leader in the more influential social, economic, scientific, and cultural areas. In my opinion, it would be more accurate to accept the collapse of the Umayyads and the rise of Abbasids in the 750s that was almost coincident with the establishment of Baghdad as the beginning of radical changes in the Islamic world, rather than the establishment of Samarra. Besides, Goitein (1949, pp. 120, 125) considers the year 750 in which the Umayyads collapsed and the Abbasids rose, signifying the beginning of the radical changes in the history of Islam in many areas, in another article named 'A Turning Point in the History of Muslim State'[2] based on 'Kitab al-Sahaba, a study of Ibn al-Muqaffa. He states that in that year, Arabian bureaucracy was replaced by a professional bureaucracy; the army composed of various tribes was replaced by a regular army composed of wage-soldiers; and Arabian sovereignty was replaced by constituents from various nations, especially the Iranians and the Turks. The changes in Islamic history in this period were far more extensive and deeper than it had been assumed (Goitein 1980, p. 57). That the year 750 in which the Abbasid state was established was a turning point in the history of Islam was emphasized by many recognized historians like André Miquel, Bernard Lewis, Carl Brockelman, Fernand Braudel, and Julius Welhausen. For the Western historians, this date symbolizes the break between the Arabian Kingdom (Umayyads) and the Islamic Empire (Abbasids) and the beginning of a new period.

Hodgson pays attention to the internal conflicts that ended in year 692 or 700 and believes that the Age of First Caliphates ended around these years. However, it cannot be claimed that this had an influence significant enough to transform the entire historical course. It is true that the Umayyads overcame all their political competitors; however, there was no development that would change the course of history that goes much deeper than the singular events and that gives the feeling that a new era has just begun. Anyway, this break point represents only an interim break in his six-age system. According to him, the essential great transition that separated the first age from the following ages and brought it to an end is the dissolution of the authority of the Caliphates (Umayyad and Abbasid) and the entrance of Buyids into Baghdad in 945.

The primary characteristic feature of the first period of the Islamic civilization that I name the 'Age of Conquests and the Foundation' is the conquests of that period. This is because many fields like state administration, finance, army, social structure, and cities were strongly influenced by the conquests. Islam laid the foundations of the Eastern and Mediterranean empires by conquering the centres of long-established Eastern civilizations and by gaining control over the intersection of the important trade routes of the ancient world. The conquests were so rapid that they were stopped only by impassable chains of mountains and or deserts (the Pyrenees mountains in the west, the Taurus mountains and Caucasus mountains in the north, the Altai and the Pamir mountains in the east, the Himalayas in the south, and the Sahara Desert and Atlantic Ocean in Africa). Muslims were minorities in the general population, and there was only one political authority. During this period, the Arabs and Arabic language were dominant in all fields. Disputes between Muslims and other religious communities had not begun yet. Different nations coexisted without interfering in each other's businesses, because they had only recently encountered each other. On the other hand, the Bedouins were urbanizing. The rapid international expansion, radical social change, and urbanization resulting from the conquests increased differences of opinion; meanwhile tension was brewing due to political factionalism between Muslim Arabs; they were shaken by the rebellions of the Shia and Kharijite tribes and deep internal depressions. We can see the reflexes like religious passion and enthusiasm, the desire for sovereignty, the sense of belonging, and low-level urbanization that are common in all civilizations at the beginning of their establishment. In the last few years of this period, due to the unrest created by the course of events, local opposition started to rise. Eventually, this period ends due to the tensions resulting from internal conflicts, rapid growth, rampancy of the Arab governors, lack of a stable management, and uncontrolled social mobility. Therefore, this period can be named as the age of conquests and foundation.

The Second Period: The Classical Age of Islam (750–1258)

There are many debates on when the first age of the Islamic history ended and which event symbolizes the development that ended this period, as well as which characteristic should be used to identify the next period. Goitein (1968, p. 124) uses the term 'intermediate civilization (850–1250)' for the stage that followed the first age. However, he emphasizes that he does not use this term as it is used in European-centred Orientalist arguments, where the real intended meaning is 'intermediary'. This is because, according to him, the Islamic civilization was not a mere transporter between the Hellenistic civilization/ legacy and the Renaissance; on the contrary, it succeeded in creating its own values. The term 'intermediate' is used more in a positional sense. Islamic civilization acted as a medium between the Eastern

Hindustan–China and the Western Africa and Europe. Besides, it had the feature of assimilating all civilizations within these boundaries. According to him, the dominant characteristics of this period were a liberal monetary economy, a social structure based on the priority of middle classes, widespread influence of the Greek secular sciences, an extraordinary creative flexibility, and richness in religious matters.

Though Miquel names this period as 'The Age of Confrontations, Meetings: The Arabian Tradition and Foreign Legacies (Centuries VIII–XI)', he prefers the term 'The Age of Baghdad Caliphates (750–1050)'. According to him, in this age Islam stabilized itself in lands where it was dominant and strengthened its foundations. Due to the establishment of Baghdad at the intersection of the trade routes and the conquest that was placed on hold, a glamorous urbanization movement took place (seventeen candles of Islam). The Muslim world dominated all the commercial intersections, and commerce was a distinctive feature of this period. Everything was on the move: humans, plants, animals, and cultures. While an Islamic sovereignty was being established in the open seas, the trade that had continued since the ancient times on the saharas was accelerating. The society transitioned from confined Bedouin life to urban life, started to encounter foreign legacies and in the process became dynamic with its traditions and innovations. Despite the political and regional divisions, there was a united Muslim society under the spiritual authority of the caliphate. On the other hand, the contact/dialogue with the foreign traditions (in terms of culture) was intensive and the old traditions were continuously being revived; in other words, the culture was still in the process of formation. The bloom in the Umayyads' times flourished with new blood from Iran and the seeds of the developments that would propel the Islamic civilization towards its cultural zenith. The author expresses this situation with the following words: 'Umayyads planted, Abbasids harvested' (Miquel 1990, p. 93). The seeds of the culture and the civilization that brought Islam to its highest state and made it such a successful religion were planted in the Age of Baghdad Caliphates.

Abbasids improved and enriched the legacy they took over from the Umayyads with the new blood they had from Iran until the middle of the ninth century. However, the Iranian culture resisted the theology, language, and culture of Islam. Political, economic, ethnic, religious, and social crises started to damage the trade routes, making holes in the glorious facades of the cities and shaking the very foundations of Islam by influencing the thoughts of the people. It did not take long for regression and collapse of the period to set in (Miquel 1990, p. 124). The destiny of the world was still in the hands of the East, but Europe had started to become active in the seas. That the Abbasid caliphates lost political authority resulted not only in the disintegration of the political union, but also initiated the militarization of the *iqta* system[3] and radical changes that would influence the socio-economic structure. This development replaced 'monetary aristocracy', which adopted a clerk–tradesman policy, with 'sword aristocracy', which adopted a military structuring. In a sense, the decayed commercial class was replaced by a land-stocker military class (Miquel 1990, pp. 164–5). Their entrance into the stage not only brought this period to an end but also changed the view of the Islamic world in the socio-economic sense.

According to Hodgson, this period is the first period of the Islamicate classical civilization that was beginning to come into existence in Marwani caliphates. Islamicate society constituted a single great state and the authority of the caliphate, with the Arabic language gradually becoming dominant as the language of science and culture. The classical formulation of the Islamic civilization was determined: Muslims, Christians, Jews, and Mazdakis. Moreover, some traditions from the pre-Islamic times were being revived, which led to a multifaceted flourishing. At this stage, an absolute bureaucratic empire was created taking the Sassanians as the model, and a civilization that found expression in Arabic language was born. Now there was formed an 'Islamic culture' that centralized on its bright culture, and a 'World of Islam' that was substantially identified by Islam. This age that was concreted by the authority of the caliphate started to collapse from the middle of the ninth century, and the political integration completely broke up in the middle of the tenth century. This collapse took place due to (*a*) the slenderness of the agricultural land and the collapse of the sprinkler system and partially due to (*b*) the failure of the clerical class that depended on the caliphate to develop ideas and models that would procure the support of the dominant social groups and hence maintain political integrity. The year 945 in which the Buyids entered Baghdad was proposed as the end of the 'age of high caliphates'.

While explaining the transition around year 945 which indicated the end of this period, Sorokin used the terms developed by Toynbee in his historical philosophy which states that the 'creative minority' around the caliphate was not able to produce ideas and models that would procure the support of the dominant social groups. And thus maintain the political integrity, and therefore they were no longer imitable to 'internal proletariats'; this situation brought the end of this period (Sorokin 1997, pp. 149–50). However, the point to which attention should be paid here is that though the high caliphate collapsed, what continued without being interrupted and formed the essential characteristic of this period were the dynamic traditions. Despite the dissolution of the caliphate, the social structures shaped by science and philosophy and by urban-tradesmen continued and, despite the political disintegration, cultural unity was maintained. Therefore, the impacts of the dissolution of the caliphate were no more than a political disintegration. Surely, there took place important developments like Muslims becoming majorities in the geographies they lived in and Islamic science and philosophy starting to produce its authentic classics; however, these were only the continuation of a process that was initiated by a great transition that had taken place long ago. Therefore, the end of the first period should be sought at a later date.

Hodgson mentions a new period that he calls the 'Early Middle Islamic Age (945–1258)', which he takes as the third stage in the history of Islam. During this period, an international civilization and society that spread beyond the Iranian–Semitic lands was established. On one hand, the political disintegration continued and on the other, thanks to the internal dynamism of the common culture and social institutions that were expressed in Arabic and Persian languages, the spread and the unity of the Muslim society was developing at the same time. In this age, another development that emerged in Islamic history was the discrimination between the *umera*, a social class composed of Mamelukes mostly belonging to nomad communities, and the 'ayan' class that was composed of *ulama*, tradesmen, craftsmen, and noblemen from tribes and religious communities, and this discrimination gradually became more apparent in time and was felt at all levels. Though the latter class procured legitimacy to the political system as an important part of Muslim society, they were segregated from the military class. Another separation was in terms of language—the courtiers and the ruling class were using Persian, especially in the Eastern regions, while the ulama were using Arabic in their religious works.

The second age that can be named as the 'second classical age of Islam' according to my classification starts with the Abbasid revolution in 750 and ends with the occupation of Baghdad by the Mongols in 1258. As has been discussed, the Abbasid revolution that led to the collapse of the Umayyads initiated great changes in political, social, and, later on, cultural areas in a broad sense and would subsequently result in changes more permanent in nature. This period was referred to as the 'Abbasid juncture' by Braudel (1999, p. 94). Just after the Abbasids came into power, the conquests that had defined the characteristic of the first century significantly decreased and a revival was initiated in urbanization and cultural life. In this period of the history, Islam became the brightest civilization that was founded on the legacy of the ancient world. The production of the constituent classics that addressed different geographies and historical ages within the Islamic cultural area with the advent of the Abbasids is the formation of a new civilization. These classics both reflect the mindset patterns of the new civilization that was in the process of formation and lay the foundation of the civilization that would be formed later. As Davutoğlu states (2007, p. 23), there is a certain era in which constituent classics of this kind are produced in the history of every civilization. In the Islamic civilization, this era starts with the establishment of Abbasid state in the middle of the eighth century and continues until the thirteenth century. In this period, the political, economic, scientific, and ideological structures of Islam were created, and basic concepts, thoughts, and schools were shaped within each settled area. This is also the period in which the system-founder philosophers and scholars flourished in almost all areas (such as *fikh*, *hadith*, *kalam*, philosophy, art, literature) and produced their studies. Islamic civilization developed its essential classical formulation in this period. Therefore, to my opinion, the most appropriate way to refer to this age would be the 'classical age of Islam'.

This age is divided into two stages within itself. The characteristic features of the first stage in which the Abbasids were ruling can be seen in Baghdad. Baghdad was both the meeting point of tradesmen and the point of confluence of ancient cultural legacies. This period came to an end with the dissolution of the 'absolute caliphate' as it lost its political power. With the collapse of the caliphate, alternative cultural regions emerged all over the Islamic world. In the second stage, hundreds of states were established between the Abbasids and the Ottomans, and a multi-centred structure was developed. After the tenth century, Buyids (945–1053) were established in Iraq and western Iran; Samanids (until 999) in Transoxiana and eastern Iran; Ghaznavids (until 1040), Seljuks, and vassal states were established in Afghanistan, Khorasan, and the Indus basin; and the Fatimid state, Almoravids, and Almurabits were established in the west. The Mongolian invasion swept all these states away like a hurricane. In this period, Persian developed as a second language. Sufi sects, guilds like *futuwwat*, and *madrasah*s came into being. In this period, philosophical kalam was developed by Al-Ghazali, and philosophical Sufism was developed by Ibn Arabi. With the contribution of the Seljuks, almost a new Muslim civilization (Turkish Islam) emerged. The conquests of Islam started again with the adoption of Islam by the Seljuks and with the Manzikert Battle against the Byzantines being won. A new 'rise and spread' age of Islam was started by the Berbers in the west and Seljuks and Ottomans in the east. Maghreb and Spain were experiencing bright ages in terms of science and intellectual tradition. Great system philosophers like Ibn Bajja, Ibn Maimoni Ibn Tufail, and the most outstanding name of this tradition, Ibn Rushd, who spent their lives in Maghreb, Spain, and Sicilia prospered. The entrance of Seljuks into the history of Islam represents the beginning of a new age due to both their political–military successes and their great attempts in the field of 'scientific thinking'. The spread of the military iqta system by Seljuks beyond the political–administrative boundaries initiated a radical change in social and economic structures. This development caused the replacement of the clerk-tradesman type by the 'military-political' elites, and this situation empowered the domination of the sword aristocracy instead of the monetary aristocracy (Miquel 1990, pp. 164–5).

While Miquel says that the process started by Turks lasted during the eighth century, Hodgson extends this age until the European geographical explorations, that is, the fifteenth century. And Goitein states that he sees no break points in this historical period; he centres his analyses on the middle-class bourgeoisie and says: 'The middle class emerged in year 750, got stronger in the third century and reached at its brightest times in the fourth and fifth centuries and became dominant and influential on the Mameluke soldiers' (Goitein 1968, p. 227). According to him, the radical change in the historical structure after the Abbasids did not take place in the years 945 or 1050, but in 1258 with the Mongolian invasion. Goitein is not the only one who thinks this way; C. Cahen (1993), B. Lewis, and F. Braudel also consider the period between years 750 and 1258 as a historical unity. According to Braudel (p. 97), this classical period ends with the death of Ibn Rushd in 1199, whereas, according to Hodgson, this age should be studied in two periods as discussed earlier. The first of these two periods is the period between years 692 and 945, and he calls it the Absolute Caliphate. After that comes the second period that ends in 1250 and he calls it the 'Early Middle Age'. However, Hodgson names the period between year 945 and 1250 as the 'First Middle Age' and the period between years 1250 and 1500 as the 'Late Middle Age' and considers the period between years 945 and 1500 as an integrated unity. According to him, the old caliphate society was replaced by a continuously expanding society that was ruled by many independent governors and had an international characteristic in terms of language and culture during the five centuries that followed the year 945 in which the caliphate collapsed. Miquel claims that this age ended in year 1050 with the arrival of Seljuks, one century later than the date presented by Hodgson.

Most historians who have studied the periodization of the history of Islam have regarded the entrance of the Turks in the Islamic world as a turning point. There is a belief that with the arrival of the moun-taineer–nomad tribes, the conditions in the Islamic world changed (Gibb 1991, p. 40). With the arrival of the Turks, the domination of the Arabs and the age of high caliphates ended, the iqta system spread, the conquests of Islam was revived after three centuries, and the nomad tribes started to dominate the settled world; and all these developments marked the beginning of a series of changes.

In the pre-Mongolian age, Kwarazmians, Karakhanids, and Ghurids were fighting each other in Asia; Anatolian Seljuks, Zengids, and Ayyubids were fighting among themselves and against the Crusaders in the Eastern Mediterranean; and the emirates in Andalusia, Almoravids, and Almohads were fighting among them-selves and against the Aragonese and Castile Kingdoms in the west.

In the meantime, another significant development took place—the Normans invaded Sicilia, Crete, and Malta, and the Islamic domination of the Mediterranean Sea was interrupted until the rise of the Ottomans. Even though the Crusaders (1095–1291) failed on land, they managed to repossess the sea and the commercial places on the Mediterranean Sea. The Crusaders lost their last castle in Akka, but they did not lose their position of superiority in the Mediterranean Sea. According to Braudel (1999, p. 83), this incident symbolizes the rise of Europe and the confinement of Muslims within its lands.

The debates on whether or not the classical Islamic civilization faced a crisis in the twelfth and thirteenth centuries still goes on. Braudel (1999, p. 109) thinks that the Islamic civilization started to regress severely in this age, which he describes as the 'age of stagnation and regression'. Various reasons were cited for this situation: (*a*) domination of nomad communities; (*b*) the attacks of the Crusaders (1095–1291) and, later, the invasion of Mongols that confronted the entire written culture and the advanced urban culture of the Islamic civilization with the danger of extinction; (*c*) Al-Ghazali's attacks on philosophy and free thought; (*d*) the spread of insightful knowledge, epistemology, and ascetism by Sufism; (*e*) the Mediterranean Sea becoming inaccessible to Muslims. Each of these reasons is worthy of being studied as an independent topic. As it was emphasized by Braudel, the depression from the thirteenth to the fifteenth centuries was not limited by Islamic geography alone. Plague, wars, population movements, economic recession, and the decrease in the working population were problems faced by the entire world, from China to Europe. However, Braudel (1999, p. 111) claims that the specific problems of the Islamic world in the thirteenth century came together with this global crisis that deepened the depression in the Muslim lands.

The Third Period: The Zenith of the Meterial Power of Islam and the Age of Empires (1258–1800)

Goitein calls the post-Mongolian invasion period the 'Institutionalized, Territorial, Non-Arabic Age (1250–1800)'. This age is primarily characterized by the rise of military feudalism (iqta army), bureaucratic state (*kuttab*), the spread of state monopoly in all areas, and the inspection of the guilds and trade bodies (*ahi* community). Everything is organized; large schools (*madrasahs*), Islamic monasteries (*zawiyahs*), a large salaried staff, large-scale encyclopedic books and epitomized manuals, and the sciences—all of these represent new institutions that were not pre-Islamic. During this period, religious creativity was substantially replaced by obscurantism. Mysticism was replaced by theosophy and Sufism was replaced by religious cults. Later on, cultural differences started to appear in areas that were dominated by the Ottoman, Safavid, Mughal, and Chagatai states. The disconnection and differentiation was not merely a matter of language anymore; there was disorder in all fields including art, architecture, and even philosophy and science.

Miquel starts this period with the year 1050 in which Seljuks entered the Islamic world and ends it at the end of the eighteenth century. Miquel uses the expression 'Turkish–Mongolian Domination and the New Face of Islam (eleventh century–end of eighteenth century)' to describe this period. According to him, the history of Islam was under the monopoly of Central Asians, especially the Mongolians and the Turks for approximately eight centuries from 1050 to 1800. The Arabs were no longer on the stage until the end of the nineteenth century; they were the audience. The new actors were the Turks, Berbers, and Mongols. This population movement that started with the Seljuks and was then followed by the Mongols and Berbers in the west, the interchange of knowledge, and economic relationships brought life to the disintegrated Old World and revived the Abbasid-age traditions. According to him, Mongols did not hinder the growth of Islam; contrary to the common claims, they conquered from inside for they broadened the movement area of Muslim tradesmen. During this age, Islam spread from Central Africa to the Far Asia and from the Indian subcontinent to China; the borders of the large empires that emerged in Egypt, Anatolia, Iran, Hindustan, and Central Asia substantially extended; due to the political stability and addition of new trade routes to the old ones, commerce improved; and thanks to the provision of institutionalization, extraordinary improvements were achieved in the sciences and arts (Miquel 1990, pp. 372–83).

Hodgson studies this period by adopting a historical categorization that is similar to European categorizations and divides it into two parts: the 'Early Middle Islamic Age (945–1258)' and the 'Late

Middle Islamic Age (1053–1258)'. According to Hodgson, the Late
Middle Islamic Age was characterized by Mongol domination and
the crises and revivals in Islamized institutions and legacy. Though
the Islamized cities were invaded and demolished by the Mongols,
Islamic norms came to be accepted and continued to spread in the
northern hemisphere. In this period, Islam spread to Anatolia, the
Balkans, Hindustan, southeastern Asia, and sub-Saharan Africa. The
Mongolian challenge resulted in the formation of a political tradition
through the spread of an unprecedentedly influential Iranian culture
in the region between the Balkans and Bengal. Hodgson refutes the
claim made by many researchers that there occurred a radical change
in the Islamic culture and society in this period and says that nothing
that can be described as a cultural decline or radical social change took
place in this age. And hence, he describes the next age as 'The Second
Flowering: The Empires of Gunpowder (1503–1789)'. According to
him, Persianized culture flourished under the rule of the great local
empires (Ottoman, Safavid, and Mughal) in this period. All of these
three bureaucratic empires that prioritized agriculture had Turkish
elites as the ruling classes. The financial power of Islam was at its
zenith, and it played its greatest role in the Old World (*oikouneme*)
during this period. There was Muslim domination in a large part of
the world; however, aesthetical and intellectual creativity was gradually vanishing. In contrast, Europe had started to awaken. Western
culture spread towards the north and the east as these bureaucratic
agricultural empires had started to lose both their cultural creativity
and power that they had gained during the Renaissance, with the
expansion of shipping trade and the Great Western Transformation in
which many other agents were shaped. This event that took place during this period at the same time brought the end of this age and the
Islamic world entered a new age approximately after the year 1800.

The dramatic transformation experienced by the Islamic world
after the thirteenth century and the influences of Mongolian invasion on this transformation have been the most discussed period of
Islamic history. Braudel (1999, p. 93) claims that the world of Islam
lost its superiority and actual regression started in the eighteenth
century. Hodgson (1992; II, pp. 409–12) states that the Mongols did
not cause a regression and the economic recession in the entire Afro-
Eurasia was caused due to other reasons like the Black Death. On

the other hand, there occurred a financial revival in the geographies united by the Mongols and spread of Islamization. According to him, the regression in the scientific creativity was about the conservative spirit that is one of the features of the agricultural-age societies. The interchange of population and knowledge brought dynamism to the Old World. According to Ahmet Davutoğlu (2002, pp. 3–4), the Mongolian invasion brought the Islamic civilization to the edge of losing its entire physical and written legacy; however, the essential spiritual and cultural parameters of the Islamic civilization continued to exist powerfully. Moreover, Islam experienced the zenith of its financial power and owed this success to the empires of the Ottomans, Safavids, and Mughals. On the other hand, it is true that there occurred a dramatic transformation in the scientific and intellectual tradition of the Islamic civilization due to the invasion. The land between the Nile and Amu Darya, which was the most dynamic region of the Islamic civilization, collapsed with regard to population and culture as a result of this invasion, and the Islamic world had a hard 'head trauma'. Many philosophical, scientific, and artistic traditions were evidently interrupted after the thirteenth century. The same regression and stagnation were seen even in the western Islamic world (Maghreb and Andalusia) that did not experience the invasion. This was apparent especially in the history of Maghreb after Almurabits (1250) (bin Nabi, 1992, pp. 17–32). After this century, the 'people who [had] ... a creative intelligence' were decreased both in number and quality (Goldziher, 1993, p. 156). The historical philosopher Sorokin, with reference to the thesis that a historical philosopher emerges after each crisis experienced by a civilization, claims that Ibn Khaldun came into the picture as a result of the crisis experienced by the Islamic civilization in the thirteenth century. However, we cannot talk about a total regression as claimed by the Orientalists through the regressive parameters; it can be mentioned as a 'loss of superiority and creativity' as stated by Braudel (1999, p. 93). In my opinion, the real regression was initiated after the eighteenth century.

However, compared to the previous ages, there was a self-enclosure and isolation of the Islamic world during the period of the Mongol invasion. It is remarkable that after the translations of the classical age came to a halt, there were no more books translated from Latin to languages that Muslims spoke until the sixteenth century (Lewis

1996, pp. 78–9). From this century on, science in the Islamic world was dominated by the conservative spirit, and renovations and creative thinking were replaced by a preference for repetition, compilation, and conservation of the old. The original books written in the classical age in various fields were mostly replaced by 'encyclopedic' works written by way of collection and compilation in this period. Some examples would be Hamawi in geography, Ibn Manzurin in dictionary work, Razi in tafsîr, Nuveyri in history, Zahabî and Ibn Hallikan in biography, Isfehani in Sufism, and Kalkashandî in literature. The creative works were replaced by systematic compilations, sharhs, and epitomizing magnificent Persian prose literature. Celalettin Suyuti (d. 911/1505) who authored approximately 300 works in total is the best answer to this description (Goldziher, 1993, pp. 156, 170). Islamic civilization left philosophical and religious discussions aside and established great and powerful empires by gunpower; as in the case of Rome, it established a world of thought, mainly based on practical occupations rather than abstract and theoretical issues, and an organized society. As mentioned earlier, ranging from madrasahs to cults, from large salaried staff to the sciences, everything was organized. Besides, Islam was being spread in the Aegean region, the Balkans, and eastern Europe by Ottomans; in Kashmir by Sufi cults; in Sudan, eastern Africa, and Malaysia by tradesmen; and in China by Turks who had followed the Mongols. Therefore, the extent of the lands dominated by Islam was now three times larger compared to that of the lands between the Nile and Amu Darya, and Islam was experiencing one of its highest points at the beginning of the sixteenth century. Hodgson describes this as 'a second flowering'. Therefore, the most appropriate name to define this period should be the Age of Empires.

When did this age end? When it comes to the eighteenth century, all of these three empires in the Islamic world were land empires. The seas that were left uncontrolled eased the victory of Portuguese sailors and other Western sailors. The Ottomans could not achieve the same success in the oceans as they did in the Mediterranean Sea. The world trade routes shifted towards the coasts of the Atlantic Ocean and the geographic explorations resulted in the gradual collapse of the economies of these three Muslim empires and the eventual dissolution of the Islamic world. However, we need further studies in this field in order to understand how these developments took place and how long they lasted. Since the impacts of the geographical explorations on the Muslim world were not sudden, we need to identify the time when these impacts became apparent in order to determine the breaking point. The Ottoman Empire did not experience a setback before the end of the seventeenth century. Its last success was the siege of Vienna. Braudel explains the death of the Ottoman world by the fact that they were not able to control the open seas—a commonly held view. If we consider this issue from the same perspective it can be seen that the indications of the institutional and social weaknesses in all three great empires had started to become apparent in the 1700s. While the Ottomans became dependent on the Europeans to protect their integrity, the Safavid Empire was demolished by the rebellious Afghan tribes. The Mongol Empire in Hindustan had already been demolished. The developments in Iran, Hindustan, and Africa paralleled each other in an interesting way. The West conquered Bengal in the Battle of Plassey and brought Egypt under their control with the Napoleonic expedition. A new era was dawning for the Muslim world that fell behind the West, which had undergone a great transformation. This era starts at the end of the eighteenth century.

The Fourth Period: Colonization by the West and the Age of Depression (1800–...)

Goitein describes the last age of the Islamic civilization as 'Transition to National Cultures: Inspiration by Origins Rather than Islam (1800–...)'. Just as he centralizes the Arabs during the categorization of Islamic history, he interprets this period based on nationalism, too. However, in this period, the nationalism wave among the Muslim peoples was not yet strong enough to determine the essential characteristic of this age. The nationalism movements within the Muslim peoples were felt only at the end of this century. Goitein analyses the activities of Christian Arabs who constituted a small group in Lebanon in the nineteenth century and extends this case to the entire Muslim world. On the other hand, Miquel identifies this period as 'Imperialism and the Arabic Renaissance (19th–20th Centuries)'. According to him, the Egypt expedition (1798) of Napoleon Bonaparte marked the beginning of a new age in Islamic history. This is because, after this incident, Muslims became embroiled in a spiritual and mental upheaval, being challenged in their own land of Islam, and they were forced towards an internal feud. There was a trend of innovativeness in both administrative–political areas and religious thinking. After this period, the Islamic world would witness movements of reformations, congresses, and innovations. Hodgson describes this age as the 'Modern Technical Age' and 'The Great Transformation of the West'. According to him, Islamic legacy was shattered in the modern technicalistic world in this period. Under the influence of the new world order controlled by the West, Islamized civilization lost its prominent position in world history. The international Muslim society that had continued without any interruption for a long time was replaced by disintegrated minorities who, living in a world governed by others, were adversely affected by the very events that had brought prosperity to the West. Islamic society was no longer a historical actor and it maintained its life not as an Islamic society, but as a society that shared an Islamic legacy. Since they were faced with a critical challenge posed by the West, all the discussions on Islamic themes were developed depending on how they would encounter this challenge.

Hodgson's explanation about the technical developments would not be an appropriate interpretation of an entire age. This is because the technical developments were not in a state to bring the West completely under its influence at the beginning of the nineteenth century. However, Hodgson's assessment presented a historical development that was still in the process of its formation in Europe as a reality within which the Islamic world was confined. The first part of Miquel's definition, 'Imperialism and the Arabic Renaissance', seems to be acceptable. This is because the undeniable reality that explained the state of the Islamic world in this period is that it was physically under European dominion and its influence. Throughout the nineteenth century, Muslim nations were being colonized one by one. Dissolution of the Islamic lands from the East to the West was taking place with regard to the standards that were being set by the elements of Western civilization. With the transition from the agricultural age, which had begun with the Sumerians, to the technicalistic modern civilization that was spreading throughout the world in this period, all the institutions, relationships, and thought processes that had been established and adjusted in compliance with the agricultural-age conditions started to lose their validity; states, administrative institutions, economic structures, and traditions were shattered. Due to these reasons, this period can be described as a period of (search for) comprehensive innovations that was accompanied by an intense Western imperialism. Therefore, I preferred to name this period as 'Colonization by the West and the Age of Depression (1800–)' within my periodization.

Exactly when the Islamic world started to decline in the face of the advancement of the West is a popular question in debates and attracts intensive attention. In my opinion, we cannot talk about a regression in the seventeenth century as has been frequently expressed. There were some indications of the internal weaknesses stemming from the internal dynamics of the Islamic world. Even in the eighteenth century, the Islamic world was at the centre of the world. Only at the end of this century, the regression of the Islamic world became apparent. The influences of the West on the Islamic societies in general and the Ottoman Empire in particular became a serious cause for concern with the Treaty of Karlowitz in 1699, following which the Ottomans started to take the West into account. This was followed by the successes of the Battle of Plassey in Bengal and the Egypt expedition. And though the Russians were advancing in Caucasia since the seventeenth century, they started to make their influence even more apparent in the second half of the eighteenth century. Under these political and military influences of the West, Muslims started to make efforts to regenerate themselves in cultural and political terms in the face of Western challenge in their own lands. All the movements that emerged in the Islamic world in this period were developed in a 'defensive' manner. The declarations of the Edict of Gulhane in 1839, the First Reform Edict in 1856, and the Second Reform Edict in 1876, and the establishment of the Constitutional Era in 1908 and subsequently the Republic in 1923 were significant in Ottoman history as steps on the way to Westernization. The Aligarh and Osmania University experiences of Syed Ahmed Khan in Hindustan, the Jadidism movement that became quite popular among the Kazan Tatars, and the reformation efforts in Egypt under the leadership of Rashid Riza and Muhammad Abduh were all consequences of the efforts to respond to the Western challenge at an intellectual level as well as at administrative and military levels. Moreover, the nationalism movements began to be deeply felt in every corner of the Muslim world from the beginning of the twentieth century and determined the history of these lands (Rahman 1984, pp. 63–83). All the movements that have been influential in the Islamic world in the nineteenth century—liberalism, socialism, nationalism, fascism, and so on—were of foreign origin.

Davutoğlu (2002, p. 7) discusses the transformations experienced by the Islamic world in the twentieth century in four different periods each corresponding to a quarter century: (*a*) the period of half-colonialism, (*b*) the period of absolute colonialism, (*c*) the period of nation-states, and (*d*) the period of political struggle and active cooperation. According to him, each of these periods reflects the different patterns of relationships with the international system and dominating power centres within itself. In the half-colonialist dependency period, whose roots were in the nineteenth century and which lasted until the end of the First World War, the entire Islamic world except for the Ottomans gradually came under colonial domination and struggles against this domination started. This period ended with the collapse of the Ottomans in 1919 and the absolute colonialist dependency period, which covered the period between two world wars, began. This period was the darkest period of Islamic history, and, except for the partially standing Iran, the mountainous regions of Afghanistan, the Rub'ul hali desert in the middle of Arabia, and the Anatolian lands, the entire Islamic world was invaded by the colonialists. Moreover, Islam became a mere Afro-Asian phenomenon in this period in which secularism made itself apparent in all fields. The third stage of the Age of Colonization by the West and the Age of Depression covered the years between the Second World War and the establishment of the Organization of Islamic Conference (OIC) in 1969. The most significant characteristic of this period was the emergence of nation states in regions whose populations were mostly composed of Muslims. Meanwhile, Muslims continued their quest for an alternative form of government. According to Davutoğlu, the last stage is the political struggle and active cooperation period that began with the establishment of OIC. The unjust attitudes and double-standards of the international power groups towards the issues faced by Muslims resulted in the rise of an anti-imperialist reactive movement in the Islamic world and the increase of the tension between the West and the Islamic communities. Despite the conflict of interests between Muslim countries, a platform of cooperation was established. Along with the economies based on crude oil, developing economies and countries in South Asia also began to draw attention. Democratization movements began against long-term dictatorships that were the remainders of the Cold War and the demands of the Islamic states simultaneously increased in a synchronized way. Academicians and intellectuals of the Muslim world started to face and question the Western social sciences about Orientalist terminology (Davutoğlu 2002, p. 19).

The last period of this age in which the Islamic world rid itself of colonialist domination, the very age in which we are still living, is also a period of transition and foundation. Through all these periods, Muslims have been experiencing a comprehensive process of transformation. In the field of the religious thinking, Muslims have been reconsidering the Islamic legacy that had been established under the conditions of the agricultural age and efforts have been made to interpret it in accordance with the need of the day. The reason for the intensity of the reformation and novation movements during the last two centuries can be seen as an effort to bridge the gap between ideals and realities. Despite efforts towards modernization in the last two centuries, the Islamic world has maintained the strongest resistance against the West. Despite facing crises like poverty, lack of education, political instabilities, and economic backwardness, the Islamic world struggles not to lose its essential values on the one hand, and endeavours to keep up with the world it lives in and find its future on the other.

***

All civilizations develop an understanding of 'daily time' in accordance with their own idealized lifestyles in order to identify and render themselves meaningful in regard to both time and space. They also develop an understanding of 'historical time' based on their historical experiences and adventures in order to identify their individuality among other civilizations. Since each civilization has its distinctive experiences, none of the advanced civilizations can establish its daily life and historical memory based on the time scale that is developed by some other civilization. It is a pity that the issue of the periods of the history and civilization of Islam has not been dwelled on sufficiently in the Islamic world until today. Muslim societies are in urgent need of a periodization based on the Islamic civilization. The inference of this study could be that Islamic civilization has survived until today by passing through four stages.

In this study, I held a discussion over the periodizations developed by three great historians and suggested a new periodization. Miquel, who is one of these historians, develops an Arabian-centred periodization, and, therefore, considers the post-classical ages of the Islamic history as a decline. Goitein takes the political events directly into the centre of his periodization and overlooks the cultural and intellectual integrity in times of dissolution. Hodgson came closest to evaluating the history of Islam in a holistic way. However, even he occasionally compared the course of the Islamic history with European history and lost his claim to authenticity. This is because according to him, Islam is a component of the fluctuations in the history of the world. Therefore, I tried to develop a holistic perspective that is not only based on the political developments, but also takes cultural, intellectual, and social factors into consideration, revealing the individual internal dynamics of the Islamic civilization; and determining its position within the same world history that claimed that the Islamic civilization is composed of four ages. The first age of the Islamic civilization is the Age of Conquests and the Foundation that starts with the divine revelation in 610 and ends with the collapse of the Umayyads. The main characteristic of this period is the conquests. The second age is the Classical Age of Islam that begins with the establishment of the Abbasids and ends with the invasion of Baghdad by the Mongols in 1258. During this period, the cultural, economic, and social structures of the Islamic world unite despite the disintegration and diversification of the political structure. The third age is the Age of Empires that starts at this date and continues until 1800 when Western colonialism begins to make inroads into the Islamic world. The primary characteristic of this age in which the second wave of the spread of Islam took place is institutionalization. The fourth and the ongoing age of the Islamic civilization is the age of colonization and depression. The essential feature of this age is the search for renovation, with Muslims seeking a way out in the face of Western civilization challenging it in all fields.

NOTES

1. 'Sahaba' is the name given to friends of the Prophet who knew him personally. 'Tabi'un' are those who knew and followed these friends in their deeds, and 'tabi' al-tabi'in' are those who knew and followed this second group of people.
2. Goitein (1949, pp. 120–35). See also Demirci (2002), *İSTEM Dergisi* (2008, pp. 217–40).
3. Iqta' (Arabic: اقطاع) was an Islamic practice of tax farming. Although the nature of the iqta changed with time and place, it was commonly a form of administrative granting. It is often (wrongly) translated into the English word 'fief'.

BIBLIOGRAPHY

Armagan, M., ed. 2006. *Osmanlı geriledi mi?* İstanbul: Etkileşim Yayınları.

Atsız, N. 1977. *Türk tarihinde meseleler.* İstanbul: Ötüken Yayınları.

Braudel, F. 1999. *Uygarlıkların grameri,* translated by M. A. Kılıçbay. İstanbul: İmge.

Cahen, C. 1993. *İslamiyet,* translated by E. M. Erendor. İstanbul: Bilgi Yayınevi

Çandarlıoğlu, G. 2003. *Tarih metodu (araştırma-yazma).* İstanbul: Türk Dünyası Araştırmaları Vakfı.

Darling, L. T. 2006. 'Osmanlı tarihinde dönemlendirme'. In *Osmanlı Geriledi mi?* içinde, edited by M. Armağan İstanbul: Etkileşim Yayınları.

Davutoğlu, A. 1997. 'Medeniyetlerin ben-idrakî'. *Divan* 2(3): 1–53.

———. 2002. 'İslam dünyasının siyasi dönüşümü: Dönemlendirme ve projeksiyon'. *Divan* 7(12): 1–50.

———. 2007. 'Küreselleşme ve medeniyetler arası etkileşim bağlamında ortak değerler'. *Anayasa Yargısı* 24: 405–14.

Demirci, M. 2002. 'Abdullah ibu'l-Mukaffa'nın Risaletu's-Sahabe adlı risalesi: Takdim ve tercüme'. *İSTEM Dergisi* XII: 217–40.

Genc, M. 2006. 'Tarihimize Giydirilen Deli Gömleği; Osmanlı Tarihinde Periyotlama Meselesi'. In *Osmanlı geriledi mi?* içinde, edited by M. Armağan. İstanbul: Etkileşim Yayınları.

Gibb, H. 1991. *İslam Medeniyeti Üzerine Araştırmalar,* II, translated by Komisyon. İstanbul, Endülüs Yayınları.

Goitein, S. D. 1949. 'Turning Point in the Islamic History'. *Islamic Culture,* XXIII: 120–35.

———1968. 'A Plea for Periodization of Islamic History'. *Journal of the American Oriental Society (JAOS)* 88(2): 224–8.

Goitein, S. D. 1980. *Dirasât fi't-Tarihi'l-İslami ve'n-Nuzumi'l-İslamiyyye*, translated by A. Kavsî. Kuveyt.

Goldziher, I. 1993. *Klasik arap literatürü*, translated by R. Er and A Yüksel. Ankara: Vadi.

Hodgson, M. G. S. 1993. *İslam'ın serüveni*, I–III, translated by Komisyon. İstanbul: İz Yayınları 1991.

———. 2001. *Dünya tarihini yeniden düşünmek*, translated by A. Kanlıdere. İstanbul: Yöneliş Yayınları.

Kafesoglu, İ. 1964. Üniversite tarih öğretiminde yeni bir plân. *Tarih Araştırmaları Dergisi*, XIV(19): 1–13.

———. 1984. 'Türk tarihinde çağlar meselesi'. *Türk Kültürü* 254: 343–53.

Kafesoglu, İ. and A. Donuk. 1990. 'Türk tarihinin taksimatı'. In *Fırat Üniversitesi Tarih Metodolojisi ve Türk Tarihinin Meseleleri Kollokyumu*, edited by A. Yuvalı and B. Kodaman, pp. 37–46. Elazığ: Fırat Üniversitesi.

Lewis, B. 1996. *İslam dünyasında Yahudiler*, translated by B. S. Şener. İstanbul: İmge Yayınları.

———. 2001. *Tarihte Araplar*, translated by H. D. Yıldız. İstanbul: Ağaç Yayınları.

Miquel, A. 1990. *İslam ve medeniyeti*, I, translated by A. Fidan. İstanbul: Birleşik Yayıncılık.

bin Nabi, M. 1992. *Cezayir'de İslam'ın yeniden uyanışı*, translated by E. Göze. İstanbul: Boğaziçi Yayınevi.

Niyazi, M. 2008. *Türk tarihinin felsefesi*. İstanbul: Ötüken Neşriyat.

Özçelik, İ. 2001. *Tarih araştırmalarında yöntem ve teknikler*. Ankara: Gündüz Eğitim ve Yayıncılık.

Rahman, Fazlur. 1984. *Islam and Modernity*. Chicago: University of Chicago Press.

Said, E. 1979. *Orientalism*. Harmondsworth: Penguin.

Saricam, İ. and S. Erşahin. 2005. *İslam medeniyeti tarihi*. Ankara: Diyanet Yayınevi.

Sorokin, P. 1997. *Bir bunalım çağında toplum felsefeleri*, translated by M. Tunçay. İstanbul: Göçebe Yayınları.

Spengler, O. 1997. *Batının çöküşü*, translated by N. Sengelli. İstanbul: Dergah Yayınları.

Togan, Z. V. 1985. *Tarihte usûl* (4th ed). Istanbul: Enderun Kitabevi.

Ülgener, S. F. 1991. *İktisadi çözülmenin ahlak ve zihniyet dünyası*. İstanbul: Der Yayınları.

Part II

Debates on Civilization in the
Contemporary Muslim World

4 The Vision of Order and Al-'Umrân as an Explanatory Concept in the Debates on Civilization*

Vahdettin Işık

'Man is civilized by nature.'
—Ibn Khaldun in *Muqaddimah*

Debates around the concept of civilization are increasing. It is natural for debates to intensify given that several disciplines such as sociology, political science, and international relations are using civilization as a unit of analysis. As Paul Ricoeur (1965, pp. 271–84) pointed out, we are in a time when a 'mediocre civilization' is gradually threatening the whole world. Paul Ricoeur (1965) in his article draws attentions to this threat and states that a standardized 'mediocre civilization' came to impose itself over the whole world. Despite his appreciation of the globalization of universal values, Ricoeur regards this 'mediocre civilization', which is produced and disseminated by modernity, and which steadily assumes a plastic-artificial character, as one of the greatest threats that humanity faces. Under such circumstances, it is beneficial to question whether the tendency to solve almost every

* I am thankful to Miriam Cooke and Tahsin Görgün who read the manuscript and offered their valuable comments.

issue through a single concept called civilization is the result of reducing thought to a standard mediocre level. Of course, every paradigm is built on 'root concepts'; however, in order to understand these clearly we must contextualize them in relation to centres of power. As a starting point, then, we can define these centres as centres of the modern Western system of thought. Thus, as modernity becomes global, non-Western societies are forced into a hierarchical relationship with the West and it would not be wrong to say that the present global regime is an outcome of Europe's re-structuring of the world.

As generally stated in the debates around the concept of civilization, the relation of non-Western societies to the West is often seen as being defensive.[1] A system of thought that places European civilization at the centre renders 'civilization' as one of the main concepts of Eurocentric thinking by grounding a hierarchical understanding of cultures and civilizations.[2]

Europe's civilizational conceptualization attempts to define human communities in terms of fixed binaries such as developed versus underdeveloped, civil versus barbarian (or wild), and modern versus primitive. These have tangible political consequences. According to Norbert Elias (2013), the concept of civilization functions to legitimize European imperialism in large geographical stretches, from Africa to the Indian subcontinent and Southeast Asia. According to him, civilization expresses Western self-consciousness.

> It is expressed with the words that the people belonging to their community 'civilize' compared to the past and the people belonging to other communities 'civilize to less' and even 'become barbarous'. (Elias 2013, p. 10)

As Elias stated, we can also call this 'national consciousness'.

> The concept is used to express the things that Western societies have believed to have for two or three centuries unlike earlier societies or 'more primitive' contemporary societies or more 'primitive' societies. Western societies try to express the things they have and pride on through this concept. For example, *their* levels of technical sophistication, *their* behavior patterns, *their* levels of scientific knowledge or *their* philosophies are some of them. (Elias 2013, pp. 73–4)

If Elias is correct, then the concept of civilization is related to a hierarchical structure, in which civilization becomes a way of favouring some at the expense of others. Therefore, similar to attitudes that conceive civilization as a picklock-concept explaining everything, attitudes that reduce all explanations to a single alternative concept that rivals civilization must equally be questioned.[3]

I believe this chapter, which consists of four sections, will contribute to the critique of the modern understanding of civilization by showing the possibility of an alternative non-reductive system of thought. In the first section, I will examine the interest in the *Muqaddimah*, which is both the main source of this study, and has an important place in Turkish intellectual history. In the second section, I will explain the historical, sociological, and intellectual backgrounds against which a foundational text like the *Muqaddimah* was produced. In the third section, I will demonstrate the relationship between Ibn Khaldun's general understanding of existence and *'umrân* as a concept that explains a social system. In this section, I will also discuss the processes through which 'umrân emerges and the different historical, sociological, and geographical possibilities in which 'umrân comes to manifest itself. And finally in the fourth section, I will explain the reasons why we need an independent discipline of *'ilm al-'umrân* in order to understand the concept of 'umrân which defines the social system.

My main goal in this chapter is to demonstrate the possibility of the existence of a social system other than the one that imposes a singular way of life defined by the modern West. By utilizing Ibn Khaldun's approach in the *Muqaddimah*, I will try to show the pluralist alternative system.

THE GROWING INTEREST IN IBN KHALDUN

The interest in Ibn Khaldun in Turkey is an old phenomenon and continues to increase even today. The Turkish secondary literature gives us insight into concepts and methods they believed were central to understanding Ibn Khaldun's work. These important indicators mediate a long-standing scholarly approach to Ibn Khaldun (more specifically, to the *Muqaddimah*).

In Pirizade Mehmet Sahib Efendi's (d. 1749) translation of the *Muqaddimah*, he states that the intellectual familiarity with Ibn Khaldun is not new. His translation of the *Muqaddimah* into Ottoman

Turkish at the beginning of the eighteenth century extended a well-established Khaldunian tradition in Ottoman thought (Câbirî 2006, pp. 9–16). He translated five out of six full chapters of the *Muqaddimah* alongside some titles from the beginning of the sixth chapter. Before completing it, he presented it to Sultan Mahmud I (1696–1754) in 1730. About a century and a half after Pirizade, Ahmed Cevdet Pasha (d. 1895) completed the full Turkish translation of the *Muqaddimah* (Hassan 1973, p. 115) by translating the remaining parts of the sixth chapter, which he described as the most difficult part of the book. Pirizade's translation was first published in AH 1274 /AD 1857 in Egypt and a year later in Istanbul.[4] Cevdet Pasha's translation was published shortly thereafter in AH 1277/ AD 1860 in Istanbul (Yıldırım 2001). There are four more Turkish translations of the *Muqaddimah*, which were done during the Republican Period. These were done by Zakir Kadri Ugan (1969), Turan Dursun (1977), Süleyman Uludağ (1991), and Halil Kendir (2004).[5]

THE *MUQADDIMAH* AS A FOUNDATIONAL TEXT

The *Muqaddimah* was written as an introduction (hence *Muqaddimah*) to Ibn Khaldun's book on history. However, like Jean Bodin's famous *Methodus ad facilem historiarum cognitionem* (1566), the book was more than a simple introduction to history. The *Muqaddimah* is laced with a rich variety of concepts and issues unprecedented at the time. The word 'muqaddimah' literally means 'preface'. As such, it can be defined as the thing on which the issues/provisions following it are based. However, the technical translation of the term 'muqaddimah' that is closest to its original meaning first used by logicians is 'a proposition suggesting an argument or a thing on which the accuracy of evidence is based without using any vehicle' (Şerif 1990, p. 118). As such, it is better understood as a 'premise' that must be correct and relevant to the problem at hand. When the premises mentioned in the First Book of the *Muqaddimah* are closely considered, it becomes clear that these propositions are in fact premises upon which the science in question, that is, 'the science of *umrân*', is based.

Modern readers of the *Muqaddimah* are often struck by an embracing vision grounded in a thorough humanistic framework that is more akin to their own sensibilities. This fascination emanates from the modern assumption that the past has teleologically progressed towards a Eurocentric present that is the only space for any kind of secular humanism. From this standpoint, it is surprising for some that Ibn Khaldun produced a scientifically rigorous explanatory framework suitable 'even today' such a long time ago in the 'East'.

However, if we approach the text from a different perspective and methodology, then we can gain insights into the text that are more helpful. First, we can start by acknowledging that an Islamic vision decisively influenced Ibn Khaldun's ability to make accurate and comprehensive inferences. The Islamic framework provided him with a general scope and an enhanced ability to comprehend the whole experience of life because it depends on an intellectual accumulation that extends beyond mere subjective ability. For those who were unable to contextualize his thoughts and rather identified him as 'an ascetic and gorgeous star in the dark night of Middle Ages; no pioneer, no successor'[6] must have been unfamiliar with his sources. For example, Imam Mawardi's concept of the relationship between the command (*taklif al-amr*) and the acquired mind (*aql al-muktasab*) with the prosperity of the world is directly related to Ibn Khaldun's concept of acquired *asabiyyah* that is based on the example of the Israelites. The similarities between the two are more than coincidental. Examples like these enable us to see the intellectual connections between Ibn Khaldun and others, and thus to shed light on each.[7] The acknowledgement of Ibn Khaldun's indebtedness to previous scholarship, something Ibn Khaldun himself clearly mentions (1969, vol. 1, pp. 94–5), should not in any way take away from his own originality.[8]

Turning to the content of the work, the author mentions that in the work he has explained the changes in the lives of the tribes who lived in past ages and the reasons behind their capturing the country. The state and characteristics of tribes, how they experience nomadic or settled life in cities and countries, their migrations and movements, how they gain power and desire, fall weak, their science and arts, trade, the stories about making profit or loss, the changes they experience in life over time, how they leave nomadic life and settle and the occurring of expected situations and cases, which belong to human communities and world, have also been explained with reasons and evidences. Khaldun also mentions that since his work includes rare sciences and marvelous wisdoms, it has become a unique and distinguished book among its counterparts (Ibn Khaldun 1969, vol. 1, pp. 13–14).

Yet we need not take Ibn Khaldun at his word. This book, like any other, bears the traces of its context. Therefore, the text can be understood better when the context is made more explicit. The spread of Islam after the seventh century provided the foundation of an empire which engulfed the Arabian Peninsula, Mesopotamia, and North Africa, ensuring the stability of trade routes between Europe and Asia. Ibn Khaldun's lifetime marks the end of this great rise. Intellectuals of his time were interested in assessing what they perceived to be a lack in visionary dynamism plaguing Muslims.

On the other hand, Islam, born in the cradle of civilization, opened new areas of scientific inquiry developed in conversation with many ancient philosophies, religious beliefs and practices. At the risk of oversimplification, one can state that Ibn Khaldun's *Muqaddimah* shows that Muslims were accustomed to keeping one foot in what they saw as Islam's original values, while keeping the other in a stream of foreign experiences.[9]

In the time of Ibn Khaldun (1332–1406), Islam geographically extended from the Maghreb to Central Asia, but was simultaneously undergoing a sort of Balkanization (Fakhry 1987, p. 257). While Muslim social organization embraced different tribes and cultures, this resulted in diversifying the sources of sovereignty. Civilizational leadership began shifting from Andalusía and the Maghreb to Anatolia and Iran.

Ibn Khaldun's life passed partly in exile or in prison, but always in contact with dynasties, and he always found himself at the centre of political struggles. Ibn Khaldun's own experiences were later embodied in the *Muqaddimah*, as a statesman who conducted negotiations between Timur and the King of Castile, as a tenured jurist who served as a *qadi*, and as a scholar competent in the intricacies of Arabic language and literature.

Another aspect of the environment contributing to Ibn Khaldun's intellectual accumulation is the philosophical spirit of his time. He drew his conclusions by reconciling with the common philosophical heritage of the period. Majid Fakhry (1987, p. 257), in his book *Islamic Philosophy*, summarizes Ibn Khaldun's contribution to Islamic philosophy in two ways: the first entails his far-reaching observations on and criticism of Greco-Arabic philosophy, and the second is an analysis of his contribution to the Islamic philosophy of history through the creation of original concepts. As Fakhry mentions, Ibn Khaldun's works can be understood in their entirety when considered together with this in his own life.

Ibn Khaldun's criticism of the explanations of philosophers about the existence of God, prophecy, the nature of revelation and afterlife were mainly epistemological. He argued that the philosopher's claims to metaphysical knowledge based on rational thought was insufficient because these issues could not be comprehended with the mind alone, and men could not say anything intellectually provable about these issues (Görgün 2009, p. 553). While Ibn Khaldun did not think philosophical explanations on these issues were epistemologically rigorous, he emphasized many a time in the *Muqaddimah* that a number of other issues should be subject to philosophical investigation. In fact, Ibn Khaldun 'demonstrated a very positive attitude in the other issues of philosophy and rational sciences. That he considered the science of 'umrân, which he founded as one branch of philosophy shows that his thinking was philosophical and he gave philosophy a very important place' (Görgün 2009, p. 553).

A VISION OF ORDER AND ʿUMRÂN AS AN EXPLANATORY CONCEPT

Ibn Khaldun argues that there exists an unbreakable bond between man, nature, society, and the Creator (Ibn Khaldun 1969, vol. 1, p. 3.). This argument is not peculiar to Ibn Khaldun. There are many thinkers—both contemporary to and following Ibn Khaldun—who have focused on this relationship. For instance, according to Ibrahim Kalın, traditional ontologies are predicated on a grand circle of existence. Traditional ontology places man and the universe within this circle. By 'traditional ontology', it is suggested that Ibn Khaldun's understanding of existence is a continuation of a larger tradition and heritage of Islamic thinkers. So the claim here is not that all Islamic thought is exactly on the same side when it comes to their comprehension of existence, but nor can one ignore that there is a shared tradition arising from belief. In addition, Kalın does not put forward a normative judgement as to the accuracy or fallacy of this tradition. On this account, existence (*wujud*) exceeds a simple referential relationship to all existing beings in the world (*mawjudat*). Because wujud's meaning goes beyond the totality of its reference mawjudat. Wujud is both constitutive and constitutional of all existing things. According to classical Islamic thought, the reality of wujud is not limited to contingent appearances alone. The wujud of contingent beings in appearance is thus simultaneously both eternal and dynamic as Kalın states; and by participating in wujud contingent beings do not circumscribe the true reality of wujud. The rich etymology of the word 'wujud' in Arabic indicates that it is a dynamic and multi-dimensional reality that is difficult to capture by the ancient Greek word for 'being', *ousia*. The word 'wujud' etymologically is derived from the root 'to find' and 'to be discovered'. This finding/discovering is always in relation to consciousness. 'To find out' requires intentionality or a 'looking for', and 'to look for' always requires consciousness (Kalın 2010, p. 38).

In this integrated understanding, what constitutes the relationship between the system *al-akhlâq* (ethics) and al-'umrân is the fact that virtues directing human life and sovereign rules and principles determining the order of the universe are derived from the same source (Ibn Khaldun 1969, vol. 1, pp. 3–5).[10] This source, together with the aforementioned virtues that direct human life and constitute the order of the universe, is ordained by Allah himself. For that reason, there is harmony and integrity among these virtues. On the other hand, according to Kalın, the description of wujud as *haqq* in classical philosophy links the ontological and epistemological aspects and levels (*marâtib-al wujûd* and *marâtib-al ulûm*) to each other. Haqq, if we express it in today's language, would refer to both truth and reality. Both 'haqq' and 'wujud' are attributes of Allah, and he is the authority (*marjia*) that defines the principles. Thus, when referring to objective reality and to principles, 'haqq' is used interchangeably with 'wujud'. While 'wujud' constitutes the reality of beings, it also imparts to them truth and meaning. Therefore, distinguishing truth and reality or being and knowledge from each other is not possible either conceptually or methodologically (Kalın 2010, p. 25).

We find a substantial sample of this conceptual framework in Farabi's *al-Madînat al-Fâdilah*. The way in which Farabi begins with the 'first principle' and brings the subject to humans and their social lives after mentioning the ranks of being is the natural outcome of this holistic approach explained earlier. His expression that all existing beings hinge on the cause of first principle and are subject to a definite ranking summarizes the framework that we mentioned here (Fârâbî 2001, p. 83). The city life and the political order formulated by Farabi rest upon a comprehensive ontology and cosmology. This holistic and integral ontology is the basic framework of the idea of order and harmony on which the 'umrân relies (Ibn Khaldun 1969, vol. 1, pp. 100–4).[11] In a similar way, Ibn Khaldun explains the formation of 'umrân in a relationship of similar wholeness. Khaldun believes that he Almighty God fashioned man in a way in which his 'need of food' would mean that he would not be able to 'live alone', nor lacking weapons, would he be able to defend himself. It is only with mutual co-operation that man obtains food for his nourishment and weapons for his defence. This is how God's wise plan that man(kind) should subsist and the human species be preserved will be fulfilled. Consequently, Khaldun believes that social organization is necessary to human species. Without it, the existence of human beings would not be complete. God's desire to people the world with human beings and to leave them as His representatives on earth would not materialize. This, he believes, is the meaning of civilization. When mankind has achieved social organization and when civilization in the world has thus become a fact, people would need someone to exercise a restraining influence and keep them apart, because aggressiveness and injustice are in the animal nature of man (Ibn Khaldun 1969, vol. 1, pp.102–3).

Ibn Khaldun states that sovereignty belongs to mankind by nature and this is realized via ideas and politics. He thinks that the state is a product of this idea and politics (Ibn Khaldun 1969, vol. 1, p. 104). Ibn Khaldun adopted the postulate that 'man is civilized by nature' in his evaluation of the nature of humans. This is also one of the basic premises of his predecessors, and it is a premise that considers 'being civilized' as related to the 'city' and 'living a social life' (Ibn Khaldun 1969, vol. 1, p. 100). This constitutive order begins with a necessity that human nature has the capacity to recognize. By being conscious of this fact, humans join the cosmic system by choosing to be natural. That is because establishing a state is a requirement of political (social) life and it is a natural need for human beings.

Here we need to emphasize that Ibn Khaldun's approach regarding man's tendency towards good rather than evil is also congruent with his approach to politics and the state. According to him, 'the good suits politics'. That is to say 'good deeds and justice are the branches of state' (Ibn Khaldun 1969, vol. 1, pp. 362–4). The ruler is the representative of God on earth. If the order is not based and maintained upon good morals and justice, the rulership granted by God will be taken back and God will give that authority to others (Ibn Khaldun 1969, vol. 1, p. 368). That is because nobility and honour are gained through exerting labour, and these assets can be preserved in a rule based on good morals and justice (Ibn Khaldun 1969, vol. 1, p. 347).

As it is understood, the 'duty of representing' (the literal meaning of 'caliphate') means the protection of existence. It is maintained when humans strengthen their tendency to do well and avoid heading towards evil falling prey to the seductions of Satan; and this corresponds to the *maqasid al-sharia* (the foundational purposes of sharia). That is to say, being a caliph or representative is an act to preserve the life, property, intellect, lineage, and religion by the will of God. Establishing this on an Islamic framework, Ibn Khaldun has to be understood within the aforementioned paradigmatic ground (maqasid) into which he was born and appropriated in time. According to Görgün, when we consider the purpose of human existence on earth as the act of establishing civilization ('umrân), it becomes more apparent. This issue is manifested in the Holy Qur'an in the distinction between *salâh* (peace) and *fasâd* (corruption), in which 'salah' may be used to define the acts carrying the being towards perfection through preserving it, while 'fasad' implies the opposite. This is what Ibn Khaldun means when speaking of the civilization of (civilizing) the earth (Görgün 2009, pp. 200–1). It does not mean treating the other with respect to the values and beliefs of one's own civilization; rather it corresponds to a wider and deeper foundation of a *hadari* civilization.

It is possible to say that Ibn Khaldun's *Muqaddimah* was written to make his system comprehensible. In fact, the content of the book has been confined to a discussion on the quality of civilization, the nomadism and settled life attached to it, seizure and occupation, earning, livestock, industry, sciences, and so on (Ibn Khaldun 1969, vol. 1, p. 82). All these elements show us the fields of human activities performed by man that are 'civil' by nature. Nonetheless, 'umrân is the manifestation of these activities. Connoting the concept of human life with *omr* and the activity of bringing life suitable for meeting vital/basic needs with *imar* displays the deep relation between these activities.

All these words etymologically stem from the verb *'-m-r*. In the dictionaries this verb means sitting down (somewhere), living long, visiting (somewhere), building, being settled (somewhere) with people and animals, residing somewhere, keeping well, keeping something or somewhere in good condition. Similarly, 'umrân means being developed, advancement, and felicity (Mutçalı 1995, pp. 657–8; Enis 1998, pp. 597–8). Ibn Khaldun uses the term ''umrân' to refer to 'peoples coming together in societies on the lively places of the earth and civilizing the world' (Ibn Khaldun 1969, vol. 1, p. 90).

'Al-'ilm al-'umrân', on the other hand, is a discipline that shows the causes behind historical events and the factors behind social relationships and stages. However, the science of 'umrân is different from the science of history which means the narration of the past events as they appear. 'Umrân represents the interior dimension of history which contains the knowledge of everything in the past as its subject matter (Ibn Khaldun 1969, vol. 1, p. 5). As indicated in the *Muqaddimah*, Ibn Khaldun is the founder of this discipline (Ibn Khaldun, 1969, vol. 1, p. 91).

According to Ibn Khaldun, the two main states of 'umrân, *badawi-yyah* and *hadarah* (sedentary), imply the states of the communities with regard to their lifestyles and manners. He asserts that both situations are natural and necessary for human beings (Ibn Khaldun 1969, vol. 1, pp. 303–4). *Bedouin* is the word for nomadic living in the desert. *Hadarî* refers to one living in the village, town, or city, in peace and security. According to him, *badâwah* or nomadism is the basic and first stage of the human communities (Ibn Khaldun 1969, vol. 1, pp. 307–8). The concept of nomadism defined the communities who adapted to the physical environment, were nomadic, had strong asabiyyah ties, and lacked the development of hierarchy. The concept of asabiyyah is one that is used and developed by Khaldun in order to express a theo-political-psycho-social phenomenon that crystalizes collective action (Ibn Khaldun 1969, pp. 364–5). This concept will be elaborated on in the following discussions, but the point here is that the ruling of these communities rests on chiefdom, which is limited only with merits and owes its legitimacy to common values. Besides nomads, the concept of badawah also refers to settled communities living in the village or rural areas, with a static or technically undeveloped economy.[12]

Hadarah, on the other hand, stands for settled societies in which the level of 'umrân is developed, and which can survive with the instruments of this development. In these societies, asabiyyah ties are replaced with 'worldly and individual desires'. Hadarah also corresponds to societies in which the level of hierarchy has taken root. Reaching the hadari stage is accompanied by the increase of property and progress of sciences and arts. In this society, sovereignty rests upon power and oppression. Even though people are not free, they cannot give up the property and the comfort they have. Also at the roots of hadarah society lies the bedouin society (Ibn Khaldun 1969, p. 309).

In Ibn Khaldun's account, the antonym of civility is savagery. Human nature does not allow establishing a life that internalizes the state of savagery (waHsh). Ibn Khaldun defines being civil as a 'natural and necessary' condition, not 'a target to be hit'. Thus, he offers a framework that is different from the modern Western understanding, in which civilization is a goal to be reached. He formulates the conditions of mankind as a historical venture under the aforementioned two categories. However, both categories are different versions of being civil. We need to pay attention to the fact that he did not define being nomad as equal to 'being savage' or as 'an uncivil situation'. And he does not consider being hadari or 'civilized' as the ultimate end of history. In these general descriptions, there is not a single form of either nomadism or urban life (Ibn Khaldun 1969, pp. 308–9).

While explaining several variables affecting these diverse human situations, Ibn Khaldun puts great emphasis on the relationship between 'umrân and geographical conditions. In the section dealing with this question, he outlines seven climates and their regional boundaries. These climates are classified according to their respective impact upon the bio-diversification, human activities, progress of sciences, arts, and religions—and the corresponding level of 'umrân/civilization in his terms. The fourth climate is the warm climate that provides the most proper conditions for human development. That is 'because the South and the North are opposite to each other—one being too hot while the other being too cold—and it was necessary for both to get equilibrium in the middle, this gradually made the fourth climate as the most developed part of the globe (Ibn Khaldun 1969, vol. 1, p. 193). The third and fifth climes are far from the circle of equilibrium. The second and the sixth climes are also far and the first and the seventh circles are the least suitable places for civil development, because with tough weather conditions—extreme heat in the South and extreme cold in the North—they are ill-suited to human settlement. Iraq and Damascus are the most moderate and suitable regions for the development of civilization. To conclude, the weather of the third, fourth, and fifth climates are moderate. Territories of East Africa, Hijaz, Yemen, Iran, India, China, and Andalusia are the remaining parts of the moderate climate zone. People living in these territories have a modest character because the conditions are optimum for shelter, clothing, tool-making, and finding sources of nutrition. The French, the Galls, and the Greeks are also people of this moderate circle. All these regions are under the third, fourth, and fifth climate regions (Ibn Khaldun, 1969, pp. 193–5). The first and second climate regions are inhabited by people of southern Africa where clothing is not vital and valuable materials such as money are not used and the settlement is undeveloped. The sixth and seventh climates are the very cold regions, such as the northern regions of Asia and Scandinavia (Ibn Khaldun 1969, vol. 1, p. 199).

Ibn Khaldun does not consider the features that emerge as a result of the geographical factors upon human beings as static or unchangeable.

> The nations are distinguished from each other with different features as well. Ascribing the nations living in a certain region to an ancestor due to adherence to the same sect or religion or due to same complexion, because of the features found in the ancestor such as religion etc. have been one of the mistakes of the unawares who do not know about the nature of the universe and the being. Because all these features change in the coming generations after fathers and it is not a lasting feature. This is a rule given by God to his Creatures. And the law of God never changes. (Ibn Khaldun 1969, vol. 1, p. 202)

His explanation of the diversity of human communities distinguishes his approach from the ones that suppose human nature to be unchangeable and consider civilization as a spiritual whole or race. For him, both civilization and the ethno-cultural diversifications appear as human differences. Skin colours, characteristics, and habits of human beings emerge and differentiate within time. Eventually, according to him, the diversity and plurality of the tribes and generations stem from the diversity and plurality of their ways and methods of livelihood. This is because the individuals coming together and living in groups is a form of cooperation for the sake of livelihood and for protecting their lives. Maintaining the things necessary for life comes before the things needed to complete the experience of living (Ibn Khaldun 1969, vol. 1, p. 302).

In addition to all these, while explaining the historical developments that are the manifestations of 'umrân, Ibn Khaldun brings the concepts of asabiyyah and mulk to the forefront. The word *asabiyyah* means a sense of solidarity or common sense, which holds the community together and makes it move as a single organism. The basic characteristics of this sense may be noted as the sacrifice of the personal for the community (Ibn Khaldun 1969, p. 365). The asabiyyah is strong in the Bedouin society and provides them with military supremacy over more settled communities. Thus, the Bedouin society exercises sovereignty over the mulk, that is, the settled community. However, in time asabiyyah dissolves and empties itself into the state and its bureaucratic apparatus. The concept of mulk is used to connote property, commodity, and all the things under the sovereignty or control of the state. For him, mulk is only possible through coming together around an asabiyyah or a thought and by hearts being united in the determination to realize it. Hearts, on the other hand, can only get closer to each other by the cooperation of the people who aim to expand the religion of God and make it sovereign (Ibn Khaldun 1969, p. 402).

The meaning of asabiyyah here extends to all forms of emotions and feelings that stand in for kinship. According to him, tribal organization does not automatically provide the necessary power to seize countries. Even if a lineage-based asabiyyah extends its political power through sovereignty over mulk/territory, this does not lead to the growth of the 'sovereign subject', but rather extends territory and human resources under it. An asabiyyah-based political organization leads to the dilution of lineage-based power over large territories because as it expands it becomes weak.

These conclusions are informed by Ibn Khaldun's larger understanding of the nature of politics. For him, the mulk/state 'can only be founded with power, authority and victory. Being victorious is only possible through convening around asabiyyah and an ideal and founding proximity among hearts to each other in order to realize that ideal' (Ibn Khaldun 1969, p. 402). Due to the very nature of this attitude, with time the state starts to act against its own existence. In this case, while asabiyyah benefits a particular group, it turns out to be a system of oppression for the ones outside this group. This is quite contrary to the raison d'être of the state. Hence, every state needs to have peculiar principles of legislation and executive power along the lines of these principles. For this reason, a need arises in every state to posit its own principles of rule and legislation and to execute these rules in accordance with those principles. If these rules or regulations are determined as 'the rules legislated by the reasoning of human beings' (Ibn Khaldun 1969, vol. 2, p. 117), then it is called 'rational politics'. The most that rational politics can achieve are worldly interests for its people. The politics constructed upon 'the principles and verdicts of sharia' on the other hand is called '*shar'i*/religious politics'. For him, only this kind of politics completely consists of the rules or principles compatible with the raison d'être of humanity as a whole.[13]

Within the sphere of religious politics Ibn Khaldun discusses the 'question of revelation' under the subject title 'The content of 'umrân, the conditions in which it emerges and the causes and reasons behind these conditions'. Khaldun mentions that after illuminating His chosen subjects with Light among whom He created, He embellished them with His *irfan* and made them 'a tool and vehicle in between'. The chosen subjects tell the created beings of God the *maslaha*, encourage them to not to go astray and protect the ones on the right way from fire. The wonders explained by them and the unknown knowledge regarding existence can only be known with the knowledge of God; it is not possible to know in another way (Ibn Khaldun 1969, vol. 1, pp. 216–17).

We may recall that for Ibn Khaldun mulk would be attained with power, and power necessarily with asabiyyah; asabiyyah could lead to oppression and injustice, and that would, in turn, threaten the survival of the state. It was compulsory for the states to set some principles and to legislate certain laws and regulations in order to get rid of this threat. God has revealed His Word and has ensured that mankind is protected from aggression and dispersion by His messengers. However, the overarching laws and regulations in maintaining this order belong to God in any case. Thus, we can say that for Ibn Khaldun, from the perspective of the science of 'umrân, religion conveyed to the people through a prophet in the realm of the social is equal to the physical–geographical and social factors (Görgün 1999, p. 552).

According to him, although humans have a disposition to evil (Ibn Khaldun 1969, vol. 1, p. 354), mankind has the capacity to lean towards good by their disposition, reason and power of speech. Man tends towards evil due to the animal powers that exist within him. 'Man's leaning towards good by being human indicates that his disposition is closer to good.' The fact that Man found state and deal with politics stems from his humanly disposition. From this perspective, then, man's inclination towards good and decent is pertinent to politics and power (Ibn Khaldun 1969, vol. 1, pp. 364–5).

As can clearly be seen, the revelatory principles are graces bestowed upon man in determining the content of the principles upon which the state and politics would be established.

According to Ibn Khaldun, the transformation brought with religion elevates the influence and qualities of sovereign power. By means of religion, different asabiyyah are dissolved and they evolve into the higher asabiyyah of belief in a single form:

> Belief in and submission to a religion ends the jealousy and competition among the owners of *asabiyyah*. All come together around the truth; the religion leads them to think for the common good and interests; since their goals are single and equally important for all, no one prevents them from attaining their goals because they embraced attaining their goals to the death. Even if the soldiers and supporters of the state they attacked outnumber them, the ones fighting for the victory of the Truth would defeat them. (Ibn Khaldun 1969, vol. 1, pp. 402–3)

The theory of asabiyyah is Islamicized by way of the idea of prophecy and religion. For instance, the visiting of angels at the time of Prophet Muhammad and keeping Muslims devoted to the cause indicate that religious politics extends beyond simple positivism into an imaginative experience of negotiating the transcendent with the immanent.

Ibn Khaldun's attitude towards the relationship between mulk and the caliphate is also directly related to this position. According to him, the concept of authority is the element that distinguishes the caliphate from mulk. Two significant aspects of the caliphate are 'the authority of religion' and the principle that no one has the right to use force on another. In this regard, authority in religion is adopted and embraced as the true religion. The submission of people to religion by free will creates the ground for unification. The power stemming from this unifying submission brings about a very strong relationship that is beyond comparison with any other kind of asabiyyah; this would, in turn, provide the constitution of the most powerful and moral society of the world. However, over time, different types of asabiyyah might emerge and this could lead to conflict. Struggle among different types of asabiyyah pressurizes political powers to force a single form and transform itself from a caliphate to a mulk. With the realization of the (secular) potential that mulk contains in its nature, it retreats from the moral virtues prescribed by religion.

Related to mulk, state, and power, another significant issue to consider is Ibn Khaldun's refusal to consider or evaluate the question of power beyond ideals, human action, and geography. As it can be better understood in this evaluation of the era of caliphs, he seemed to adopt a consensual formula between the requirements of power relations and the ideals. His interpretation of the conflict (the first civil war among Muslims) between two close friends of the Prophet, Ali and Muaviyah, provides strong evidence for this claim. He states that both Ali and Muaviyah tried to unite the Muslims under their leadership. According to Ibn Khaldun, they wanted this for the sake of Islam and both of them were right. Ibn Khaldun wrote:

> When the second caliph Umar visited Damascus and saw the governor Muaviyah in unaccustomed clothes to the Muslims and asked 'O Muaviyah! Do you follow the Iranian rulers?' and Muaviyah responded to him 'O the leader of the believers! We are in the border area next to the enemies and have to take pride in our war customs and accessories', Umar remained silent and did not refuse his argument based on righteous and religious concerns. (Ibn Khaldun 1969, vol. 1, pp. 512–13)

It is clearly stated in the introduction and definition of the concept of 'umrân that it is a comprehensive concept that regulates and organizes both systems of thought and ways of life. Thus, another point emphasized by Ibn Khaldun is the correlation between the development and diversification of the arts and sciences and the progress of 'umrân. Khaldun believes that the people living in the cities in the progress towards sedentary life are concerned about the basic needs of life and these are wheat and other foods to eat. After cities develop and production increases, the income of the people exceeds their basic needs. People start spending this extra income to procure objects of luxury. Besides, industry and science is the product of reason and reflection, which differentiate humans from animals. Since humans are a kind of animal, they need food and nutrition. Yet the necessities of life come before industry and sciences. Science and industry is something needed after the basic needs of living have been met. Industries and the development of cities ensure that progress is in accordance with its need for luxury. The building of cities necessitates the progress of art and industry (Ibn Khaldun 1969, vol. 2, p. 369).

According to Ibn Khaldun, when the needs of the people are met, new opportunities for human beings emerge. Prosperity is directly related to mobilizing resources and opportunities, and creating new ones. Thus, he says that God makes the earth prosperous via the hand of humankind.

Ibn Khaldun confined the sixth book of *Muqaddimah* to the issue of sciences. In the introduction of this chapter, he emphasizes the naturalness in the development of knowledge and sciences and points to the necessary conditions for the development of the sciences within the theory of 'umrân. According to him, the preconditions for the progress of sciences are absent in villages or rural nomadic settlements, since these communities cannot sustain production beyond vital needs (Ibn Khaldun 1969, vol. 2, p. 453). Methodologically, Ibn Khaldun uses a descriptive approach and reflects on the phenomena as they are, but, when needed, he also uses a normative approach and makes judgements upon his phenomenology of the political. While talking about the sciences, he acts as an observer on the one hand, and as a critic on the other, and sometimes even as a scholar contributing to the production of knowledge (Bedir 2006, p. 18).

Ibn Khaldun's classification of the sciences begins with two branches. The first is the category of wisdom-related philosophical sciences (Ibn Khaldun 1969, vol. 2, p. 455). These sciences are natural sciences for the people, and they learn these by themselves with their own reason and capacity. The second is the category of revelational-constructive sciences, and people can learn these from a teacher or instructor (Ibn Khaldun 1969, vol. 2, p. 455). For Ibn Khaldun, these sciences are peculiar to the Islamic community. Ibn Khaldun notes that every nation has such sciences peculiar to them, but he argues that the Islamic community has two advantages in this regard. In the Islamic community, these sciences progressed to a level that had not been seen in any other nation (Ibn Khaldun 1969, vol. 2, p. 458).

Ibn Khaldun discusses the methods of philosophical and constructive sciences in several places within the text. One of the contexts he discusses is how the natural process of thinking in humans turns into a rigorous science. According to Ibn Khaldun, because they have the ability to think, human beings achieve two things:

1. They can build a worldly life via cooperation, solidarity, and living together, and
2. they can comprehend the message of Prophets in order to prepare for the life hereafter.

Therefore, Ibn Khaldun takes two socially significant phenomena into consideration while classifying the sciences: designing the world and understanding the message of the Prophets. According to Görgün (1999, pp. 538–55), while in the first phenomena humans play a founding role, in the second role humans limit comprehension. In his emphasis on deductive reasoning, humans point to the role of comprehension. One of the sciences he includes in this classification is the science of 'umrân that was first developed by him. The basic feature of the science of 'umrân, which is a metaphysics of society, is that it considers the subject matter as a social existence which went unnoticed by the metaphysicians. Ibn Khaldun's true success is not his emphasis on treating historical events with a methodology based on causality, but to invent the field of social existence. There, he considers the science of 'umrân as a part of philosophy as well as history. In this regard, 'umrân can be considered as a philosophy of history on the one hand, and, through the study of history, a philosophy of social science on the other. However, it is possible to say that beyond these two disciplines, 'umrân is essentially a social metaphysics expressed in the tradition of classical philosophy (Görgün 1999, pp. 538–55).

According to Ibn Khaldun, to raise professionals specialized in science, regular education is required. This is only possible if society has developed to a certain level in demography, prosperity, and economics. The society that promotes the progress of sciences, by transferring funds and resources to the study of the sciences, is the most powerful and thereby exercises dynastic control over the mulk. The establishment of foundations and the rise of the arts and sciences in the East and the West formed the apogee of state power (Ibn Khaldun 1969, vol. 2, pp. 441–52). According to his theory of 'umrân, as the rise and fall of the civilizations necessarily follow each other, the arts and sciences also follow this cycle, and with the decay of the civilization, the sciences also fall (Ibn Khaldun 1969, vol. 2, p. 452).

Ibn Khaldun considers the arts resulting from this process and classifies them according to their different aspects. The first classification is based on meeting the needs. The art that exists for meeting basic needs are 'simple arts', while the ones for meeting luxurious needs are 'complicated arts'. In another classification, the arts are distinguished as ones peculiar to sustenance, politics, and reflection. Arts and crafts like textile weaving, sericulture, carpentry, and ironworking are peculiar to sustenance. Military service and its equivalents are peculiar to politics. The sciences and arts peculiar to reflection are classified as music, poetry, and teaching.

The relationships of the arts with bedouin, hadari/sedentary, and civilization/'umrân, are also treated in the sixth chapter. The classification of basic arts with respect to their contents is as 'essential' and 'honorable and significant by subject'. The essential arts are farming, architecture, tailoring, carpentry, and weaving. The arts that are honorary and significant by subject are midwifery, authorship, book selling, music, and medicine (Ibn Khaldun, 1969, vol. 2, p. 368).

THE NEED FOR THE SCIENCE OF 'UMRÂN

While forming the science of 'umrân, Ibn Khaldun distinguishes two realms of existence. The first of these, the 'realm of elements', constitutes the subject matter of the metaphysical, and as its extension, of the physical or the natural sciences (*tabiiyyat*). The second realm, the 'realm of occurrences/events' constitutes the subject matter of the science of 'umrân. The realm of events is the realm of being/existence and annihilation. It is directly related and dependent on humans and can exist solely alongside humans; likewise humans cannot exist without the realm of events. The essential difference between these two realms of existence is that humans belong to the first realm with their physical entity and individuality, yet the second realm of existence exists necessarily as a result of the human existence, that is to say, it belongs to humans. As the realm of events arises from within the society, it is social; as it exists and ceases to exist within time, it is inside the society, and, therefore, the realm of the events is a social realm of existence. Things like asabiyyah, mulk, and state, which do not exist in the physical world, arise out of people living together. Therefore, by acting and interfering in the physical world, humans reconstruct it in accordance with their means and purposes. 'Umrân arises as a result of this reconstruction (Görgün 1999, p. 544).

As also understood from the lines just quoted, according to Ibn Khaldun (1969, vol. 1, pp. 66–7), as every entity undergoes change in the realm of events 'umrân also goes through changes. Khaldun mentions that one should know that the duty of man is to talk about the reconstruction of (imar/'umrân) the habitable places of the world by living in communities, and the savageness which occurs in the native state of this reconstruction and gaining familiarity (habituation) within the community, and the asabiyyah in which humans protect themselves and the families and populaces they belong to. It is one's duty to inform about every kind of aggression and invasion of people against each other, and the founding of the states as a result of these invasions, and the degree of the power and glory of these states, and humans earning and making a living through labour, the sciences, the skills, and the arts, typically the industry, and naturally the civilized productions coming into existence as a result of this prosperity and to narrate and relate any knowledge regarding these subjects (Ibn Khaldun 1969, vol. 1, p. 82).

It can be inferred from this quotation that narration and rumour, due to various reasons,[14] are methods that could lead to delusions.[15] Especially in the calculation of goods, money, and armies, historians have narrated so many rumours that did not make sense that these narrations have to be analysed in accordance with rules and principles of reason and laws (Ibn Khaldun 1969, vol. 1, pp. 19, 88–9). Ibn Khaldun (1969, vol. 1. pp. 91–2) expressed that since these rules and principles could not be studied by existing sciences, a new science was needed. He recites the characteristics of this new science and accentuates its peculiarities, differentiating it from other sciences.

The science of 'umrân is the reconstitution of events and the social existence of humans within this multilayer conception.

In this chapter, the concept of 'umrân and its significance in understanding the term 'civilization' from the point of view of Ibn Khaldun is explained. 'Umran is a sophisticated concept and it has a certain relation to religion, nature, arts, science, and state politics. It is, thus, a regulatory concept that conforms above all to God's rules and then to the order that humans have founded on earth in accordance with those rules. In light of this, it is possible to evaluate what we have written so far in four points:

1. Ibn Khaldun thinks that everything happens in accordance with destiny and the situation we are now facing is the realization of this destiny. As there is an order in the sphere of physical existence, the sphere in which mankind lives has a similar order. And Khaldun's term the 'nature of 'umrân' indicates that the rules of 'umrân can be explored (similar to rules of the physical world). The subjects of the science of 'umrân are the analysis of this nature, the accidents that befall this nature, and the relations between these accidents. The core principle of the explanation for how 'umrân came into existence can be stated as 'needs properly met produce new potentials'. So, throughout the *Muqaddimah*, Ibn Khaldun set forth that Allah constructs the earth via the hands of man and prosperity is realized by mobilizing existing potential and producing new potential. Among the wisdoms of *i'mar* (reconstruction and prosperity) are the different dispositions: the need for nutrition and the sheltering of humans. These necessities help humans to voluntarily realize the maqasid al-shari'a. This is both a state of necessity and a realization of the freedom of man's actions that are shaped by his preferences.

2. The basic feature of the science of 'umrân, which is a kind of 'metaphysics of society', founded by Ibn Khaldun, is that it takes as its subject matter the historical–social existence which had not been noticed until then by the metaphysicians. The actual success of the science of 'umrân comes from this genuineness. Ibn Khaldun's metaphysics of society enables a two-layered and two-phased thought. The first of these is that with reference to the unity of humans, it identifies that the realm of historical–social

existence consists of human actions and in this context it states that the realization of social order needs no other reason than that of one being human. Second, it states that as humans gravitate towards perfection, they necessarily need religion, and the ethical perfection in human actions adds a different dimension to the cooperation among people.

3. According to him, humans are civilized by nature, but here 'civil' means humans living in society with other people. Thus, the word here has a meaning quite close to that of being culti-vated. However, every group of people does not have to necessar-ily establish the same social order, because establishing a social order runs in a 'voluntary' way based on 'free will' (Şentürk 2006). Ibn Khaldun mentions the stages experienced by humanity in its historical journey: badawiyyah and hadarah. However, he regards these two situations as manifestations of being cultivated under different conditions. It has to be pointed out that he does not define badawiyyah as being savage or as an uncultivated state. In this case, the ultimate goal of the human history is *not* evaluated as 'being cultivated' or 'being hadarî'. According to his explana-tion, the opposite of being cultivated is 'being savage', yet man-kind has not constituted a lifestyle which leaves a possibility to internalize this situation. With this approach, Ibn Khaldun has presented a framework that is explicitly different to the modern Western system of thought.

4. For Ibn Khaldun, mulk signifies a second level of existence. As he considers humans as a part of existence, Ibn Khaldun evalu-ates humans' *'inshâ'î* (constructive/constitutive) activities not as a matter of domination over nature but as a matter of rights and responsibilities of a representative in his capacity of being God's caliph (representative) on earth. According to him, mulk cannot be the ultimate goal of history. The ultimate goal of history can be understood by the expression 'God, completes/perfects his com-mand (*'amr*) through the caliphate.' This becomes more evident especially if we think that the purpose of the existence of man-kind in the world is to bring about 'umrân, that is to say, make the earth prosperous. This question/subject shows up in the dif-ferentiation of 'salah' and 'fasad' which are used in the Qur'an in a widespread manner. While salah is subject to and the proper

way for divine guidance, the quality of the actions that preserves the existing and carries them to perfection, fasad means the exact opposite. By the construction (i'mâr) of the world, Ibn Khaldun exactly means this (Görgün 2009, p. 200).

All of these points suggest why 'umrân appears as a unique concept in Ibn Khaldun's thought and why this chapter hesitated to translate 'umrân simply as 'civilization'. Unlike 'umrân, the concept of civilization has been immersed in discussions of progress and modernization—something that still continues. Ibn Khaldun, however, one should re-emphasize, developed the concept of 'umrân with the purpose of understanding the cycle of civilizations in their natural context, far from responding to the modern crisis of Muslim societies.

In a nutshell, what I have summarized in four points leads us to the conclusion that social life is a phenomenon which is constructed through free human agency and which can manifest itself in different forms under different circumstances. Therefore, it is necessary to see different social manifestations and ways of life as totally natural. And the concept of 'umrân constantly promotes this understanding.

Along with this, another conclusion might be that just as the current social system is constructed by human agency, other forms of social life can be constructed in a similar manner. Detailed examples given in the *Muqaddimah* clearly demonstrate this point. Therefore, contemporary social, economic, and political forms are not ultimate and eternal. In any case, everything has an end; eternity and constancy/stability are qualities that befit no form or mode of existence less than it does God himself.

NOTES

1. Ottoman–Turkish modernization is a remarkable experience that can be examined from this perspective. Moreover, as the modernization in Ottoman as a general frame was a Europeanization–Westernization disseminating from the political centre towards the periphery, the concepts of being civilized and civilization were used in a Eurocentric context in nineteenth-century Ottoman thought, and the measure of civilization was generally defined as 'vulgar Westernization' (Kalın 2010, pp. 13–14).
2. For an attractive evaluation about 'Letâifu'l-efkâr ve kâşifu'l-esrâr' by Semerkandi as an example of different ways of understanding the history of humanity and its condition, see Kavak 2012, p. 467.

3. As an example to facilitate the understanding of the mental clutter, the main function of Halil Halid's 'civilization' expression is to adopt and understand civilization as the common heritage of humanity instead of rejecting it in spite of the awareness of the fact that it justifies European colonialism: 'Let Europeans not forget that Easterners are fond of their independence and freedom just like themselves and hate a foreign country to boss them with the claim of "good will" or "civilizing mission" with all their hearts' (Hâlid, 2008, p. 211).

4. Latinized copy of this work was also published by Klasik Yayınları. See Ibn Khaldun and Pîrîzâde (2008).

5. Although I have utilized Pirizade's, Kendir's and Dursun's translations for this chapter, I prefer to quote from Ugan's translation alongside the Arabic text (Ibn Khaldun 1981). There are various questions concerning all of these translations. For example, the concepts of *civilization* and *state* which have different connotations today were frequently used in the translations interchangeably. On the other hand, some parts of the text were translated incompetently without mentioning the fact that some parts had been skipped during the translation. For an assessment of this translation, see Kırbaşoğlu (1985, pp. 363–98).

6. Cemil Meriç evaluated Ibn Khaldun in his book *Umrândan Uygarlığa*:

> Darkness falls on Maghreb.... A man in Ibn Selame castle.... Sounds of hooves and screams in his ears and bitter taste of defeats in his lips. He has been fighting with history for more than 20 years. He has been a player in or a spectator for very major disaster of his era. Palaces, wars, dungeons.... And the destiny, which razes the most proud towns to ground, wakes up before consciousness cliffs. Thought, son of crises. The man's gazes pierce the mists. The man places law in the place of destiny, the law in other words, manifestetion. He understands that there is no place for giants in this war where dwarves have the victory. He conquers with his pen the countries which he cannot conquer with his sword, the countries and eternity. Ibn Khaldun (1332–1406), an ascetic and gorgeous star in the dark night of Middle Ages; no pioneer, no successor. *Muqaddimah*, a dawn enlightening ages, whirlpools, caves, summits. (Meriç 1996, p. 139)

Although this evaluation of Cemil Meric is popular and attractive, it is not accurate. Indeed, it is known today that different names especially Fahreddin Razi and Al-Ghazali are his sources (see Fakhry 1987, pp. 256–64; Görgün 1999, pp. 533–44).

7. See İmam Mawardi (2012, pp. 13–14); Ibn Khaldun (1969, p. 360).

8. For a vision which uses his classical metaphysical language but is not a repetition of his classical metaphysics, see Görgün, 2009, pp. 354–6.

9. Ibn Khaldun (1969, vol.1. pp. 5, 93–5) mentions the reflections of this situation on scientific activities partly.

10. Imam Mawardi also implied that all blessings are from Allah and the more men do favour, the more result they get. According to him, the improvement of world and afterlife occurs this way (Maverdi 1969, p. 5).

11. Likewise, it should be expressed that the circle of adalah, commonly known in the way Kınalızade formed and one of the most comprehensive and concise expression of Ottoman social order as well as Classical Islamic political thought, has also been used by Ibn Khaldun (Mukaddime, v. 1, p. 94). In Kınalızade's expressions the circle of justice (*'adalah*) is expressed in the following way (emphasis are our own):

   adldir mucib-i salâh-ı cihân/cihân bir bağdır divânıdevlet/devletin nâzımı şeri'attır/şeri'ate olamaz hiç hâris illâ **mülk**/mülk zabt eylemez illâ **leşker**/leşkeri cem edemez illâ **mâl**/mâlı kesb eyleyen **ra'iyet**tir/ ra'iyyeti kul eder pâdişah-ı âleme adl. (Ahlâk-ı Alâî p. 539)

12. As happened in Ugan's translation of *Muqaddimah*, the term 'badawî' being translated as 'nomad' leads to semantic restricton.

13. For the details of these politics and about the 'al-siyasah al-madaniyah', as told by Ibn Khaldun and based on spiritual virtues, see Ibn Khaldun (1969, vol. 2, pp. 117–37).

14. For the details of these reasons, see Ibn Khaldun (1969, vol. 1, pp. 18–19, 82–90).

15. The situation can be different for shar'i issues. See Ibn Khaldun (1969, vol. 1, p. 89).

BIBLIOGRAPHY

Bedir, M. 2006. 'İslâm düşünce geleneğinde naklî ilim kavramı ve İbn Haldun'. *İslâm Araştırmaları Dergisi* 15: 5–31.

el-Câbirî, Muhammed Âbid. 'Niçin İbn Haldun?' [Why Ibn Khaldûn?]. *Dîvân Dergisi* 21 (2006/2): 9–16.

Elias, N. 2013. *Uygarlık Süreci*, translated by E. Ateşman. İstanbul: İletişim.

Enis, İ. 1998. *El-mu'cemu'l-vesît* (2nd ed.). Beirut: Mektebetu'l-Asriyye.

Fakhry, M. 1987. *İslâm felsefesi tarihi*, translated by K. Turhan. İstanbul: İklim.

Fârâbî, 2001. *el-Medinetu'l-fâzıla*, translated by N. Danışman. Ankara: MEB.

Görgün, T. 1999. 'İbn Haldun'un görüşleri'. In *TDV İslam Ansiklopedisi* vol. 19, pp. 543–55. İstanbul: TDV.

———. 2009. 'İbn Haldun'un toplum metafiziğinin güncelliği ve günümüzde toplum araştırmaları açısından önemi'. In *Güncel İbn Haldun Okumaları*, edited by R. Şentürk, pp. 169–203. İstanbul: İz.

Hâlid, H. 2008. *Bir Türkün ruznamesi*, translated by R. Bürüngüz. İstanbul: Klasik.

Hassan, Ü. 1973. 'İbn Haldun'un Mukaddime'si metninin yaygınlık kazanması üzerine notlar'. *Ankara Üniversitesi SBF Dergisi* XXVIII(3–4): 111–26.

İmam Ebu'l Hasan el-Maverdi. 1969. *Edebü'd-dünya ve'd-din*. Beirut: el-Mektebetu'l- Asriyye.

Kalın, İ. 2010. 'Dünya görüşü, varlık tasavvuru ve düzen fikri: medeniyet kavramına giriş'. *Dîvân* 15(29): 1–61.

Kavak, Ö. 2012. 'Zaman Osmanlı'ya doğru akarken: bir osmanli âliminin penceresinden dünya'. *Hece Dergisi* 186–8: 463–9.

Ibn Khaldun. 1969. *Mukaddime* (3rd ed.), translated by Z. K. Ugan, vols 1–2. İstanbul: MEB.

———. 1977. *Mukaddime*, translated by T. Dursun, vols 1–2. Ankara: Onur.

———. 1981. *Mukaddime* (3rd ed.), edited by Ali Abdulvahid el-Vafi. Cairo: Daru'l Nahda.

———. 1991. *Mukaddime* (4th ed.), translated by S. Uludağ, vols 1–3. İstanbul: Dergâh.

———. 2004. *Mukaddime*, translated H. Kendir, vols 1–2. İstanbul: Yeni Şafak.

Ibn Khaldun and M.S. Pîrîzâde. 2008. *Mukaddime: Osmanlı tercümesi* (1st ed.), vols 1–3. İstanbul: Klasik.

Kınalızâde Ali Efendi. 2007. *Ahlâk-ı Alâî*, edited by M. Koç. İstanbul: Klasik.

Kırbaşoğlu, M. H. 1985. 'İbn Haldun'un Mukaddime'sinin yeni bir tercümesi üzerine'. *Ankara Üniversitesi İlahiyat Fakültesi Dergisi* XXVII(1): 363–98.

Meriç, C. 1996. *Umrandan uygarlığa*. İstanbul: İletişim.

Mutçalı, S. 1995. *El-mu'cemu'l-Arabi'l-hadîs*. İstanbul: Dağarcık.

Ricoeur, P. 1965. 'Universal Civilization and National Cultures'. In *History and Truth*, edited by P. Ricoeur, pp. 271–84. Evanston: Northwestern University Press.

Şentürk, R. 2006. 'Medeniyetler sosyolojisi: Neden çok medeniyetli bir dünya düzeni için yeniden İbn Haldun?' *İslâm Araştırmaları Dergisi* 16: 89–121.

Şerif, M. M. 1990. *İslam düşüncesi tarihi* (vol. 3), translated by M. Armağan. İstanbul: İnsan.

Yıldırım, Y. 2001. 'Türkçe'de İbn Haldun üzerine yapılan çalışmalar ve bibliyografya denemesi'. *İstanbusl Üniversitesi İlahiyat Fakültesi Dergisi* 4: 139–74.

5 Beyond Civilization*

Pan-Islamism, Pan-Asianism, and the Revolt against the West

Cemil Aydın

The idea of Europe among non-Western elites from the early nineteenth through the mid-twentieth centuries embodies one of the most arresting paradoxes of modern global history. From the 1880s to the 1930s, non-Western elites contributed to the 'end of European hegemony in Asia' with their 'revolt against the West', while at the same time their own legitimacy and self-identity were initially shaped, and continued to be strongly influenced by, Eurocentric notions of civilization and modernity. Did the various visions of the world and of modernity that non-Western intellectuals developed during the era of decolonization transcend the Eurocentric discourse of civilization and the notion of Europe's universality? What was the international impact of this non-Western intellectual engagement with the ideals and idea of 'Europe'? Did it make any significant impact on the process of decolonization?

In this chapter, I shall argue that the concept of a single universal civilization—initially formulated to define the content and justify the politics of European hegemony in the world—was preserved by

* This chapter was first published in 2006 in the *Journal of Modern European History*, 4(2): 204–23.

non-Western elites when they challenged the idea of the 'civilizing mission' contained in discourses of East–West 'civilizational' synthesis. This chapter will focus on pan-Islamic and pan-Asian ideas, which were highly influential intellectual and political forces from the 1880s through to the 1930s. For a long time, many advocates of pan-Islamist solidarity saw the Ottoman Empire as a natural leader of the Islamic world, while pan-Asianism had a strong stand that saw Japan as the leader of Asian cooperation against Western hegemony. This chapter will focus on pan-Islamic thinkers in the Ottoman Empire and pan-Asianist thinkers in the Japanese empire, partly to show the appeal of these ideas as reflections of a global consciousness even among non-Western intellectuals who were not directly colonized. The pan-Islamic and pan-Asian critiques of the supposed 'universality' of the West were of significance in the formulation of non-Western discontent about the late-nineteenth-century international order. These two transnational visions of anti-Western solidarity helped to articulate non-Western discourses on civilization(s), modernity, and internationalism. Their trajectory from the 1880s to the 1920s illustrates what happened to the discourse of civilization when it was an intense topic of debate in the global public sphere, and how the politics of new 'civilizational' identities functioned in relation to rising nationalist movements and changing power relations between Europe and Asia.

THE GENESIS OF ANTI-WESTERN UNIVERSALISMS: PAN-ISLAMIC AND PAN-ASIAN DISCOURSES ON CIVILIZATION

The first important characteristic of both pan-Asianism and pan-Islamism is their commitment to European-inspired modernizing reforms. Early pan-Asian and pan-Islamic thinkers were modernist, and not reactionary, conservatives. They believed in the necessity of Westernizing reforms, almost in terms of a self-civilizing discourse, to uplift Asia or the Islamic world from their backward condition. Their main thesis was that European imperialism was hampering, not fostering, pro-European style reform and, thus, there was a need for anti-imperial solidarity to achieve the desired civilizational progress.[1] More importantly, advocates of pan-Islamic and pan-Asian solidarity perceived a contradiction between the idea of the universality of Eurocentric modernity and the increasingly popular European discourses of the permanent and eternal inferiority of Muslims, or the yellow race. The recognition of the contradictions in the ideology of the civilizing mission of European imperialism led pan-Islamic and pan-Asian thinkers to search for a more inclusive definition of universalism and internationalism. In this process, Asian intellectuals redeployed Orientalist notions of Eastern and Western civilizations for anti-colonialist political purposes, and, by the end of World War I, were forcing European intellectuals to revise their ideas about race, civilization, and human diversity.

The timing of their rise, the late 1870s and early 1880s, is the best indication that neither pan-Islamism nor pan-Asianism was a natural response to European expansion in Asia, which had already been happening since the early nineteenth century. In fact, at the time of the French invasion of Algeria, British expansion in India, and the Opium Wars, there certainly were expressions of anger or reflection, but not any developed notion of Asian or Islamic solidarity as a response. The response of various Asian societies to the continuing Western expansion took many different forms of resistance, including calls for *jihad* (holy war). Yet, these early attempts at resistance did not carry the notion of a systematic challenge to the imagined global legitimacy of the Eurocentric world order (Dale 1988, pp. 37–59; Keddie 1994, pp. 463–87). Instead, many intellectuals of the Ottoman Empire, and later the Japanese empire, accepted the idea of a universal European civilization and even the benevolence of European imperialism in offering to uplift the level of civilization in the rest of the world.[2] Following the paradigm of liberal civilizationism, this ideology allowed the Ottoman and Japanese elites to challenge the new European international society to be more inclusive by asking European powers to accept the multi-religious Ottoman state ruled by a Muslim dynasty or the non-Christian Japanese state ruled by a Shinto emperor as equal members of the new system, upon the fulfilment of the required reforms. Appropriation of the notion of a Eurocentric but universal civilization by the Ottoman and Japanese elites, also empowered these same elites in domestic politics as they could justify the imposition of centralizing radical reforms upon their own populations as a civilizing mission.[3] The Ottoman elites in Istanbul, through the liberal ideology of Ottomanism, could ask Muslim and non-Muslim subjects to become citizens of the new 'civilized' Ottoman nation, while simultaneously asking them to make sacrifices for the costly and painful process of modern state building. Istanbul- or Tokyo-human-centred self-civilizing projects also meant that nomadic populations had to be settled, peasants had to pay more taxes, and families had to send their male children to the army, while diverse sub-national lifestyles had to be sorted out for the homogenizing projects of the central government.

While the assumptions of liberal civilizationism continued, the moment of the 1880s represented an important rupture in the Asian perception of Europe, which began to be seen as more imperialistic, aggressive, and racially and religiously exclusive.[4] The turn to the 'scramble for Africa' and more competitive imperialism, accompanied by much more rigid theories of Orientalism and race ideology, established a permanent identity-barrier between Christian white Europeans and the coloured races, which included the black race, the yellow race, and an imagined Muslim race. Muslim responses to the invasion of Tunisia and Egypt in the early 1880s were different from their response to the invasion of Algeria about fifty years earlier, because, in the early 1880s, European expansion and hegemony were seen as part of a global pattern of uneven and unjust relationships. Similarly, pro-Western liberal intellectuals of Japan, such as Fukuzawa Yukichi, began to perceive the threat from the West as much greater in the 1890s than it had been during the 1860s, because—despite the fact that Japan was militarily stronger at the latter date—Westernization was now accompanied by increasing disparagement of Japan's 'yellow race' identity (Craig 1968, pp. 99–148; Sannosuke 1967, pp. 168–9).

Both Ottoman and Japanese elites perceived the later nineteenth-century European discourses on the 'yellow race', the Muslim world, and the Orientals, in connection with the predominant notions of Darwinism and other scientific paradigms, as a judgement that they could never perfectly fulfil all the required standards of civilization due to defects in their racial make-up, religious beliefs, or cultural character. In addition to the infuriatingly racist anti-Muslim speeches of British Prime Minister William Gladstone and anti-yellow race expressions of German Kaiser Wilhelm, popular writings in the European media, and more scientific writings of well-respected European scholars on human diversity and progress led to objections and disillusionment among non-Western elites. Many Western-educated Ottoman and Japanese elites began to perceive a non-transcendable racial and civilizational barrier between their own societies and Europe, and expressed a strong sense of being pushed away by the European centres towards which they had been looking to for inspiration. Nevertheless, these non-Western elites did not give up on the ideals of progress and one single universal civilization.

It was in this context that pan-Islamic and pan-Asian ideas were developed by the Western-educated generation of the Meiji era in Japan and the Tanzimat era of the Ottoman state: as a rethinking of the relationship between civilizing processes, the international order, and predominant forms of racial and religious identities. The first pan-Islamic magazine *al-Urwat al-Wuthqa* was published in Paris by Jamal ad-Din Afghani and Muhammad 'Abduh in the early 1880s (Keddie 1968). Ottoman Sultan Abdulhamid II, whose reign from 1876 to 1909 overlapped with the most turbulent period of European imperial expansion, began to be identified with either pan-Islamic sympathies or pan-Islamic peril, despite the fact that he continued a cooperative diplomacy towards the Western powers. Similarly, the first pan-Asian-ist organization, Koakai, was established in 1880 (Tikhonov 2002). The first major book on pan-Asianism, *The Theory of Uniting the Great East*, was written in 1885 by Tarui Tokichi (Tadashi 1968). From the early 1880s, many in Europe and Asia spoke of the potential peril or benefits of Asian and Islamic solidarity. Pan-Islamic and pan-Asian ideas gradually entered into the vocabulary of writings about international affairs, often paralleling the ideas of pan-Slavism, pan-Germanism, and later pan-Europeanism.[5] Yet, for a long time, the political projects of pan-Islamism and pan-Asianism, as a challenge to the Eurocentric world order, were not officially endorsed by the governments of the Ottoman and Japanese empires. In accordance with traditions of Meiji diplomacy or Tanzimat diplomacy, these two governments were very careful in fostering friendly cooperation with Western powers while attempting to prevent Western suspicions that they could be behind a 'reactionary' alliance against the West. They believed that it was in many ways better in the national interest of the Japanese and Ottoman Empires to dispel fears of the 'yellow peril' or the Muslim peril in European public opinion. The ideas of pan-Islamic and pan-Asian solidarity, which were themselves partly responses to yellow peril and Muslim peril discourses in Western public opinion, were seen as likely to confirm and strengthen the same peril discourses.[6]

Reformist elites of the Ottoman and Japanese empires had a shared interest, however, in challenging, modifying, and revising predominant European notions of Oriental inferiority. From the 1880s to the 1910s, there was never a blanket rejection of European-originated 'scientific' ideas of race or civilizational relations. Yet, most non-Western intellectuals offered internal critiques and revisions of these theories, where possible in dialogue with European intellectuals. It is in this context that the very flexibility of the concepts of Asian, Eastern, or Islamic civilizations, and their contents in relation to the idealized European civilization, allowed non-Western intellectuals to inject their own visions and subjectivity into these notions that had originated in Europe. Ottoman and Japanese intellectuals accepted that they belonged to an Asian, Islamic, or Eastern civilization different from the Western civilization, yet they did not have to concede that their civilization was morally inferior and eternally backward. It should be underlined that both the notions of 'Asian civilization' and 'Islamic civilization' were products of the second half of nineteenth century. There had been a strong Muslim identity and intra-Islamic world interaction before the nineteenth century via trade, education, and pilgrimage networks. Yet, this pre-nineteenth-century religious identity had not carried the same connotation of the term 'Islamic Civilization' as that which was to set in during the late nineteenth century. The famous fourteenth-century world traveller Ibn Batuta, for example, who had visited all the major centres of the Islamic world at that time, could converse with educated Muslims in Arabic all the way from Morocco to India and China. Yet, his pride in the cosmopolitan Muslim networks of the fourteenth century had not involved any conception of a 'civilization' defined in relation to its inferior or superior others (Dunn 2004). In contrast, the writings of pan-Islamic travellers of the late nineteenth and early twentieth centuries, such as Abdurreşid Ibrahim, exhibit a strong consciousness of belonging to an oppressed Islamic–Eastern world in relation to a Western 'other'.[7] Similarly, despite the fact that there had been a long tradition of education or pilgrimage-oriented travels within the Confucian or Buddhist lands of Asia, it was the late-nineteenth-century Asian travellers who exhibited a new notion of belonging to an Asian, Buddhist, or Confucian civilization, defined in relation to its Western counterpart (Jaffe 2004, pp. 65–96).

Muslim intellectuals in the era of late-nineteenth-century imperialism rightly viewed Ernest Renan as the most representative name
of the new European Orientalism, in which Renan championed the
intellectual trend to 'Hellenize Christianity and Semitize/Arabize
Islam'.[8] Before the 1870s, Muslim reformists had assumed that the
Muslim world shared the same cultural legacy as modern Europe,
namely Hellenism and monotheism, and thus believed that they had
strong innate capacities for progress and civilization along European
lines. After all, they reasoned (echoing dominant European views of
world history at this time), it was the Arabic-Muslim civilization that
had preserved the Hellenistic legacy of science and philosophy and
transferred it to modern Europe, thereby directly contributing to the
birth of European modernity, while illustrating the fact that there
was nothing contradictory in being a Muslim and being civilized and
progressive. If Muslims had once been great in producing science
and philosophy, their religion could not be an intrinsic impediment to
adopting and excelling in modern science and thought as well (Adas
1989, pp. 11–12). In response to these optimistic Muslim modernist
ideas, Ernest Renan argued that science in the medieval Muslim world
had developed despite Islam and the Arabs, not because of them.
Already famous for his claims that Christianity had been Hellenized
despite its Middle Eastern and Semitic origins, Renan argued that
Islam, as the religion of Semitic Arabs, could never be compatible
with modern progress, and that Muslims had to shed their religion
in order to adapt to modern life.[9] As a student of Islam, Renan noted
that if there were great scientific and cultural achievements in medieval Islam, this was due either to Christian Arabs, whose Hellenistic
Christian faith had controlled their Semitic Arab side, or to Iranian
Muslims whose Aryan race had cancelled out the negative aspects of
their Semitic faith.

Muslim intellectuals perceived Renan's well-publicized speech and
writings as the most eloquent formulation of the prevalent European
image of the Islamic world as an inferior race, justifying European
colonialism in the Muslim world just a few years after the invasions
of Tunisia and Egypt (Cündioğlu 1996). Muslim intellectuals not only
responded to Renan directly by publishing refutations of his ideas,
they also searched for venues and means to engage in a dialogue
with European intellectuals in general. Leading pan-Islamic figure of

that time, Jamal ad-Din al-Afghani sent his response to Renan to the same French journal that had published Renan's speech, in which he endorsed Renan's thesis on the clash between religion and modern science but vehemently rejected the claim that Islam or Muslims were inferior to Christianity or Christians in their attitude towards modernity.[10] Congresses of Orientalist scholars in Europe presented good opportunities for various Muslim intellectuals to address European scholars directly and to convince them that the Muslim world was indeed capable of civilizational progress. The Ottoman government sponsored trips to these congresses for prominent intellectuals such as Ahmed Midhad Efendi, and at other times sent bureaucrats to read semi-official papers (Findley 1998). For example, the Ottoman bureaucrat Numan Kamil presented a paper at the Tenth Orientalist Congress in Geneva in 1894, criticizing the anti-Muslim writings of Volney, Chateaubriand, Renan, and Gladstone, and asking the European Orientalists in the audience to be 'objective' in their judgements about the question whether Islam was the 'destroyer of civilization' or a 'servant of civilization' (N. K. Bey 1316 [1898– 9]).[11] It was in the same spirit of dealing with Orientalism that all the major pan-Islamic books on the international order felt obliged to devote sections to Islam and modernity, and to often say something apologetic about the situation of women, polygamy, and other cultural differences of Islam, while being very assertive about the compatibility between Islam and modern civilization in general.[12] Parallel to this apologetic effort, which conceded Europe's superiority in civilizational progress but insisted that Muslims have the racial and religious capacity to emulate this progress, Muslim intellectuals gradually developed a discourse that underlined the moral and aesthetic vitality of Islamic civilization.

Non-Muslim Asians also struggled with similar discourses about Christianity's superiority to Buddhism and Hinduism, or the white race's superiority to the coloured races. Hence, prominent Buddhist and Hindu intellectuals of Japan and India appeared at the Chicago World Parliament of Religions in 1893 to assert the equality and comparability of their religions to Christianity (Ketelaar 1990, pp. 136–220; Snodgrass 2003). In fact, the generation of very Westernized Japanese intellectuals during the 1890s, such as Miyake Setsurei and Inoue Enryo, developed powerful anti-Christian notions of world civilizations and progress (Burtscher 2006). This mood of challenging

European imperialism, which used critiques of Orientalism and of European discourses on race to affirm the universality of Eurocentric civilization and modernity, characterized the writings of all pan-Islamic and pan-Asian thinkers until World War I.[13] These pan-Islamic and pan-Asian engagements with Orientalism and race ideologies demonstrate that Orientalist notions were omnipresent but not omnipotent. They could be redefined and re-employed for purposes very different from those intended by the original European formulators of the universalist claims of Western civilization. And, concurrently with this non-Western challenge to the contradictions of the 'modernist' version of the civilizing mission ideology, the ideas of Asian 'romantic traditionalists' in Europe and America were also appropriated by Asian intellectuals. The pan-Asian ideas of Okakura Tenshin and Rabindranath Tagore, for example, cannot be understood without considering the influence of European and American pessimists who condemned Western civilization, and searched for a solution to humanity's crisis in the spiritual traditions of Asia (Hay 1970).

This Euro-American influence on pan-Asianism and pan-Islamism may perhaps appear as little more than yet another form of Western influence on the East. Starting from the late 1890s, however, Muslim intellectuals began to perceive international relations as a global encirclement of the Muslim world by the Christian West in an illegitimate manner (Halid 1907a). While European authors perceived the emerging Islamic solidarity as xenophobic anti-Westernism, Muslim writers either denied the existence of any reactionary alliance against the West or noted that it was the only way to overcome the unjustified rule of the imperial world order. Around the same time, East Asian intellectuals were increasingly emphasizing the conflict between 'the white and yellow races'.[14] It is during this period that pan-Islamist and pan-Asian thinkers began to develop the narrative of a sinister Western expansion in Asia since the eighteenth century, employing Hegelian notions of continuous conflict between the East and the West. Shared experience of engaging European ideas of Orient–Occident brought the predominantly Muslim Middle East and non-Muslim East Asia together around the notion of a shared Asian–Eastern identity and prompted their alternative internationalism. Early pan-Asianism focused on the Chinese cultural zone of

East Asia, China, Japan, and Korea, with their identity based on the same 'Chinese' culture and the same yellow race (*dobun–doshu* in Japanese). Gradually, the scope of Asian solidarity and identity was extended, first to India via Buddhist legacy arguments, and then to the whole of West Asia, including the Islamic world via a concept of the shared destiny of non-Western Asians.[15] It was not the legacy of common culture, history, or religion, but the geopolitics of Western imperialism that was shaping the imaginations of non-Western intellectuals to conceptualize an anti-Western alliance. A similar expansion of the notion of the East occurred in the Muslim 'mind'.

European discourses about racial hierarchies, due to their underlying scientific claims, were harder to challenge than the ideas of Orient and Occident, which were flexible enough to be redefined and used against the legitimacy of colonialism. In the political domain, the idea of the yellow race's inferiority and the discourse of the yellow peril led pan-Asianists to respond with their own theories of a 'white peril' in Asia (Shinichi 1994, pp. 33–4).[16] One should remember that one of the most influential pan-Asianist arguments for Japanese–Chinese racial solidarity was written by Prince Konoe Atsumaro upon his return from a long stay in Germany during the 1890s, at the peak of German yellow peril debates.[17] Konoe predicted an inevitable racial struggle in East Asia between the white and yellow races, with the Chinese and the Japanese siding with each other as sworn enemies of the white race. Similarly, since the Muslim world was often construed as equivalent to a category of race, even those Ottoman intellectuals who were not very religious, such as Ahmed Riza, felt compelled to write apologetic pieces defending Islam against Orientalist positions (Riza 1979; Riza and Urban 1992). More important for Asian intellectuals, however, was the issue of racial classification in the writings of Darwin, Spencer, Gustave Le Bon, and others. The first generation of Ottoman and Japanese reformists had dealt with questions of geographical, climatic, and religious determinism by engaging the writings of Buckle, Guizot, and Montesquieu, among others.[18] With regard to new and more scientific ideas on race determinism, Asian intellectuals generally preferred the theories of Herbert Spencer, in particular his notion of racial self-responsibility, because they could accept that in reality the coloured races were underdeveloped, but denied that this was a permanent inferiority. The idea of biological self-responsibility meant that intellectual elites could intervene, by various forms of social engineering and calls for a reawakening, in order to put an end to the decline of their racial or religious communities.

It should be noted that pan-Asianists and pan-Islamists were themselves not immune to contradictions and internalized racism. In fact, pan-Islamists like Halil Halid noted that if European racism and the civilizing mission ideology were limited to the natives of Australia, the Caribbean, and Africa, he would not have had any objections to it (Halid 1907b, pp. 185–8). He, however, noted the un-acceptability of the civilizing mission ideology for Muslim, Indian, and Chinese societies, which had had their past greatness in civilizations and a continuing legacy of higher moral values. Thus, he objected to their depiction as uncivilized savages in need of colonial intervention for progress and development. Even though Ottoman and Japanese elites insisted on their civilizational equality, at least in potential, with the West, they developed a civilizing mission ideology in their own regions: the Ottomans claimed that they had a mission to civilize backward Muslim regions, while Japan expressed hopes to civilize East Asia.

AWAKENING OF THE EAST—REVOLT AGAINST THE WEST

It is against the backdrop of this long tradition of engagement among Asian elites with the European discourses of Orient and race, and Western intellectuals' awareness of this challenge, that the Russo-Japanese War of 1905 became a turning point in the history of decolonization, and thus the political destiny of Western hegemony in Asia. Despite the fact that the Japanese won the war with the support of the British Empire, non-Western elites saw this war as a crucial turning point in their struggle against the civilizing mission ideology of European colonialism. Upon the Japanese victory, all previous European discourses about the inferiority of the Asian and yellow races were proven to be invalid. In fact, the reconsideration of the scientific literature on racial characteristics, to which the Japanese victory contributed immensely, would lead to the 1911 Universal Races Congress, an event that indicated the global impact of the ideas and critiques of non-Western intellectuals (Holton 2002).[19] Against the prevailing vogue for Social Darwinism, the Russo-Japanese War confirmed the earlier preference of non-Western intellectuals (and of many Westerners as well) for the idea that the existing underdevelopment of Asian or Muslim societies should not be seen as permanent due to race or religion. Following the model of what Japan had done in four decades, Asian societies could awaken, exercise self-strengthening, and catch up with the developed societies of Europe in an equally short period of time. In that sense, however, although the Japanese victory was viewed by anti-colonial nationalists as a sign of the awakening of Eastern civilization or the revival of Asia, it also confirmed the universality of the European-inspired vision of progress and civilization. After all, Japan was proving that a single civilization and modernity, which had gained perfection in Europe, was the universal legacy of humanity, and that it could be adopted by and successfully merged with the local cultures in Asia (Aydın 2007).

The slogans of the 'Awakening of the East' associated with the Russo-Japanese War are indicative of the agency of non-Western actors in the history of decolonization and the end of Western hegemony, both intellectually and politically. Western civilization did not have to 'decline' for Asia to gain liberation from Western hegemony. A series of constitutional revolutions, partly inspired by the Japanese model, in Iran (1906), Turkey (1908), and China (1911) also signalled the modernist content of the Asian reawakening (Sohrabi 1995).[20] It was led by Young Turks, Iranians, or Chinese, who were well trained in European thought and who aimed to reform their societies along European lines, even though an emphasis on cultural authenticity and civilizational values accompanied the process of modernization.

Thus, the subsequent impact of World War I on alternative visions of world order, especially in pan-Islamic and pan-Asian thought, has to be considered in relation to 1904–14 as an era of Asia's self-conscious revival and awakening. By 1914, Ottoman and Japanese intellectuals had already developed their alternative discourses of civilization, in which the East and the West both had their virtues, and their synthesis or harmony would result in a higher level of world civilization. In fact, members of the Japanese elite insisted that Japan would assume leadership in carrying out this East–West synthesis, thus assuring both its equality with the West and its leadership in the East (Shigenobu 1990). It was at this juncture that Ottoman and

Japanese intellectuals developed highly sophisticated theories about the indispensability of following the European civilization and the inevitability of this process, while at the same time underlining the insufficiency of the European model in the Asian context. Ziya Gokalp, a sociologist of the Late Ottoman period, with references to both the Japanese example and European theories, formulated a new vision of authentic modernity based on the trinity of Islamic identity, Turkish nationalism, and European-inspired universal civilization, whose synthesis would be necessary to resolve the tensions between the indispensable and insufficient aspects of Western civilization as a model for Turkish reform.[21]

The influence of pan-Islamic ideas, especially the diagnosis of international relations as a modern crusade of the West against the Muslim world under the pretext of civilization, became crucial for gathering Ottoman public support for entering World War I on the side of Germany (Aksakal 2003). Young Turk leaders of the post-1908 Revolution Ottoman government initially hoped to establish an alliance with the British Empire.[22] Yet, the invasion of Ottoman Libya by Italy in 1911 and the Balkan War in 1912, which started with an attack against the Ottoman State by an alliance of Christian nations, led to a great disillusionment about the 'West' when none of the great powers intervened to stop these violations of international law (Aksakal 2004). Rising anti-Western emotions in Ottoman public opinion aroused the concern of the leading Ottoman Westernist Abdullah Cevdet. For example, in a polemic between Abdullah Cevdet and Celal Nuri, it became clear that Cevdet did not want a radical condemnation and hatred of the imperialist West, as that might have led to the rejection of the Enlightenment West as well. In response, Celal Nuri noted that he made a distinction between the 'good' Enlightenment West and the 'bad' imperialist West, and that his anti-Westernism did not extend to everything about Western culture, much less to modernity.[23]

Many Ottoman opinion leaders reasoned that they had to use the intra-European rivalry as a chance to take their revenge upon the modern and secular 'crusade' led by the British, French, and Russian empires against the Islamic world. This was a drastic change from the nineteenth-century Ottoman foreign policy of cooperation with the leading Western powers while implementing 'civilized' reforms. In some ways, the Ottoman insistence on securing a formal alliance with Germany as a precondition for entering the Great War was a continuation of this Ottoman desire to be a part of rather than remain outside European diplomacy, and to resist being treated like the colonies in Africa and Asia. However, beyond this diplomatic calculation, popular notions of pan-Islamic solidarity provided Ottoman policy makers with the vision that upon entering the war they would be able to utilize the contradictions and weak points in the imperial world order by encouraging Muslim disobedience to and, if possible, open revolt against it. One major problem for the Ottomans in imagining a military confrontation with Britain and France was the sour feeling of fighting against a civilization that had introduced them to modernity. Indeed, in a patriotic and pan-Islamic play *Halife Ordusu Mısır ve Kafkas'da* (Caliphate Army in Egypt and Caucasia) depicting discussions among Ottoman military academy students around the time of the Ottoman decision to join the Great War, there is a scene expressing this Ottoman dilemma. In response to excited anticipation that the war would bring doom to Europe and salvation to the Ottoman state, a student named Subhi, who had previously studied in Europe, asserts that he is not happy to see the 'bankruptcy of a great civilization' from which the Ottomans learned so much (Baha [Pars] 2003). The dilemma of Westernized Ottoman intellectuals in advocating a war against the cradle of the modernity that they emulated could only be resolved by the fact that by 1914 the Ottomans had already made a sharp distinction between the ideal of universal modernity and its specifically Western version.

The Japanese empire, as an ally of the British Empire, was on the opposite side of the Ottoman Empire during World War I, and thus it did not try to mobilize any pan-Asianist revolt. Yet, pan-Asianist intellectuals were very active in Japan and elsewhere in Asia during World War I, emphasizing Western subjugation of the coloured Asian races as the main conflict in international affairs and urging the Japanese empire to break its alliance with Britain in order to become the natural leader of rising Asian nationalism (Shûmei 1915, pp. 40–4; 1916, pp. 47–55; Tokutomi 1917, pp. 121–7). Although Japan's pan-Asianists were in opposition during World War I, they did conduct a successful public opinion campaign in cooperation with Asianists in China and India, underlining the continuing racial discrimination by whites even against their Japanese allies and emphasizing that it was better for Japanese national interests to be the leader of a free Asia than to be a second-class member of the all-white superpowers club (Das 1918).

World War I immensely affected the destinies of the pan-Asian and pan-Islamic revolts against the West. The visible destruction and barbarity of the Great War in Europe strengthened pan-Asian and pan-Islamic discourses, as more and more intellectuals in Asia emphasized the idea of a 'declining' Europe. Instead of claiming to civilize others, Europe now needed to learn moral civilization from Asia. In fact, the counter-discourse of the morally superior East saving the West from its own decadence, and thus saving humanity from the West, was shared by 'pessimist' groups in Europe as well as by various Asian intellectuals. However, the Bolshevik Revolution in Russia on the one hand, and Wilsonian Principles of national self-determination and the League of Nations on the other undermined the previous notion that pan-Islamic or pan-Asian solidarity was the only way to overcome colonialism. There were now two viable 'Western' alternatives to the declining imperialist world order. In a sense, Western civilization was offering its own solutions to the globally acknowledged crisis of international order: either a new sense of normative liberal internationalism, or a socialist alternative.

Thus, socialist internationalism, calling for a complete end to imperialism, promised that the unjust Western hegemony over Asia would end both through the agency of the European working classes and the solidarity of Asian nations. Initially, the Bolsheviks tried to benefit from the accumulated anti-Western sentiments of Asian societies and the tide of pan-Islamic activism by organizing the 1920 Eastern People's Congress in Baku, where leading pan-Islamic personalities such as Enver Paşa appeared (Riddell 1993). The new Bolshevik government in Russia was also supporting the anti-colonial nationalist movements in the Muslim world. Yet, the Bolsheviks could not accept the idea of an alternative Eastern civilization entrenched within pan-Islamic and pan-Asian discourses, and gradually socialists distanced themselves from pan-Islamic and pan-Asian movements, due to their fear that instead of using them, they might themselves become instruments of these two rival internationalisms.[24] On the other side, the initially positive pan-Islamic and pan-Asian interest in the Bolshevik Revolution also gradually turned into animosity and competition. Both in Japan and the Ottoman state, internationalist visions before World War I had generally concurred on racial and religious identities, but both societies witnessed the rise of socialist internationalism among their own citizens in the aftermath of the Bolshevik Revolution. Similarly, the pan-Asianist moments within Indian, Chinese, and Vietnamese national movements from 1905 to 1914 were replaced by the attraction for socialist alternatives felt by nationalists of a newer generation.[25]

The relationship between the pan-Islamic and pan-Asian revolt against the West and Wilsonianism was equally complex. Many pan-Islamic and pan-Asian intellectuals admired Woodrow Wilson and saw him as an exceptional Western leader who tried to introduce normative principles into international affairs (Kimitada 1967). There was also the paradox of a widespread nationalist utilization of the Wilsonian principle of the right to self-determination against the imperialist legacy of the 'universalist' standards of civilization, as seen in the biographies of Ho Chi Minh, Sa'd Zaghlul, and other nationalists in Asia (Manela 2003). If independence from colonialism was congruent with the natural right to national self-determination, intellectuals of the colonized nations could argue that they did not have to prove that they had the merit of civilization to deserve equal treatment by the Western powers.

In the context of the Ottoman defeat in World War I, Muslim leaders of the Ottoman state found Wilsonianism to be a means to gain independence and secure a new national state in areas where Muslims were a majority. Hence, some of the most articulate advocates of pan-Islamism in the Ottoman state, such as Celal Nuri İleri, became founders of the 'Wilsonian Principles Society' in Istanbul and asked for American intervention and a mandate for a national Turkey against a potential 'imperial' settlement of cross-national Ottoman lands (Erol 1966). Yet, the demands of the Ottoman Muslim leadership to have the Ottoman state recognized as the national home to its Muslim majority was rejected at the Paris Peace Conference, again with arguments about the civilizational inferiority of the Turkish Muslims. It was in this context (of the Conference's endorsement of Greek, Armenian, and Kurdish nationalism and its rejection of Ottoman Turkey's Wilsonian demands) that the Turkish national movement became the focus of a new post–World War I pan-Islamism, a development most clearly embodied in the Khilafat Movement of India.

Initiated by Indian Muslims and supported by leading Hindu nationalists such as Gandhi, the Khilafat Movement symbolized a paradoxical merger between the ideals of Islamic solidarity, anti-colonial nationalism, and Wilsonian notions of legitimacy. While collecting enormous sums of material donations for the Turkish war for independence, the Khilafat Movement leaders asked the British government, the colonial rulers of India, to recognize the right to self-determination of the Muslim majority in Turkey. Even though the name of the movement was 'Khilafat', implying that it aimed to liberate the seat of the Muslim caliphate in Istanbul from allied occupation, it was sending its aid to the national government in Ankara and it received the moral support of non-Muslim Hindu nationalists. Ultimately, the fact that the Turkish national movement achieved its goals was partly due to moral and material support from the pan-Islamic movement. Nevertheless, the elite of the new Turkish Republic decided to abolish the caliphate and disavow its pan-Islamic claims to leadership in the Muslim world, thus indicating their own self-conscious preference for a Wilsonian direction in the interwar international order. Turkey remained outside the League of Nations for another decade, perceiving the League as a new way of justifying British and French colonial interests in the region. Yet, its decision to abolish the caliphate ended the peak of post–World War I realpolitik pan-Islamism.[26] It is important to note that at this crucial moment of abandoning the pan-Islamic discourse of civilization and world order, the leaders of the Turkish Republic did not abolish the discourse of civilization itself. Instead, they emphasized that the Eastern–Islamic civilization could not be a true alternative to the West in terms of carrying out concrete modernizing reforms and that a secular national Turkey could and wanted to be a member of the Western civilization. In many ways, Kemalism demonstrated the triumph of the Eurocentric concept of a singular and universal civilization embedded in earlier anti-imperialist thought. Kemalist thinkers continued to depict the Western powers as sinister, unreliable, and untrustworthy, but nevertheless identified with the superiority of the Western civilization in carrying out radical projects of transforming a Muslim majority society into a 'civilized' modern one (Berkes 1975; Bora 2002, p. 251).

Pan-Asianist responses to Wilsonianism travelled along a similarly twisted road. When the Japanese government, partly under the influence of earlier pan-Asianist propaganda, proposed a race equality clause at the Paris Peace Conference, Japanese pan-Asianists were mobilized in support of this proposal, suggesting that it would be the litmus test for the sincerity and credibility of the moral principles underlying the League of Nations. The rejection of the race equality proposal was indeed depicted by pan-Asianists as a proof of the continuation of white supremacist ideology and Western hegemony under the mask of the League (Shimazu 1998). On the other hand, the Wilsonian idea of national self-determination, in inspiring the Korean national revolution and the May Fourth Movement in 1919, revealed the contradictions between nationalism and pan-Asianism in Japan, as most of the Japanese pan-Asianists in their vision of Asian solidarity had imagined that Korea would forever be part of the Japanese empire. In that sense, Wilsonian internationalism weakened the pan-Asian challenge to Western hegemony in Asia. Ideas of Asian solidarity survived throughout the interwar era, with effective critiques of both the League of Nations and the Socialist internationalism. Yet, the pan-Asian revolt against the West, too, became overshadowed by the two Western alternatives to the crisis of Western imperialism, namely Wilsonianism and Socialist internationalism.

A counter-discourse of civilization around redefined notions of an East–West distinction thus survived World War I and became dominant in the interwar period, though interpreted very differently. Even though political activism in the name of Asian or Islamic solidarity did not have much of an influence in international politics during the 1920s, the visions of a revival of Asia, the idea of Eastern and Western civilizations, and the diagnosis of the conflict of civilizations began to be shared by many Japanese intellectuals (Naoki 1994).[27] It was this legacy of civilizational thinking and anti-Western historical memory that the Japanese elites of the 1930s were able to utilize at the moment of crisis in Japanese imperialism. Japan's 'return to Asia' and its challenge to the remaining European hegemony in Asia was not an outgrowth of the long-standing pan-Asian movement, but rather an appropriation of those earlier ideas by various state agencies during the 1930s. Similar to that earlier pan-Asianism, which had emerged during the era of European high imperialism (1882–1914),

Japan's official Asianism displayed an ambivalent attitude to the idea of Europe's universality. While claiming to overturn modernity and to end European colonialism in Asia, the Japanese empire in fact embodied a most radical experiment in modernization (Garon 1994; Young 1998; Harootunian 2000).

***

The story of the pan-Islamic and pan-Asian revolt(s) against the West illustrates the ways in which non-Western elites contributed to the process of decolonization by challenging the legitimacy of Eurocentric world order with values inspired by the idea of a universal West. In this process, non-Western elites became active subjects in the appropriation of European ideas of history, race, and civilization, forming their own counter-narratives, and refashioning their own visions of modernity and universality. Their re-employment of Orientalist knowledge categories of the East and the West for anti-colonial and nationalist purposes brought about the somewhat paradoxical emphasis on the Islamic, Asian yellow race or Eastern identities at a time when these elites were self-consciously Eurocentric in their vision of reform and modernization. During the interwar period, both the Turkish and Japanese were familiar with the discourses of the 'decline of the West', but this did not lead them to abandon the Eurocentric notions of civilization and modernity. In Turkey, the elites who once mobilized the ideals of a pan-Islamic revolt against the West during World War I became staunch Westernizers, contributing to the confidence of Europeans who believed in the universality of their own experience. Similarly, Japanese pan-Asianists were proud of Japan's achievements in appropriating Western modernity and in spreading the merits of Western civilization in 'underdeveloped' Asia. Even when the Japanese elites of the late 1930s utilized ideas of pan-Asian solidarity as a solution to the crisis of their imperial expansion in East Asia, Japan's achievements in Eurocentric modernity were presented as the reason for its leadership in Asia.

In short, non-Western elites delegitimized the Eurocentric imperial order by reorienting European discourses of civilization, Orient, and race. Yet, in all of these non-Western challenges, the idea of Europe's universality was preserved and recreated, to the extent that Europe was reborn in non-Western discourses at a time when European pessimists were declaring the 'decline of the West'. It is in this spirit that peaks of anti-Western and anti-imperial emotions and ideas in Asia were also moments of powerful pro-Western ideological trends, such as in the aftermaths of the Russo-Japanese War and World War I.

NOTES

1. For early pan-Islamic and pan-Asian ideas, see Tadashi (1968), Tikhonov (2002), Yoshimi (1993, pp. 337–40), Landau (1990, pp. 1–72).
2. For a formulation of a universal theory of civilization by the most prominent early Meiji-era intellectual, see Yukichi (1973). For examples of Ottoman theorization of the process of civilization, see N. Kemal (1880, pp. 381–3), M. Paşa (1862, 26–7).
3. For aspects of the Ottoman civilizing mission for its own populations, in the form of reapplying European Orientalism for domestic political purposes, see Makdisi (2002, pp. 768–96). For the Japanese version of a similar process, see Kyoko (2003, pp. 179–96).
4. For the changing global image of the West and transformation of world order during the 1880s, see Arendt (1962, p. 123).
5. For an example of the appeal of pan-Islamic ideas in Morocco, outside of Ottoman domains, in this same period, see Burke (1972, pp. 97–118).
6. There was a policy vision of Muslim solidarity during the reign of Abdulhamid II, but this mainly aimed to solidify the citizenship base of the Ottoman Empire among various Muslim ethnicities. Abdulhamid II was very cautious about not directly challenging the legitimacy of the Eurocentric imperial order. Even the idea of Islamic solidarity within the Ottoman Empire, at the expense of Christian subjects, was not official, since this would have been a violation of a policy of Ottomanism. For Abdulhamid's concern about the civilized image of the Ottoman state, see Deringil (1998). For an assessment of Abdulhamid's policies from a world historical perspective, see Akarli (2002, pp. 261–84).
7. For the civilizational consciousness in the extensive travels of a prominent pan-Islamist activist all over Asia, see İbrahim (1910–11).
8. For a broader world historical assessment of Ernest Renan's ideas on the Aryan race, see Kaiwar (2003, pp. 13–61).
9. Renan gave his speech on 'Islam and Science' on 29 March 1883 at the Sorbonne and published it in the 30 March 1883 issue of *Journal des Debates*. Soon afterwards in the same year, the speech was published as a

twenty-four-page-long separate booklet. For its English language translation, see Renan (2000).

10. For Afghani's response, see Afghani (1968).

11. For a current edition of the text, see N. K. Bey (2002).

12. Even Qasim Amin, famous for his book *Liberation of Women* advocating the reform of the status of Muslim women of Egypt at the turn of the century would argue, in his writings addressed to European audiences, that Islam does not oppress women and it is not an inferior religion. See Cole (1981).

13. Halil Halid, one of the most prolific pan-Islamic thinkers in Europe, consistently wrote in European papers about the issue of Islam and modernity and attended the Fourteenth Orientalist Congress in Algeria in 1905. See Wasti (1993).

14. Tokutomi Soho (1863–1957) advocated the term 'Yellow Man's Burden', giving voice to an alternative to the idea of the 'White Man's Burden' (based on Rudyard Kipling's famous poem of 1899). See Sohô (1906) quoted in Sukehiro (1987, p. 29).

15. For the development of shared Eastern identity in different parts of Asia around the turn of the century, see Karl (2002). For the development of cooperation between Japanese Asianists and Muslim activists around the notion of shared Eastern identity, see Esenbel (2004).

16. For the continuing relevance of this idea of 'white peril' in Japan throughout the interwar era, see Duus (1971, pp. 41–8).

17. Konoe Atsumaro's article, published in *Taiyo* in 1898, was titled 'Dôjinshu Dômei: Shina Mondai Kenkyû no Hitsuyô' [We Must Ally with Those of the Same Race, and We Must Study the China Problem]. See Jansen (1980, p. 113).

18. François M. Guizot (1787–1874) first published the *Histoire de la Civilisation en Europe* in 1828. For a recent English language edition, see Guizot (1997). Montesquieu (1689–1755) wrote *The Spirit of Laws (De l'Esprit des Lois)* in 1748. See Montesquieu (2002); Buckle (1913) (originally written in 1857). For a critique of these European thinkers of civilizational progress by non-Western intellectuals, see Yukichi (1973); Hiroaki (1984).

19. For a recent reassessment of the London Universal Races Congress of 1911, see Fletcher (2005); Pennybacker (2005); Bonakdarian, 2005; and Gregg and Kale (2005).

20. In the aftermath of the Chinese Revolution, Lenin also noted the 'awakening of Asia' as a contemporary observer.

21. For the subaltern split in the thought of Ziya Gökalp, see Davison (2006).

22. Two Young Turk leaders, Ahmed Riza and Dr Nazim, mentioned the formula of making Turkey 'The Japan of the Near East' in their interview

with British Foreign Secretary Sir Edward Grey in 1908. See Hanioğlu (2001, p. 304, 492). Also quoted by Ahmed and Kent (1984, p. 13).

23. For Celal Nuri's critique of Abdullah Cevdet's pro-Westernism during the Balkan Wars, see Nuri (1914).

24. For the separation between communism and pan-Islamism, see Malaka (2001).

25. For example, interest in Japan among leading Vietnamese nationalists from 1905 to 1914 was replaced by Wilsonian and Socialist inclinations after World War I. For the pro-Japanese trend in mainstream Vietnamese nationalism, see Marr (1971, p. 113). Ho Chi Minh's biography illustrates the appeal of both Woodrow Wilson's principle of self-determination and socialist internationalism (see Bradley 2000).

26. For examples of the post–World War I pan-Islamic movement and its ideas, see Kidwai (1919a and 1919b); Minault (1982).

27. For an example of the dominance of this civilizational paradigm, see Takashi (1921).

BIBLIOGRAPHY

Adas, M. 1989. *Machines as the Measure of Man: Science, Technology and Ideologies of Western Dominance.* Ithaca: Cornell University Press.

Afghani, J. 1968. 'Answer of Jamal ad-Din to Renan'. In *An Islamic Response to Imperialism*, edited by N. Keddie, pp. 181–7. Berkeley: Calif.

Ahmed, F. and M. Kent, eds. 1984. *The Great Powers and the End of the Ottoman Empire.* London, Boston: George Allen and Unwin.

Akarli, E. D. 2002. The Tangled End of Istanbul's Imperial Supremacy. In *Modernity and Culture from the Mediterranean to the Indian Ocean, 1890–1920*, edited by L. Fawaz and C. A. Bayly, pp. 261–84. New York: Columbia University Press.

Aksakal, M. 2003. 'Defending the Nation: The German–Ottoman Alliance of 1914 and the Ottoman Decision for War'. PhD dissertation, Princeton University.

———. 2004. 'Not by Those Old Books of International Law, but Only by War: Ottoman Intellectuals on the Eve of the Great War'. *Diplomacy and Statecraft* 15(3): 507–44.

Arendt, H. 1962. *The Origins of Totalitarianism.* New York: Meridian Books.

Aydın, C. 1999. 'Nihon Wa Itsu Toyo No Kuni Ni Natta No Ka? Chuto Kara Mita Kindai Nihon' [When Did Japan Become an 'Eastern' Nation? Modern Japan in the Imagination of Middle Eastern Nationalists]. *Atarashii Nihongaku no Kiochiku—Constructing Japanese Studies in Global Perspective*, pp. 81–6. Tokyo: Ochanomizu University Press.

Aydın, C. 2007. 'A Global Anti-Western Moment? The Russo-Japanese War, Decolonization and Asian Modernity'. In *Competing Visions of World Order: Global Moments and Movements, 1880s–1930s*, edited by S. Conrad and D. Sachsenmaier, pp. 213–36. New York: Palgrave.

Baha (Pars), M. 2003. 'Halife ordusu Mısır ve Kafkas'da'. In *Hilafet risaleleri*, Vol. 3, edited by İ. Kara, pp. 383–426. Istanbul: Klasik.

Berkes, N. 1975. *Türk düşüncesinde Batı sorunu*. Ankara: Bilgi Yayınları.

Bonakdarian, M. 2005. 'Negotiating Universal Values and Cultural and National Parameters at the First Universal Races Congress'. *Radical History Review* (92): 118–32.

Bora, T. 2002. Milliyetçi muhafazakar ve İslamcı düşünüşte negatif batı imgesi. In *Modern Türkiye'de siyasi düşünce 3: Modernleşme ve Batıcılık*, edited by U. Kocabaşoğlu, pp. 251–68. Istanbul: İletişim.

Bradley, M. 2000. *Imagining Vietnam and America: The Making of Postcolonial Vietnam, 1919–1950*. Chapel Hill N.C.: University of North Carolina Press.

Buckle, H. T. 1913. *History of Civilization in England*. New York: Hearst's International Library.

Burke, E. 1972. 'Pan-Islam and Moroccan Resistance to French Colonial Penetration, 1900–1912'. *The Journal of African History* 13(1): 97–118.

Burtscher, M. 2006. 'Facing "the West" on Philosophical Grounds: A View from the Pavilion of Subjectivity on Meiji Japan'. *Comparative Studies of South Asia, Africa and the Middle East* 26(3): 367–76.

Cole, J. R. 1981. 'Feminism, Class, and Islam in Turn-of-the-Century Egypt'. *International Journal of Middle East Studies* 13(4): 387–407.

Craig, A. M. 1968. 'Fukuzawa Yukichi: The Philosophical Foundations of Meiji Nationalism'. In *Political Development in Modern Japan*, edited by R. E. Ward, pp. 99–148. Princeton NJ: Princeton University Press.

Cündioğlu, D. 1996. 'Ernest Renan ve "reddiyeler" bağlamında İslam-bilim tartışmalarına bibliyografik bir katkı'. *Divan* (2): 1–94.

Dale, S. F. 1988. 'Religious Suicide in Islamic Asia: Anticolonial Terrorism in India, Indonesia, and the Philippines'. *The Journal of Conflict Resolution* 32(1): 37–59.

Das, T. 1918. *The Isolation of Japan in World Politics*. Tokyo: Asiatic Association of Japan.

Davison, A. 2006. 'Ziya Gökalp and Provincializing Europe'. *Comparative Studies of South Asia, Africa and the Middle East* 26(3): 377–90.

Deringil, S. 1998. *The Well-Protected Domains: Ideology and the Legitimation of Power in the Ottoman Empire, 1876–1909*. London: I.B. Tauris Publishers.

Dunn, R. E. 2004. *The Adventures of Ibn Battuta: A Muslim Traveler of the Fourteenth Century*. Berkeley and Los Angeles: University of California Press.

Duus, P. 1971. 'Nagai Ryutaro and the "White Peril", 1905–1944'. *The Journal of Asian Studies* 31(I): 41–8.

Erol (Sümer), M. 1966. 'Wilson Prensipleri Cemiyeti'nin Amerika Cumhurbaşkanı Wilson'a gönderdiği muhtıra'. *Ankara Üniversitesi Dil ve Tarih Coğrafya Fakültesi Tarih Araştırmaları Dergisi* 3(4–5): 237–45.

Esenbel, S. 2004. 'Japan's Global Claim to Asia and the World of Islam: Transnational Nationalism and World Power, 1900–1945'. *The American Historical Review* 109(4): 1140–70.

Findley, C. V. 1998. 'An Ottoman Occidentalist in Europe: Ahmed Midhat Meets Madame Gulnar, 1889'. *American Historical Review* 103(1): 15–49.

Fletcher, I. C. 2005. 'Introduction: New Historical Perspectives on the First Universal Races Congress of 1911'. *Radical History Review Spring* (92): 99–102.

Garon, S. 1994. 'Rethinking Modernization and Modernity in Japanese History: A Focus on State–Society Relations'. *The Journal of Asian Studies* (53): 346–66.

Gregg, R. and M. Kale. 2005. 'The Negro and the Dark Princess: Two Legacies of the Universal Races Congress'. *Radical History Review* (92): 133–52.

Guizot, F. M. 1997. *The History of Civilization in Europe*. London: Penguin Books.

Halid, H. 1907a. *The Crescent versus the Cross*. London: Luzac and Co.

———. 1907b. *Hilal ve salib münazaası*. Cairo: Matba-i Hindiye.

Hanioğlu, Ş. 2001. *Preparation for a Revolution, the Young Turks, 1902–1908*. Oxford: Oxford University Press.

Harootunian, H. D. 2000. *Overcome by Modernity: History, Culture, and Community in Interwar Japan*. Princeton: Princeton University Press.

Hay, S. N. 1970. *Asian Ideas of East and West: Tagore and His Critics in Japan, China, and India*. Cambridge, Massachusetts: Harvard University Press.

Hiroaki, M. 1984. 'Varities of Bunmei Ron' (Theories of Civilization). In *Japan in Transition: Thought and Action in the Meiji Era, 1868–1912*, edited by H. Conroy, S. T. W. Davis and W. Patterson, pp. 209–23. London: Associated University Presses.

Holton, R. J. 2002. 'Cosmopolitanism or Cosmopolitanisms? The Universal Races Congress of 1911'. *Global Network* (2): 153–70.

İbrahim, A. 1910–11. *Alem-i Islam ve Japonya'da intisari Islamiyet*, vols 1–2. İstanbul: Ahmet Saki Bey Printing House (vol. 1) and Kader Printing House (vol. 2).

Jaffe, R. 2004. 'Seeking Sakyamuni: Travel and the Reconstruction of Japanese Buddhism'. *Journal of Japanese Studies* 30(1): 65–96.

Jansen, M. 1980. 'Konoe Atsumaro'. In *The Chinese and the Japanese: Essays in Political and Cultural Interactions*, edited by A. Iriye, pp. 107–23. Princeton: Princeton University Press.

168   *Debates on Civilization in the Muslim World*

Kaiwar, V. 2003. 'The Aryan Model of History and the Oriental Renaissance: The Politics of Identity in an Age of Revolutions, Colonialism and Nationalism'. In *The Antinomies of Modernity*, edited by S. Mazumdar and V. Kaiwar, pp. 13–61. Durham: Duke University Press.

Karl, R. 2002. *Staging the World: Chinese Nationalism at the Turn of the Twentieth Century*. Durham: Duke University Press.

Keddie, N, ed. 1968. *An Islamic response to Imperialism*. Berkeley and Los Angeles: University of California Press.

Keddie, N. R. 1994. 'The Revolt of Islam, 1700 to 1991: Comparative Considerations and Relations to Imperialism'. *Comparative Studies in Society and History* 36(3): 463–87.

Kemal, N. 1 Safer 1297/14 January 1880. 'Medeniyet' [Civilization]. *Mecmua-i Ulum* (5): 381–3.

Ketelaar, J. E. 1990. *Of Heretics and Martyrs in Meiji Japan*. Princeton: Princeton University Press.

Kidwai, S. M. H. 1919a. *The Future of the Muslim Empire: Turkey*. London: Central Islamic Society.

———. 1919b. *The Sword against Islam or a Defence of Islam's Standard-Bearers*. London: Central Islamic Society.

Kimitada, M. 1967. 'Japanese Opinions on Woodrow Wilson in War and Peace'. *Monumenta Nipponica* 22(3/4): 368–89.

Kyoko, U. 2003. 'Ino Kanori's "History" of Taiwan: Colonial Ethnology, the Civilizing Mission and Struggles for Survival in East Asia'. *History and Anthropology* 14(2): 179–96.

M. Paşa, Muharrem 1279/ June 1862. 'Mukayese-i ilm ve Cehl' [A Comparison of Knowledge and Ignorance]. *Mecmua-i Fünûn* (I): 26–7.

Makdisi, U. 2002. 'Ottoman Orientalism'. *American Historical Review* 107(3): 768–96.

Malaka, T. 2001. 'Communism and pan-Islamism'. *What Next? Marxist Discussion Journal* 21. Retrieved from http://www.whatnextjournal.org.uk/Pages/Back/Wnext21/Panislam.html.

Manela, E. 2003. 'The Wilsonian Moment: Self-Determination and the International Origins of Anticolonial Nationalism, 1917–1920'. Unpublished PhD thesis, Yale University, New Haven, US.

Marr, D. 1971. *Vietnamese Anti-Colonialism*. Berkeley: University of California Press.

Minault, G. 1982. *The Khilafat Movement: Religious Symbolism and Political Mobilization in India*. New York: Columbia University Press.

Montesquieu. 2002. *The Spirit of Laws*. Amherst, NY: Prometheus Books.

———. 2002. İslamiyet ve Devlet-i Aliyye-i Osmaniye hakkında doğru bir söz: Cenevre'de Müsteşrikin Kongresi'nde irad olunmuş bir nutkun tercümesidir. In *Hilafet Risaleleri 1. Cilt*, edited by İ. Kara, pp. 353–71. İstanbul: Klasik Yayınları.

N. Kamil Bey. 1316 [1898–9]. *Islamiyet ve Devlet-i Aliyye-i Osmaniye hakkında doğru bir soz*. Istanbul: Tahir Bey Yayınevi.

Naoki, M. 1994. 'Senkyûhyaku Nijû Nendai Nihon, Chosen, Chûgoku ni okeru Ajia Ninshiki no Ichidaimen: Ajia Minzoku Kaigi o Meguru Sankoku no Roncho'. In *Kindai Nihon no Ajia Ninshiki*, edited by F. Tetsuo, pp. 509–44. Kyôto: Kyoto Daigaku Jinbun Kagaku Kenkyujo.

Nuri, C. 1914. *Müslümanlara, Türklere hakaret, düşmanlara riayet ve muhabbet*. İstanbul: Kader Publishing House.

Pennybacker, S.D. 2005. 'The Universal Races Congress, London Political Culture, and Imperial Dissent, 1900–1939'. *Radical History Review* 92: 103–17.

Renan, E. 2000. Islamism and Science. In *Orientalism: Early Sources, Volume I: Readings in Orientalism*, edited by B. S. Turner, pp. 199–217. London: Routledge.

Riddell, J., ed. 1993. *The Communist International in Lenin's Time. To See the Dawn: Baku, 1920–First Congress of the Peoples of the East*. New York: Pathfinder Press.

Riza, A. 1979. *La faillite morale de la politique occidentale en Orient*. Tunis: Editions Bouslama.

Riza, A. and I. Urbain. 1992. *Tolerance de l'Islam*. Saint-Ouen: Publication du Centre Abaad.

Sannosuke, M. 1967. 'Profile of Asian Minded Man V: Fukuzawa Yukichi'. *Developing Economies* 5(1): 168–9.

Shigenobu, O. 1990. *Tozai Bunmei no Chôwa*. Tokyo: Waseda Daigaku Shuppansha.

Shimazu, S. 1998. *Japan, Race and Equality: The Racial Equality Proposal of 1919*. London: Routledge.

Shinichi, Y. 1994. 'Ajia Ninshiki no Kijiku'. In *Kindai Nihon no Ajia Ninshiki*, edited by F. Tetsuo and Y. Shinichi, pp. 33–4. Kyoto: Kyoto University Press.

Shûmei, O. 1916. 'Kunkoku no Shimeï'. *Michi* (93): 47–55.

――――. 1915. 'Sekai ni Okeru Nippon no Chiï'. *Dôwa* (52): 40–4.

Snodgrass, J. 2003. *Presenting Japanese Buddhism to the West: Orientalism, Occidentalism and the Columbian Exposition*. Chapel Hill: University of North Carolina Press.

Sohô, T. January 1906. 'Kojin no omoni'. *Kokumin Shimbun*.

Sohrabi, N. 1995. 'Historicizing Revolutions: Constitutional Revolutions in the Ottoman Empire, Iran and Russia, 1905–1908'. *American Journal of Sociology* 100(6): 1383–447.

Sukehiro, H. 1987. 'Modernizing Japan in Comparative Perspective'. *Comparative Studies of Culture*, 26.

Tadashi, S. 1968. 'Profile of Asian Minded Man, IX: Tokichi Tarui'. *Developing Economies* 6(l): 79–100.

Takashi, H. 1921. 'Harmony between East and West'. In *What Japan Thinks*, edited by K.K. Kawakami. New York: Macmillan Company.

Tikhonov, V. 2002. 'Korea's First Encounters with Pan-Asianism Ideology in the Early 1880s'. *The Review of Korean Studies* 5(2): 195–232.

Tokutomi, I. 1917. 'Japan's Mighty Mission'. In *Is Japan a Menace to Asia?*, edited by T. Das, pp. 121–7. Shanghai: Japan Chronicle.

Wasti, S. T. 1993. 'Halil Halid: Anti-Imperialist Muslim Intellectual'. *Middle Eastern Studies* 29(3): 559–79.

Yoshimi, T. 1993. *Nihon to Ajia*. Tokyo: Tokyo University Press.

Young, L. 1998. *Japan's Total Empire: Manchuria and the Culture of Wartime Imperialism*. Berkeley: University of California Press.

Yukichi, F. 1973. *An Outline of a Theory of Civilization [Bunmeiron no Gairyaku]*. Tokyo: Columbia University Press.

6 Interaction of Concepts of Progress and Civilization in Turkish Thought

Necmettin Doğan

The idea of progress is one of the basic assumptions of modernism. It can even be claimed that it is the civil religion of Western civilization. The idea of progress was uttered by European thinkers in the 1680s, whereas it was formulized into today's context mostly by French encyclopedists such as Turgot, Condorcet, and others. The word 'progress' can be defined as the cumulative process that is based on the acceptance that the last stage is more preferable and qualitatively more superior compared to the previous stage. Moreover, this definition implies that the change is a constant evolution in one certain direction: irreversible and inevitable (de Benoist 2008, p. 7). According to de Benoist, the idea of progress, that is, an expression of Christian theology in secular terms, became the most common belief among Western thinkers in the nineteenth century. From Hegel to Marx, from Comte to Popper, many thinkers shaped the idea of progress in a way that included the idea of civilization as well. Comte tried to spread positivism as a religion of civilization in the real sense of the word and accepted it as the last stage of the history (Comte 2000, pp. 174–5). Hegel, one of the thinkers who left his mark on nineteenth century's thinking, claimed that *Geist*, which realized and externalized itself in the philosophy of history, reached perfection in the modern

Western civilization, whereas he considered Islamic civilization as a detail in the historical process that could be summarized in a few pages by himself (Hegel, 2004). Marx adopted a similar perception of history and considered capitalism that emerged after the collapse of feudalism as a compulsory connecting station that prepares the proper conditions for the rise of communism. This belief in historical progress resulted in him favouring the emergence of capitalism. For this reason, he even criticized English imperialism for causing great poverty by destroying traditional sprinkler systems and agricultural systems that depended on the central government in India. Because of his 'stationary Orient' perception that is a component of the idea of progress, he states that English imperialism served historical progress for in the nineteenth century it brought a change into this country, which he described as one that had been stable for thousands of years (Marx 1853).[1] Elias claims that these shortsighted progressive social philosophies that emerged in the nineteenth century lost their effectiveness in the twentieth century despite the acceleration of technical and scientific improvement, and this was mainly due to the structure that the modern nation states adopted, along with factors like wars, authoritarian states, nuclear weapon threats, and so on (Elias 2002, pp. 28–31). However, Popper (1979), who criticized the thinkers mentioned earlier for assigning the task of predicting the future to social sciences and thoughts, and approaching history and the future in an integrative way, gives us one of the very recent and striking examples of the imputed relationship between the idea of progress and civilization and shows how political this relationship is by claiming that with the collapse of the Soviet Union, supporting Pax Americana is necessary for realizing Pax Civilitatis and for the salvation of humankind (Ihlau 1992). Huntington's famous thesis of the clash of civilizations is one of the latest examples of this mode of thinking. In short, the concept of civilization internalized the idea of progress.

   In this scope, many thinkers and social scientists have expressed the belief that other societies should become Westernized first in order to become civilized. In this sense, the concept of civilization is used as a functional tool in order to legitimize Eurocentrism and European imperialism (Kalın 2010, pp. 1–61). While the theories and practices are not expressed in a civilization-based discourse back in ecclesiastic eras when feudalism and scholastics were ruling, the idea of civilization is attributed to capitalist modernism later, from Hegel's history of philosophy to Goethe's world literature (*Weltliteratur*), from Herder's world history to Kant's philosophy of ethics. According to Dabashi, this is related to the shift of power relations in Europe due to which power shifted from the hands of the aristocrats and the church to the bourgeoisie. The emergence of capitalism changed the power relations, and bourgeoisie and national discourses substituted for the discourses based on lineage and church. The expression of Western civilization is a new discourse that is based on the concept of a nation that emerges because of this social change. The discourse is related to the idea of enlightenment and attempts have been made to universalize it. In this scope, the idea of non-Western societies is invented from an Orientalist perspective in order to emphasize the authenticity of Western civilization by Westerners themselves, and the discipline of Orientalism is developed in this context as well. According to Dabashi, Islamists adopted the concept of Islamic civilization as a means of resisting the West (Dabashi 2001, pp. 363–6). While doing that, they benefitted from Western criticism in Western thinking itself, especially from Nietzsche, Heidegger, the Frankfurt School, and theories of reification and alienation in leftist ideology. However, approaches towards the concept of civilization in Turkish thinking are not limited by Western influence. Historical experiences and ideological discussions in Turkey affected the approach towards this concept, which is the main subject of this chapter. I will try to explain how the concept is considered in Turkish thinking, especially by Islamism in Turkey, and how it functions as a 'utopia' as pointed out by Mannheim.

THE CONCEPTS OF PROGRESS AND CIVILIZATION FROM THE OTTOMAN EMPIRE TO THE TURKISH REPUBLIC

The word 'civilization' (*madaniyyah*) was used in Turkish for the first time in 1838. While this word is of Arabic origin, it was used by the Ottomans as the word corresponding to 'civilization'. The word 'civilization' has been used to mean manners, courtesy, and so on for a long time. Mustafa Rashid Pasha (1800–1858) defined civilization as *terbiye-i nas ve icra-yı nizamat* or the good manners of human beings and the practice of etiquettes (Baykara 1992, pp. 2–12). However, the word began to be used to mean Western civilization in today's context and is related to the concept of progress in time. There are not many concepts that have left as lasting an impression as the concept of progress has in Turkish thinking. The number of political parties, associations, and periodicals that have adopted words such as *terakki* (development), *ileri* (progressive) can give us an idea of how great the impact has been of this concept in Turkey. The words 'progress' and 'civilization' have become complementary to each other in time.

Ottoman politicians, who were disheartened and surprised by the consecutive defeats against Western countries, started to think that the only way to save the state was to first have whatever things the West had and become one of them later. This way, the context of civilization in Ottoman gradually contained within itself the idea that Westernization was necessary and progress was possible only in that way. Damat Ibrahim Pasha assigned the mission of 'comprehending the tools of civilization and education thoroughly and submitting the ones that are applicable' (Karal, 1999 p. 19) to Yirmisekiz Mehmet Celebi who was sent to Paris on his own as a delegate in 1790. After a century, the idea of leaving the ones that were adopted here immediately took the place of the idea of submitting the applicable ones from there. Hence, one of the politicians in Tanzimat era, Fuad Pasha (1814–1868), argued that in order to continue its existence in Europe, a country needed to obtain the necessary and compulsory political and administrative organs and break connections with the old ones for the sake of Islam. 'Saving the Mighty State' and following 'the needs of modern times' were the discourses used to legitimate the idea in question. At this stage, establishing a one-to-one relation between law and order and development must be accepted as an important mental change. According to Sadık Rifat Pasha (1807–1858), who had an important role in the preparation of Tanzimat, 'progressing in accordance with the current civilization in Europe depends on the procurement of absolute security of life, property, honor, and dignity of everyone; in other words, it depends on the practice of required freedom rights properly' (Çetinsaya 2001, pp. 55–61). Comte praised the reforms implemented in the letters that he wrote to Mustafa Rashid Pasha, and the French media considered the Tanzimat as a set of steps leading towards civilization (Siyavuşgil 2009, pp. 750–5).

The Young Ottomans, with motivations that were similar to that of the leaders of the Kuleli Case, adopted a critical stance against the Tanzimat bureaucracy that remained incapable of solving the problems of the country and gradually felt the impact of Europeans. Probably, the fact that Young Ottomans supported constitutional regime with Islamic principles was closely related to the reactions that were sparked against the Tanzimat reforms. As some claims about the relation between Islam and progress that had been brought forward in Europe began to have their impacts among Ottomans as well, Young Ottomans developed a more concrete and defensive attitude towards this matter. The claim made by Renan that Islam is a religion that is against progress and the discussions created by this claim in Ottoman intellectual circles are well known. Namik Kemal's 'Statement of Defence against Renan', which he had written to prove that Islam and Ottomans were open to progress, was influential in the Second Constitutional Period. In this booklet that was written in reply to Renan's speech entitled 'Islam and Science', Namik Kemal claimed that Renan's anti-Islamist expressions stemmed from the fact that he was biased against all religions in general. Because, according to Namik Kemal, Renan's views about Christianity were mostly about the wide dominance of the religion in Middle Age Europe. Moreover, Namik Kemal gives examples of successful philosophic, scientific, and literary works presented by Muslims in history, in order to disprove Renan's claims. In the following chapters of his book, he stated that Muslims could adopt and practise the science of the West. This book of Namik Kemal could only be printed in 1908, many years after his death. However, Kemal introduced similar ideas in his article published in the *Ibret* newspaper in 1873. In his article titled 'Civilization', he argued that the Western concept of civilization indicates the level reached by humanity in art, architecture, industry, science, and so on, and ignoring civilization in this sense is against human nature (Kemal 1289). The point that draws our attention is that in his article he defended civilization against conservative people who had rejected civilization for many reasons, especially because they thought Western civilization contains moral corruption within itself. According to him, moral corruption (prostitution, drinking, and so forth) is not a fundamental element of civilization. It is not necessary to imitate the West in all aspects in order to adopt its civilization. This approach of Namik Kemal contains a question that will be raised even more after the Second Constitutional Period (1908): We need to adopt civilization, but how?

In the Second Constitutional Period, this problem was intensified even more by the arguments of a group of people who were called 'Westerners'. Abdullah Cevdet (1869–1932), in contrast to many other Ottoman intellectuals who were pointing out the necessity of Westernization of the Empire, claimed that civilization is not only about the practice of techniques from the West and suggested that the country should Westernize culturally, too. According to Abdullah Cevdet, the traditional features of Ottoman society could not evolve, and as it is not possible to utilize these elements even as tools to realize the civilization, it is required to replace them with their European counterparts which can meet the requirements of modern times (Hanioğlu 1981, pp. 360–1). In the case of Ziya Gökalp (1876–1924), who expressed his thoughts just after the 'Balkan War' and whose impact lasted into the Republic period, made a sharp distinction between 'culture' and 'civilization' and suggested that Western civilization should be adopted. Gökalp (1976) says:

> The scientific notions, technical successes, economic productions of a civilization pass from one nation to another through imitations and interchanges, and the civilization of one community, starting from a local nature, embraces other countries, continents and eventually the entire humanity step by step.... It can be understood from this description that the concept of modernization occupies a superior position when it comes to adopting the maturing sciences and skills of the ruling civilization so as not to fall behind any other nation. It is not against the privacy of lives of any family or state, nor contradicts the cultural solidarity that any nation or community possess, to have mutual human lives as civilized communities.

And he continues, 'Turks should be equipped with the intelligence and science of the ruling civilization, and form a Turkish–Islam culture at the same time' (Gökalp 1976, pp. 33–42). In other words, Gökalp claims that civilization is universal, whereas culture is local. According to him, Turks accepted Islam and embraced its civilization that helped them improve themselves, but also enabled them to conserve their culture, especially at the community level. Therefore, they must do the same thing now, and while conserving their culture, they should adopt the civilization that belongs to the entire humanity and emerge into the West for this time (Gökalp, 1976). This idea was accepted especially in nationalist circles, and though Islamists appropriated it in a general sense, they were disrobed by the secular views of Gökalp.

Islamist writers of the Second Constitutional Period generally adopted a position against the West and the Ottoman intellectuals who believed that Western civilization is the only way to follow in order to progress. However, they also accepted the superiority of the West in technical–scientific areas without questioning it, and related their 'progress and future' visions to the gains of technology and science. Many writers in the *Sebilürreshad* magazine argued that Ottomans could adopt only the technology of the West and preserve the moral and cultural values of their own, just like the Japanese nation had done. In this sense, Islamists were more likely critical against Europhile Westerners who had a 'Tanzimat mentality', and at some point their thoughts were in a line similar to that of Gökalp. This shows that their perspective on the issue of progress in the Ottoman region was not different from that of N. Kemal. The following verses of M. Akif (1873–1936) support this argument:

> Do not aspire to seek
> The secret to progress in other places.
> A nation to rise will find it within itself.
> For imitating everything does not mean acting always.
> Take the science of West, take its art
> And work on it very hard.
> For it is not possible to live without these.
> For art and science belong to all human beings.
> But remember well the words I just said.
> In order to go beyond the development,
> Keep the nature of your spirit as your guide,
> For it is meaningless to hope salvation without it
> —Debus (2009, pp. 195–8)

On the other hand, Islamists criticized many writers, from Gökalp to Abdullah Cevdet, regarding phenomena like secularism and cultural Westernization, despite their sympathy for development and civilization. On the underdevelopment of Islamic world, Islamist writing in *Sebilürreshad* often states that Islam or being Muslim is not against development. According to them, the real causes of this situation were the self-complacency and arrogance of Muslims, not Islam itself. Besides, they considered imitating the West as part of these reasons. That Islam is not against development was argued by various Islamists, and scientific successes in the history of Islam, moral standards of ancient Muslim societies, and the great cities of old were presented as evidences for their argument. They frequently emphasized that blaming Islam and trying to eliminate it was meaningless for Muslims who had brought civilization to Europe in the first place; they clearly adopted a defensive stand on this issue and the relation between civilization and progress was concretized (Debus 2009, p. 205).

One of the leading names of Turkish liberalism who also issued a magazine named *Terakki*, Sabahattin Bey (1878–1948) identified the problem as 'communitarian structure of the society' and claimed that to prevent the collapse of the country, this structure should be converted into an individualistic structure. According to Sabahattin Bey, civilization cannot be improved by importing science and technology or preserving or changing culture, but it is possible only by transforming the social structure. He also asserts:

> Our reformists who are increasing in number since the Tanzimat period have had sincere intentions for regeneration; but they could not figure out how to realize this regeneration. However, first freedom, then constitutionalism, education, ethics, and eventually westernization, have been suggested as the condition to progress—these all are still being argued! But all these arguments contributed nothing to the community or to the mentality trying to regenerate it, because the realization of the details mentioned above does not generate a social structure. On the contrary, a social structure would generate these details in a positive or negative way. (Sabahattin, 1950, p. 22)

In order to accomplish his ideals, Sabahattin Bey propounds the use of education and a decentralized method. However, his thoughts had an influence only in a limited environment.

When it came to the Republic period, the reforms that were implemented as a result of the ideological background explained previously added different dimensions to the classical *avam–havas* (commoners–educated class) separation in Ottoman. The protagonist of *Yaban*, a novel by Yakup Kadri (1889–1974), one of the important names associated with the magazine *Kadro Dergisi* that had a Kemalist stance, Ahmet Celal, is a half-intellectual military officer who takes it upon himself to bring civilization and development to the country. As a civilized man, he despises the underdeveloped and ignorant peasants of Anatolia and takes it as his duty to lick them into shape and raise their awareness. The following sentences are from the article of Vedat Nedim Tor from the same magazine, *Kadro Dergisi* (1932–5), whose objective was to turn Kemalism into a doctrine, explaining how to renew this peasant represented in the novel *Yaban*: 'We will vaccinate them with technology.... Would the peasants who will pick the ripe fruits of high technique with their own hands and see them with their own eyes pay attention to bigots and fanatics? Would the peasants who will witness the superiority of reformist mind over the tradition and custom call high intellectuals as yaban (stranger)?' (Moran 2011, pp. 164–5). Kemalist nationalism identifies its opposition as underdevelopment and objectifies it, and just like the approach that science developed against nature, aims to transform it. Peyami Safa's (1899–1961) *Turk Inkilabına Bakışlar* (Reviews of Turkish Reform) reveals the civilization and progress perception of Kemalism in a more concrete way. According to Peyami Safa, Europe means *kafa* (the mind) both as a continent and in areas like idea, understanding, spirit, intelligence, and so on. Everything about culture and civilization in Europe was born from the blood of Greeks, Sionians, Romans, and 'barbarians' on the shores of a classical sea. Europe was born of Greeks, Romans, and Christians, and the ones who have not been under the impact of these three would have no reason to change to be European. According to him,

> The East has neither science nor criticism. Therefore, we cannot talk about an ideological life or intelligence there. Science and criticism does not constitute the whole knowledge, but there is no knowledge without geometry or criticism: the whole science is nothing but criticizing nature. The East is religious, but not philosophical. At the point it has to describe something, its mind goes blank. The metaphysics of Hindustan and the Far East is just a play on the words and except that it has no value at all. It always makes claims that cannot be proved. Its impact on nature is all witchcraft. When the East has to talk about the freedom, rights and laws, science, ethics, all it does it to imitate the West. But it does not understand the thing it is talking about. (Safa, n.d., p. 103)

After these words, Peyami Safa claims that the East can be separated into two, as Buddhists and Muslims, and that the fatalism and other negative attributes that come to one's mind when talking about East in the West belongs mainly to Buddhist East. According to him, these half-colonized 'primitive Asian nations' cannot be ranked with the Turkish nation. Then, he asks if the people of the Turkish nation who for centuries have been brought up in Islamic East with Arabic and Persian cultures are able to adopt the European mentality which is nothing but the production of Greece, Rome, and Christianity, and he answers 'yes'. Because, according to him, Islam and Turkish intellectual traditions did more than acquainting themselves with Greek philosophy and introduced it to Europe in the Middle East. And Islam is not the antithesis of Christianity, but its maturation (Safa, n.d., pp. 103–33). In short, he means modern Western civilization is not unfamiliar to us, it is already ours. There is no reason that we cannot be like them. It can be concluded that according to him there are two main principles of reform: nationalism and civilizationism. Nationalism will take us to our roots in Middle Asia and the East, to our history and brothers in language; and civilizationism will take us to the European method, intellectual traditions and social connections. Sovereignty of the nation, the establishment of a Grand National Assembly, abolition of the sultanate and caliphate, national economy, considering Turkish history within the framework of the Ottoman Empire, and extending it to the roots in Middle Asia, the language and pure Turkish surname reforms, the translation of the Qur'an and Turkish *azan* are the several reforms that nationalism inspired. On the other hand, civilizationism-based reforms are secularism, Latin alphabet reforms, and the removal of the alaturca branch of Darulelhan, and the establishment of the conservatoire that teaches only Western music, the adoption of the Western calendar, English weeks, and Sunday holiday, and the officializing of Western clothing (Ayvazoğlu 2000, p. 114).

Niyazi Berkes (1908–1988), who was influential in leftist and academic circles in Turkey especially after 1960 and who was writing daily articles in newspapers, comes to the fore as a typical representative of 'Leftist–Kemalism'. Even though there can be found an anti-West, mostly nationalist and anti-imperialist discourse in his writings that can be seen in the case of many other 'Leftist–Kemalists' as well, ultimately Berkes also emphasizes that Western civilization is universal and Westernization is compulsory. He considers civilization as a matter of progress and modernization. He criticizes the environments that place themselves in opposition to Western civilization to the point of almost insulting them (Berkes 1975). Berkes' 'enlightened despotism' or his ideas that remind of a radical social engineering can still be seen in Leftist–Kemalist circles today.

The civilization and progress perception of Kemalism created a distance and hierarchy between them and the conservative communities and their values, and that was the cause of many objections being raised against this understanding. One of these objections was by Mumtaz Turhan (1908–1969), who had a rightist–nationalist political view and a stance more like Ziya Gökalp. Turhan claims that real Westernization added only a new factor, namely science, to the culture of our nation. According to him, Westernization is imperative. However, Westernization does not mean imitating the Western way of living or randomly importing their technology or institutions. He believed this to be a matter of mentality. When science and technology are correctly accepted as the measure of Westernization, according to him, the West will not be considered as a geographical concept anymore (Özakpınar 2000, pp. 207–11). Turhan negates such an oppressive and authoritarian Westernization in this sense; he claims that it is possible to achieve civilization (this is Western civilization, needless to say) by developing a scientific mentality.

CIVILIZATION-PROGRESS AND CONSERVATIVE-ISLAMIST THINKING

Most of the Islamist writers also attribute a positive meaning to the concept of civilization. However, in this case it is not Western civilization in question, but Islamic civilization that needs to be developed as an alternative. This effort was also a political opposition to Kemalist reforms. One of the radical criticisms against the official opinion of civilization in the Republic period belonged to Necip Fazil (1904–1983) who has been quite influential on Islamists in Turkey. Necip Fazil, like Peyami Safa, also says that the East represents the spirit and the West represents the materiality. However, according to him, the West is disabled by corruption and has lost its spirit (Kısakürek 2002, pp. 50–2). Moreover, Necip Fazil criticizes imitation and rootlessness. His perspective on the concepts of civilization and progress is different from that of Kemalist and nationalist intellectuals. He states that the material means of civilization should be sought in our roots, in an Islamic renaissance (Kısakürek 1982, p. 215). In short, according to Necip Fazil, the civilization to achieve is not Western civilization, but Islamic civilization. What is introduced by the West as progress is mostly a moral corruption. Therefore, the policies implemented in the Republic period are completely false. It should be indicated that even though Necip Fazil claimed that the West is in the process of a moral collapse, he refers to its material development in a positive way and prescribes a similar development for Islamic civilization to be revived.

One of the other important names that have had a remarkable effect on the conservative thought, Nurettin Topçu (1909–1975) was not of the opinion that the West was in a state of moral corruption. Because, according to him, it is not the culturally deprived parts of the society that develop Western ethics, but the men of church, science, and art in the West. Topçu states that these are the factors constituting Western civilization. According to him, science is not the property of the West. It sprung to life at the hands of Asian people when humanity was in its childhood period. However, it developed its full characteristics and gained consciousness of its own will after the Renaissance in European civilization, that we call Western civilization. Topçu claims that we misunderstand the science and the ethics of the West, and that the factors behind the science of the West are the love of truth and freedom of thought and expression that is necessary for the development of this love. According to him, if there is any super-ficial corruption in the West, the ones responsible are those who are shaping the morality of the West—the universities, intellectuals, and philosophers. The foundations of morality are respect, community consciousness, and rebellion against the ambitions of the human soul and the cruelty created by these ambitions. After these words, Topçu does not prescribe Westernization as the solution. In fact, Topçu does just the opposite and emphasizes the necessity for 'revival', just as Necip Fazil did: 'Let us turn back to our own selves. What [do] we have in our spirit that is our own, that is the product of our power?' (Okay 2009, p. 173). On the other hand, Topçu adopts some arguments that were raised by some German thinkers about technology and says that technology starts to operate independently from the culture, makes the human its slave, and eventually the human is described through matter. According to him, 'Today, American technology that is putting everything under the order of the matter is ruling in our world. Actually, this is the victory of the matter over the human; a victory that was being prepared for centuries in Europe' (Topçu 1998, pp. 17–19). Unlike many other conservative thinkers, Topçu relates the situation described in the quotation above with communism of the capitalist system. According to Topçu, Turkish intellectuals were mistaken by thinking that technology can be exported. But there is no way that a technology that does not emanate from the culture of a nation will benefit the nation. Besides, the produced technology must be a reflection of the culture. And for that, a philosophy that is based on the historical values of the Turkish nation should be developed (Topçu, 1998, pp. 21–3).

One of the important names of Turkish Islamism and Turkish poetry, Sezai Karakoç (b. 1933) also seeks the reconstruction of Islamic civilization around the concept of 'Revival'. According to him, contemporary Turkish thinking is all about transferring everything from abroad. The roots and sources of our thinking are dysfunctional now. Turkey is drowning in the missionary mentality and the preconceptions generated by the shallow knowledge provided by the West. Instead of developing a real intellectual tradition, we just drift with the tides of the trends and imitations. Karakoç acknowledges thinkers like Necip Fazil, Sayyid Qutb, and Mawdudi who are in search of an ideology alternative to capitalism and communism that emerged after the Second World War, and says they are the rising generation of Islamic thinkers. Karakoç thinks that the awaking and the spread of Islam is a sign of the revival of Islamic civilization. These thoughts of Karakoç are best expressed in his booklet *The Economic Structure of Islam*. According to him, when Islam is studied as a civilization different from Western civilization, it will be seen that Islam suggests an economic system that is completely different from both capitalism and socialism. Moreover, the principles of Islam flies in the face of the West, which is having various problems for it cannot define the correlation between economics and ethics and religion as lifesaving symbols; their pride makes them blind. According to him, Islam does not only have an understanding of the economics, it is the source of civilization and a wholly different world view. Islam grants humans the right of disposition over properties. However, the property is only a means, an opportunity, and a tool for a Muslim to get closer to the creator. The reason for that is that s/he accepts and even asks for the responsibility of having properties for the peace s/he will find in the eternal life by fulfilling the tasks that come along with these properties, more than the pleasure that will come with it (Kara 1998, pp. 381–408). According to him, a civilization is an action realized by the great sacrifices of men who have their ideals. It was created by the efforts of mankind to search and realize their main objective. Civilization and culture are not two separate things, as Gökalp claimed. If there is a civilization in question, it has to have a culture, too. Civilization is the effort of mankind to be as God wants him/ her to be, it is the monumentization and the institutionalization of this effort. According to him, for this reason Islamic civilization is an apocalyptic civilization (Karakoç, 1986, pp. 9–11). Therefore, Karakoç speaks of revival and rejuvenation in relation to civilization. A materialist progress or Westernization is not on his agenda.

Due to his critical approach towards the concept of civilization, Ismet Özel (b. 1944) holds an anomalous position in Turkish thinking. However, as Özel indicates in the preface of his book *Uc Mesele* (Three Problems), most of the articles arguing about civilization, technology, and alienation bear the traces of the criticisms about the alienation, civilization, and technology in German and French thinking. Besides, the books of the thinkers that criticize the concept of civilization in an Islamic perspective were translated into Turkish in this period. Therefore, what Ismet Özel does in general is to interpret these discussions within the frame of an Islamic reasoning (Özel 1995, pp. 14–15). Accordingly, Özel claims that considering Islam within the issues of civilization and culture means loading it too much with the institutional interpretation of the history of humanity. According to him, once we perceive Islam within the context of civilization, we restrain ourselves in time to see it in certain categories and interpret it within today's conditions only. Thus, we are fixated on the idea that the future society will be an Islamic society instead of a socialist one. However, those that shape the behaviour of a Muslim are the commands and prohibitions of Islam, not human-made notions.

Therefore, civilization as a concept can be understood completely within historical and social conditions, and it cannot have the opportunity and the privilege of being a determining factor of human behaviour. According to Özel, the efforts of Muslims to establish an Islamic civilization are inflamed by the reaction against Western imperialism and the West's intentions to diffuse its culture to other corners of the world. Besides that, the one who is speaking of other civilizations and praising them is again the West. But it forms a hierarchical relationship between its own civilization and that of others (Özel, 1995, pp. 123–4). Nedvi, whose book *On the Religion and the Civilization* was translated into Turkish, questioned the concept of civilization too. According to him, most of the palaces, castles, architectures, and art works that are presented as the symbols of Islamic civilization belong to a pompous period that does not suit Islam (Nedvi 1976). Özel refers to this book and says that the establishment of the civilizations is based on the formation of social classes and exploitation of humans by other humans. Therefore, no matter how well intentioned they are, the claims to establish an Islamic civilization presents a danger. Objecting to the claim that civilization pertains to Europe and attempting to compete with it will serve the ones who want to make Islam blend in with other social structures and turn it into an ideology that would act as stuffing to support those structures (Özel, 1995, p. 140). Özel develops a similar approach towards the issue of technology. According to him, technology is a sign of overstepping the limits as the servants of Allah. Therefore, Western technology, as it is now, cannot have a place in the patterns of an Islamic life and it differs from the science whose main objective is to find the truth. According to him, civilization in today's context accords an important place to the idea of progress in the education it provides. Civilization adopts it as its duty to carve the thought into the minds of people that human beings are in a continuous process of development and moving towards a better future. That means nothing but the legitimization of a certain tyranny (Özel 1995, pp. 177–85). In conclusion, Özel follows a different path by critiquing the concepts of progress, civilization, and technology that were hitherto mostly discussed only so that ways to obtain them could be found. However, he did not develop these thoughts in the following year; on the contrary, he abandoned them.

TRADITIONALISM: REVIVAL OF THE CIVILIZATION

Rosemary Hicks tells an interesting story about the establishment of the Center of Islamic Studies in the US. According to her, after the Second World War, people like Wilfred Cantwell Smith (1916–2000) and H. A. R. Gibb played an important role in the establishment of the centres for Islamic studies in various universities in America and Canada. The main objective of the centres established in the universities like Princeton, Harvard, McGill, and Yale with the support of various foundations, particularly Rockefeller and Ford Foundations, was to do research on the current movements of thought and political structures in Islamic geography in order to create an Islamic world that is in line with democracy and capitalism. For that purpose, it also aimed to collaborate with Islamic organizations that are adaptable to modernization. Especially Sufism in Iran and Hindu–Islam geography was considered as the Islamic movement most adaptable to the modern world. Gibb and Smith were cooperating within this scope, and Fazlu'r-Rahman and Seyyed Hossein Nasr were among the people whom Gibb introduced to Smith. Smith believed that Islamic liberalism could be realized through Sufism. But this Sufism was not the Sufism of the Middle Age that is focused on the hereafter, but was a 'liberal neosufism', adaptable to the modern world. According to Hicks, Nasr became distant to this modernization project in the 1950s and because he was especially impressed by the writings of Europeans on Sufism, he claimed that Sufism was the common point of all religions and contains a universal truth, and he developed an antimodernist stance. However, this antimodernist stance of his was politically in tune with liberal Islam. Later on, Nasr did research on Ibn Arabi and Mulla Sadra, who is an Iranian scholiast of Ibn Arabi's works, together with Toshiko Izutsu. Hicks mentions that Smith and Fazlu'r-Rahman were not pleased with the antimodernist stance and his commitment to Sharia, but they perceived it as a modernist Sufist initiative against reactionary approaches (Hicks 2011, pp. 141–58). Hicks's expressions place the traditional understanding of Islam that created a great impact in Islamic world on a quiet political ground and brings it under suspicion in many aspects. But Nasr claimed that his purpose was not the modernization of Islam as of Smith's, but the revitalization of Islam (Hicks 2011, p. 159). In a chapter titled 'What

Is Traditional Islam?' in his famous work named *Islam in the Modern World*, Nasr first explains what tradition means to him. He uses this word in the same sense as René Guénon did: tradition to him is various expressions of the humans' understanding of the revelation in the historical process. And Nasr defines traditional Islam as the summation that has shaped people's lives and world views for fourteen centuries, free from the limitations of time and space. According to him, traditional Islam is a whole that is constituted by the Qur'an and Sunnah, particularly *tawhid* belief (belief in the indivisible oneness of Allah), authentic hadith books, the Sharia, classic *fiqh* and *kalam* schools, Sufism and *hikmah* (Islamic philosophy), and Islamic art and architecture. According to him, various forms of Islam, including Sunnism and Shiism, are a unique synthesis of Al-Ghazali, Sheikh Bahaddin Al-Amili, Mulla Sadra, and others, and the art and architecture of Ottoman and Safavid Empires have arisen from the Qur'an and Sunnah. Therefore, the tradition represents the divine, eternal unchangeable truth for Nasr (Nasr 2010, pp. 1–3). Nasr claims that his work is an effort to reveal the value of traditional civilization that has been neglected, unlike reactionary, fundamentalist, and modernist understandings of Islam. Nasr states that there are many schools and disciplines differing from and even criticizing each other within the scope of traditional Islam, and that a traditionalist defends them all. He says that this is because the traditionalists assess the various schools of kalam, philosophy, and Sufism with an Islamic world view. In short, these all are the different interpretations of the universal Islam. A traditionalist strives for the revitalization of Islam. What distinguishes traditionalists from modernists and fundamentalists is that they believe in the importance of the tradition and highlights the inner spiritual courses. Yet the modernist and fundamentalist approaches may highlight an external power that is above the will of God and based on fear. Besides, their approaches to technology and science result in the secularization of knowledge, just like in the case of Western civilization. Even though they claim that they are based on the Qur'an and Sunnah in politics and deny Western ideas, they just adopt the most radical political views in Europe since the French Revolution and produce ideologies similar to Western ones. However, traditional Islam is against considering Islam as an ideology (Nasr 2010, pp. 3–5).

Ahmet Davutoğlu, in an article he wrote in 1997, explains the resistance of the non-Western civilization against Westernization and their effort to regenerate their own civilization by developing a different sense of self. According to Davutoğlu, the sense of self is the reflection of the perception of self-existence and self-consciousness of the culture, the environment s/he is living in and society. It is culture that has a meaning. The ultimate factor that is needed for the formation of the sense of self is not institutive of a formal area, but a world view that places the existence problem of the individual in a framework meaningfully (Davutoğlu 1997, pp. 10–13). Ibrahim Kalın, reflecting on the ways to revive Islamic civilization, discusses the philosophical means of the revitalization of Islamic civilization on the grounds of the idea of Davutoğlu according to which the sense of self impacts civilizations and the conflict between tradition and modernism. This effort of Kalın is a continuation of the Islamist approaches of N. Fazil, I. Özel, and S. Karakoç, but it also represents differentiation from that line. In this sense, it is important to understand the ideas of Kalın in order to understand the differentiation in question.

According to Kalın, civilization is

> manifestation and embodiment of a world view throughout time and space. The world-view asks the most basic and general questions about the existence and its meaning, whereas existence perception represents the summation of approaches and stances developed in the face of existence. In this sense, the world view and the existence perception of a civilization contain both the theoretical and practical principles within itself. (Kalın 2010, p. 21)

Kalın claims that Ottoman intellectuals who could not understand Western world view and existence perception believed that they could take part in modern civilization by adopting the industry, technology, and European details in daily life, but the world views, existence perceptions, understanding of the universe, and the concepts of humans in the civilizations do not allow such a superficial adoption (Kalın, 2010, p. 16). According to Kalın, civilization refers to the whole that contains both metaphysical principles and concrete approaches and actions. Unless the beliefs, ideas, and actions that we define as civilization are conceptually clear on the issues of practical existence and universe by the world view, it is not possible to understand existence of the level to which the human belongs. While modern humanism that was developed under the impact of Cartesian subjectivism places the human at the centre of existence and meaning, modern cosmologies that were shaped under the impact of positivism consider the human as a meaningless entity in the universe. The contradiction of modern thought causes great confusion in the mind, to put it mildly, and people shuttle between being a half-God and nothing. According to Kalın, the perception of existence that is seeking the essence of the matter is somewhere out of humans' depth and he accepts that from non-living things to plants and animals, each entity has a personal meaning and value. This acceptance is, then, adapted to the social and physical life of Islam civilization comprehensively. The idea that each entity has an essence more than what is seen contributed to the science and aesthetics of Islam and prevented the reduction of the truth to one level of existence (Kalın 2010, pp. 24–6).

Kalın explains the meaning of his thoughts narrated earlier by making a similar differentiation of Nasr's dichotomy of the modern and the traditional. According to him, the source of the meaning in modernity is the individual who is detached from any relation and context and his/her subjective choices, therefore, freedom and meaning should appear simultaneously in the choices and the actions of the individual. What modernity promises is not the meaning but the freedom. Modernity gives all kinds of rights of choice to the individual who became the subject and, in this way, it frees him/her, however, the responsibility of imparting meaning to existence and life is left to the individual. Tradition, standing opposite to the modernity that embraces freedom against meaning, offers a meaningful life in exchange for the limitation of the freedom. Tradition considers the individual in a broader context of existence and society and opposes the atomized social structure models. The individual, who is part of a greater unity, can be an entity that has a meaning and is rational, only if s/he acts in concordance with this unity. The freedom of the individual is not defined by his/her ability to make limitless and unconditional choices, but by his/her ability to realize his/her own potential within this unity. This is because making unlimited and unconditional choices is not only impossible and but can also cause the termination of the existence of the individual. In short, while modernity offers a freedom deprived of a meaning, tradition says that freedom must be limited for the sake of a meaningful life (Kalın 2010,

p. 42). According to Kalın, a comprehensive and sustainable change in physical, political, scientific, and artistic areas will be possible only if we can change our point of view and approach towards existence, in the light of the philosophy of Molla Sadra. This is a process that will begin when the human makes peace with his/her existence again and comprehends that s/he is a part of a unity. The cosmological perspective, demolished by modern science in theory and the technology–civilization in practice, is in a position to be an essential part of this new perception of civilization (Kalın 2010, p. 59).

***

The main purpose of Turkish thought in the pre-Republican period was 'to save the state'. Therefore, modernization appears in its various forms in different ideological environments. Kemal and Islamists of the Second Constitutional Period tried to prove that Islam is not against progress in reaction to Renan and the 'Westerners'. For this reason, Islamists in the Second Constitutional Period had a modernist and progressive perspective in general. They stated that they should also renew their understanding of Islam as a part of their resistance against Western imperialism and domination. They neither criticized the capitalist system nor did they have an idea about the relation between capitalism and secularism. In the case of Kemalists, they denied the culture of Gökalp and argued that salvation is possible only through Westernization based on a nationalist discourse. According to them, Western civilization is the only universal civilization. In the case of conservative Islamist thinking in the Republican period, two main characteristics come to the fore. Topçu, Karakoç, and Necip Fazil advocate civilization but talk about a revivalist movement, not including capitalism and socialism. They claim that capitalism is based on the exploitation of both nature and the human, and they say it should be substituted by an Islamic economic system. In this sense, they represent the search for a system that would be an alternative to modern civilization both in philosophical and economical areas. Ismet Özel adopts a different approach by claiming that efforts of reconstruction, by centralizing the concept of civilization, will result in similar outcomes to those of other secular ideologies. Nevertheless, the common ground of all these views, including that of Özel, is that they represent a search for system that can serve as an alternative to capitalist and socialist systems and the fact that they developed an ideological stance against the modern capitalist system (West) within the concept of civilization. Because, according to them, a Muslim individual cannot adapt to the capitalist system and Islam civilization cannot be regenerated in this sense.

Nasr, one of the traditionalist thinkers, and his follower Kalın also seek the revival of the Islamic civilization, which can be an alternative to the West. However, unlike others, they do not politically challenge modernity or Western civilization in a direct way or focus on developing an alternative to capitalism. In other words, even though they do not put this into words politically. According to them, the revival of civilization is possible if the perception is changed and an Islamic perception of existence is developed first. Though traditionalism criticizes capitalism indirectly, it does not seek to construct a political–economical alternative like Islamists do. And it opposes to that consciously. That brings a question to one's mind: Can an Islamic perception of existence and the sense of self transform the system in the long term, as a traditionalist expects it to, and build an Islamic civilization? Or will the system transform the individuals who are not after developing an alternative to itself at the macro level? Many individuals who studied the nature of capitalism in the history of thinking, like Marx, Simmel, Weber, and Lukacs, emphasized the transformative, reifying, secularizing power of capitalism. For example, according to Simmel, one of the most important and identifying characteristics of capitalism is that it caused society to transition from a largely monetized exchange system to another system that is almost completely ruled by money. The logic of the money reduced everything to numbers and calculations, and the relationships between people are being monetized and materialized as well (Simmel 1900, pp. 90–8). Weber points out that one of the most important outcomes of the capitalist system is that things that were unacceptable before, like saving, stocking, and chasing after profit, are now seen as attractive, both morally and emotionally (Macfarlane 1993, pp. 263–4). Islamist movements that were named fundamentalist by Nasr started to go through a crisis after the 1990s, and considering their claims and their assertions about producing an alternative to Western modernity and the capitalist system, they fell quite short. Traditionalism is not directly in contest with the West and seeks a civilization by developing a new perception of existence in the face of the current system. This will determine the outcome of the efforts to build another civilization as well.

While Kemalist reforms that were implemented in the Republican period brought alienation into the circles of Islamist intellectuals against the new political system, the search for authenticity came to the fore (Aktay 1997). The most concrete expression of the search is embodied in the concept of modernization. The concept of civilization is ascribed a function that Mannheim attributed to the concept of 'utopia' in Islamic thinking. Mannheim says that in case utopia disappears, humans will be objectivized and a static situation will be created. Therefore, utopia represents the search for a better world that challenges the status quo (Mannheim 1995). The concept of modernization appears in Islamic discussions mostly as a 'utopia' against a Kemalist–secularist system and modern Western capitalization. An enlightened progress ideology does not play a part in the ideal of civilization among Islamists, but the impact of progressive thinking on them can be seen through the emphasis on material development, particularly made by individuals like Mehmet Akif and Necip Fazil. The sign of criticism towards the concept of civilization is Western thinking, as can be seen in the works of Nurettin Topçu and Ismet Özel. The concept of civilization has political, economic, and cultural dimensions for Islamists. Traditionalism that is more influential in recent times places utopia on a more apolitical ground by lightening the activist–political language of Islamists and represents a more intensive intellectual search. From this point of view, the rise of traditionalism can be interpreted as the decline of politically driven discourse as well.

NOTES

1. The most striking words of Marx are the following:

   England, it is true, in causing a social revolution in Hindustan, was actuated only by the vilest interests, and was stupid in her manner of enforcing them. But that is not the question. The question is, can mankind fulfil its destiny without a fundamental revolution in the social state of Asia? If not, whatever may have been the crimes of England she was the unconscious tool of history in bringing about that revolution.

BIBLIOGRAPHY

Aktay, Y. 1997. 'Body, Text, Identity: The Islamist Discourse of Authenticity in Modern Turkey'. Unpublished PhD thesis, Middle East Technical University, Ankara, Turkey.

Ayvazoğlu, B. 2000. *Doğu-Batı açmazında Peyami Safa. Doğu Batı*, 11: 107–31.

Baykara, T. 1992. *Osmanlılarda medeniyet kavramı ve on dokuzuncu yüzyıla dair araştırmalar*. İzmir: Akademi Kitabevi.

de Benoist, A. 2008. 'A Brief History of the Idea of Progress'. *The Occidental Quarterly* 8(1): 7–17.

Berkes, N. 1975. *Türk düşününde Batı sorunu*. Ankara: Bilgi Yayınevi.

Çetinsaya, G. 2001. 'Kalemiye'den Mülkiye'ye Tanzimat zihniyeti'. In *Tanzimat ve Meşrutiyet'in birikimi*, edited by M. Gültekingil and T. Bora, pp. 55–71. İstanbul: İletişim Yayınları.

Comte, A. 2000. *The Positive Philosophy of the Auguste Comte*, vol. III, translated by H. Martineau. Kitchener: Botoche Books.

Dabashi, H. 2001. 'For the Last Time: Civilizations'. *International Sociology* 16: 363–6.

Davutoğlu, A. 1997. 'Medeniyetlerin ben-idraki'. *Divan* 1: 1–53.

Debus, E. 2009. *Sebilürreşad, Kemalizm öncesi ve sonrası dönemdeki İslamcı muhalefete dair karşılaştırmalı bir araştırma*. İstanbul: Libra Kitapçılık.

Elias, N. 2002. *Uygarlık süreci*, vol. I. İstanbul: İletişim Yayınları.

Gökalp, Z. 1976. *Türkleşmek, İslamlaşmak, muasırlaşmak*. Ankara: Kültür Bakanlığı Yayınları.

Hanioğlu, M. Ş. 1981. *Bir siyasal düşünür olarak Doktor Abdullah Cevdet ve dönemi*. İstanbul: Üçdal Neşriyat.

Hegel, G. W. F. 2004. *The Philosophy of History*. Mineola: Dover Philosophical Classics.

Hicks, R. R. 2011. 'Comparative Religion and the Cold War Transformation of Indo-Persian "Mysticism" into Liberal Islamic Modernity'. In *Secularism and Religion-Making*, edited by M. Dressler and A. P. S. Mandair, pp. 141–58. Oxford: Oxford University Press.

Kalın, İ. 2010. 'Dünya görüşü, varlık tasavvuru ve düzen fikri: Medeniyet kavramına giriş'. *Divan* 15(29): 1–61.

Kara, İ. 1998. *Türkiye'de İslamcılık düşüncesi*, vol. III. İstanbul: Dergah Yayınları.

Karakoç, S. 1986. *Düşünceler I*. İstanbul: Diriliş Yayınları.

Karal, E. Z. 1999. 'Tanzimattan evvel Garplılaşma hareketleri'. In *Tanzimat*, vol. I, edited by Y. Abadan, pp. 13–30. İstanbul: MEB.

Kemal Namık. [1289] 1873. 'Medeniyet, İbret, No: 84, Zilkade 1289'. In *Namık Kemal, Osmanlı Modernleşmesinin Meseleleri*, edited by N. Y. Aydoğdu ve İ. Kara, pp. 358–61. İstanbul: Dergah Yayınları.

Kısakürek, N. F. 1982. *Batı tefekkürü ve İslam tasavvufu*. İstanbul: Büyük Doğu Yayınları.

———. 2002. *İdeolocya örgüsü*. İstanbul: Büyük Doğu Yayınları.

Kompridis, N. 2006. Re-inheriting Romanticism. In *Philosophical Romanticism*, edited by N. Kompridis, pp. 1–19. New York: Routledge.

Ihlau, O. 1992, March 23. Kriege führen für den frieden, der philosoph Karl R. Popper über den kollaps des kommunismus und die neuen aufgaben der demokratie. *Der Spiegel*. Retrieved from http://www.spiegel.de/spiegel/print/d-13682439.html, accessed 10 January 2015.

Macfarlane, A. 1993. *Kapitalizm kültürü*, translated by R. H. Kır. İstanbul: Ayrıntı Yayınları.

Mannheim, K. 1995. *Ideologie und utopie*. Auflage: Klostermann.

Marx, K. 1853, June 25. 'The British Rule in India'. *New-York Daily Tribune*. Retrieved from https://www.marxists.org/archive/marx/works/1853/06/25.htm, accessed 5 January 2015.

Moran, B. 2011. *Türk romanına eleştirel bir bakış*, vol. I. İstanbul: İletişim Yayınları.

Nasr, S. H. 2010. *Islam in the Modern World, Challenged by the West, Threatened by Fundamentalism, Keeping Faith with Tradition*. New York: HarperCollins.

Nedvi, Ebu'l H. 1976. *Din ve medeniyet üzerine*, translated by E. Harman. İstanbul: Kaynak Yayınları.

Okay, M. O. 2009. 'Batının iki yüzü'. In *Nurettin Topçu*, edited by İ. Kara, pp. 107–15. Ankara: Kültür ve Turizm Bakanlığı Yayınları.

Özakpınar, Y. 2000. Türkiye'de bir Mümtaz Turhan yaşadı. *Doğu-Batı* 12: 207–11.

Özel, İ. 1995. *Üç mesele*. İstanbul: Şule Yayınları.

Popper, K. R. 1979. *Das elend des historizismus*. Tübingen: J. C. Mohr (Paul Siebeck).

Sabahattin, P. M. 1950. *Türkiye nasıl kurtarılabilir?* İstanbul: Türkiye Yayınevi.

Safa, P. t.y. *Türk inkılabına bakışlar*. Ankara: İnkılap Kitabevi.

Simmel, G. 1900. *Philosophie des geldes* [Paranın Felsefesi]. Berlin: Duncker and Humblot Verlag.

Siyavuşgil, S. E. 2009. Tanzimat'ın Fransız efkarı umumiyesinde uyandırdığı akisler. In *Tanzimat*, vol. II, edited by Y. Abadan, pp. 750–5). İstanbul: MEB.

Topçu, N. 1998. *Kültür ve medeniyet*. İstanbul: Dergâh Yayınları.

7 The Rise and Demise of Civilizational Thinking in Contemporary Muslim Political Thought

Halil Ibrahim Yenigun

> *It is not a little characteristic of the structure of the Western society that the*
> *watchword of its colonizing movement is 'civilization'.*
>
> —Norbert Elias, [1939] 2000

Very few modern political concepts have gained such a degree of near-consensus among Muslim political thinkers as has *civilization*. Indeed, the trajectory of contemporary Muslim political thought can be reconstructed through various narratives, each of which attests to a shifting trail of key concepts. For instance, a student of intellectual history can point out how the 'Liberal Age' (Hourani 1983, p. iv)[1] was receptive to such European socio-political concepts as liberty, patriotism, parliamentary democracy, and nationalism. Yet this reconciliatory attitude gave way to blatant rejectionism from the mid-twentieth century onwards, only to witness liberal Muslims entertain a revival of democracy towards the end of the century. Other scholars, such as Roxanne Euben, might deploy the Weberian idea of 'disenchantment' to construct another narrative to demonstrate how Afghani's disenchanted understanding of Islam revived reason's cherished position

196 Debates on Civilization in the Muslim World

vis-à-vis revelation (Euben 1999, pp. 15, 17, 86). However, this would be supplanted by the re-enchantment project undertaken by Sayyid Qutb, who criticized his predecessors for elevating reason to the same level as revelation, thereby multiplying the foundations that inform the ethico-political level of a Muslim's system of thought (Qutb 2005b, pp. 18–20).

One can complement Euben's alternative narrative by pointing out the recent trend that some Islamic scholars have resumed by deconstructing many traditional and Islamist concepts in order to distinguish 'the human understanding of religion' from 'religion itself'.[2] Hence, a new trend of disenchantment can be observed. Another case in point is my own dissertation 'The Political Ontology of Islamic Democracy', which seeks to frame an ontological narrative of contemporary Muslim political thought by identifying its shifting onto-political constellations related to the idea of democracy. This work has demonstrated that the Islamist rejection of democracy was neither a defining feature nor the result of a consensus among different thinkers and attitudes towards democracy at any particular point in time (Yenigun 2013).

Each of these attempts confirms the fluctuating nature of contemporary Muslim political thought as regards the thinkers' attitudes towards such borrowed concepts and ideas as democracy, nation, liberty, and homeland. However, the concept of 'civilization' proves to be an interesting exception, even though it is no less borrowed from the modern European socio-political vocabulary. Quite strikingly, Muslim thinkers ranging from the liberal to the fundamentalist parts of the political spectrum have embraced and defended this very concept in the form of a unique 'Islamic civilization'. Remarkably, in his book *Milestones*, Sayyid Qutb entitled one of his chapters 'Islam is *the* Civilization' (Qutb 1986, p. 105), even though this particular work stands out as one of contemporary Muslim thought's most serious attempts to purge Islamic thought of its borrowed and 'inauthentic' concepts and ideas.

This chapter is an attempt based on the emerging field of comparative political theory (CPT) to trace civilization's trajectory throughout the contemporary era, beginning with Rifa'a Rafi' al-Tahtawi (1801–1873) up to and including Hamid Dabashi. Although it analyses the rise and demise of this concept, among my chief concerns is to discuss this concept's current descriptive and normative value. I argue that for the last two centuries, the term *civilization* has possessed a primarily rhetorical value, for it functioned as a defensive tool that subjugated Muslims could use against the Western colonial discourse that helped justify and perpetuate colonial domination. Thus, the term *Islamic civilization* itself emerged as a defensive discourse constructed by Muslim apologists to counteract the project of the 'West',[3] which had first constructed 'the Orient' as a foil to represent its distinct and inferior 'other'. Beyond this, I maintain, civilization has had little descriptive and normative value for Muslims' self-understanding or self-projection. Moreover, I argue that its current deployment as both a descriptive term for various Muslim cultures' self-understanding, as well as a normative goal for Muslims to pursue a socio-political project in the form of constructing or revitalizing an 'Islamic civilization', is obsolete and must be overcome. Towards this end, I will pay particular attention to the work of Dabashi (Dabashi 2001, 2008), who has consistently sought to deliver a coup de grâce to this well-worn concept. Accordingly, I view all attempts to formulate a unique 'Islamic civilization' vis-à-vis Western civilization as futile pursuits of an outmoded way of thinking about oneself and the other. By the same token, the concept of dialogue among thinkers who draw upon different ontological sources should not be considered a dialogue among civilizations, a concept that is itself a power-effect. Any truthful and reasonable theoretical endeavour that aims to establish dialogue and peace among groups of people, therefore, must first debunk such essentialist concepts. My stance can better be characterized as 'post-Western', a post-Orientalist overcoming of the categories of 'Western', 'Eastern', or 'Islamic' civilizations.

In the first part of this chapter, I will lay out how the concept of civilization was constructed as both a universalizing and a colonizing discourse. Thus, as Brett Bowden duly notes, civilization must be taken first and foremost as an 'empire of civilization', that is, as an imperial idea (Bowden 2009). To illustrate this point, I will analyse John Stuart Mill's account of civilization to reveal several neglected dimensions of the concept. The second part will be devoted to snapshots from several Muslim thinkers' view of civilization in order to outline a trajectory characterized by the rise and demise of this discourse. Although the term *demise* does not insinuate a generalization for Muslim political thought concerning a wholesale abandonment of this idea, I would like to show how an idea that was once almost universally embraced by leading Muslim thinkers who wanted to construct a specifically Islamic discourse, eventually came under serious challenge. As the critique of the project of the 'West' is expressed more vocally, along with all of its essentialisms, foundations, binary divisions, and discursive effects, it is time to put the concept of 'Islamic civilization' under the same critical and post-foundationalist lens.

THE 'WESTERN' PROJECT AS AN 'EMPIRE OF CIVILIZATION'

Civilization's (*hadara* or *madaniyya* in Arabic) privileged status among all modern borrowed vocabulary in contemporary Muslim discourse might be somewhat related to Muslim thinkers' familiarity with Ibn Khaldun's (1332–1406) renowned theory of '*umrân*, which is the core of his philosophy of history. A family resemblance can be considered between civilization and '*umrân*, in which Ibn Khaldun argues for a dialectical relationship between Bedouins (*badawi*) and city-dwellers (*hadari*). In this frame of thought, the key explanatory variable for the rise and fall of '*umrâns* (regimes/civilizations) is social cohesion ('*asabiyyah*).[4]

However, the modern genealogy and discourse of civilization and Muslim thinkers' embrace of the concept does not seem to be a direct legacy of '*umrân*. In fact, civilization's emergence and global spread during the early modern era proves that it is something more than simply a descriptive tool for social scientific analysis, just like the emergence of the concept of culture[5] was not simply a response to the need for an analytical tool for ethnographic and anthropological research. The identification of the distinct stages of human progress provided the foundations of these research fields that, in turn, served as the sources of the theories of human progress (Bowden 2009, p. 53).

Bowden sets out to document how 'civilization' as a word conceals an imperial idea behind its known family of meanings, such as 'advancements in comfort, increased material possessions and personal luxuries, improved educational techniques, "cultivation of the arts and sciences", and the expansion "of commerce and industry"' from its initial introduction into the French language, after which the word entered the English language circa 1750s to 1770s (Bowden 2009, p. 31). Eventually, and especially during the prime time of the Enlightenment, the constellation of culture, civilization, and progress[6] was consolidated at a critical conjuncture of 'Western' ascendance and domination. Therefore, as Nisbet puts it, 'From at least the early nineteenth century ... belief in the idea of *progress* of mankind, with Western *civilization* in the vanguard, was virtually a universal religion on both sides of the Atlantic' (Bowden 2009, p. 74).[7] These related concepts, consequently, reflect how that project's adherents imagined the particular shape of international society and continue to mould it via the deployment of these grand ideas, which are now taken as universal standards (Bowden 2009, p. 67). As Zygmunt Bauman also holds, the concept of civilization 'entered learned discourse in the West as the name of a conscious proselytizing crusade waged by men of knowledge and aimed at extirpating the vestiges of wild cultures' (Bowden 2009, p. 74).

Thus, it has been deployed over a long period of time and across vast spaces to describe, explain, rationalize, and justify interventions and sociopolitical engineering (Bowden 2009, p. 227). The imaginary of civilization does this first by dividing the world into hierarchies of *civilization*, levels of *progress*, and the concomitant enforcement of civilization accompanied by imperial civilizing missions directed those branded as 'uncivilized' or 'barbarians' (Bowden 2009, pp. 227–8). In this sense, deploying the concept of civilization almost always carried an implicit, if not explicit, dichotomy of civilized versus barbarian/savage, which then justified forceful civilizing missions. This, all the more warrants the view that the debate on *civilization* should not be discussed merely as a conceptual debate on its analytical precision, but, in the terms of Quentin Skinner, as an 'evaluative–descriptive' concept.[8] Simply put, this suggests that 'taken as a value, civilization constitutes a political and moral norm. It is the criterion against which barbarity, or non-civilization is judged and condemned' (Starobinski 1993, p. 31).[9]

It is widely noted that just as the Great Depression, two world wars, the Holocaust, and the environmental challenges made some people question the idea of progress, the ideal of civilization was also tarnished (Bowden 2009, p. 72), while such decline narratives as Oswald Spengler's *The Decline of the West* (1926) was already in circulation.[10]

Yet modernization theory furthered the concomitant ideas of civilization and progress as specifically prescribed for the development of non-Western people. In this sense, placing modernization, or the ideal of becoming 'modern', could not be contextualized without referring to what was previously called 'civilization' and the ideal of becoming 'civilized' (Bowden 2009, p. 70).

Interestingly enough, the collapse of communism and the end of the Cold War revived the concept of civilization, as did the global debates broached by the highly polemical works of Francis Fukuyama and Samuel P. Huntington (Fukuyama and Bloom 1989; Fukuyama 1992; Huntington 1993, 1996). As I will discuss later on when analysing Dabashi's approach to this renewed debate, although these works did not enjoy as much esteem among academics as much as they were able to set a new agenda for reviving the civilizational debate, the concept of civilization seemed to have re-emerged as a tool of social scientific analysis and policymaking. But apart from breathing new life into this well-worn concept in the so-called West, these new trends also found their more formidable interlocutors in Muslim-majority countries.[11] Apart from those polemical interests, even in a critical research area such as the emerging field of 'comparative political theory', most scholars unquestioningly adopted this concept as the unit of analysis for comparing 'Western' political theories with those developed in the Islamic, Indian, Chinese, African, and other 'civilizations'.[12] The critical issue, then, is whether this concept's descriptive or normative efficacy has any role to play in the desired 'inter-civilizational dialogue,' as long suggested by policymakers and academics alike. In a nutshell, can civilization be salvaged in this form despite its historical baggage that continues to draw upon dichotomies that subjugate the other?

Mill's Parental Despotism and Civilization as the 'Capacity for Social Cooperation'

We can turn to Mill and his piece 'Civilization' (Mill [1836] 1977) for an interesting illustration of these issues. His endorsement of the European powers' paternalistic despotism over their colonies is often cited to undermine his credentials as a defender of liberty (Moloney 2011). Following in Tocqueville's footsteps, Mill also drew attention to the danger of social tyranny and the increasing predominance of mediocrity in the democratic age. In this particular essay, he distinguishes between two senses of civilization: 'it sometimes stands for human improvement in general, and sometimes for certain kinds of improvement in particular'. In its second sense 'it distinguishes a wealthy and powerful nation from *savages* or *barbarians*' (Mill 1977).[13] His aim is rather to talk about the vices of civilization, in a sense revealing the disruptive and contentious moments of the presumed link among civilization, progress, and Enlightenment thought. However, just like his cautionary remarks on democracy's levelling tendencies that end up in social tyranny do not impede his commitment to the democratic ideal, here his concern must be differentiated from a counter-Enlightenment or Romanticist challenge against civilization. For him, civilization's defining feature is 'the ability to act in concert' as opposed to savagery, a condition in which each person shifts for himself. Thus, 'wherever ... we find human beings acting together for common purposes in large bodies, and enjoying the pleasures of social intercourse [for example, agriculture, commerce, and manufactures], we term them civilized' (Mill 1977). Therefore, the most accurate test of civilization's progress for Mill is the power of cooperation, as 'it is only civilized beings who can combine'. The downside of this trend, however, begins to surface as the diffusion of property and intelligence transfers power from individuals to the masses, who are doomed to drive individuality into greater and greater insignificance. This also has moral costs, for these processes that eventually render individuals sluggish and unenterprising also make them stoical under inevitable evils (Mill 1977).

Although this piece appears to be more a critique of mass society, one has to note the distinction he maintains between savagery and barbarism. In his mind, savage societies are characterized by primitive individualism, which contrasts with a civilized condition. Yet he finds therein some virtue of 'original and vital expression of freedom' that he wants to retain under civilized conditions (Moloney 2011). Moreover, as civilization only denotes progressive development and not racial superiority, savages also have the potential of becoming civilized. In other words, they are in need of 'parental despotism,' even though this might amount to a differential treatment compared to that meted out to barbarians. In any case, at the end of the day we reach the same conclusion: Civilization signifies a people's capacity for socio-political cooperation and self-government and therefore renders several groups of 'barbarians' or 'savages' targets of various civilizing missions.

From this account of civilization in modern Euro-American thought, it is clear that the evaluative–descriptive concept of civilization carries a quite violent historical baggage, one that is hard to put aside when someone wants to embrace it either as a normative ideal or a descriptive term. The intrinsic distinction that civilization makes between civilized and uncivilized (barbarian or savage), as well as a constructed hierarchy of cultures that almost always accompanies the civilizational imaginary, readily appears as a hurdle to any meaningful dialogue with one's 'other'. In addition, it purveys a distorted image of one's own self. Apart from its historical baggage, the post-structuralist deconstruction of civilization's essentialist structure, as well as the 'intra-civilizational' contention and violence often overlooked by the celebratory treatment of civilizations, will be my focus while I seek to account for civilization's contemporary rise and decline in the Muslim world.

THE 'CIVILIZATION' THAT WE CALL ISLAM

The Early Nahda Period and the Discovery of Civilization as a Panacea

Rifa'a Rafi' al-Tahtawi (1801–1873), the pioneering figure of the *Nahda* (Arab Renaissance), is renowned for introducing modern French political vocabulary into Arabic, thus building a modern political discourse in Arabic. As he shared his observations on each and every aspect of French life in his *The Extraction of Gold, or an Overview of Paris* (Ṭahṭāwī and Newman 2004), he suggested using *watan* (fatherland) for *patrie* and *hurriya* (liberty) for *liberté*. His vocation was, in a sense, to act as a practitioner of comparative political theory in both its classical Greek sense and in the way his mind proceeded by identifying functional equivalents for the borrowed terms he introduced. Thus, he would suggest, 'what they hold dear and call liberty is what we call equity and justice' (Kurzman 2002, p. 32) and 'what we call the branches of *fiqh* [jurisprudence], they call civil rights or laws. What we call justice and benevolence, they call freedom and equality' (Kurzman 2002, p. 36).[14] Along the same lines, he embraced civilization wholeheartedly, for 'as civilization advances among the kingdoms of earth, wars diminish, hostility decreases ... unlawful enslavement and bondage end, and poverty and humiliation vanish' (Kurzman 2002, p. 36). Interestingly enough, he cited 'adhering to *shari'a'* along with 'promoting science and knowledge', 'advancing agriculture, commerce, and industry', and last, but not least, 'justice' and 'public freedom' as being among civilization's root causes or foundations (Kurzman 2002, pp. 36–7). In his mind, the laws delivered by the prophets were without a doubt 'the essence of true civilization' and Islam's principles have 'certainly civilized all the countries of the earth' (Kurzman 2002, p. 35).

Khayr al-Din Tunisi (c. 1820–1899), another prominent Nahda figure and pioneer of civilizational thinking, was a leading Tunisian–Ottoman reformer and statesman. Among his accomplishments was arguably his effective role in declaring the first constitution and parliament in a Muslim-majority administration: Ottoman Tunisia. In addition, he was known for considering parliament the embodiment of *shura*, the Islamic principle of consultative deliberation. He carried on Tahtawi's reform agenda *(islah)* and was fond of liberty and civilization, just like his predecessor. In a quite Millean fashion, he was strongly convinced that liberty was 'the basis of the great development of knowledge and civilization [*'umrân*]' (Tūnisī and Brown 1967, p. 160).[15] The decline of the Muslims was, in essence, political in nature and thus the solution would be of that kind as well: 'Europe has attained these ends and progress in the sciences and industries through *tanzimat* based on political justice' (Kurzman 2002, p. 44).[16]

Jamal al-Din al-Afghani and the Introduction of 'Islamic Civilization'

Jamal al-Din al-Afghani, the renowned philosopher, activist, and a founding father of the anti-imperialist Islamist struggle, was a heir of the Nahda's prevalent view that sought to reconcile modern European and Islamic concepts. He effectively combined the Nahda's modernizing views with the accomplishments of Islam's eighteenth-century indigenous revival movements, most specifically that of Shah Waliyullah al-Dihlawi (d. 1762). His ambitious reform agenda comprised theological, social, and, most significantly, political aspects in an integrated fashion. Perhaps one of the most remarkable features of his reform was his view on civilization.

Inspired by both Guizot[17] and Ibn Khaldun (Kohn 2009, p. 399), he was arguably the first Muslim scholar to formulate Islamic civilization in a way that subverted the unitary conceptions of civilization. This understanding would eventually become an essential trait of the goal held by almost the entire reform movement and Islamism: to revive Islam as an Islamic civilization. However, Afghani retained the Western dichotomy between civilization and barbarity only to exclude certain Easterners from the 'barbarian' category. Thus, he did not question this discourse's central categories, but only reclaimed them for certain Easterners in a counter-narrative. In a remarkable passage, Afghani, posing as an Indian, says:

> What has brought us to poverty and need, with our wealth exhausted, our riches ended, and many of us dead, consumed by hunger? And if you claim that that is due to a defect in our nature, and narrowness in our mental power, it is surprising from the sons of Brutus, who suffered for long ages and wandered in wild and barbaric valleys, that they should believe in the deficiency and unpreparedness of the sons of Brahma and Mahadiv, the founders of human *shari'as* and the establishers of civilized laws.[18]

One can recognize in Afghani the same admiration of a universal conception of 'civilization' (that is, human accomplishments in the arts and sciences) as well as a general increase in the planet's welfare and development. However, he is also quite critical of those Europeans who denied Muslims and Easterners the progress they themselves had achieved. Afghani's challenge, then, does not take issue with the civilized versus barbarian binary, but seeks to prove that some of the civilized Easterners had been misclassified and thus did not need this supposed civilizing mission. Even further, in some cases it is the colonizers themselves, as opposed to the colonized, who represent barbarity. After giving an account of the costs and benefits of Western civilization by juxtaposing its scientific accomplishments with its war-related destructiveness, he claims to see nothing but barbarism and savagery: '[T]herefore in this fashion and given these consequences, progress, science and civilization are nothing more than the abyss of barbarism and savagery. To me, today's human is below the level of the age of ignorance [*jahiliyyah*],[19] and even below the level of braying animals' (Mahzumi [Makhzumi] 2006, p. 118). His major objection to foreign domination was likewise based on its dehumanizing effects, as it 'turns native people into beasts of burden, who lose their higher human capacities of imagination and wisdom' (Kohn 2009, p. 410).

Imperialism, therefore, corrupts and dehumanizes both the colonized and the colonizer by removing both from the civilized level of humanity and returning them to the level of animals. Although Afghani never adopts a self-righteous stance of blaming the 'other' for the East's long-standing ills, he boldly diagnoses what colonialism costs both sides. Far from civilizing the East, he contends, Western colonialism produces systematic poverty and political decline.[20]

Afghani's appropriation of this discourse brings to mind certain problems that are intrinsic to civilizational thinking. Most importantly, by adopting this discourse as a rhetorical tool, he reproduces the above-mentioned binary only to remove certain Easterners (for example, Muslims, Indians, and Chinese, more specifically) from the barbarian category while referring to others, the Zulus for instance, as savages. [21]

His philosophical treatise *Refutation of the Naturalists* [Neicheriyye], which seeks to prove that religion is the true pillar of civilization, is his most obvious case of civilizational thinking. The Naturalists, Afghani's transnational and ahistorical arch-enemy, were doomed to corrupt morals and cause the decline of civilization. In other words, they were the targets of his invective not only because they were anti-Islamic in their creed, but also because their path was the major impediment blocking the progress of civilization. This was due to an imagined causal mechanism, whereby a false creed would corrupt morals and lead to political decay. He actually sums up his book's objective as unveiling the damage Westerners have done to civilization (Afgani [Afghani] 1997, p. 103n). As a case in point, the way he portrays the levelling tendencies of the communists, a branch of the Neicheriyye, is quite telling in terms of its civilizational language:

> This weak species [humanity] will be brought to the vale of perdition and will disappear completely.... All external and internal perfections, all material and moral progress, and science, knowledge and the arts would be destroyed. Man's throne of glory and nobility would be over-turned and he would dwell in the desert of savagery like the other animals.... When privilege and distinction are removed, souls are stopped

from the movement toward eminence and minds neglect to penetrate the truth of things. (Afghani, 'The Truth', in [Keddie 1983, p. 150])

Afghani uses this moral and universal language as his primary means to promote his reform agenda as a discourse of resistance against European imperialism and as the universalizing language of civilization. Hence, in contradiction to the claims of European 'civilization' about how it has benefitted humanity, despite the fact that the damage it has caused has obviated those very self-proclaimed benefits, he states that religion, the most superior form of which is Islam, must serve as civilization's true foundation. Many future Muslim intellectuals and scholars, inspired by Afghani, would put forth similar arguments to defend Islam as an 'Islamic civilization' without calling into question this discourse's essentializing tendencies and intrinsic false binaries. Islamizing the civilizational discourse by adding 'Islamic' would suffice for most of them, including the foremost rejectionist thinker: Sayyid Qutb.

Sayyid Qutb and 'The Civilization' Survives the Authenticity Test

Sayyid Qutb represents a paradigm shift in contemporary Muslim political thought from the more reconciliatory approach to Western ideas, which is observable in Afghani, towards an almost-total rejectionism. I would prefer to call his project a fundamentalist version of Islamism due to his anti-hermeneutic stance as much as his purgative attitude that seeks to construct an all-authentic Islamic *weltanschauung* (world view).

Qutb had his own reasons for this, most of which were firmly rooted in his strong foundationalist view of Islam. For him, the problem with Muslim societies went far deeper than Afghani or his closest disciple Abduh ever anticipated. Awakening Muslims from their apathy, cleansing the religious culture from superstitions and false innovations, and attaining political unity and good government were all necessary conditions for their revival; however, the problems went deeper. In his eyes, traditional oppressive and modern secularist digressions from Islam at the societal level had been so insidious that Islam itself needed a literal revival from its extinct state. Only a complete mental break with existing social norms at the foundational level could save Muslims.

This system (*nizam*) is clear-cut in its formation and perfect in its configuration. Anything minor or major in it is integrated with each other and is on a *foundation* upon which it rests, and it is from its preciseness that any element that is foreign to the nature of its complexion will change [the system's] nature. This system cannot accept any [foreign] patch ... because its creed and worship, the mode of behavior and interpersonal relations, all of them are connected to each other, are integrated and interacting, and each of them springs from a single creed with definite goals that *found* its social offshoots on its intrinsic complexion. Thus no social offshoot emanating from foreign philosophies or positions can go with it, even if in appearance it is distant from the subject of creed, such as economic or financial issues. We shall soon see that all parts of the system's components, whether they seem distant from the creed or not, are bound with a firm bond to and deeply touched by this creed. (Qutb 2008, p. 115)[22]

This holistic view (*al-wahdah al-kubra*) centred on God's unity (*tawhid*) seems to be the most purist form that a religious world view could attain. However, one chapter in his most purist work, *Ma'alim*, is titled '*Al-Islam Huwa al-Hadarah*' ('Islam Is *the* Civilization') (Qutb 1986, p. 105). Thus, one wonders, why does Qutb not classify civilization as a 'foreign patch'?

As puritan and fundamentalist as he sounds, Qutb actually never gave up his commitment to certain modern values, a reality that makes his thought more like an amalgamation of both emancipatory and fundamentalist moments. His endorsement of the French Revolution's values of liberty, justice, and equality, alongside the ideal of civilization, is a striking point for his students. For Qutb, Islam is an 'emancipatory revolution' (*thawrah tahririyyah*) (Qutb 1995, p. 76) and the 'freedom of thought from any delusion and superstition that would prevent it from improving life on Earth' (Qutb 2008, p. 30). Even during the last and most radical stage of his life, he never renounced his commitment to human liberation or civilization. Given this, how does one solve this seemingly paradoxical aspect of his thought?

One must regard Qutb not as a fanatic who would take Muslims as his primary audience and incite them to hatred of everything 'alien' (Western), but as one who appears more like speaking to a global audience and trying to explain what went wrong with Western civilization and how to fix it: 'We do not call for intellectual and mental social isolation from the rush of humanity. We are part of the caravan,

partners in the human civilization' (Qutb 2006b, p. 28). His solution—Islam—is the best way for humanity to overcome animality and
achieve civilization and progress, but only when it is properly understood.[23] Therefore, Qutb's aim for an all-Islamic world view does not
mean that he thinks totally outside the modern frame of mind, but
that he shares some of its ideals and poses Islam as the best way to
realize them. If so, what is the problem with 'Western civilization'?

For Qutb, who was writing during the Cold War, both capitalism
and communism represented the two paths of Western civilization.
He maintained that both of them have led humanity down the wrong
path. After the meaning of the French Revolution's goals was worn
out and drained of any new ideals, Euro-American civilization became
fixated on material development and industry. However, 'humanity
cannot live on industrial production alone. It is in constant need of
new principles and ideas, ones that will give it stability, *change, progress,* and *development*' (Qutb 2008, pp. 18–19).[24]

As if Islam were at the end of a dialectical process, Qutb maintains
that liberal capitalism and communism, which made up for some of
capitalism's deficiencies, have reached a stalemate: 'Communism is
the endpoint of the natural course of material civilization.... Thus a
new system and a new thought are needed, in the shade of which
humanity will sustain itself', namely, Islam (Qutb 2008, p. 27).

At this point, Qutb reiterates the Qur'anic conception of the
human being as God's vicegerent (*khalifah*) who has been entrusted
with modifying, transforming, developing, and progressing humanity (Qutb 2005a, pp. 175–6). While discussing this obligation, Qutb
also draws upon a certain view of human nature, one that has been
either fulfilled or negated by modern Western civilization. His major
inspiration here is Alexis Carrel, another 'Western' thinker.[25]

As his point of departure, Qutb takes Carrel's idea that despite our
vast knowledge of the natural sciences, we have not made—and probably will never make—enough progress in the human sciences.[26]
Thus 'we are in absolute ignorance about the human'. Then how is
a human being going to discharge his duty as God's vicegerent? In
Qutb's view, the vicegerent can manage Earth's affairs; however, the
method (*manhaj*) of life is posited by God, who rules over this life
as well as the hereafter. Modern civilization, by defying this absolute
ignorance and purporting to know human nature and the method

of life through the modern sciences, in fact dehumanizes, alienates, subjugates, and undermines individuality by depriving humans of their spirituality (Qutb 1967, pp. 124–31).

A human civilization will be built on the basis of these given premises, thereby saving the human individual's 'true nature' (Carrel 1935, pp. 286–99). Only Islam, in its role of humanity's leader, can transform the sciences and discoveries into means of compassion, civilization, and peace (Qutb 2006a, p. 167), because no other religion was revealed to build a civilization for a certain society and show its people how to live within it. If human beings submit to the method of life revealed by God, a moral and sustainable civilization will ensue, one that the two Western alternatives have failed to deliver. This is the meaning of his declaration that 'Islam is *the* civilization'. Yet the fact that Islam is constructed as a civilization, a quite modern construct with its questionable historical legacy, is nowhere mentioned in his purgative attempts to create an all-authentic Islamic world view absolutely based on Qur'anic conceptions.

Shariati and Ozel: Shattering the Civilizational Discourse

Ali Shariati (1903–1977), an Iranian sociologist and author of *Civilization and Modernization* (Shariati [1984]) stands out as a far more eclectic thinker than Qutb, even though both share quite a strong commitment to social justice as an Islamic ideal. Shariati is not particularly known for his emphasis on Islamic authenticity and, thus unlike Qutb, did not declare many Euro-American concepts and ideologies as alien and heretical. Nonetheless, he managed to pose a timely challenge to the discourse of civilization for the false hierarchies it implies and the violence it has committed, even though he did not subvert or abandon civilizational thinking altogether. In this short sketch I will bring up the disruptive moments in two of his works, namely, *Civilization and Modernization* and *Reflections of a Concerned Muslim on the Plight of Oppressed People* (Shariati [1977]), in order to outline his stance towards civilizational thinking.

As a sociological category, civilization seems to bear an objective reality in Shariati's mind, as he does not hesitate to refer to a 'genuine' civilization: 'A more important issue is the relationship between an imposed modernization and genuine civilization. Unfortunately modernity has been imposed on us, the non-European nations, in the guise of civilization' (Shariati [1984]). Here, while he recognizes culture, civilization, and modernization as objective and descriptive categories, he is more interested in distinguishing between modernization and civilization. In this, he resembles many other non-Western intellectuals of his time who resisted modernization theory's attempts to impose a unilinear path on their peoples' movement towards modernization, development, civilization, and Westernization, all of which meant one and the same thing:

> Therefore, the Europeans had to make non-Europeans equate 'modernization' with 'civilization' to impose the new consumption pattern upon them, since everyone has a desire for civilization. 'Modernization' was defined as 'civilization' and thus people cooperated with the European plans to modernize.... Civilization and culture are not European-made products whose ownership makes anyone civilized. But they made us believe that all modernization nonsense was a manifestation of civilization! (Shariati [1984])

Here Shariati seeks to disentangle civilization and modernization in order to oppose the latter and affirm a 'genuine' human civilization. The very category of 'civilization' does not seem to have been contested. However, one can find a more radical challenge to it in his later work, where he relates a story of his journey to Africa. As he introduces himself as a person who is 'deeply interested in human civilization and heritage' (Shariati [1977]) he decides to see the pyramids of Egypt, 'this great monument of civilization' (Shariati [1977]). While he was amazed by that wonderful work, he learns that 'a few stones' located around the pyramids indicated the mass graves of slave labourers who were crushed under the heavy loads during the construction of these monuments of civilization. He then relates his feelings:

> I looked back to the Pyramids and realized that despite their magnificence, they were so strange to and distant from me! In other words, I felt so much hatred towards the great monuments of civilization which throughout history were raised upon the bones of my predecessors!... This was how all the great monuments of civilization were constructed at the expense of the flesh and blood of my predecessors! I viewed civilization as a curse. I realized that the feelings of all those people buried together in the ditches were once the same as mine. I returned from

my visit and wrote one of them a letter describing what had transpired in the past five thousand years. He was not living in those thousands of years, but slavery existed in one form or another! (Shariati [1977])

As Shariati points out the inherent violence involved in the construction of civilizations, he identifies himself with the slaves and distances himself from civilization altogether—perhaps the first time in contemporary Muslim thought that civilization in and of itself is not celebrated. The more important element of his subversion is that his anti-civilizational stance does not challenge Western civilization in the name of a more spiritual, superior, humane Islamic civilization. In his critical take, he neither spares 'Islamic civilization' nor seems to have any intention of replacing a false Islamic civilization with a true one:

I believed in the prophet Mohammed since his palace was no more than just a few rooms constructed of clay.... The great contests to build splendid mosques, magnificent palaces, beautiful houses for the Caliphs in Damascus [Umayyads] ... were all done at the expense of our blood and lives; but, this time it was pursued in the name of God!... The civilizations, educational systems, and religions have made human beings into animals interested only in financial security or selfish and heartless worshippers or men of thought and reason who lack feeling, love and inspiration as well as knowledge, wisdom, and logic. (Shariati [1977])

Shariati's search for an alternative—a saviour for humanity—finally ends not in the construction of an 'Islamic civilization' but in a vision for humanity that is characterized by the wisdom and action represented by Imam Ali (d. 661):

My friend, all those who remained loyal to Ali belonged to our suffering class. He did not adopt his beautiful sermons ... in order to make excuses for our deprivation nor the excesses of those who seek power.... He thinks better than Socrates, not for the sake of demonstrating mortal virtues of the noble classes in which slaves have no share, but for the sake of values which we possess. He was not an heir of the Pharaohs or those of similar class. He symbolized thoughts and considerations, not in closed libraries, schools, and academic centers like those who acquire knowledge, as an end in itself, living in the world of theories while remaining indifferent to the starving and suffering classes (Shariati [1977]).

In this latter piece, Shariati voices a view that is more radical than the eclectic character of his overall body of thought. Intra-civilizational violence and subjugation, which is arguably intrinsic in constructing any notion of civilization, had perhaps never been taken up so strikingly to dismiss the ideal of civilization itself. For instance, while Afghani called upon scholars to be socially concerned and said that they are wise only if they look for the cause and cure of poverty (Keddie 1983, p. 120), he still maintained an organic view of society in which some people had to perform the menial tasks for those who deserved distinction. Accordingly, his defence of civilization envisioned a division of labour without being very concerned about some people's subjugation. Qutb was a very strong defender of an egalitarian society, inasmuch as his view of Islam had a clear injunction to attain social justice. But this did not lead him to question the very basis of the concept of civilization, which might as well have been an 'unIslamic' concept that concealed the violence against and subjugation of certain people by others. After all, his overarching principle of liberty was that Islam had been revealed to emancipate humanity from being enslaved by other human beings and that any subjugating force would block the direct relationship between God and the human being. Shariati differed from both of them by arguably being the first to identify the intrinsic violence inherent in the very concept of civilization.

Ismet Ozel (b. 1944), the Turkish poet, thinker, and author of *The Three Problems: Technology, Civilization, and Alienation* (1978), is by far a lesser-known Islamist figure. However, his work deserves some attention here because of his uncompromising dismissal of the idea of civilization, perhaps taking it even further than Shariati had. An important detail of his challenge 'Against All Sorts of Civilization'[27] is that he wrote his essays on this subject right after he left socialism for Islamism. It might be hypothesized that his dismissive attitude may have to do with his surprise at Islamists' pervasive celebratory attitude towards civilization despite its antiquated and tarnished image among the wider domestic and international intellectual circles.

Reflective of his new commitment to the Islamic world view and the political goals of Islamism, Ozel contends that

> [I]t is vain to wish that the Islamic struggle that we are trying to actual-ize or undertake is going to end up in an Islamic civilization.... This

is not an attempt to revive the old Islamic civilizations, imitate them, or institute another Islamic civilization under the new circumstances. Just to the contrary, we must thoroughly comprehend how the Islamic state had been civilized and it is essential to move towards an Islamic society that would be in constant struggle to forestall such a civilizing temptation. (Ozel 1978, pp. 81–2)

Ozel thus not only rejects utilizing the discourse of civilization, but also suggests taking an active position to prevent the emergence of any Islamic civilization. For him, 'the caveat is that our Islamic concerns to construct an Islamic society will be overwhelmed by humanly concerns and the principles of establishing a civilization' (Ozel 1978, p. 112). Thus, it seems that if Muslims formulate their mission as not constructing an Islamic society but as establishing a civilization, this will be tantamount to striving for a secular goal. Ozel sees no other form of civilization like that of Qutb, a civilization built on the basis of revelation: 'Civilization is a natural consequence of assigning the supreme value to human reason in the arrangement of life and to the temptations of the appetitive soul as regards the fulfilment of human needs' (Ozel 1978, p. 110). Furthermore, he is of the opinion that 'in all civilizations, social organization tends to divide the society into categories based on wealth and to reinforce the institutionalization of inferiority and superiority. For this reason, being civilized amounts to a set of distorted and unjust human relationships' (Ozel 1978, pp. 80–1).

Ozel, who provides a genealogy of the term *civilization* from Mirabeau onward, concludes that it is an imperial term and emphasizes that even when Western civilization finds something of value in other civilizations, it views itself as the only one qualified to lay down the terms of the particular relationship in question. He goes on to claim that Western people have given up on using 'civilization' as their excuse for dominating the world and now employ 'culture'. But in either case, the current shape of the world, whether one calls it 'culture', 'civilization', or nothing at all, is stamped by the West (Ozel 1978, pp. 102–3). Drawing on Ibn Khaldun's analysis of *'umrân*, Ozel sums up his position by what he deems as three features of civilizations:

1. Civilization paves the way for stratification and exploitation of one person by another.

2. Civilization embodies human vulnerability towards matter and its dependency upon material development.
3. Civilization corrupts the social structure and human personality (Ozel 1978, pp. 107–9).

Therefore, Ozel views the belief that an Islamic struggle will culminate in an Islamic civilization as misguided. Moreover, any argument along the lines that existing civilizations are based on false premises and that Islamic civilization will spring from revelation, and thus will be superior to others, is nothing but empty words. If authority belongs only to God in an Islamic society, then no added benefit can be drawn from describing this state of affairs as 'civilization' (Ozel 1978, p. 111).

In many ways, Ozel's provocative anti-civilizational discourse is ahead of its time but little known outside his native Turkey. At the time of his writing, the self-deconstruction of the Western project from within through post-structuralist and *postmodern* critiques of the essentialist categories, as well as their discursive effects, was not so recognized. Only with Hamid Dabashi would one finally observe the deadly blow delivered to civilizational thinking. In this task, he draws on some of the earlier critiques as well as Western post-structural and *postmodern* thought.

Hamid Dabashi and Overcoming 'Civilizational Thinking'

Dabashi (b. 1951), an Iranian–American scholar at Columbia University, joined the Muslim debate on civilization by authoring several articles and books, including 'For the Last Time: Civilizations' (Dabashi 2001) and *Islamic Liberation Theology* (Dabashi 2008). His larger project is, without a wholesale dismissal of earlier attempts to formulate an Islamic ideology of resistance to imperialism, to formulate a new mode of Islamic liberation theology. His efforts stand out due to his participation in other modes of revolutionary resistance to the predatory empire. For him, this new resistance has to deal with the major novelty of our times, namely, the collapse of binary oppositions along with the demise of civilizational thinking.[28] Accordingly, he develops a different narrative of both the discourse of civilization and the Islamic reactions to it: Islamic ideology as a site of resistance.

Dabashi, very much in line with Bowden's conclusions, loudly proclaims that civilizational thinking is an Enlightenment invention that is 'contemporaneous with the growth in power of the globalizing empire of capital' (Dabashi 2001, p. 361). In a quite functionalist analysis based on how capital has operated throughout history, Dabashi argues that what European and North American people called 'Western Civilization' is a universalizing abstraction of the new class of bourgeoisie as a substitute for Christendom (Dabashi 2001, p. 363). Over time, this new construct had to invent various counterparts in the form of Islamic, Chinese, and Indian civilizations to both authenticate and superordinate what it called 'Western civilization'. In the colonial context of Muslim peoples, such colonial discursive efforts were opposed by developing an Islamic ideology that emerged as a mutation of the colonially constructed site into a site of resistance (Dabashi 2008, pp. 85, 171).

According to Dabashi's list, Afghani is the major figure who started the civilizational line of thinking as well as Islamic ideology. Thus Afghani 'set the discourse for almost two centuries of incessant re/formulations of an "Islamic Ideology", in direct and dialectical conversation with European colonial modernity' (Dabashi 2008, p. 41). As Dabashi himself sets out to formulate an Islamic liberation theology, he hails Afghani as the thinker who provided Muslims with a legitimate liberation theology that was compatible with their contemporary historical predicament at that point in time (Dabashi 2008, p. 41).

Dabashi's narrative of Islamic ideology and liberation theology continues with Sayyid Qutb, who reformulated Islam as a moral domain for a legitimate defiance of injustice. This is tantamount to a Qutbian liberation theology. But Dabashi does not adopt a static view by sticking with Qutb, for he contends that what is needed now is the reformulation of a liberation theology into a liberation theodicy, one that would be the legitimate successor of those devised by Afghani and Qutb and would not fall into the trap of 'an absolutist, puritanical, and totalistic disposition' (Dabashi 2008, p. 9). It would be designed 'to liberate humankind from everything that dehumanizes it' (Dabashi 2008, p. 257). He then proceeds to elaborate this new liberation theodicy's character. However, the new circumstances surrounding this task have to be delineated because the intellectual scene has witnessed the re-emergence of the civilization discourse and of Muslim polemicists who want to carry on that kind of talk.

For Dabashi, the resurgence of 'civilization' through Huntington is nothing but a defence mechanism to salvage an outdated mutation of capital and culture inaugurated during the eighteenth century (Dabashi 2008, p. 133). Even worse is the fact that the reaffirmation of civilizational thinking by Muslim interlocutors in response to Huntington is not only 'conservative' but also 'retrograde' (the result of the clash between ideological power and seismic changes in the material basis of cultural formations). Intellectual positions that seek to replace the 'clash of civilizations' with the 'dialogue of civilizations' fare no better in his view. He readily dismisses civilizational dialogue as 'a latter-day collapse into the bare necessity of will to power disguising itself as will to truth, pragmatics of power selling itself as political theory' (Dabashi 2008, p. 138).

Chief among the targets of Dabashi's condemnatory language are such thinkers such as Abdolkarim Soroush and Tariq Ramadan. He declares their attempts to be retrograde because, according to him, they have once again re-fetishized 'the West', which is nothing but a colonial concoction that had been all but surpassed in the works of Ali Shariati and that had never even been a factor in the more advanced project of Malcolm X (Dabashi 2008, p. 100). In order to surpass this new regressive thinking while articulating the emerging terms of a new liberation theodicy, Dabashi suggests that we cross over the recent works of thinkers like Soroush and Ramadan and go back to those of Ali Shariati and Malcolm X in order to resume a conversation with their unfinished projects (Dabashi 2008, p. 100).

All in all, for Dabashi civilizational thinking played a short but crucial role in the course of the Muslim world's colonial encounter with European modernity. However, it has already exhausted its uses and abuses 'in facilitating the operation of the globalized capital' (Dabashi 2008, p. 34). As a result, the West as a civilizational category has long since ended. As the iconic referent of European Enlightenment modernity, it has self-destructed in what is now code-named postmodernity (Dabashi 2008, p. 12). For the new participants of this discourse, civilizational talk, therefore, is nothing but an outmoded way of trying to talk with a dead interlocutor. In his materialist analysis, Dabashi finds it even more ironic that the new material configuration of capital and labour is already generating its own culture, which is at once post-national and post-civilizational (Dabashi 2008, p. 143). This will render any ongoing talk of civilization among Muslims even more redundant. What is needed for a liberation theodicy is a perspective that would not just realize but also embrace its normative shadows for those people who draw on different ontological commitments and come from different cultures and religions (Dabashi 2008, p. 168).

AFTER THE DEMISE OF CIVILIZATIONAL THINKING

Muslim and Western apologists alike can still argue for the existence of distinct and unique Muslim, Judeo-Christian, Western, or some other categories of civilization. In fact, it is not so far-fetched to assert that a good part of the people living in the purported borders of these civilizations still maintain a self-perception that confirms these categories. On the other hand, there might have been countless examples of non-Western polemicists who, in one way or another, responded to the likes of Huntington or Fukuyama by reproducing the very questionable categories that they presupposed (yet never proved). However, when it comes to providing empirical evidence or a normative justification for the concept of civilization with clear-cut borders and definitive foundations, hardly any intellectual endeavours can sustain it as an operational and meaningful category.

Among the European and American thinkers covered in Bowden's survey of Muslim thinkers I discussed in this chapter, hardly any of them embrace civilization and articulate a vision of civilization that does not essentialize either a religion or an intellectual heritage code-named 'civilization'. Likewise, it is hard to come by with any conception of civilization that is not defined against the conception of 'barbarian' or 'savage', or that provides a reasonable justification for the intra-civilizational hierarchies it presupposes. In short, we have not yet stumbled upon a formulation of civilization that could sustain any conceptual vigour or analytical precision and yet does not draw upon false binaries or essentialisms.

In contrast, sufficient examples exist to allow us to conclude that the discourse of civilization almost always served to justify the naming of a specific group of people as 'barbarian' or 'savage' and thereby to portray them as ones in need of parental despotism or some other kind of colonial intervention. At this stage, it is the defenders of civilization who have to show that they have conceptualized a notion that is immune to these problems.

It is essential, then, for Muslims or any other adherents of these civilizational constructs to revisit the analytical value or normative worth of perceiving oneself as part of a civilization and defining one's normative goal as building a civilization. All functionalist and materialist premises aside, it is hard to disagree with Dabashi's conclusions that those who continue to talk against the West are talking to a dead interlocutor, as no contemporary efforts can intellectually sustain a category of the 'West' apart from its received, customary use as a relic of the past.

For Afghani's contemporaries, it seemed relatively reasonable to assert the existence of specific civilizations against the dominant universalizing conception of civilization and even to assert a superior role for Islamic civilization as a defensive and motivational discourse. However, its endless and fruitless repetition at this point in time reveals a perspective that is stuck in a worn-out conceptual framework, if not in outright intellectual poverty. After all, even Huntington acknowledged the existence of civilizations—in the plural—regardless of his perception of them as essentially inimical to each other.

Therefore, it is time for the CPT project to draw upon more robust categories than the essentialist category of civilization, in the name of which countless discursive and physical violence has been committed. This is of crucial significance, given that CPT has been calling for *dialogue* among different traditions of political thought. Constructing and acknowledging civilizational identities at the expense of overlooking intra-civilizational hierarchies and violations will hardly improve the lot of a more and truly globalized political theory.

As this chapter has made clear, 'Islamic civilization' itself seems to be nothing more than a defensive discourse constructed by Muslim apologists to counteract the project of the 'West,' which constructed 'the Orient' to serve as its distinct and inferior 'other'. During Orientalism's prime, this Muslim discourse appeared to be a byproduct of a siege mentality, as well as a defensive rhetorical tool of Islamic apologetics used to prove that Muslims were also civilized. However, scholars and thinkers failed to sustain any intellectual gain for the concept of civilization beyond its motivational and defensive value.

Instead, the demise of this discourse brought about by Shariati, Ozel, and, most recently, Dabashi is a significant gain for the contemporary Muslim reform (*islah*) movement. A meaningful dialogue needs to do more than just overcome the essentialist categories of national culture or the pretentions of a universal civilization; it needs to do away with the far larger and essentialist category of 'civilization' altogether.

***

In this comparative political theory chapter, which has focused on the category of 'civilization', I argued that a 'post-Western', post-Orientalist overcoming of the categories of 'Western', 'Eastern', or 'Islamic' civilizations is an urgent step that must be taken and that this step is now more feasible than ever thanks to the recent efforts of some Muslim thinkers. In the first part, I provided a narrative of the concept of civilization in Western political thought, most recently surveyed by Bowden. This proved civilization to be little more than an imperial relic that continues to dominate subjugated people by imposing its standards of civilization upon them. On the other hand, attempts by non-Western constituencies to counterbalance the damage incurred thereby manifested themselves as mere inverted versions of the same essentialized categories.

Nonetheless, the construction of Islamic civilization has served as a discourse of resistance against the incursions of Western powers. Afghani's effort to posit a distinct and unique Islamic civilization was perhaps reasonable for his time; however, it is now obsolete and must be overcome. Qutb carried on this attempt by formulating an all-harmonious, all-authentic, strong foundationalist, and revelation-based conception of Islamic civilization, but his affirmation of the concept itself went against this goal. Moreover, he could sustain this concept only by imagining a category of *jahiliyyah*, which, in my view, is best translated as 'savagery' (Yenigun 2013, p. 214n). Over time, the subsequent challenges launched by Shariati, Ozel, and Dabashi as regards the very concept of civilization have helped debunk this obsolete construct of the early modern era. What I suggest to those students of comparative political theory who are seeking a genuine dialogical political theory is that they will gain nothing by pursuing 'civilization' or any other essentialist category that has been complicit in the discursive violence of the past and present. The task of a truly globalized political theory involves debunking and doing away with certain constructs of the colonial discourse.

NOTES

1. He admits his reluctance to use this term because, at least for him, the agenda of that age was not limited to such liberal themes as individual rights and democratic institutions. Although I also employ this term only to follow their convention, I would much rather characterize this era as a 'Rational Salafi' period, as I did in my dissertation. See Yenigun (2013).

2. Among the several hermeneutical approaches found in this deconstructive trend, Abdolkarim Soroush makes use of this particular distinction.

3. The West as a 'project' clearly draws on Asad's understanding of modernity and/or the West. See (Asad 2003, pp. 12–16). Accordingly, throughout the chapter my use of 'Western' must be taken as either the self-perception of those who see themselves as part of it or the perception of those who use it to denote their antagonistic 'other'.

4. For the complete exposition, see Ibn Khaldun, Rosenthal, and Dawood (2004).

5. For the German intellectual class' attempts to distinguish between *Kultur* and *Zivilisation* and to subordinate the superficial *Zivilisation* that deals with external appearances to the 'authentic' *Kultur*, which has to do with the intellectual, artistic, and religious facts or values, see Bowden (2009, pp. 34–40).

6. As Nisbet identifies its five major inherent premises, the idea of progress implies 'belief in the value of the past; conviction of the mobility, even superiority, of Western civilization; acceptance of the worth of economic and technological growth, faith in reason and the kind of scientific and scholarly knowledge that come from reason alone, and finally, belief in the intrinsic importance, the ineffaceable worth of life on this earth' (Bowden 2009, p. 74).

7. Emphases added.

8. (Bowden 2009, p. 8). This refers to concepts that perform evaluative as well as descriptive functions in natural languages. Apart from describing their object, they both 'commend and condemn' (Bowden 2009).

9. Cited by (Bowden 2009, p. 43).

10. '"[T]he Decline of the West" comprises nothing less than the problem of Civilization' (Spengler, Atkinson and Hughes 1991, p. 24).

11. For instance, subsequent to its introduction to Turkish intellectuals' circles, several edited volumes that brought together writers who

debunked the 'clash of civilizations' thesis appeared. In fact, 9/11 itself was viewed in this light by several inquiries as to whether this event confirmed Huntington's thesis. Turkey took a leading role in the 'Alliance of Civilizations' initiative, which was apparently an effort to counter the 'clash of civilizations' as worded by Turkish prime minister Erdoğan himself ('Erdoğan: İyiler Kazanacak', 2012).

12. See, for instance, (Dallmayr 2002).
13. Emphases added.
14. For an interesting comparative political theoretical account of Tahtawi, see Euben (2008).
15. He continues, 'the countries which have progressed to the highest ranks of [umra[n] are those having established the roots of liberty and the constitution' (Tūnisī and Brown 1967, p. 164). His use of the Khaldunian term 'umrân must be noted.
16. For him, it is a social law that God ordained for earth that 'justice, good management, and an administrative system duly complied will be the causes of an increase in wealth, peoples, and property' (Kurzman 2002).
17. As Hourani pointed out, French historian and conservative statesman Francois M. Guizot's (1787–1874) *History of Civilization* was held to have made a definitive impression on Afghani (Hourani 1983, p. 114). In parallel to Afghani's discourse against the *Neicheri* sect, in which he also rebuts positivists and nihilists, Guizot played an important role in the apologetic fight against French positivism. A believer in civilization as a total way of life, Guizot narrated European history as a continuous process of social progress (Jung 2011, p. 240). His *Cours d'histoire moderne* also impacted Tocqueville, Mill, and Marx (Jung 2011, p. 231). Afghani and his closest disciple, Abduh, read Guizot's work in its Arabic translation in 1877 and became rather fond of it. Afghani even inspired the latter to write an article welcoming its translation and expounding upon its doctrine (Hourani 1983, p. 114). Guizot's argument that the Reformation was the major force that enabled modern European civilization to arise must have been quite appealing to Afghani. Also, his holistic conception of civilization amidst European diversity might have accounted for Afghani's idea of proposing Islam, the religion of numerous politically fragmented countries, as 'Islamic civilization' probably for the first time (Jung 2011, p. 241).
18. 'The True Reason of Man's Happiness,' cited by (Keddie 1972, p. 105). The same sentiments are also discernible when Afghani relates Abduh's encounter with Lord Harrington, the British defence minister. According to this story, when Harrington asserted that Egyptians would prefer British to Ottoman rule, Abduh reproached him by arguing that Egyptian

patriots would never desire foreign rule. This time, Harrington claimed that Egypt's level of ignorance disallows such a differentiation between native and foreign rule in the minds of the populace, for this insight applies only to 'civilized countries'. After relating this story and Abduh's response to it, Afghani calls the readers' attention to how the British people see Egyptians and Easterners—as having descended to the level of pets and horses that are led by nothing but their instincts. Thus, the solution is to stick together and save their dignity and humanity. 'Here is the British and Their Views!' in Afghani and Abduh (1987, pp. 546–9).

19. This term will frequently appear in Qutb's theory of *jahiliyyah*. Note how it functions here as a rhetorical tool to invert the categories of 'civilized' and 'barbarian.'

20. Afghani provides several illustrations of how British imperialism, both structurally and systematically, produces poverty in India. For instance, see Afghani and Abduh (1987, p. 449).

21. Afghani and Abduh (1987, p. 547). While Abduh was arguing with Harrington about whether patriotism was an innate feeling, Abduh reproduced the very same antinomy by calling the Zulus a very savage but still patriotic people. According to his concept of an infinitely perfectible human nature, it can be inferred that Afghani does not see this as a permanent condition. But given his objection to imperialism, one wonders what, in his opinion, how 'savages' could progress and attain civilization.

22. Emphases added.

23. 'The human being spends all of his energy to nourish, modify, improve, and advance things on this Earth, and to undertake creations in the matter by God's will' (Qutb 2005b, p. 187).

24. Emphases added. It is fairly obvious that at this point Qutb criticizes the current human civilization from within, as a modern man, for not living up to its Enlightenment ideals. He demands not the abandonment of such principles as liberty, equality, justice, and progress as 'foreign' imports, but rather seems to embrace them as humanity's common ethical goals that Western civilization cannot deliver.

25. The book's preface states that it was written for those who are bold enough to understand the necessity 'to overthrow the industrial civilization and of the emergence of another conception of human progress' (Carrel 1935). In a sense Qutb takes up this task.

26. Qutb relates Carrel's argument that 'Our knowledge about ourselves will never reach the simplicity, refinement, and abstraction of the science of matter. The factors that have delayed its development are permanent. We have to frankly realize that the science of humanity is the most difficult science' (Qutb 2005a, p. 24). (He does not cite page numbers.)

27. This is the title of a chapter in his book (Ozel 1978, p. 80).

28. 'Civilizational thinking had a very short but crucial role in the course of the colonial encounter of Muslims with European modernity, but that it has now effectively exhausted its uses and abuses in facilitating the operation of the globalized capital' (Dabashi 2008, p. 34).

BIBLIOGRAPHY

Afgani [Afghani], C. J. 1997. *Dehriyyun'a reddiye: Natüralizm eleştirisi*, translated by V. İnce. Istanbul: Ekin.

Afghani, J. and M. Abduh. 1987. *El-urvetu'l vuska*, translated by İ. Aydın. Istanbul: Bir Yayıncılık.

Asad, T. 2003. *Formations of the Secular: Christianity, Islam, Modernity.* Stanford: Stanford University Press.

Bowden, B. 2009. *The Empire of Civilization: The Evolution of an Imperial Idea.* Chicago: University of Chicago Press.

Carrel, A. 1935. *Man the Unknown.* New York: Harper and Brothers.

Dabashi, H. 2001. 'For the Last Time: Civilizations'. *International Sociology* 16(3): 361–8.

———. 2008. *Islamic Liberation Theology: Resisting the Empire.* London: Routledge.

Dallmayr, F. R. 2002. *Dialogue among Civilizations: Some Exemplary Voices*, first edition. New York: Palgrave Macmillan.

Elias, N. [1939]2000. *The Civilizing Process*, translated by E. Jephcott, revised edition. Oxford: Blackwell.

Erdoğan, İyiler Kazanacak. 2012, May 31. ElTurkNews. Retrieved from http://www.elturknews.com/article/Erdogan-Iyiler-kazanacak.html, accessed 24 July 2016.

Euben, R. 1999. *Enemy in the Mirror: Islamic Fundamentalism and the Limits of Modern Rationalism.* Princeton: Princeton University Press.

———. 2008. Travel in Search of Practical Wisdom: The Modern Theoriai of al-Tahtawi and Tocqueville. In *Journeys to the Other Shore: Muslim and Western Travelers in Search of Knowledge*, edited by R. Euben, pp. 90–8. Princeton: Princeton University Press.

Fukuyama, F. 1992. *The End of History and the Last Man.* New York: Maxwell Macmillan International.

Fukuyama, F. and A. Bloom. 1989. *The End of History?* vol. 16. National Affairs, Incorporated.

Hourani, A. 1983. *Arabic Thought in the Liberal Age, 1798–1939.* Cambridge, UK: Cambridge University Press.

Huntington, S. P. 1993. 'The Clash of Civilizations?' *Foreign Affairs* 72(3): 22–49.

Huntington, S. P. 1996. *The Clash of Civilizations and the Remaking of World Order*. New York: Simon and Schuster.

Ibn Khaldun, F. Rosenthal, and N. J. Dawood. 2004. *The Muqaddimah: An Introduction to History* (abridged ed.). Princeton, NJ: Princeton University Press.

Jung, D. 2011. *Orientalists, Islamists and the Global Public Sphere: A Genealogy of the Modern Essentialist Image of Islam*. Sheffield, UK: Equinox.

Keddie, N. 1972. *Sayyid Jamal ad-Din 'al-Afghani': A Political Biography*. Berkeley: University of California Press.

————. 1983. *An Islamic Response to Imperialism: Political and Religious Writings of Sayyid Jamal ad-Din 'al-Afghani'*. Berkeley: University of California Press.

Kohn, M. 2009. 'Afghānī on Empire, Islam, and Civilization'. *Political Theory* 37(3): 398–422.

Kurzman, C. 2002. *Modernist Islam, 1840–1940: A Sourcebook*. Oxford: Oxford University Press.

Mahzumi [Makhzumi], M. 2006. *Cemaleddin Afganî'nin hatıraları*, translated by A. Yerinde. Istanbul: Klasik.

Mill, J. S. 1977. *The Collected Works of John Stuart Mill, Volume XVIII–Essays on Politics and Society Part I*, edited by J. M. Robson. Toronto: University of Toronto.

Moloney, P. 2011. *John Stuart Mill on Savagery, Slavery and Civilization*. Retrieved from http://ssrn.com/abstract=1976870, accessed 24 July 2016.

Ozel, I. 1978. *Üç mesele: Teknik, medeniyet, yabancılaşma* [The Three Problems: Technique, Civilization, and Alienation]. Istanbul: Düşünce.

Qutb, S. 1967. *Islam ve medeniyetin problemleri*, translated by M. Varlı. Ankara: Hilal.

————. 1986. *Ma'alim fi al-tariq* [Milestones]. Istanbul: Risale.

————. 1995. *Dirasat Islamiyya* [Islamic Studies]. Cairo: Dar al-Shuruq.

————. 2005a. *Al-Islam wa mushkilat al-hadharah* [Islam and Problems of the Civilization]. Cairo: Dar al-Shuruq.

————. 2005b. *Khasais al-Tasawwur al-Islami wa Muqawwimatihi* [The Islamic Conception and its Charararacteristics]. Cairo: Dar al-Shuruq.

————. 2006a. *al-Salam al-'alami wa al-Islam* [Universal Peace and Islam]. Cairo: Dar al-Shuruq.

————. 2006b. *Ma'rakat al-Islam wa al-Ra'simaliyyah* [The Battle between Islam and Capitalism]. Cairo: Dar al-Shuruq.

————. 2008. *Nahw mujtama Islami* [Towards an Islamic Society]. Cairo: Dar al-Shuruq.

Shariati, A. 1977. *Reflections of a Concerned Muslim on the Plight of Oppressed People*. Retrieved from http://www.shariati.com/english/reflect/reflect1.html, accessed 24 July 2016.

Shariati, A. 1984. *Civilization and Modernization: Reflections on Humanity.* Retrieved from http://www.shariati.com/english/machine.html, accessed 24 July 2016.

Spengler, O., C. F. Atkinson, and H. S. Hughes. 1991. *The Decline of the West* (abridged ed.). New York, Oxford: Oxford University Press.

Starobinski, J. 1993. *Blessings in Disguise; or the Morality of Evil,* translated by A. Goldhammer. Cambridge, MA: Harvard University Press.

Ṭahṭāwī, R. R. and D. L. Newman. 2004. *An Imam in Paris: Account of a Stay in France by an Egyptian Cleric (1826–1831).* London: Saqi Books.

Tūnisī, Khayr al-Dīn and L. C. Brown. 1967. *The Surest Path: The Political Treatise of a Nineteenth-Century Muslim Statesman: A Translation of the Introduction to the Surest Path to Knowledge Concerning the Condition of Countries.* Cambridge, MA: Harvard University Press.

Yenigun, H. I. 2013. 'The Political Ontology of Islamic Democracy: An Ontological Narrative of Contemporary Muslim Political Thought'. Unpublished doctoral dissertation, University of Virginia, Charlottesville, Virginia.

8 Revisiting Shariati

Probing into Issues of Society and Religion

Seyed Javad Miri

RE-PRESENTING SHARIATI

My approach in this chapter is to discuss Ali Shariati's main ideas in relation to my own conceptual framework by demonstrating his existential concerns and the relevance of such concerns in an inter-civilizational dialogue. It is argued that Shariati's point of departure is a religiously grounded one, but this, unlike the main argument of modern thinkers, does not prevent him from being engaged with the social self, which is grounded in an understanding of the dynamics of the historical process. This chapter is an illustration of how a Muslim intellectual can come to terms with modernity.

The *ulama* (religious scholars) in Iran considered Shariati to be a Marxist who blended Islam with Marx's notion of a socialist society and attempted to reformulate the Iranian idea of nationhood based on a Sartrean notion of 'authentic' by dressing it up in Shia terminology. His supporters venerated him as Muslims' Luther and hence a true reformer. Here, I do not attempt to solve these historical disputes or address Shariati's relevance in terms of 'traditional theology' or 'modernist theology' and their importance to the question of state on contemporary Iran. This is not to say that one should disregard the entirely relevant question of 'class' and 'power' raised by these opposing parties, who three decades ago gathered their respective ideological troops around the positions formulated by Shariati (such as the role of ideology and religion in modernity, tradition and modernity in relation to the state, and so on); indeed, Shariati's memory lives on in today's post-Khomeinian Iran and these political positions seem to be of profound importance to the modern clergy and their lay religious counterparts. These are significant issues but they have already been discussed and fall outside the parameters of this particular study, which takes as its focus the questions of social theory in an inter-civilizational perspective by emphasizing the convergence of social theoretical reflections in Western and Islamic traditions in existential terms. I would like to begin with a brief account of Shariati's biographical background before tackling his ideas and thoughts in relation to social theoretical concepts of modernity.

Ali Shariati was born on 3 December 1933 into a religious and learned family in Mazinan, a suburb of Mashhad, Iran. His father, Mohammad-Tagi Shariati, was a religious scholar with a strong social activist philosophy based on anti-Marxism. He hoped that by establishing an Islamic centre at the border of the former Soviet Union he would be able to educate Muslim youth about the erroneous beliefs of the Tudeh party, which represented Marxist–Stalinism in Iran. The young Shariati's first teacher was his father, who taught him about Islam and its social teaching versus Marxism. Ali Shariati completed his elementary and high school education in Mashhad. At teacher training college, he came into contact with young people from the lower economic strata of society and became more aware of poverty and hardship. At the age of eighteen, he started his career as a teacher in the north-eastern province of Iran. After graduating from college in 1960, he won a scholarship to pursue graduate studies in France. He received his doctorate in hagiology in 1963 from the University of Paris by submitting a partially annotated translation of a medieval Persian manuscript entitled *Fazael-e Balkh* (*The Meritoriousness of Balkh*) as his dissertation. In France, he got acquainted with five different discourses of modernity: Marxism, Orientalism, academic sociology, existentialist philosophy, and the postcolonial ideologies of Fanon and the Algerian Freedom Movement.

When he returned to Iran, he was arrested at the border and imprisoned on the pretext of having participated in political activities while studying in France. Released in 1965, he began teaching again at Mashhad University. As a Muslim sociologist, he sought to explain Muslim society in the light of Islamic principles, explaining and discussing the issues with his students. He soon gained in popularity with students and with people from different social classes in Iran.

As a result, the regime discontinued his courses at the university and Shariati was transferred to Tehran. There he continued his active and brilliant career. His lectures at Houssein-e-Ershad Religious Institute attracted not only thousands of students who were registered for his summer classes, but also thousands of people from different backgrounds who were fascinated by his teachings.

His book *Hajj* sold more than sixty thousand copies in its first print run, despite the obstructive interference by the authorities in Iran. The Iranian regime was so threatened by the popularity of Shariati's courses that the police surrounded Houssein-e-Ershad, arrested many of his followers, and put an end to his activities. He was imprisoned again for eighteen months in extremely harsh conditions. Popular pressure and international protests finally obliged the Iranian regime to release Shariati on 20 March 1975, but he remained under close surveillance by security agents. This wasn't really freedom, since he could neither publish his thoughts nor contact his students, and he finally escaped to England. Three weeks later, on 19 June 1977, he died under suspicious circumstances in London. However, his memory lives on in post-revolutionary Iran, where debates on modernity versus tradition, democracy versus theocracy, and modernist Islam versus Islamic modernity reign supreme in a chaotic manner both in the streets and in the universities.

In situating the significance of Shariati, many critics have argued that what he advocated was 'radical Islam', as opposed to the 'militant Islam' expounded by Ayatollah Khomeini. Shariati, in this depiction, made bold innovations in the interpretation of Shia doctrine, particularly in the way it applied to the relationship between religion, religious reformation, politics, and community. It is also argued that he advocated the use of violence to transform society into an Islamic utopia. Shariati's version of utopia was an Islamic state ruled by enlightened thinkers, with no room for the ulama; while Khomeini's, for instance, was an Islamic state ruled by the ulama, as representatives of the hidden Imam. Shariati's ideology is understood as a blueprint for the radical transformation of the social order. The agenda for Shariati was social revolution, whereas Khomeini had political revolution in mind, aimed at the young intelligentsia, many of whom found their organizational base in Mojahedin-e Khalq (Banuazizi 1999).

Challenging the widespread assumption of modernist thought that 'only the West has produced political theory', Robert Lee (1997), another exponent of Shariati, poses fundamental questions about the nature and degree of common political and philosophical quandaries across civilizations. He does so by tracing the contours of the modern Islamic search for authenticity against the backdrop of analogous pursuits by Western political theorists, from Rousseau to Charles Taylor. His discourse serves as a timely reminder that those who dismiss the pursuit of authenticity as the machinations of wild-eyed Islamists fail to recognize the way in which 'authenticity' acts as a familiar trope in modern and contemporary Western social thought, and also the fact that we need to attend to the nuances and complexity of Islamic attempts at pursuing theories of authenticity. At times, one may argue, the analysis founders in its attempt to turn similarities between radically different critics of modernity into a trans-civilizational search for authenticity, defined not only by common dilemmas but also by unswerving themes and analogous solutions.

The discourse on Shariati begins by identifying four crucial themes in the pursuit of authenticity as articulated by modern Western theorists: a concern for individual and cultural particularity; a radicalism defined by a struggle against both tradition and modernity; an emphasis on human autonomy in the creation of identity and history; and the 'unicity' of human experience.

Some may regard the decision to analyse Shariati in terms of themes derived from Western debate as problematic and biased. But Lee, for example, insists that advocates of Islamic authenticity must be understood, at least in part, in terms of their profound engagement with Western debates. He sidesteps the all-too-common temptations to essentialize what is often called 'the Islamic impulse' or to assume an undifferentiated, homogeneous West. He provides admirably clear and nuanced exegeses of Shariati's significance, while associating with 'the West' a mixture of arguments and anxieties that nevertheless reveal common preoccupations with the darker side of modernity. Lee (1997), despite his complex theoretical approach, seems to be unconcerned about finding the right balance between striving to understand what he calls 'authentic thought' on its own terms and practising inter-civilizational dialogue. There are other thinkers who have criticized Shariati from a liberal perspective based on what they believe to be his anti-progressive sociology. In analysing the problem of development in terms of transition from tradition to modernity, Ghaninejad (2003) argues that if we want a brief definition of the term 'development', we could say that it is an economic, social, and political process that leads the members of a given society to better economic and socio-political conditions. Through such a process, the standard of prosperity, well-being, per capita income, and education of citizens improve and they achieve modern and prosperous living conditions as a result.

This may lead one to question what this process is. It is, in fact, a transition from a traditional to a modern economy, and the achievements gained from it are the products of this process. The question for Ghaninejad (2003) is why this process is so slow in Iran. The reason is that our knowledge and understanding here have been lacking. Who is responsible for the country's backward condition? Ghaninejad blames modern Iran's intellectuals and scholars. He argues that those who have taken up this problem of underdevelopment have never presented a comprehensive, systematic, and acceptable theory about the causes of poverty and lack of progress in Muslim countries in general, and Iran in particular. When studying the works of these intellectuals, time and again we come across a number of simplified reasons for Iran's lack of progress and development, such as foreign elements, foreign exploitation, and imperialism. Ghaninejad argues that while it is unwise to deny the important role played by other nations in Iran's underdevelopment, to attribute it to foreign influence alone is a sign of intellectual naiveté and deprivation, and it is the latter that is a more problematic aspect of modern times. Ghaninejad argues that such intellectual poverty has prevented Iranian thinkers from impartially analysing and judging the reasons for this underdevelopment and the causes that prompt them to point the fingers of blame at others and avoid responsibility. Ghaninejad believes that if we cannot appreciate the realities of a situation, we cannot find a remedy for our problems. According to him, the main problem with Iranian intellectuals is that they have not had a sound understanding of realities and, therefore, have not been able to put forward reasonable theories.

Ghaninejad (2003) contends that Shariati, instead of outlining concrete and well-founded explanations for these problems of modernism and development, presented a series of fictions and illusions aimed at provoking people. He did not present an accurate evaluation of modern society, but mimicked the arguments of leftist critics—without taking any initiative on his own—and repackaged them as Islamic socialism. In attempting to explain why intellectuals such as Shariati had difficulty in understanding the concept of development, Ghaninejad argues, that rather than becoming familiar with the essence of Western thought that is based on liberty and rationalism, Iranian intellectuals have been influenced by a leftist form of postmodern socialist theory. He argues that this outlook is more compatible with the values of Iran's traditional society and, by putting aside the original modernism, these intellectuals have been unable to understand Western society adequately.

In order to tackle the contradictions between tradition and modernism, Ghaninejad suggests that Muslim nations should know that tradition is an amalgamation of beliefs and values that are often contradictory in nature. It is possible to extract many elements of tradition that are compatible with modernism, but, in order to do this, Ghaninejad suggests getting rid of models that are in principle leftist and clad in Islamic jargon by people such as Shariati, whom he views as being responsible for keeping Iran in its current intermingled and eidetic situation.

Ghaninejad goes even further and dismisses the very notion of religion held by Shariati, arguing that the Islam that Shariati introduced cannot be the real Islam because he censored himself and never tried to understand this reality. According to Ghandinejad, Shariati had the wrong idea about modern society; he believed that socialism was the ultimate aim of advanced society and since Islam is just, so is socialism.

In other words, Shariati is criticized by intellectuals such as Ghaninejad (2003) because of a perceived anti-liberalism and lack of traditional understanding of Islam (which is in fact capitalist-friendly in its attitude towards private property). On the other hand, among leftists such as Ali Mirfetros (1979), liberal democrats, and progressive secularists, there is a deep-rooted hatred of Shariati. They tend to view him as the prophet of retrogression, who, along with Jalal Al-e-Ahmad (1923–1969), another Iranian intellectual, attacked democracy and modernism and, in doing so, did a great disservice to Iran and the Iranians. The main thread of this historiography is that it was a mistake for Iranian intellectuals to fall for Shariati's version of Islamism in the 1970s and attack secular liberalism and democracy through anti-Western slogans, because it achieved nothing but reactionary backwardness for Iran (Ghaninejad 2003). There are also those who place Shariati's work in the wider context of Islam and modernity, and argue that he belonged to a particular school of Islam and modernity and that he belonged to a particular school of Islam that goes back to Seyyed Jamal al-Din al-Afghani (1838–1897), who was extremely critical of traditional ulama because, in his view, they discouraged any new creative thought among Muslims. Shariati, as a member of the Afghani school, believed that medieval mentality was primarily responsible for the decline of the power and the influence of Muslims in the contemporary world. The proponents of this position argue that for Shariati, Islam is the religion of action and must be energetic too. They argue that Shariati supported an action-oriented view of religion by quoting from the Qur'an that 'God changes not what is in a people until they change what is in themselves'. In following the Afghani school of thought, Shariati believed that Europeans embraced change and Muslims must achieve that in their own way by revolutionizing their cultural life (Hopwood 2000, pp. 1–2).

Lily Zakiyah Munir (2003) suggests that Shariati attempted to reform Islamic thought within Muslim communities through reason and revelation, by advocating the convergence of Islamic and universal ethics. In other words (like Seyyed Jamal, Abduh (1848–1905), Muhammad of Sudan, and Muhammad Abed Al-Jabri and Abdurrrahman Wahid of Indonesia), he was a modernist who did not fear or dislike the ways of the West. On the contrary, he welcomed non-Islamic ideas and practices that he considered beneficial to the progress and prosperity of Muslim societies. Munir holds that Shariati imaginatively synthesized Islamic and Western ideas to produce a valid and relevant interpretation of Islamic reasoning with an enlightened cosmopolitan, liberal, and realistic perspective (Munir 2003).

Within this perspective, Shariati is interpreted as a modernist, who believes in tolerance for diversity and is willing to adjust rapidly to a changing environment that may contribute to the emancipation of the individual Muslim and to the progress of Muslim societies (Husain 1995, p. 110).

Apart from these liberal and leftist critics, Shariati had his enemies within the camp of what could be called, religious intellectuals, for example, Soroush. In Soroush's view, Shariati belongs to the category of intellectuals who favour extracting their political doctrines from religion, in contrast to mystics, who argue that the world is an impermanent domain to be abandoned in favour of an inner journey (Sadri 1999). Religion for mystics, unlike intellectuals such as Shariati, considers the affairs of the world and those of religion as mutually exclusive. But for Shariati, argues Soroush, the abandonment of the worldly aspect of religion by Muslims and the abdication of political and social struggle are inimical to religiosity and religious order. Thus, what Shariati proposes is a new understanding of religiosity that embraces these neglected aspects.

But by doing this, argues Soroush, Shariati presents an ideology of religion that is the opposite of pluralism, and, in doing so, binds it to a single interpretation and generates a class of official interpreters—a result that, in Soroush's view, is not what Shariati had in mind. But this result is inevitable, according to Soroush, because Shariati 'wanted to make religion plumper' (Sadri 1999). In other words, many claims have been made in the name of religion and many burdens are put on its shoulders, and this is a direct consequence of presenting an ideology of religion that intellectuals such as Bazargan (1907–1995), Jalal Al-e-Ahmad, and Shariati have been instrumental in disseminating among Muslims, and is one of the great dangers in post-Revolution Iran (Sadri 1999).

Although these discourses on Shariati are of great significance, it should nevertheless be noted that none of these critics have looked at his discourse in terms of cross-cultural issues that contain themes of common interest across different intellectual traditions based on 'existential concerns'. But before exploring this aspect and addressing how my own understanding differs from the current view of Shariati in the literature, let us look at Shariati's thought in terms of an overarching frame of analysis based upon the concepts of self–community, sacred–secular, and religion–authenticity.

SELF AND COMMUNITY

There can be no more splendid a question than what 'man' is in Shariati's entire work (based on *Kaviriyat* or gnostic reflections, *Islamiyyat* or Islamic reflections, and *Ijtima'iyat* or social reflections) and in his religious-cum-political activist life. The very distinction between the different dimensions of his collective work betrays Shariati's view of the perfect man and ideal society: the fact that he viewed the self as a three-dimensional being with a social aspect, a divine nature, and an inner world that together constitute the unique nature of the human ego.

The human is a being-in-becoming who is in dire need of intro-spection, objective investigation, and projection (of his/her own ide-als and dreams in the world). That is to say that one needs to know the nature of one's own dualistic self through an inward journey (the path of Gnosticism or Sufism) to realize the historical dimension of divinity in one's own social setting (the path to becoming acquainted with the religious mode of society and hence Shariati's appropriation of Islam) and the application of one's internal and external struggles in the realms of society and history. Shariati's view of society includes the three dimensions he would probably prefer to call the 'Holy Trinity', that is, (*a*) a spiritual preoccupation among individuals in human society concerned about the meaning of 'revealed religion' at the heart of historical process, which would and should re-channel the spiritual force of humanity into life-giving and self-enhancing resources, rather than unawareness-inducing and self-alienating ide-ologies (which would become opium for the people); (*b*) a constant application and dutiful engagement with society; and (*c*) a belief that the results of individual gnosis and revealed truth of monotheistic religion should be tested in the laboratory of community. This is Shariati's view on self and society in a nutshell. I shall now turn to the underlying assumptions in Shariati's discourse on society and self and analyse its implications for his ideological construction in terms of wider socio-political issues of relevance for social theorization from an inter-civilizational perspective.

There is a longstanding tradition in modern social theory of arguing that empirical findings should not disobey the logic of discovery, which means that research should be conducted on descriptive terms and rendered analytically, without normative biases, be they positive or negative. In Shariati's discourse, the 'real' and the 'ideal', 'fact' and 'fiction', 'myth' and 'history' are not separable realms but poles of being or becoming, and the boundaries dividing them are surmountable by the will of the 'committed man' (*insane-e mote'ahed*) such as Abu Zar. In his view, the human being is a *mojod* (being) in the geography of *vujud* (existence). The very phenomenon of vujud is a spark of *eshq* (divine love) and the human being is the only 'spark' able to enhance the scope of her/his existence and aspire to the highest form of being, which is distinguished by the degree of *agahi* (consciousness/awareness). In order to understand Shariati's view of the human being, one should remember that he is a man of ideology—and I use this term in a very peculiar sense, which is uncommon in modern sociological parlance—that is, knowledge of the very setting of ideas as a carrier of a meaningful message. The idea of self in his discourse can be extracted from his view on the nature of *haq* (Allah) or reality. Shariati provides a key to understanding and unveiling his 'idea-logy'. He makes a distinction between false and improper realities and between belying occurrences and truthful unrealities. In his view, only a naïve person believes that all that is real is truthful and all that is unreal and has not actually happened is a lie. For Shariati, contrary to popular opinion, there are many truths that are lies since they never happened, and many lies that are real. 'There are so many truths. Absolute, proper and becoming truths that have not attained body, weight, color and presence' (Rahnema 1998, p. 161).

What is essential to Shariati is not the actual occurrence of an event or the authentic existence of a character, but the necessity of conceiving, developing, and depicting a significant occurrence, individual, art form, or message. The ideal individual, the exemplary poetic verse, the perfect gnostic love story portraying the depths of metaphysical attraction and divine beauty are true in Shariati's eyes (Rahnema 1989, p. 161). This methodology gives him a powerful tool in approaching social issues in a tripartite sense, that is, from the perspective of the ideal, the actual, and the revolutionary. The ideal is a desirable mode of being not yet actualized; the actual is the degrading or realized form of the ideal depending on its content; and the revolutionary act is the distinguishing feature of the self as a bridge-builder between angelic forces and Luciferious ones. To understand the ideas, one should rely on the symbolic universe of the holy tradition; to learn about the actual context of human life, one should learn sociology and history; to bring desirable changes into the society of people and within the selves of society, one should practise *Khodsazi-e-Enqlabi* or realize one's spiritual abilities and live accordingly (Shariati 1980a, p. 131).

There is continual reference to this trinity of ideal–actual–revolution in Shariati's anthropology. What the self should be is based on Qur'anic discourse, but what the self is is based on his modernist reflections (here one can find traces of Hegel, Marx, Bergson, Nietzsche, Fanon, liberation theology, existentialism, Hinduism, Buddhism, and so on). In addition, how the actual self can attain the state of the ideal being is based on Shariati's unique approach to the riddle of life. This tripartite methodology reflects the way he came to view his own life-long intellectual, political, and religious struggle— *Kaviriyat*, *Islamiyyat*, and *Ijtima'iyat*. These three elements collectively express his world view (*tawhid*) and, in turn, inform its modalities and practicality in a changing world.

The human being is a creature capable of elevating his/her lowly, animal-like existence to the level of God—the absolute manifestation. Man/woman, in Shariati's view, is a maker of ideals who possesses superior virtues and desires. The basis of Shariati's ideology is tawhid, a mystical–philosophical world view that sees the universe as one living organism, imbued with self-consciousness and will, evolving in a pre-determined direction towards a utopian goal. Tawhid allows no dichotomies—it is a 'unity in trinity' of the three hypostases, God, nature, and man. No matter how the observer perceives reality, tawhid states that the universe is a harmonious whole. One's responsibility is to recognize and accept this model of reality and move with its flow (Shariati 1980j pp. 308–9).

The apparent discord in the world is not an inherent tawhid trait, but stems from an opposing world view—that of *shirk*—imposed on the universe by those who reject the tawhid model. The world view of shirk is idolatry and sees creation as full of many equal but opposing forces. Shariati thus views history as an eternal dialectical struggle between tawhid and shirk. Tawhid is the 'natural', God-given order of things, while shirk is the enemy who has to be fought and eliminated. In Shariati's discourse, there are major concepts that reflect his religious anthropology, such as the path (*tariqa*), the pilgrimage (*hajj*), and the journey (*suluk*) to God. The human being is on an inward pilgrimage, returning from the exile of sin to God who is his original home and friend, and the hajj to Mecca is its symbol. Man is 'the way, the wayfarer, and wayfaring, engaged in constant migration from his clay self to his divine self' (Ahmadi 2002, p. 73). This religious anthropology comes to the fore more vividly when Shariati reflects on the dynamism of the human self within society and history. A human, he claims, is dialectic reality created of clay and spirit, a contradiction causing inward struggle and constant movement.

In the creation myth of Islam, clay symbolizes stagnation while spirit symbolizes a movement towards perfection. A human being's natural condition (*fitra*) lies between two opposite poles, a combination that creates an evolutionary movement of the human towards perfection. The real battle of Satan against God is not waged in nature, but within the human heart as one's clay nature strives to overcome one's spirit (Shariati 1980j, pp. 42–7).

Shariati thinks he has discovered in the Qur'an a humanistic philosophy of the great dignity, God-like essence, and spiritual nature of human beings. Adam symbolizes the human species created as God's vicegerent (*khalifa*) and superior to the angels. Man is the bearer of God's trust—free will—a trust that no other part of creation was willing to accept. God gave Man the knowledge of names, significantly scientific truths that even angels are unaware of, and a mission to perform God's will and create a paradise in the place of exile. Man is not merely God's trustee on Earth; he is also God's relative, partner, and friend. *Insan* (human being) is not a fixed biological reality but an existential choice. Insan is the sum of struggle and effort, and the result of *shenakht* (knowledge). Insan is an 'eternal be-coming'—an 'infinite emigration'. In short, insan is a dialectical being (Shariati 1980j, p. 44).

What makes Man superior to other creatures, in Shariati's view, is his sense of 'choice', as he can rebel and choose between good and evil. God's spirit within draws him up to perfection, while the opposing clay principle drags him down to stagnation. In the process of overcoming his lower nature, Man evolves and draws nearer to God. But God is not a theological substance as advocated by ulama. On the contrary, Shariati's God is a vital reality that lives in history and is different from the Aristotelian prime mover of metaphysical nature (Shariati 1980q, pp. 304–5).

It could be said that Shariati has a vision of the evolution of the 'ideal' human in whom spirit has overcome clay, freeing him from doubt and contradiction and enabling him to enjoy both nature and spirit. He is wise and artistic, not moulded by his environment, but forming it, creating a paradise on Earth. Shariati's ideal self is a philosopher and a political soldier and Sufi. Shariati was aware of the critical writings of modern intellectuals such as Herbert Marcuse, Heidegger, and Horkheimer (there are many occasions where he mentions them by name) who decried the one-dimensionality enveloping 'modern man'. To impede this global process among Muslims, Shariati urged his audience to aspire to become multi-dimensional beings and build a multi-dimensional society based on *irfan* (gnosticism), *azadi* (freedom), and *barabari* (justice) (Shariati 1980d p. 36). These three dimensions are for Shariati 'innate needs' that have been historically separated from one another (Shariati 1980a, p. 78). Freedom, justice, and gnosticism, he argued, constitute the inseparable triad assuming human happiness as well as communal welfare (Shariati 1980a, p. 78).

For Shariati, the notion of 'heroic Sufism' was an individualizing force rooted in the notion of spiritual chivalry of *futuwwat* (*Javanmardi* in Persian). Members of this Sufi order were called *fatiyan*, a word derived from the Qur'anic term *fata*, which the ninth-century Sufi master Qusheri defined as 'he who breaks the idols'. Shariati's Sufism, therefore, taught the individual how to win freedom from the chains of religion, as the prophet Abraham, the model *fata* had done. Moreover, Shariati was convinced that such a religious ideology was indispensable for developing the ideal Islamic individual who, through a fusion of reason and gnosis, would 'liberate God and His love from the monopoly of religion, freedom from the monopoly of capitalism, and egalitarianism from the monopoly of Marxism' (Shariati 1980b, pp. 48–9). Precisely for these reasons the Marxists detested Shariati, because in their view, he was 'Islamizing their ideas', although in his own view he was reclaiming lost religious territories intellectually.

Religious fundamentalists, meanwhile, despised him for 'liberalizing, democratizing, and socializing religion' (Rahnema 1998, p. 226).

Man is an extremely important subject in Shariati's social theory, because his world view is based on the axiomatic principle that perceives the mental rather than the natural universe of Man as the battleground of God and Satan, clay and spirit, polytheism and monotheism. This is another way for Shariati to unveil his normative view about society and the ideal form of a communal system. In Islam, as Shariati understands it, Man is not subjugated by God, since he is the Lord's associate, friend, trustee, and kinsman on Earth. God taught Man and all the angels prostrated themselves before him. Such a two-dimensional being needs a religion that will protect him from the extremes of asceticism and worldliness, and keep him at a constant equilibrium. Only a two-dimensional religion is able to give reality to Man's great responsibility (Shariati 1980d, p. 48).

What distinguishes Man from other animals is Man's ability to bestow meaning upon his own death by dedicating his life to a cause. To demonstrate this aspect of his anthropology, Shariati focuses on the notion of *shahid* (martyr) to depict the role of 'cause' in shaping of the human self. The 'cause' in his view is always intertwined with a sense of 'pain' due to the very fact that Man is a *mojod* and the story of 'being' is sad and mysterious. This idea of cause is extended to the communal dimension of humanity, where he argues that 'a nation is the sum total of all human beings who feel a common pain' (Shariati 1980t, p. 317). This understanding of nation and the human self opens up many paths in an inter-civilizational dialogue where issues of an existential nature can bring intellectuals of various traditions into a global debate in which points of departure are not the only determinants in the process of dialogue.

In order to understand the notion of community in Shariatian discourse, one needs first to define the human self and how he or she comes into being. The 'beingness' (*mujodiyat*) of insan is not an accidental phenomenon based on a purposeless whim of unknown forces. Being an insan is in its truest sense an act of 'choice'. This choice (*entekhab*) is covenantal and demands committed allegiance, setting before insan a constant challenge (called life). This challenge requires profound endurance or *sabr*. To realize this is to be conscious of the very 'painful' fact of life in exile, that is, insan's separation from

God. The story of being is the painful reminder that insan is 'separated' from his/her Love and exists in *kavir* (the vast desert of being). The notion of pain is at the heart of Shariati's religious anthropology and this is carried into his reflection on the sociological dimension of being as an individual self, as well as a communal being (Shariati 1980h, pp. 73–4).

The notion of community, however, is not a descriptive concept in Shariati's thought. That is not to say that he is unaware of descriptive sociological concepts such as 'society', 'nation state,' or 'world system'. On the contrary, one should credit him as one of the few Third World Muslim intellectuals in the 1960s and 1970s who was aware of both Western schools of thought and Eastern religious philosophies. At the heart of Shariati's normative notion of community is the idea of 'cause' that gives birth to a community or notion (Rahnema 1999, p. 120). To help understand this idea, it may be useful to introduce two concepts rooted in the religious tradition of Islam that were dear to Shariati's social philosophy: *shahadat* and Hajj.

One could hastily translate these terms as 'martyrdom' and 'pilgrimage', respectively, but to do so would be unfair to the 'semantic revolution' of the Shia tradition that Shariati brought about by fusing the ethos of existentialism and the piety of Shi'ism in the spirit of revolutionary socialism. By shahadat, Shariati meant a way of being and by Hajj, he meant a way of becoming. A martyr or shahid is not someone who wages a holy war and dies a mortal death. On the contrary, shahid is someone who lives for a 'cause' and Hajj is living one's life faithful to this cause. Hajj is not the annual pilgrimage to Mecca, which involves circling the House of *Ka'abe* and observing various religious rituals and rites. It is the act of becoming a traveller through the desert of life, a witness of the primordial covenant. Shahid is a man or woman who is like a 'sign' (*ayat*), displaying the path to those who are not yet initiated in the theophany of existence. Shahid is a person who intends (*ahang Hajj karsan*) to walk on the path of the divine (*Hag*) and bear witness to the primordial covenant (*mithaqe azali*). To do this is tantamount to carrying a weight unbearable to all those in the entire universe of being except insan. Insan sets forth and accepts this responsibility unknowingly, but once the realization dawns he or she experiences pain (*dard*), anxiety, worry, and *qamm* (a sense of spiritual pain that results in consciousness of frustration) (Shariati *Jihad and Shahadat; Hajj*).

This pain is not tantamount to *poena* (punishment), however. The *dard* Shariati is referring to here—and in fact prescribing for the *rushanfekr* (the ideal modern man who understands his time and society, a true intellectual whose existential being has been lit up by the spark of God's love of His people)—is neither trivial nor a *poenaical* kind of pain (a kind of penalty). Rather, he is envisaging an uplifting spiritual pursuit in the midst of communal life, which tackles the obstacles of societal life in a divine sense and turns them into an arsenal of self-construction or self-realization; this can be achieved by finding an outlet for the social ills one encounters, thus avoiding 'indifference' (Mohammad Ali 1994, p. 60). This is the kind of dard Shariati calls *dard-e deen*, which needs to be incorporated in the psyche of the *rushanfekr-e-deeni* (religious intellectual).

To undertake the burden of this pain is not a punishment but a higher form of 'consciousness' (similar to the one Jesus demonstrated before His enemies and those who crucified Him), which displays a profound 'insight' into the nature of reality that is beyond mere 'bookish understanding' or discursive rationality. This kind of pain is a gift and the beginning of true self-realization amid seemingly secular socialization because the real is Haq, and Haq is another name for God in Shariati's religious parlance (Shariati 1980n, p. 129).

It is impossible to form a community of selves in the school of pain without recognition of the categorical significance of 'cause' and the intention of bringing this ideal into the body of communal life. For Shariati, a 'human thing' (*bashar*) is not automatically a 'human being' (insan) endowed with the extra dimension of 'self-consciousness', which can only be realized by experiencing 'felt pain'. He then moves on to define a community or nation (*ummah*) as the sum of all human beings who feel a common pain (Shariati cited in Rahnema 1998, p. 120). If that pain is felt across contemporary borders of current nation states and throughout history, then Socrates could be described as a closer disciple to Buddha than his contemporary Rajas, and Gandhi a closer guru to Shariati than the mullahs in Iran. Similarly, a community of oppressed people in the colonial countries of Latin America could be said to be closer to Shariati than the affluent Muslim aristocracy who happened to inhabit the same geographical space as him.

The idea of pain in Shariati's view of the self is expressed within his discourse on society too. The concepts of shahid and Hajj also apply to the community, and the ummah should be a witness with the intention (*ahange Hajj nemodan*) of sustaining the heavy weight of 'cause' (Shariati, *Hajj*). Such a nation can be born regardless of national, ethnic, religious (in the traditional sense), political, ideological, and geographical boundaries. The pain felt by Shariati in his time was caused by *este'mar, estekbar, estesmar* or *zar, zur*, and *tazvir* (colonialism, capitalism, and religious stupefaction or Mammon, coercion, and hypocrisy). He saw great souls such as Fanon, Che, Mao, Lumumba, Sartre, and Massignion fight against these forces around the world; he identified profoundly with their pain and felt an affinity towards each of them.

It seems Shariati is suggesting that a nation can be born if a common pain generates a sense of commitment and the kind of dynamism that can produce *agahi* in those who vow to renounce all polytheistic allegiances and adopt a tawhidic world view. This cannot be accomplished without the necessary 'ideological apparatus'.

The mere existence of a group of people is not enough to generate the type of dynamic nationalism that produced Protestant Europe, for example. In Shariati's view, a 'human being' cannot fully emerge if he or she has no consciousness of self. A human organism does not automatically qualify as a human self unless he or she is acculturated or socialized, and it seems as if Shariati applies the same reasoning to human community or what he calls ummah (Shariati 1980o, pp. 494–5). Before Europe became largely Protestant, there were different tribes and groups of people who were unconscious of their own 'nationality' and 'language'. The colonial mentality of Catholic imperialism deprived them of their own vernacular dialects in their self-education. What led to the birth of Protestant Europe was the commonly felt pain, which brought people such as the English together and liberated them from the yoke of the Catholic Church (Shariati 1980p, pp. 86–122).

In other words, a group of people can become a nation and a community when they realize they share the same destiny and that arriving at their chosen destination will cause pain and require more than a verbal commitment to the cause. The cause demands total commitment, which is tantamount to a complete renouncement of life in death, not in the sense of glorification of death but upholding life without oppression. By shedding

> his own blood, the *shahid* ... condemns the oppressor [which is one of the forces that distorts the historical destiny of the community of God that intends to realize the tawhidi system on earth] and provides commitment for the oppressed. He exposes aggression and revives what has hitherto been negated. He reminds the people of what has already been forgotten ... the [upholding of the covenantal cause or *shahadat*] blood of the *shahid* is a candle-light which gives vision and saves as the radiant light of guidance for the misguided who wander amidst the homeless caravan, on mountains, in deserts, along by-ways, and in ditches. (Shariati, *Jihad and Shahadat*)

In Shariati's view, insan is a 'sign' in the theophany of existence and living up to such an ideal demands Hajj—a sense of purpose, and the intention to embark on a purposeful life—which elevates the man of clay to the heights of performer of purposeful life, that is, *Hajji* through *arafat* (knowledge), *mash'ar* (consciousness and understanding), and *mina* (love and faith). As a man of covenant cannot be born without a sense of purpose and the will to live life for the cause, a community of covenantal people will differ from a contractual society where the communal cause is a secular convention devoid of divine purpose. Ummah is another name for a covenantal community where men and women intend to embark on the path of becoming signs of God or performers of Hajj (Shariati 1980e, pp. 31, 43, 77). The symbolic stage of pilgrimage is traditionally set in Mecca and it seems Shariati is suggesting that it would be a grave mistake to limit the revolutionary performance of authentic existence to a few days of the year and to a small place in Arabia (Shariati 1980m, pp. 156–7).

Hajj (or living life as witness to God by achieving the heights of divinity) is performed on the stage of life itself and its borders are as wide as the world. Shariati implies that Ummah has no geographical boundaries. For him, community is not bound to a place in the way that the concept of 'nation' in modern social theory is. On the contrary, he is envisaging a group of men and women embarking on a journey that does not recognize geopolitical boundaries but takes humanity as its audience and the world as its home (Shariati 1980e, p. 43).

As man in the true sense of the word must gain knowledge, consciousness, faith, and love (the stages of becoming a *hajji* or performer of the divine covenant), so must the community. When Shariati turns his attention from abstract issues to concrete problems such as colonialism and underdevelopment, he has explanations that are different from those provided by modern intellectuals in Third World countries. He argues that colonized societies will remain stagnant if they do not aspire to pass through the stages of Hajj and shahadat, which are universally incumbent upon men and women in these societies who are nothing but consumers imprisoned by machinery or *assimile* (Shariati 1980g, pp. 72–3). Such consciousness can only be achieved through *madhab* (religion), which itself, in his parlance, is another name for 'self-consciousness' or *khod-agahi*. It should be noted that Shariati does not take a scholastic view of religion, nor does he accept the traditional religious dictums prescribed by Shia clergy. He seems to argue that although we need a methodology to study religion, the methods need not necessarily be extracted from the religious tradition itself (Mohammad Ali 1994, pp. 61–2).

SACRED AND SECULAR

Shariati's entire work could be deciphered through an understanding of his view of insan and her/his nature in the scheme of reality. This is one of the most salient entries into his theoretical, social–philosophical, and ideological reflection. In his view, Man has a primary 'essential' character and a secondary 'shaping' character. With respect to the former, every person is the same. But, Shariati argues, what forms a person's true character and makes him distinct from other beings is his spiritual qualities—the things that cause a person to sense his particular being ('I'). He becomes conscious of his 'self', and says 'sum' ('I am') (Shariati, *Jihad and Shahadat*).

This distinction in Shariati's anthropological methodology serves fundamentally as a touchstone in assessing both modernity (European civilization) and traditionalism (contemporary Iran and, by extension, the Islamic world) and exposing what he saw as the social vices and malpractices of both. He is of the view that there are societies, philosophies, ideologies, religions, intellectual positions, and economic systems that are based mainly on furthering and nourishing the 'primary essential' needs of Man while neglecting or even distorting his fundamental role and diminishing the substantial importance of his 'secondary shaping character'. Shariati's dualistic definition of Man's being gives him a tool to argue that it is possible to identify two movements in history. On the one hand, there is Man's orientation based on an ideology, where the ultimate goal is the fulfilment of 'essential needs' and the extension and proliferation of those needs in a consumerist society. On the other, there is a society where essential needs are considered but spiritual concerns are the leitmotif of social rationality, a society where the rationale of historical change is not merely the result of blind faith, but of authentic choices made by *ummatan wasatan* or 'a community justly balanced' (the ideal society) (Shariati 1980e pp. 40–2).

History, society, and the entire cosmos of a human being could be seen as warring forces on a battlefield, vying over the soul of 'direction' and the means of controlling the 'end'. In a society structured mainly on 'primary essential needs', where material welfare takes precedence over existential well-being (the latter, in Shariati's view, requiring a deep sense of religious anxiety), the significance of 'secondary shaping needs' gradually disappears and diminishes. The lack or presence of these secondary character-inducing needs produce different models of existence: the monotheistic Man (society, religion, world view, and history) and polytheistic Man (society, religion, world view, and history), respectively (Shariati 1980j, pp. 147–8).

The notion of secular (in its meta-theoretical sense) in modern social theory can be seen as a belief in the independence of the social universe as a unit unto itself, governed by its own set of rules and not reliant on any transcendental guidelines, which in Islamic parlance is called *vahy* or revealed tradition. Shariati, unlike traditional Muslim thinkers, does not approach modernity from the naïve viewpoint that the West is a materialist civilization and the East is a spiritual culture, and never the twain shall meet. His approach is subtler.

First, he de-legitimates the traditional point of departure in Muslim intellectual tradition by arguing that the conventional distinction between 'here' and 'hereafter', or *dunya* and *akhirat*, is merely figurative and at best has an 'existential relationship' to the vital process of *hayat*, or life. Dunya and akhirat are not geographical realms, separated spatially and temporally. On the contrary, they are qualities (*sefat*) that become meaningful in relationship to the acts committed by human subjects (Shariati 1980s, p. 101).

To understand the world view of Islam in such a dualistic sense is to miss the point about the very fact of life, the very act of creation, and the importance of Man in the theophanical cosmos. By introducing a particular kind of gnostic monism (which is different from both Spinotzian monism and Russellian neutral monism), Shariati attempts to not only shatter the traditional distinction between here and hereafter, but also argue for religious activism in the matter of society, which is linked to the birth of the 'existential character' of Man. Once he has demolished the concepts of traditional Islam, he begins to question the very ontological basis of modernity, relegating matters of spiritual concern to the private sphere and contrarily establishing a *sui generis* realm called the 'secular'.

If the true expression of secular rationale is to be found in economics, civil society, and political life where there is no place for religious intrusion and spiritual anxiety, it is clear that Shariati also has a different opinion of capitalism and class—which are not issues that figure in late modernity, although they had serious social consequences at the early stage of modernity in European countries such as France. The refutation of the traditional world view of life and afterlife does not lead Shariati to materialism in philosophy, capitalism in economy, or secularism in politics (Eshkevari 2001, p. 232).

The sacred–secular distinction is based on a particular 'vision' of reality (in its metaphysical sense), which can be extended to various aspects of reality (such as epistemology, ontology, politics, ideology, society, and so on) and can condition the perception of one's praxis. One of the most salient features of this distinction is the peripheral role assigned to 'religion' and 'religious concern' in the political scene and the rationale of policy in the modern context. In fact, as stated earlier, the emergence of 'secularism' within the political arena in Europe was profoundly related to the role of religion, which at the time was deemed destructive for the health of civil society and nascent nation states. But it seems Shariati has a different understanding of religion and the role assigned to religious thinking and 'religious sensibility' in the affairs of society and in the construction of the human self.

In Shariati's view, the categorical 'distinction' between the secular and the sacred, which allows for the systematic regulation of the affairs of life to various dimensions, is only possible for an ideology based on *shirk*—that is, polytheistic in nature rather than monotheistic. Let us now explore these two concepts in detail and find out what impact they have had on the notions of sacred and secular in Shariati's social theory.

The secular is a domain where the affairs of civil society are of central importance and the 'managing rationality' is devoid of any 'religious' or 'divine' concerns. The notion of 'accountability' is mundane and unrelated to extra-social concerns, which (the same concept), in religious world view, is contingent upon a system conceptualized as 'creation'. The domain of being is the created domain because the creatures of this universe are all part of a divine melody. There is only one being capable of disobeying the theophanical rhythms of this melody and that is the human being. The very act of disobedience brings a peculiar kind of mentality that can serve as the basis of the historical process, and for Shariati it is illustrated in the story of Adam, in its metaphorical sense, and Abel and Cain, in its sociological sense.

Man is the battleground of the 'spirit of God' (which represent creativity, consciousness, knowledge, love, and forgiveness) and the 'stinking mud' from which human beings were made (in the anthropology of the Qur'an) and which represents stagnation and inertia. Abel and Cain represent these respective forces, and the subsequent socio-economic systems resulting from them, in turn, mirror the 'spirit of God' or the 'stinking mud'. The Cainian system is a 'property system' and a subsequent class system, and thus represents the secular with its distinction between 'matters of life' and the 'affair of afterlife'. Shariati goes on to argue that the property system gives rises to a tripartite hegemony where capital, ideology, and power constitute a whole that could be seen as having a world view in it. Today, one could be misguided by what is called religion (organized religion and a clerical class) and anti-religion (society without religion and non-religious classes), as the very basis of secularism or the distinction between the matters of polity and the affairs of religiosity are inauthentic. For Shariati, the whole raison d'être of Islam was to demolish the distinction between 'spiritual, ethical, and metaphysical' on the one hand and 'social and political' on the other. The greatest and most revolutionary contribution of Islam to human history, he held, was that it channeled the

> power of religious love and the miraculous force of gnostic feelings, which had always existed within individuals, guided them towards rev-olution, sacrifice, the welcoming of death and martyrdom and towards the attainment of power to create a human society based on justice and dedicated to material and spiritual progress in this world. (Shariati 1980d, p. 48)

Within modernity, the 'social' emerges in its most progressive sense when the political notion of religion is relegated to a pre-modern communal system, but Shariati seems to be suggesting that in Islam, the best form of humanity can be achieved in 'communal form' and only in the ummah, which is a divinely guided community. Shariati's notion of tawhid prevents him from conceiving of a sphere where the affairs of the 'social' can be conducted, the rationality of capitalism acceded, and 'reform' chosen as an option to rectify the drawbacks of the system. He is essentially a *mosol parast* (utopian), an ideologue rather than a modern *academic sociologue*.

For Shariati, the whole of creation is an expression of the sacred or *Tajalli-e-Haq*, but it is only within insan that this divine expres-sion can be realized. Within human society, that expression, or the lack of it, is apparent on a global scale, and this affects the 'cause' of creation. If Man is a dual reality then the two dimensions of profane and sacred are not external forces but aspects of Man himself that are vying for *supremacy*. When the allegiance to 'stinking mud' overtakes the 'spirit of God', or when within society the principles of polytheism overshadow the reality of tawhid, then in Shariati's normative analy-sis, the consequences become visible in all spheres of life (Shariati 1980i, pp. 318–20).

Shariati goes on to argue that this world and the hereafter, natu-ral and supernatural, spirit and body, matter and meaning are all integrated, and each is a dimension of a single 'existing truth'. This existentially imperative life principle cannot be laid at the doorstep of one of the noblest dimensions of man's activity, that is, the affairs of the City or Medina. The search for this life-generating principle and world-shaking energy requires a special kind of vision, which is beyond the grasp of reason or philosophy. Shariati calls this vision *hikmat* or theosophy (Rahnema 1998, p. 151).

Shariati seems to suggest that the methodological distinction between secular and sacred is a by-product of a historical and sociological process in a European context that has come to occupy a semi-philosophical position in terms of the fundamental issues of epistemology, ontology, the nature of the world, and the character of history in general. Shariati argues that if the problems of modernity in terms of world view are context bound, then Muslim intellectuals do not need to adopt secular positions in encountering the challenges of modernity or describing Islam in terms set by secular ideologies (Shariati 1980f, p. 4). Shariati, apart from his categorical refutation of imitation of Western historic-socio-political destiny, both in form and content, refuses to acknowledge this distinction and instead argues that the world is a purposeful and continuous entity with an 'ideal and an objective' (Rahnema 1998, p. 289). The principle of tawhid is not a concept limited only to the belief in one God. Shariati perceived monotheism not only as a world outlook, but also as a philosophy of history, a sociological outlook, an ethical doctrine, and finally a social mission (Shariati 1980j p. 232). On the basis of his tawhid world view, Shariati rejects the traditional dichotomies between soul and the body, material and spiritual, sacred and profane, physical and metaphysical, here and hereafter, without realizing that his refutation is the result of an ideological commitment that lacks explanation.

Shariati's understanding of monotheism was not a logical construction aimed at re-emphasizing the 'existence of God', but had specific social, political, economic, and ethical implications. It was more of a re-establishing of the human self in the scheme of modernity, as well as an attempt to rescue the human being from the stifling grasp of traditionalism by refusing the inevitability of materialism and idealism on the one hand and the opium-inducing character of traditional religion on the other (Rahnema 1998, pp. 287–8).

Shariati's principle of 'unity of being' or *wahdat al-vujud*, gave him a tool to view the whole phenomenon of life as a single organism connected in its entire diverse dimension by the very principle of 'being', or *vujud*. This principle conditioned his view by imposing unity upon objective diversity within all dimensions of life. Whatever unity was absent (such as in Iran's economic system during Pahlavi), Shariati wished to impose it without any regard to the internal logic of the system (be it social, economic, or political) (Shariati 1980d, p. 25). There is no single 'sphere' that could claim 'independent logic' (and hence

unconditional allegiance, as was demanded by the Shah-regime during
the pre-Revolutionary modernization of Iran) from tawhidi principle.
This can be interpreted as the denial of any special claim or prior
concession to secular logic and the refusal to concede that the sacred
logic is irrelevant or of limited relevance. Shariati tried, albeit polemi-
cally, to de-legitimize the claim for any special kind of secular logic and
extended his notion of monotheism to envelop all areas of communal
life and international struggle. But how does he accomplish this? The
notions of *ikhlas* and *deen* are the keys to deciphering this conundrum.

AUTHENTICITY AND RELIGION

What is ikhlas? The direct translation is 'sincerity', 'loyalty', or 'devotion'. In the religious discourse of Islam, it is said that leading a
religious life requires sincerity and loyalty as well as devotion. In
rejecting loyalty to religious establishments, Shariati declares that
the search for attaining an authentic sense of being and leading an
integral life requires a process of personal soul-searching based on
absolute sincerity in one's intentions and actions, both in solitude
and among the multitude (Shariati 1980t, p. 338). He distinguishes
between faith and religion by explaining that faith has an external
(*zaheri*) and an internal (*bateni*) dimension. For him, the essence
of faith is gnosticism (*irfan*) reached via the oath of tariqa (Shariati
1980t, p. 339). To express this mode of being, Shariati uses the symbolic ritual of pilgrimage, Hajj, and transforms its entire semantic
universe in order to demonstrate his sense of authenticity and the
way he conceives deen, or religion, both in solitude and multitude
(Rahnema 1998, p. 151).

The ritual of Hajj begins with a conscious act of *niyyat* or 'intention'. Before setting off on the path, the pilgrim should make some
'preparation' in order to be eligible to arrive at *miqqat*, the 'trysting-
place'. The symbol of Hajj is used to formulate the notion of an
'existentially responsible' lifestyle, which Shariati deems is correct
and conforms to the Qur'anic notion of *mithag*, or covenantal trust.
The substantial dimension of a life in pilgrimage, as in the ritual of
Hajj, is the very notion of 'consciousness', which is a self-conscious
seeking of 'authentic existence' by renouncing all kinds of allegiance,
whether psychological or socio-political, that claims a God-like sense

of submission without having any divine credibility (Shariati 1980m, pp. 116, 156–7).

Shariati seems to overturn the semantic universe of the term 'pilgrimage', bestowing a new identity on the 'pilgrim' by exhorting his audience to abandon the traditional sense of understanding—which confines religious mode to a ritualistic machinery without individual spirit—as well as the modern one that deprives Man of the spirit of religion in the name of modernity (Shariati 1980g, p. 238).

The lexical translation of ikhlas, however, is not to make sense of what Shariati means by this concept (ikhlas) in relation to authentic action and religious thinking. It is tempting to compare his notion of ikhlas to 'integrity', which constitutes the spirit of ikhlas even if it belies the lexical meaning of the term. Shariati's religious integralism implies that the human person is both material and spiritual, and can become more than a merely self-interested individual by acquiring and practising the habits necessary for actualizing his humanity. Indeed, Man may rise to the heights of reason and purpose latent within his nature most efficaciously through playful communion with other persons under divine guidance. Shariati goes so far as to suggest that man has a substantial dimension that can be termed 'gnostic substance', which can be activated through sensible education that acts as an antidote to fallacious ethics symbolized by Marxist materialism and Western bourgeois capitalism (Shariati 1980b, pp. 51–3).

Shariati shares an essential notion with many other modern Muslim thinkers who embarked upon a quest for authenticity (Safi 1994). This is the notion of 'individual authenticity' based on sacred morality, summed up by the belief that 'I as a person (and by extension a culture) should be who I am and not anybody else'. An authentic person should not follow external recipes for ethical behaviour and moral vision (such as institutional *mullahism*, a sign of tradition, or statism, a sign of modernity) but should be guided by arafat, *mash'ar*, and mina (Shariati 1980l, pp. 374–7). The argument put forward by Shariati is not only about personal salvation; he also attempts to formulate a recipe for social salvation from the hazards of modernity (by the capitalism of the West, the Marxist Leninism of the former USSR, traditionalist Islam, or Iranian nationalism) (Shariati 1980c, p. 31).

How successful he was in this attempt is a matter of great controversy among scholars of both East and West. One issue is undisputed, however: the 'essential' link between 'individual authenticity' and 'societal authenticity' based on sacred morality. Shariati, like Jacques Maritain (1946, 1973) in his religious and neo-Thomistic anthropology, preferred to describe this as *dard-e deen* (religious concerns) for the right ordering of public life, which without individual life or life itself would go away. As Jacques Maritain argued that the best political order would encourage the view that religion and metaphysics are an essential part of human culture, primary and indispensable incentives in the very life of society, so did Shariati maintain that the 'religious dimension' is truly the only essential human dimension. Without this, society would be destroyed, Man would be at a loss, and history would become a dungeon. Shariati alludes to this in his philosophy of supplication in a very poetical manner:

> My Lord, inspire our 'open minded' ones who consider economics essential that economy is not the goal, and inspire our clergy and religious ones that economy is also essential.... An empty stomach lacks everything. A society which has economic problems also lacks spiritual wealth. Whatever is called ethics in a poor country is nothing but deviant customs and habits, not spirituality. (Shariati 1980c, p. 31)

What does Shariati mean by the term 'religion' and how does this relate to the idea of authenticity (*bazgasht be-khishtan*)? Since Kant, Religionskritik has signified the abandonment of religious consciousnesses (as a factor to be reckoned with in the matters of social engineering). For David Strauss, Ludwig Feuerbach, and Karl Marx, this was tantamount to false consciousness, devoid of any cognitive dimension (or an irrelevant truth-claim in Durkheim's sociological investigation on religion as a societal cohesive element). In a similar vein, Dewey followed Feuerbach and Strauss in admitting that the ultimate reality of religious yearning is not a being or a living reality, but the unity of all ideal objectives arousing us to desire and action, best described as human subjectivity. This modern discourse takes natural science or scientific rationality as its point of departure, stripping religion of any a priori claim to objective understanding and truthful consciousness.

If Man is a social animal whose interests are best served in a political order as a citizen, what he needs most is accurate and truthful consciousness to enable him to realize his most humane potential and achieve his social needs. The way to achieve the heights of social

consciousness and political maturity is through science and philosophical rationality (or modern mode of consciousness). Within this
framework (based on *Religionskritik*), there is no place for 'religious
consciousness'. Religion is a figment of imagination and a product of
social 'unawareness' or, at best, a tool for moulding communal nation
states into a cohesive form rather than a 'force' to be reckoned with in
the progression of humanity in a historical sense.

Scientific rationality needs to be applied to the social fabric and
individuals need to reacquaint themselves with modern consciousness through science. But Shariati, as much he revered science and
modern philosophy, did not appreciate modern Religionskritik. On
the contrary, he accused modernists of being naïve and not getting to
the heart of 'historical truths' in relation to religion and 'religious consciousness'. Such truths could awaken Man to a nobler form of being,
unattainable to science and philosophy and necessary for a cohesive
public life in particular, and for humanity in general (Shariati 1980l,
pp. 81–4; 1980h, pp. 46–7).

Further strengthening his position, Shariati uses historical
characters such as Abu Zar, Salman, and Avicenna as ideal types to
demonstrate that what brings dynamism into history is not 'philosophical consciousness' or 'scientific consciousness'. If political order
is impossible without the integrity of individuals in possession of
the 'self-consciousness' evident among religious men such as Abu
Zar or Salman as symbols of authentic personalities of the highest
order without the slightest sense of social responsibility (rather than
the consciousness found among scientists and philosophers such
as Avicenna), then the path to authenticity is not through science or
modern rationality (which disregard the essential of religious thought
and mode).

To understand Shariati's argument in relation to modern
Religionskritik, it is necessary to find out what he means by religion
and how it is different from the modern view conceived within the
sociology of religion. His understanding of religion is imbued in the
complex notion of dialectic (half Hegelian–Marxist and half gnostic)
that informs his anthropology and cannot be considered independently. As mentioned earlier, Shariati's view of Man is a dual reality,
the battlefield of God and Satan in dialectic mode (Rahnema 1998, p.
291). Using the dialectical method, he refers to human beings as the

union of Lucifer and Allah. The 'spirit of Allah'—representing creativity, consciousness, knowledge, love, and forgiveness—is the thesis, while the 'stinking mud' from which human beings are made represents the antithesis, stagnation, and inertia. The struggle between the two in the nature of human beings and their history has created an ascending, deterministic, and dialectical movement. In Shariati's scheme of thought, as Rahnema rightly notes, the path leading from the 'stinking mud' to 'God' is called 'religion' or deen (the primordial nature) (Shariati 1908j, p. 47).

However, the main point is that the demonstration of the 'Lactiferous religiosity or religious conception based on false consciousness' does not remain in the individual realm but manifests itself at various social and historical stages in increasingly complex ways. Shariati sets out to describe the most vicious forms of Lactiferous mentality that creep into the framework of 'true religious ideology' by domesticating people and depriving them of an original 'personality' and an ideal 'society', attainable only when the transition from 'mud' to God produces a God-like creature able to use her or his free will and ingenuity to successfully construct a human paradise on earth (Rahnema 1998, p. 292).

Shariati fights on two fronts (traditional and modern) to make the distinction between monotheistic and polytheistic religion. While arguing that philosophy and science are forms of 'consciousness', he contends that if the war of 'religion against religion' is not properly understood in a historical context, two significant facts, which would mean nothing without humanity, end up being neglected.

The first of these is that while science and philosophy are important in the history of humanity, they only lead to a 'consciousness' devoid of political and social significance. This can only be achieved when an individual of historical nature attains a form of 'self-consciousness', demands his rights, and pays his dues. Shariati equates this form of self-consciousness with religion and considers it to be the true source of 'authenticity' (Borojerdi 1996, p. 115). The self-consciousness of an Abu Zar or a Salman is related to their God-consciousness and it can only be realized through the negation of the self in God and subsequent living with people within society (Rahnema 1998, pp. 159, 247).

The second fact concerns polytheistic religion—the opium of the people—viewed as the primordial nature of man advocated by Islam.

Shariati claims that religious wars have raged continually through-out history. Each war represents a total ideological system (comprising economy, world view, religion, society, philosophy, anthropology, politics, and ideal) symbolically termed Abelian or Cainian. Shariati accuses the intellectuals of the Enlightenment (or Rushanfekran in Iran) of disregarding this significant fact (that is, the distinction between religion and anti-religion that is socially represented as religion), and hence depriving the masses of a powerful place of 'self-consciousness' that could be instrumental in bringing about an authentic socio-political revolution in Iran or the colonized world. He attempts to delegitimize the accuracy of Marxism in a Muslim context in general, and an Iranian context in particular, and uses Shi'ism as a native cultural framework in order to galvanize revolutionary fervour in Iran. By doing so, he hopes to demonstrate that the 'opium of the people' is not a monotheistic religion, but a poly-theistic one. He also attempts to convince Third World intellectuals that social progress achieved at the expense of the abandonment of religion, as had happened in Europe, should not be imitated at any cost. Instead, one should reconsider Occidental religious experience and the importance of the nature of 'European rejection' (Shariati 1980i, pp. 45–6).

Shariati argues that a distinction should be made between mono-theistic and polytheistic religions, the true cause of wars in human history, without clarifying whether this distinction is based on an intra-religious approach or on his sociological methodology. Monotheistic religion is championed by the prophets of the Abrahamic religions. Polytheism, meanwhile, has always challenged and fought against monotheism in the name of religious custody. Shariati distinguished between false polytheistic and true monotheistic religions on the basis of their position in relation to socially significant issues. Polytheism was characterized as a creed that propagated acquiescence and inau-thenticity, while monotheism was defined as a revolutionary creed based on defiance and a source of authentic being.

The term 'religion' is a normative one saved for 'true monothe-ism' and in this true sense, it has a spiritual aspect based on belief in one God and a material and worldly aspect representing human unity or oneness. But Shariati seems to argue that there is no distinction between dunya and akhirat if both aim to reach the same destination where man is delivered from 'stinking mud' and turned into the representative of Allah on earth. Since human beings are creatures of a single ultimate reality, Shariati argues, they must be of the same kind and equal value. From a sociological point of departure, therefore, monotheism represents the belief in the unity of humanity, irrespective of race, ethnicity, nationality, and class. Monotheism's invitation to obedience towards God is also an invitation to rebel against any authority that deprives people of being true and authentic unto themselves; the only relevant authority is *Ruh-e-Khoda* or the spirit of God.

Monotheism is thus a 'revolutionary religion', which urges its adherents to change and destroy whatever they find to be false and unacceptable to the rule of God. Polytheism is as old as monotheism but not in the sense used by Hume. The long history of polytheism is evidence of oppression and suppression of the masses by *zar* (an economic system based on expropriation), *zur* (a political systems based on oppression), and *tazvir* (an ideological system based on false consciousness). Polytheistic religions, Shariati claims, distort all religious principles and deprive the Muslim community of any truthful means to regain its authenticity by adhering to the principles of religion. In Shariati's view, Muslims adhere to distorted ideas and misconstrued ideals in the name of religion, ideas that induce nothing but acquiescence to widespread social injustice, inequity, and inequality in the name of *qaza* and *qadar* (pre-determined fate) (Shariati 1980k, p. 274). Shariati, concurring with modern intellectuals who called religion 'the opium of the masses', berates Muslims for not distinguishing between the religion of *tawhid* and anti-religion of *shirk*, which is founded on ignorance, fear, discrimination, and property laws characteristic of the feudal era (Rehnema 1998, p. 249).

The institutionalization of polytheistic traits and their application as social norms deprives Man of the sense of authenticity that is a prerequisite for any ideal city. For Shariati, polytheistic religions that distinguish between *Islam-e-Aqideh* and *Islam-e-Farhang* (a belief that comes from within and is a constitutive factor of one's personality versus a cultural feature that one is born into without any personal realization, or put simply, dialogical Islam versus traditional Islam) are enemies of progressive systems and alienating social conditions (Shariati 1980q, pp. 144–8).

If the path from 'stinking mud' to 'spirit of God' is called religion and leads Man to the highest form of consciousness, which is an expression of authentic being, then Shariati reminds us that this pilgrimage cannot be accomplished while the social condition is in tatters. In the story of Hussain (a historical personality in Islam), who leaves his ritual pilgrimage in order to encounter Yazid (a ruler in the early days of Islam), Shariati introduces his concept of 'religious consciousness' and its significance on social revolution and the birth of Hurrs (a historical figure, who in Shariati's hands became an ideal for authentic being and action—an 'authentic personality').

Authenticity or *bazgasht be khishtan (Esalat)* cannot be achieved without a profound sense of *khudi*, or 'self'. The process of being aware of one's own self as a purposeful reality situated at the heart of history and ingrained with a divine purpose is impossible without a sense of 'self-consciousness', or *khod agahi* tantamount to *khoda agahi*, or 'God-consciousness'. Awareness of this dimension of Man's being cannot be brought about by either science or philosophy; Shariati equates the emergence of self-consciousness in the heart of Man with religion, but not any kind of religion. His is a normative religion, which has tawhid as its sole principle. The product of this religion is a *muvahhed*, or an authentic man, who is freed from the four prisons of 'nature', 'history', 'society', and 'self', and capable of recreating himself in the form that Allah originally created him—not as a social animal who adapts to the environment, but one that can make his environment adapt to the needs of the authentic man of tawhid (the philosophy of supplication).

This is a man with ikhlas who practises isar (or self-consciously practises selflessness for the cause of the oppressed), in whom the 'spirit of God' has prevailed over Man's basic 'mud'-like element. This ideal man, who represents the noblest form of authenticity, permanently revolts against the Cainian status quo in order to establish the Abelian society (Rahnema 1998, p. 294). What are the principles of the Abelian society? Who are the examples of this ideal society and how can one know about the ideology of monotheism?

Islamshenasi, or knowledge of Islam (its history, society, principles, book, significant personalities, culture, and so on), is the key to a successful revolution and the creation of the promised human paradise on earth. Here again, Shariati takes the opposite view of the traditional clerical concept of religion, which bases its ideology for lay people on the 'principle of imitation'. He also disagrees with modern intellectuals who argue against 'religious thinking' in toto. His own position is that of shenakht which enables the authentic man of religion (as personified by Abu Zar, Hossein, Fatima, Ali, Muhammad, Hurr, Zeynab, Salman, and Meqdad in history and in concrete social situations, where the real essence of human self can show itself) to believe that Man is not a plant that grows because of a coincidence of nature, history, and society (or what Shariati takes for the materialist position within modern discourse). At the same time, shenakht also enlightens Man to the fact that the *only* path towards God (and authentic self-consciousness) passes through the Earth, that is, it is a path that involves living within history and being concerned about historical realities. That is to say, Shariati holds that traditional religious people have forgotten that Man is made of dust, which is an indication that material phenomena imply God's existence as much as inexplicable unseen ones.

In other words, the road to authentic life, as demonstrated by Abraham in Shariati's view (Shariati 1980r), both in its individual and communal sense, follows the principles of material reality, which is an expression of the ultimate reality. Shariati yearns for an existential kind of life—not something that will make him resentful of its worthlessness or mourn its uselessness on his deathbed, but something endowed with the 'gift' of choice, which is the only salient feature of mankind. But the choice Shariati endorses is not of the Sartrean kind, devoid of divine concerns or *dard-e deen*; on the contrary, his is a choice different from traditionalists' notion of *ekhtiyar* (free will) or *jabr* (determinism), and also unlike the Fanonian concept of 'personal choice'.

In the philosophy of Supplication, Shariati expresses this notion very eloquently by saying to God, as the ultimate ego or the absolute 'other':

My Lord, grant me ... a life ... [and] let me choose ... but in the way that please[s] you the most.... You teach me how to live ... I shall learn how to die. (Shariati 1982)

Although the road to authenticity is through 'knowledge', the kind of knowledge Shariati deems significant for a true religious life, either individual or communal (as expressed in the symbolic form by the image of a pilgrim), is not a modern objective secular kind of epis-teme. On the contrary, he depicts a kind of knowledge that is 'useful' to the communal being of mankind. This 'usefulness' in Shariati's view is not individual 'elated feelings of the heights of lofty under-standing [represented by fine arts, which would disable one] to see the depth of hunger in the eyes of the hungry or the black bruises of an abused human'.

The kind of knowledge advocated by Shariati is *ma'rifa*. This is essential for an authentic life and is the fruit of religious thinking, which is distinguished from discursive thinking but not independent from it, and the philosophy or the spirit of supplication (the philoso-phy of supplication). Religion, in Shariati's view, is an existential yearn-ing, which turns into praxis through Man's actions in the world. The vocation of Man on Earth is to work and fulfil God's message. The fulfilment of the message (religion) is another name for authenticity. Religion is a direct call for action, and action is a manifestation of faith. Action involves men and women alike, hence Shariati's attention to Ali and Fatima as ideals of the Muslim community and their ways of deal-ing with vital issues of life, as the norms of authentic action. Action is the only legitimizing device for sovereignty on Earth. The revolution of transcendence appears in society for the implementation of social justice and the foundation of an egalitarian society. As Shariati asserts, transcendence means universal equality between all individuals in the same society. Prophets did not only preach the revolutions but they also led them. They enter into the political struggle and take the side of the poor, the oppressed, and the wretched of the Earth.

To conclude this exploration and evaluation of Shariati, the key point to be underlined is that this theorist has presented a distinctive modernist normative agenda for Muslim/Iranian social (as opposed to political) revolution through fusing existentialism and the piety of Shi'ism. In the context of the three themes of inter-civilizational dialogue, as with Iqbal, controversy abounds about Shariati's (notably different) theoretical groundings. But despite—or perhaps because of—his transcendental world view that sees the universe as one living organism, his essentially existentialist approach provides substantial commonalities for cross-cultural discussion. Specifically, in terms of self-community, humans are uniquely three-dimensional dialectics of clay and spirit, who, through self-conscious monist gnosis and a common cause/destiny, achieve communal consciousness. In terms of sacred–secular distinction, despite constant internal human conflict between fulfilling essential/consumerist needs and fulfilling spiritual concerns, the holy and the profane are not distinguishable in an ideology based on divinely guided monotheism. For the final distinction, that between religion and authenticity, in an 'existentially responsible' lifestyle, self-consciousness through religious knowledge is by definition seeking both individual and societal authenticity based on sacred-normative morality.

BIBLIOGRAPHY

Ahmadi, H. 2002. *Shariati der Jahan* (Shariati in the World). Tehran: Sherkat Sahami Enteshar.

Banuazizi, A. 1999. 'Islamic States and Civil Society in Iran'. Paper delivered at the Seventeenth Annual Joseph (Buddy) Strelitz Lecture on 18 April, Boston College.

Borojerdi, M. 1996. *Iranian Intellectuals and the West: The Tormented Triumph of Nativism.* Syracuse: Syracuse University Press.

Eshkevari, Y. H. 2001. *Shariati va Naghde Sunnat* [Shariati and his critique of tradition]. Tehran: Yadavaran Publisher.

Ghaninejad, M. 2003. 'Transition from Tradition to Modernity'. *Iran International,* 26: 1–8.

Hopwood, D. 2000. 'Introduction: The Culture of Modernity in Islam and the Middle East'. In *Islam and Modernity: Muslim Intellectuals Respond,* edited by R. L. Nettler, M. Mahmoud, and J. Cooper, pp. 1–19. London: I. B. Tauris.

Husain, M. Z. 1995. *Global Islamic Politic.* New York: HarperCollins College Publishers.

Lee, R. D. 1997. *Overcoming Tradition and Modernity: The Search for Islamic Authenticity.* Boulder, Colo.: Westview Press.

Mahmoud, S. 1997, March 11. 'Intellectual Autobiography of Abdolkarim Sorosh: An Interview'. Retrieved from http://www.drsoroush.com/English/Interviews/E-INT-19970311-Intellectual_Autobiography_An_Interview_of_Abdolkarim_Soroush.html, accessed 6 June 2016.

Maritain, J. 1946. *True Humanism,* translated by M. R. Adamson. London: Geoffrey Bles, The Centenary Press.

———. 1973. *Integral Humanism, Temporal and Spiritual Problems of a New Christendom,* translated by J. W. Evans. Notre Dame, Indiana: University Press of Notre Dame.

Mirfetros, A. 1979. *Moghadamehi der Islamshenasi* [A prolegomena to Islamology]. Tehran, Iran.

Mohammad Ali, M. 1994. *Deenshenasi Mo'aser* [Contemporary Religionwessenschaften]. Tehran: Aftab Publisher.

Munir, L. Z. 2003. 'Islam, Modernity and Justice for Women'. Paper presented at the Islam and Human Rights Fellow Lecture, 14 October, organized by the Islam and Human Rights Project, School of Law, Emory University, Atlanta, GA.

Rahnema, A. 1998. *An Islamic Utopia: A Political Biography of Ali Shariati*. London: I.B. Tauris.

Sadri, M. 1999. 'Intellectual Autobiography of Abdolkarim Sorosh'. www. drsoroushc. om/Interviews.htm.

Safi, L. 1994. *The Challenge of Modernity: The Quest for Authenticity in the Arab World*. Lanham, MD: University Press of America.

Shariati, A. 1980a. *Ba mokhtabhaye ashena* [A dialogue with familiar audience] (Collected Works 1). Tehran: Entesharat Mona.

———. 1980b. *Khod-sazi-e enghelabi* [Revolutionary reconstruction] (Collected Works 2). Tehran: Entesharat Mona.

———. 1980c. *Bazgasht* [Authenticity] (Collected Works 4). Tehran: Entesharat Mona.

———. 1980d. *Ma va Iqbal* [We and Iqbal] (Collected Works 5). Tehran: Entesharat Mona.

———. 1980e. *Shia* [Shia] (Collected Works 7). Tehran: Entesharat Mona.

———. 1980f. *Jahatgiri tabaghati Islam* [The class issues within Islamic frame of reference] (Collected Works 10). Tehran: Entesharat Mona.

———. 1980g. *Tarikhe tammadon* [A treatise on civilization] (Collected Works 12). Tehran: Entesharat Mona.

———. 1980h. *Tarikhe shenakhte adyan* [History and study of religion] (Collected Works 13). Tehran: Entesharat Mona.

———. 1980i. *Tarikh va shenakhte adyan* [History and study of religion] (Collected Works 14). Tehran: Entesharat Mona.

———. 1980j. *Islamshenasi* [Islomology] (Collected Works 16). Tehran: Entesharat Mona.

———. 1980k. *Hossein varase adam* [Hossein: The Archetype of Just Human Ideals] (Collected Works 19). Tehran: Entesharat Mona.

———. 1980l. *Che bayad karad?* [What Should Be Done?] (Collected Works 20). Tehran: Entesharat Mona.

———. 1980m. *Mazhab bar alayhe mazhab* [Religion against religion] (Collected Works 22). Tehran: Entesharat Mona.

———. (1980n). *Jahanbini va ideology* [World view and ideology] (Collected Works 23). Tehran: Entesharat Mona.

Shariati, A. 1980o. *Ali* (Collected Works 26). Tehran: Entesharat Mona.

———. 1980p. *Bazshenasi hoviate Irani-Islami* [The reconstruction of Irano-Islamic identity in the matrix of modernity] (Collected Works 27). Tehran: Entesharat Mona.

———. 1980q. *Raveshe shenakhte Islam* [Some methodological and epistemological issues in the study of Islam] (Collected Works 28). Tehran: Entesharat Mona.

———. 1980r. *Mi'ad Ba Ebrahim* [A Convenant with Abraham] (Collected Works 29). Tehran: Entesharat Mona.

———. 1980s. *Honar* [Art] (Collected Works 32). Tehran: Entesharat Mona.

———. 1980t. *Asare gonegon* [Miscellaneous Work], vol. 2 (Collected Works 35). Tehran: Entesharat Mona.

———. 1982. *The Philosophy of Supplication.* Tehran, Iran.

9 Culture and Civilization in the Thought of Alija Izetbegovic

Mahmut Hakkı Akın

The twentieth century was a time in which Western civilization faced criticism both internally and externally. Western civilization, up until then, had experienced historical and cultural events such as the Renaissance, the Enlightenment, the Age of Discovery, the French Revolution, and the Industrial Revolution. It had greatly influenced vast areas of the world with its ideas, and technical and practical knowledge. Technical superiority had given it an opportunity to gain power and expand like no other civilization before. When compared with the past civilizations that lost their power and influence, Western civilization has a very distinct structure. One of the most important factors that differentiates Western civilization from previous civilizations and cultures is how it transforms, and even destroys, the cultures it interacts with. On the other hand, in non-Western societies, desire to become a part of the Western civilization has become a policy valued by many intellectuals and politicians. However, there has been debate among intellectuals with different dispositions over how the relationship with Western civilization should be. Contemporary Muslim thinker Alija Izetbegovic made a distinctive and important contribution to this debate from within the Muslim world. In this chapter, I will discuss his dual criticism of Western civilization and of Muslim societies, with regard to the relationship that he constructed between culture and civilization.

Alija Izetbegovic is generally known as the president of Bosnia and Herzegovina and a politician of the late twentieth century. He actively participated in politics for around ten of his seventy-eight years. Almost half of his lifetime was spent at war. Izetbegovic expanded his world of thought by reading on many different fields. He joined the Young Muslims organization as a youngster. In the organization, he actively fought against communism and atheism and made an effort to educate himself. The influence of these early years is reflected in the opinions he discusses in the books published in his adulthood. Izetbegovic experienced arrest and imprisonment for the first time when he was a member of the Young Muslims. When the communist regime that was established in Yugoslavia after the Second World War increased the oppression of Muslim Bosniaks, Izetbegovic was imprisoned for three years.

In 1970, as a call to intellectuals of all Muslim societies, Izetbegovic published a declaration that analysed the situation of being stuck between modernity and tradition, and the state of relationships of the Islamic world with Western civilization. In this book, called *Islamic Declaration*, he wrote about the dilemma of Muslim societies and of possible solutions to general issues. He also wrote articles on Islam and the problems of Muslim societies of this period. In these articles, he focused on general issues that had been discussed among intellectuals in Muslim societies for a long time. Why did the Islamic world fall behind? Is becoming part of Western civilization the only way for Muslim societies to develop? Is an Islamic Renaissance possible? These were among the questions he discussed and sought answers to. Unlike the representatives of the first Islamist generation such as Muhammad Abduh, Jamal ad-Din al-Afghani, Muhammad Iqbal, and Mehmet Akif Ersoy, Izetbegovic had the opportunity to analyse the conditions of Muslim societies that had experienced modernization. Being a European Muslim thinker who was raised in Europe itself, Izetbegovic was also distinct from these individuals. He showed regard to the modernization experiences in nation states of the Muslim world throughout the twentieth century and identified important issues in Muslim societies caused by nationalism, conservatism, and an imitation of the West. In his book *Islamic Declaration*, he claimed that there was no road to freedom for Muslim societies except through Islamization and a realization of an Islamic Renaissance.

His main work, *Islam between East and West*, was published in the early 1980s in the United States while he was in prison. In this book, Izetbegovic revealed his comprehensive knowledge of the main thoughts of Western civilization and the Islamic creed. He argued that essentially there are only three standpoints represented by Judaism, Christianity, and Islam. According to him, considering the dualist nature of being, neither materialism nor idealism suffices to explain issues pertaining to man, and Islam is the third way that accepts man with all his physical and spiritual aspects.

In 1983, Izetbegovic was sentenced to prison in the Sarajevo Islamism case because of the ideas he defended in the *Islamic Declaration*, along with many opinion leaders of Bosnia and Herzegovina. He spent almost six years in prison. He continued reading and writing in this period and worked on the humanitarian issues he had discussed in *Islam between East and West*. The time he spent in prison was a period of New World Order debates. In fact, a year after he left the prison, the Berlin Wall was torn down and a search for a new order started in Yugoslavia in the post-communist period, as it did in other socialist countries. Izetbegovic founded the Party of Democratic Action with his friends to actively participate in the politics of the new regime. He was elected as the leader of the party, and after general elections was elected as the president of Bosnia and Herzegovina. Soon after, on 1 March 1992, the Bosnian War broke out, which would only end after four years, with the Dayton Agreement, on 14 December 1995. The fact that a war had broken out in the middle of Europe after the Second World War was perceived as an unexpected situation in the debates regarding Western civilization and the New World Order. Global public opinion had to face the reality of genocide once again. Many Western states and international organizations chose to simply ignore all these events.

Izetbegovic, who passed away in 2003, was a thinker who earned respect both because of his opinions and his attitude in the Bosnian War as a Muslim intellectual and a politician. He can essentially be defined as a Muslim intellectual who was interested in human philosophy. In his works, the subject of civilization, together with culture, was discussed as a part of human philosophy. He did not reject Western civilization as a whole, despite everything that he experienced. For the sake of his own intellectual principles, he wanted to comprehend the issue with all its different aspects. He argued that it was wrong to blame everything on the image of 'the bad West', and the Muslim world should benefit from the experiences of the Western civilization. He emphasized that some of the dynamics and cults that created Western civilization are virtues of past Islamic civilizations. His call to Muslim societies to choose Islamization, beyond positive or negative sanctions, was created to understand Western civilization. It is necessary to interpret his thought and struggle as an effort in this sense.

Islamization refers to a political philosophy based on making contact with the Western civilization as Muslims. Most Muslim societies established their first contact with the West through colonialism. One of the greatest risks that awaited these societies was alienation. On the other hand, a similar issue stands out in the relationship that independent Muslim states had established with Western civilization because of their own underdevelopment. Particularly in the nineteenth century, Western educated intellectuals in independent Muslim states, like Turkey and Iran, tried to be integrated with the West through its imitation. Islamization policy accepts a limited relationship with Western civilization. Early Islamists express that this relationship should be limited to scientific and technical developments. One of the most important debates of the time was built around the question of whether Islam was an obstacle to development. When Izetbegovic joined this discussion as the thinker of a few generations later, the global situation had shifted. Nevertheless, similar issues, especially the nature of the relationship with Western civilization, continued to be discussed in this new era.

Izetbegovic's Islamist views and his call for Islamization in politics, economy, education, and culture in Muslim societies were not well received by many Westerners. Izetbegovic was accused of being a fundamentalist and a radical during the Bosnian War. However, when one looks into his works, tolerance and coexistence stand out as a base for his understanding of politics, which is based on his interpretation of Islam. For those who accused him, the fact that he chose to take Islam as a reference was more important than what he actually said. Izetbegovic states, 'The fact that the main point of the protested book, *Islamic Declaration*, is Islamic, makes the book unacceptable by the West' and that he 'is not forgiven' because of this (2003, p. 30). This fact is notable in terms of the New World Order and the clash of civilization debates. Huntington's mention of Bosnia and Herzegovina is one of the fault lines of the clash of civilizations, because this region is at the crossroads where Islamic, Slavic-Orthodox, Catholic, and Western civilization in general meet. The Bosnian War happened in the midst of these discussions. Izetbegovic, who was always known as a pro-peace politician, was labelled as a dangerous politician in Western public opinion because of his thoughts and Muslim identity (Mestrovic 2010, p. 140). The negligence and negative propaganda of Western public opinion led to the killings, forced migration, and suffering of countless innocent people.

In Izetbegovic's thought, culture and civilization have equivalents in different contexts. He primarily discussed why these notions are a problem of human philosophy. His being the president of Bosnia and Herzegovina and his position in the Bosnian War made the culture–civilization debate more meaningful for Izetbegovic. He constructed the relationship between man and history on the basis of God as the primary ruler, and likened this relationship to the relationship between fish and the sea. History is moving towards its target. According to Izetbegovic, people's responsibilities and efforts have little effect on this continuity. Yet a sense of responsibility and effort are in the nature of a human being. Izetbegovic's understanding of civilization discusses the opportunities of agreement and coexistence, not conflict. Accepting both the opportunities and the risks of civilization involves societies with different accumulations of culture and civilization to overcome difficult situations together. He tried to follow this understanding as a policy during the years of the Bosnian War and in the post-war period.

DEBATES ON CULTURE AND CIVILIZATION IN THE TWENTIETH CENTURY: FROM OPTIMISM TO PESSIMISM

Discussions on the concepts of culture and civilization have an important position in social sciences literature. People interested in these concepts have submitted many different ideas on them. It could be said that there is extensive literature on culture and civilization today. With all the contributions from different fields of research, this literature has a complicated structure. While some have separated these two concepts, others have used them with the same meaning. To define also involves a limitation or to point out the limits of the object that is sought to be known.

There are hundreds of definitions of the terms 'culture' and 'civilization' in sociology and anthropology books. When the close relationship between these two concepts is considered, the complexity of the situation can be realized (Berger 1995; Meriç 2002; Sorokin 2008; Toynbee 1991). But be it in culture or in civilization, as situated beings, human beings always necessarily experience a process of acculturation. Everything that is part of and has been produced by human beings (including civilization) is somehow cultural and related to culture.

Which properties separate culture from civilization? Can these two concepts be used interchangeably? Is the relationship between culture and civilization unidirectional? It is possible to multiply these questions. Thinkers who have been interested in issues related to culture and civilization have tried to emphasize and answer these questions. In general, these keynotes and issues can be identified from the texts of contributors to the issues of culture and civilization:

1. It is not possible to identify the concepts of culture and civilization clearly. There are numerous definitions made for both concepts.
2. It is hard to determine the extent and structure of the relationship between culture and civilization.
3. It is not clear which concept is more inclusive.
4. It is controversial if there is continuity from culture to civilization, or from civilization to culture.

Of course, the main issue in this topic is not just a debate related to description. It is worth noting that these two concepts have been used to specify categorical differences between Western and non-Western societies for the past two centuries. Technical developments experienced in Western societies have been voiced as 'progress' and 'civilizing' by many intellectuals of both Western and non-Western societies. In many non-Western societies, the mentality of civilization and progress has been made a state policy and modernization has been accepted as a process to integrate oneself with Western civilization. It is possible to see this mentality in many Muslim societies and the important social changes that have been experienced under its influence.

Considering the dualist character of the being in question, Izetbegovic accepted that the concepts of culture and civilization reflect the dualism in the nature of a human being. According to him, culture has a structure that is fed by the human soul. On the other hand, civilization can be explained through the human body and it is a result of the material relationship established between human beings and nature. But human beings are both spiritual and material beings. As a contemporary Muslim thinker, Izetbegovic tried to explain the concepts of culture and civilization and the situation of Muslim societies against Western societies from this point of view. Izetbegovic's review of culture and civilization could be accepted as an original contribution regarding this issue in Islamic societies. The question whether Islam can be 'an alternative to Western civilization' is one of the significant issues that Izetbegovic was interested in. The aim of this chapter is not to discuss what the concepts of culture and civilization are, but to identify Izetbegovic's original contributions to the issue. A chapter of his book *Islam between East and West* was exclusively devoted to the issue of culture and civilization.

The humanity ideal of Western civilization and its emphasis on freedom, along with technical developments and achievements, created an optimistic view of the future in the minds of many thinkers. Since the Enlightenment, the emphasis on man using the power of the mind and intellect gave the human mind a special and privileged status. It is striking that most of the thinkers and philosophers of the time carried an optimistic belief that a new political and social order shaped by mind and science, which were regarded as the safeguards of freedom, would overtake the place of the religion of the past and traditional authorities (Sorokin 2008, pp. 322–3). Naturally, there were some objecting opinions. Alongside ideologies like conservatism that aim to protect tradition and traditional institutions, Romanticism's criticism of the development of the Western civilization in art and literature should be noted. In both Western and non-Western societies, science, technical knowledge, and positivism as a scientific approach have had a considerable influence on the creation and expansion of a new understanding of civilization. The belief that science and technical development enrich Western societies and make them more powerful and progressive became the prevailing opinion for most Western and non-Western intellectuals.

This understanding carries the utopian idea of 'a better world' of the future, shaped by science and technical knowledge. In the process that led to the Enlightenment and modernization, Western civilization, with the influence of Renaissance, was constructed as a utopia. Utopias were the most important structures of creating 'a better world' or 'heaven on earth', and they developed anthropocentrically with the period's emphasis on humanism.

As metaphysics lost its value and natural sciences (especially physics) rose in the concept of civilization, utopian thought found a new opportunity. This opportunity was the social sciences, which would establish the discipline and control mechanism that the natural sciences had established over societies. Social scientists had been pursuing scientific knowledge by taking natural sciences as a model. In this sense, it is meaningful that the founders of sociology, Saint-Simon and Auguste Comte, are also the founders of positivism. It is possible to make a close connection between the optimism of early social scientists regarding the future of modernity and the utopian mindset of Western civilization. On the issue of civilization, positivism also reflects an understanding of philosophy of history that is periodized, progressive, and evolutionist.

From the point of positivist understanding that identifies and generalizes cause-and-effect relationships between events, man is, in a way, a factual being that behaves according to determined rules. At least, this is the main topic in which positivism is interested when dealing with man and his productions. The physical world is accepted as the only world of which knowledge has to be attained, and this is done with the purpose of keeping away metaphysics and speculation.

This new understanding created a legitimacy crisis for societies, which led to an epistemological power struggle. Science was accepted as the winner of this power struggle and as the authority that would resolve the legitimacy crisis. The defenders of this opinion believed that it was the duty of science to determine the politics, economy, law, and social institutions of the future. It can be said that the optimistic view of a future that asserts that science will work at the disposal of humanity, continued through the nineteenth century, even though it became the object of criticism at times.

The tragic events experienced by Western civilization in the nineteenth and twentieth centuries led to the questioning of many formerly unquestioned realities and, particularly, the breaking of routines in modern times. When the subject of civilization was accepted as a matter of human philosophy, the status of the modern man, in the wake of progression, improvement, technical and scientific development, started to be discussed again. Experiences in the world wars, genocides, nuclear arms race in the years of the Cold War, and social problems arising from growing individualism led man to question his raison d'être. It began to be expressed more clearly that a mentality that was only interested in factual reality would be unable to understand the diverse aspects of man. The emphasis on metaphysics made by philosophers discussing ontology like Bergson, Heidegger, and Sartre contributed to the rise of anti-positivism. In fact, even science and technical knowledge, the most important tools of the nineteenth century, and the concept of Western civilization itself started to be questioned and criticized more strongly with regard to human philosophy. The twentieth century became a period when the optimism about Western civilization disappeared. One of the most important indicators of this were the anti-utopias written in this period: *We* by Yevgeny Zamyatin, *1984* by George Orwell, and *Brave New World* by Aldous Huxley. They represented the loss of hope for a better future and the pessimism of civilization.

The discussions in the philosophy of science that started after the Second World War are remarkable within the context of critical contribution to the Western civilization. The fact that Western civilization depends on scientific thought has been regarded as one of its distinctive properties. Mind and science, which became unquestionable authorities with the influence of positivism in the second half of the twentieth century, started to be questioned. The positivist approach, which regards scientific knowledge as superior to all the other kinds of knowledge, was harshly criticized. In this process, one of the most important authorities of the Western civilization was seriously questioned. Thomas Kuhn and Paul Feyerabend's criticism of 'scientism' are particularly important. The fact that the understanding of the world constructed by mind and science in theory and in belief that resulted in the destruction of the world is one of the most important reasons why optimism about the Western civilization turned into pessimism. Civilization, along with technical opportunities and wealth, became a process that speeded up the alienation of man.

Technical developments and the transformation of the production system is another aspect of the civilization debate. The relationship between man and nature was established and processed like it had never been done before in the modern era. According to Heidegger (1998, p. 56), in the modern era, technical knowledge turned everything into a motorized industry. Technical knowledge, which used to be a means for nature to reveal its secrets to man, turned into an industry that accelerated the alienation of man.

Modern technical knowledge produced a mechanical system in terms of human relations not only in workspaces but wherever else it was used. This experience involves the paradox of 'being the slave of the machine while becoming the lord of the world and nature' (Sorokin 2008, p. 136). The city, which is one of the most important elements of the civilization debates, turned into a place where authenticity was damaged by modern technical knowledge. Man lost his belongingness to a community or culture and became a part of the mass. All of these adverse events led to the questioning of linear progressive history, which was valued by Enlightenment and post-Enlightenment thinkers. In the twentieth-century philosophy of history, the strong emphasis on cyclic history against progression has a particularly significant place in the debates on Western civilization.

IZETBEGOVIC'S DISTINCTION OF CULTURE AND CIVILIZATION

Culture is always about humans and human interactions. It is significant that the most important characteristics of human beings are cultural ones, and that cultural accumulation is transferred from generation to generation. This accumulation provides the continuity of culture as a humanistic and social reality. Things, rituals, people, history, society, and religion have acquired a meaning in culture. This production of meaning is a process of cultivation. As every human grows in a cultural reality, cultivation is found everywhere human beings exist. The reason for this is that human beings ascribe meanings to themselves, to other human beings, and to objects. The continuity, through rules and laws of a social organization based on attributing meaning, enable humans to live together in harmony. Production of meaning and living together could be accepted as the two most important characteristics of cultural reality and accultura-tion (Hall 2006, p. 134). However, culture and acculturating processes differ according to time and space.

The concept of civilization has been referred to in order to empha-size the difference between city life and city culture, which is one of the aspects of the diversity of culture and civilization. One of the first uses of civilization in social science literature emphasizes the 'culture of city'. City life refers to the construction of human relations and cultivation in different ways, and in the presence of a combination of cultures. Diversifications of the division of labour, technical devel-opments, and the coexistence of cultural differences have also been attributed to civilization. But human beings experience cultivation in all conditions and in this way cultures exist in civilization. It is possible to say this condition has not changed today for discussions on Western civilization. There are diversifications of the division of labour and technical developments during the development of Western civilization. However, the coexistence of different cultures has been one of the most important problems that Western civiliza-tion has faced and continues to face. Culture and civilization reflect the dualism of human reality. Izetbegovic has accepted human dual-ism as the source of both culture and civilization, and developed an original interpretation of it.

Izetbegovic was a Muslim thinker who lived in the West and had understood Western civilization very well. His works and general thoughts could be accepted as contributions from the West to contem-porary Islamic thought. Although, in terms of spiritual and emotional aspects, he felt that he belonged to the East, in terms of reasoning and nationality, he felt that he belonged to the West. In general, Izetbegovic's thoughts were based in Islam, they were 'between East and West'. In *Islam between East and West*, Izetbegovic discusses many issues such as human beings, culture, civilization, art, history, ethics, religion, philosophy, and science. Principally he evaluates the basic thesis made on these issues before and then he offers his alternative thoughts that were based on an Islamic approach. According to him, there are basically three mentalities or philosophies in the world: Christianity, Judaism, and Islam. In other words, there is spiritual-ism and materialism, and there is Islam, which accepts and partially rejects the other two mentalities and could be accepted as a third way between them. This work is also a human-centred Islamic philosophy book. Izetbegovic has maintained an Islamic perspective for all issues that he was interested in.

Izetbegovic has placed emphasis on the idea that everything that exists has been created with a dual nature. This emphasis is directly based on the Qur'an. This recognition has a central position in his thoughts. The dualist character of being reveals itself not only in the human as a historical, sociological, biological, and ethical reality but also through the products of human beings. Humans are composed of body and soul. The body is the biological and material part of the human, while the soul is spiritual. Only human beings have two environments in all beings. They reveal their beings in two environments and produce a unique reality from the relationships established. One of these environments is natural, and the other one is social. In their relationships established with nature, human beings transform and take control of it. On the other hand, human beings interrelate with each other and these relationships produce the social environment. But in the relationships between nature and other humans, human beings do not act by instinct, but in reality are made up of existing norms, values, and beliefs. Here, it can be seen that natural and social realities reflect the ontological dualism of man as two realities which envelop its existence.

According to Izetbegovic, the concepts of culture and civilization can also be explained by the dualism of humans. As distinct from the biological reality of human beings, cultural space includes elements such as the soul, ethics, freedom, and art that distinguish human beings from other beings. Civilization corresponds to the relationship established between human beings and nature through technology. A stone or a piece of wood can be used as a technical tool and can obtain a sacred meaning by being attributed a meaning that is symbolically not of itself. In the first case, its function gives the object the characteristic of being a tool and thus a technical meaning. The technical relationship between man and nature is the source of the meaning it receives. In the second case, it is impossible to find another being, besides man, that attributes a holy characteristic to a stone or another object. The stone acquires that sacred meaning from a spiritual source. Both culture and civilization exist as significant realities. But as its source, civilization comes alive through the inclination of humans towards a natural reality outside of itself, and culture is the inclination of man towards itself and to the reality of mankind. Both culture and civilization are necessities for man (see Karaarslan 2013). People are neither formed by material bodies alone nor only by the soul. Man cannot subsist by simply supplying his material needs; he also requires spirituality and truth. Because human beings have both material and spiritual aspects, culture and civilization are experienced in every society that is formed by human beings at different times and in different forms.

The meaning of a poem or a novel addresses the cultural aspect of people. A spiritual emphasis on giving up pleasures is also cultural. On the other hand, an understanding that has stopped listening to its inner voice and turned simply to constructing the world belongs to civilization.

That opposition includes the elements shown in the following table that are identified in Izetbegovic's works (see Table 9.1).

In some communities, it can be observed that culture precedes civilization. The cultural abundance of tribes and cultures worldwide is notable; however, most of these tribes have reached a very simple technical level. Thus, they were defeated when they were confronted by Western civilization, which was technically stronger than them. According to Izetbegovic (1993, p. 45), progress belongs to technique and civilization. It is otherwise impossible to talk about progress in cultural space. It cannot be said that civilization is good or bad in itself. But culture does not belong to this world and depends on the truth that distinguishes human beings from other beings. Thus, one of the biggest risks of the civilization is the limiting of people within a material reality and a determined space. Izetbegovic emphasizes the diversity of human beings that cannot be derived from their biological properties. Morality, spiritualism, art, and religion do not acquire their meanings from this world. These cultural elements have an effect on both interpersonal relationships and interactions between humans and nature.

Because of its humanistic character, Izetbegovic accepts (1993, p. 49) culture as a way of self-discovery for people, but civilization, according to him, considers society as based on persons, and mass education transfers this thought. Compulsory and national schooling is an important process that enables the transference

TABLE 9.1 Izetbegovic's Culture–Civilization Differentiation

Culture	Civilization
Spiritual	Material
Feeling	Observation
Art	Technical knowledge
Literature	Positive science
Ethics	Ethical indifference
Afterlife	World
Drama	Utopia
'Snap out of it'	'Dominate the nature'
Make do	Consumption
Thinking	Teaching
Soul	Body
Fate/Indeterminism	Determinism
'Look for knowledge in yourself'	'Look for knowledge in nature'
Personality	Uniformism
Individual	Mass
Mediation	State and School
Sacred	Profane
Village	Urban
Community	Society
Motherhood	Gender
Michelangelo	Darwin
Authentic life	Mechanical life
Man	Citizen
Authentic culture	Mass culture
Verbal communication	Mass communication

Source: 'Table of Opposites' (Izetbegovic, 1993, pp. 293–5)

of Western civilization. Especially schools that educate by Western education systems have played important roles in aiding the modernization processes in non-Western societies by modelling the system on Western-civilization societies. Izetbegovic (1993, p. 52) identifies a wide difference between thinking about the self, existence, and the soul of a person and learning what is being taught in the modern education system. The fact is that this difference is the difference between culture and civilization. According to him, thinking and meditation present to human beings a possibility of finding an answer to the question Who am I? via freedom and spirit. But because the belonging of man to a working social system or to a government is given importance, he is prevented from asking the question 'Who am I?' In fact, ready answers are provided which do not allow any questions.

WESTERN CIVILIZATION AND MASS CULTURE

Izetbegovic was a thinker of the Cold War period. Representing two opposing political orientations, capitalism and socialism competed with each other in this war (Sunar 2010). When we look at their origins, it is possible to identify both these ideologies as results of important changes that created the Western civilization. Fascism, socialism, liberalism, and nationalism are different ideologies that emerged in the West during this civilizational change process. The experience of the West is a transformative process from culture to civilization. So, science, materialism, the laws of human origin that order human relations, experiments, and observations have gained more importance than religion, spiritualism, morality, and feelings. According to positivism, the physical world is the only reality about which we may discover information and talk about. This approach means accepting only one aspect of human reality. According to Izetbegovic, humans will always remain incomplete in a world where God, belief, and spirituality are rejected.

It is possible to say that Izetbegovic follows Oswald Spengler in his thoughts on culture and civilization, and especially in his findings on Western civilization. Spengler, in his work *The Decline of the West*, accepts that a culture turning into a civilization is both an obligatory process and one that leads to its extinction, based on the cyclical conception of history. He argues that Western civilization, which reached the civilization cycle in the nineteenth century, will eventually decline (Spengler 1997, pp. 45–6). This idea refers to societies experiencing a movement from culture to civilization during the course of history. Becoming a stronger civilization means losing the power and spirit of culture. In other words, although civilization occurs by the spirit of culture, when civilization becomes stronger, culture loses power. There is an inverse ratio in the relation between these two realities.

Technology, with its development through civilization, became more dominant on culture, and the cultural aspects of the human continue to be an important problem. Despite wealth and financial satisfaction, an unstoppable increase in crime, divorce, alcoholism, drug addiction, suicide rates, psychological disorders, gambling, and other practices that damage the social structure indicate another aspect of civilization. According to Izetbegovic, the technical development of Western society is a progress that is anti-human because, as opposed to materialist ideology, civilization and comfort are not suitable for human nature (Izetbegovic 1993, p. 67). Civilization addresses the material aspect of humans but misses their spiritual aspect. The increase in the above-mentioned practices inevitably takes the human problem over and above the civilization because all these are common ethical problems of humanity. Moral discussion, even though it has material aspects, is basically spiritual and belongs to the realm of culture.

Reflecting on the meaninglessness and worthlessness of social life produces a continuous moral exhaustion. The transformation of life into a mechanical one results in an alienation of humans that, according to Izetbegovic, is a completely moral issue. Cult is about objects acquiring a symbolic meaning and is human-centred. Mechanical life which emerges through the development of technology makes culture lose its meaning. In line with this, objects lose their real meaning because of their instrumental meaning and, therefore, stop being cultist. The relationship between an increasing interest in mystical teachings and an increase in rates of crime, alcoholism, and drug addiction in the West is notable. This condition in the thoughts of Izetbegovic means seeking the spirit of the body. The body that cannot find its spirit sinks to the excesses and becomes valueless. Based on these thoughts, Izetbegovic describes mass culture as a result of civilization and a 'fake culture'. Mass culture grew immensely, while the alienation of human beings continued in both capitalist and socialist countries during the Cold War years. In place of authentic culture, a mechanical culture that has needs but not a spirit is being produced. Technical developments also support this process of alienation. Mass media tools, especially television, aid the destructive effects of Western civilization on authentic cultures. Mass culture works as a reality against the real man and soul.

ISLAMIC CULTURE OR ISLAMIC CIVILIZATION?

Culture and civilization issues have occupied the thoughts of contemporary Muslim thinkers, in line with the progress and growing influence of Western civilization. Questions such as 'Why have Islamic societies lagged behind Western civilization?' and 'Is Islam an obstacle to progress?' have been and are still discussed in Muslim countries, Turkey, Egypt, Pakistan, Iran, and Malaysia being among them. As a Muslim thinker from a bipolar world in the twentieth century, Izetbegovic contributed to these discussions, initiated by previous Muslim thinkers, and produced original approaches to culture and civilizational issues that can be accepted as important contributions to Islamic thought.

Izetbegovic does not accept Islam merely as a religion. According to him, Islam is beyond a religion. Islam has a strong connection to this world in the practices of morality, law, and politics. Thus, it does not correlate a metaphysical relationship in believers, nor does Islam limit the sacred as only metaphysical. At the same time, Islam wants believers to observe the world and reconstruct it. In other words, introspection, which has inspired culture and religion, is not enough for Islam. Human beings are not only composed of soul and spirituality. Being more than a religion, Islam does not sacrifice culture to civilization, nor civilization to culture because it faces this world. It is possible to accept Islam as a belief and practical system, and as something that is between culture and civilization, something that accepts these two human factors but keeps from their extreme interpretations in Izetbegovic's thought.

Continuity from culture to civilization can be identified in practices existing in the history of Islam. But a mentality based on imitation and memorizing have replaced creativity and dynamism in Islamic societies. All revolutions have experienced this process of change in the course of history. Even though a revolution is realized through a revolutionary spirit, the concept of freedom, sacrifice, and struggle, it begins to lose these properties due to worldliness. Eventually, due to reasons such as power struggles and fanaticism, this revolutionary spirit disintegrates. According to Izetbegovic (1993, p. 60), 'both religion and revolution are born in pain and suffering and die in well-being and comfort. Their true life is as long as their struggle to be realized. Their realization is their death. Both religion and revolution, in their stage of becoming real, produce institutions and structures which eventually suffocate them'. He asserts that the history of Islam has experienced a similar process. A culture centred on the Qur'an, the human, justice, and morality has begun to lose its human-centred approach and the value system it was based on in Islamic history.

Praising the dynamism of Islamic civilization that existed in the early Islamic period, Izetbegovic asserts that with time, the culture–civilization balance has changed in favour of civilization and against culture. Can this be avoided? Izetbegovic is not positive about the answer. Based on a cyclical conception of history, he accepts that as cultures expand to different geographies and generations in history, through a revolutionary spirit of sacrifice and faith, it loses its authenticity. The suppression of the creative elements of culture by civilization is a human condition. According to Izetbegovic, the idea of the 'Islamic civilization' carries many risks and contradictions in itself within this context. He points out the distinction between an Islamic civilization fostered by Islamic culture and an Islamic culture sacrificed to Islamic civilization. He accepts that Islamic culture today is a matter of concern and sees the Islamization of Muslim societies as a primary problem. Izetbegovic's emphasis on Islam is that the culturalization of civilization, which has digressed from culture (Aydin 2013, p. 111). According to him, a culture that is first and foremost based on the original source of Islam should be reclaimed by Muslim intellectuals against the efforts of keeping up with Western civilization (Izetbegovic 1990, p. 25). Technical or scientific issues are important for him, but they come second.

As an Islamist thinker, Izetbegovic thinks that Islam carries an alternative potential against Western civilization. Against the degeneration of Western civilization, Islam has conserved the possibility of a counter position. According to him, it is possible for Muslim societies to keep up with technical progress. However, because this superiority is basically technical, what first needs to be done is not to create the conditions that produce the superiority of Western civilization as has been attempted in many non-Western societies. Based on this mentality, Izetbegovic first tries to identify the possibilities of cultural transformation and his work *Islamic Declaration* is a manifesto for all Muslim societies (Izetbegovic 1990). But, for Islamic societies, he attaches importance to giving up a mentality of imitating and placing importance to values such as belief and morality of their own cultures, instead of trying to compete with Western civilization technically; for one of the most important matters of concern for Muslim societies is following a traditional practice that is far from their own belief principles. Unless they are themselves and unless there is the experience of a moral renaissance, it would not be possible to produce an Islamic alternative for Muslim societies against the West.

Izetbegovic (1993, p. 74) refuses to totally reject the idea of civilization. Religious influences are evident in sources of Western civilization. Later on with the acquiring of meaning and value of work, producing and accumulating capital as a cult shows the move from a culture to a civilization (Izetbegovic 2005, p. 112). But, problems such as the rise of materialism and the instrumentalization and alienation of the human being require a culture-based criticism of civilization. According to Izetbegovic, ideas such as nihilism, existentialism, and revolt philosophies of Western civilization, which express an uprising against the alienation of the human and the optimism of Islam regarding man find meaning in the same rebellion. While pessimism allows a negative criticism of Western civilization, Islam is the possibility of its culture-based positive criticism. The turning of culture into civilization is not an event that can be waited for. But Izetbegovic claims that Islam may put forward culture-based critiques and interpretations of civilization.

It is not possible to make the world better through only the development of civilization. Making the world better is possible through the realization of good, through faith in belief and practice (Izetbegovic 2007, p. 130). Izetbegovic warns that one should watch out for an excessive emphasis on culture which could turn into an ignorance of the world, and an emphasis on the world could turn into an extreme worldliness. He accepts that both extremisms are deviations for humans and attaches importance to dualism, which distinguishes people. If this is not fulfilled, interpreting civilization without referring to culture will be only in terms of utopias. And creating an order with reference to utopias is not humane in Izetbegovic's thought (Akin 2013). In a culture isolated from civilization, there are the risks of becoming a closed society and the inability of man to carry out his duty of changing the world. Such societies have always been societies with civilization. What is important is to carry out a renaissance based on the reality of human beings. In the thought of Izetbegovic, an Islamic renaissance based on Islamic culture corresponds to a possibility that may create harmony between culture and civilization.

***

As a thinker who has contributed to discussions about culture and civilization in contemporary Islamic thought, Izetbegovic has given importance to the source of culture and civilization, and has accepted these concepts as two realities that reflect the dualist structure of human reality. Both realities are ones that could only be put forward by human beings. These two realities organize, change, and produce human relations, and both are necessary for human beings. Izetbegovic accepts the process that progresses from culture to civilization. Returning from civilization to culture is not possible, but a dialectical relationship between these two human realities can be identified. This is because people always experience and create a cultural reality with others even if they are in different times, conditions, and situations. This situation continues in periods when civilization is at its peak.

One of the original dimensions of the issue is emergence of Western civilization and its relation with modernity. The development of modernity in the West and its spread in the world has been regarded as an important stage in civilization. The strengthening of Western civilization has brought about risks as well. Progressing through its reliance on cults such as work ethic and critical thinking, Western civilization has experienced two world wars during the twentieth century. Having encountered issues such as the Holocaust, weapons of mass destruction, increasing crime-rates, alcoholism, suicides, the breaking of the intergenerational bonds, and the weakening of human relationships, Western civilization has been reliving the experiences of the past civilizations. Izetbegovic interprets the condition of Western civilization as the decline of culture due to the development of civilization. One of the important results of the decline of culture is the development and spread of mass culture as a counterfeit culture.

One issue, which makes this topic distinct, is how people experienced a similar kind of alienation in capitalist or socialist countries. Actually, in both types of societies, authentic cultures have been replaced by a counterfeit and mechanical culture. Mass culture works through a mentality mainly based on providing for material needs. Many behaviours that have been accepted as crime and deviance in the past are now regarded as the norm. Izetbegovic thought that change is the result of destruction of authentic culture and the acceptance of a one-dimensional human reality.

Modernization and Westernization processes have taken place through an aim to 'civilize' non-Western and Islamic societies. Izetbegovic argues that the main problem of the Islamic world is a matter of civilization, but he also identifies the estrangement of Islamic societies from Islam as a cultural matter. According to him, in Islamic societies practices based on Western civilization have further increased cultural alienation. On the other hand, an emphasis on Islamic civilization by Islamist thinkers is derived from looking at only one aspect of the condition. According to him, Islamic societies have no other way to produce an Islamic renaissance other than through Islamization. If Islam is not also seen as a cultural matter, most of the negative conditions in Western civilization will be experienced in Islamic societies as well, and it will not be possible to counter these negative issues. Izetbegovic emphasizes that the most important property that differentiates Islamic civilization from others is not technical superiority, but Islamic culture. Islamic culture organizes interpersonal relationships as well as the relationship between humans and all existence. So the difference and superiority of Islamic civilization depends on Islamic culture that produces its own values. But, like in other civilizations in history, as the Islamic civilization settled down, creativity and sacrifice were ignored, wars were fought in line with political disintegration, essence was replaced by form in faith, and worship and moral corruption spread in society. Throughout the history of Islamic societies, culture was sacrificed to civilization and civilization was defeated by another stronger civilization. Thus, in terms of Izetbegovic's approach to the issue of culture and civilization, the matter of the underdevelopment of Islamic societies is not only an issue of civilization, but it is an important issue of culture.

284   *Debates on Civilization in the Muslim World*

BIBLIOGRAPHY

Akin, M. H. 2013. 'Aliya İzzetbegoviç'in siyaset felsefesi ve İslam'. In *Doğu ve batı arasında İslam birliği*, edited by M. A. Güvendi, pp. 55–63. İstanbul: İlmi Etüdler Derneği.

Aydin, M. 2013. 'Kültür ve medeniyet ikilemine farklı bir bakış'. In *Medeniyet tartışmaları*, edited by S. Güder and Y. Çolak, pp. 101–12. İstanbul: İlmi Etüdler Derneği.

Berger, B.M. 1995. *An Essay on Culture: Symbolic Structure and Social Structure.* Berkeley: University of California Press.

Hall, J. A. 2006. 'Culture'. In *The Blackwell Dictionary of Modern Social Thought* (4th ed.), edited by William Outhwaite, pp. 133–7. Malden: Blackwell.

Heidegger, M. 1998. *Tekniğe ilişkin soruşturma*, translated by D. Özlem. İstanbul: Paradigma.

Izetbegoviç, A. 1990. *The Islamic Declaration: A Programme for the Islamization of Muslims and the Muslim Peoples.* Sarajevo.

———. 1993. *Islam between East and West*, third edition. Oak Brook IL: American Trust.

———. 2003. *Tarihe tanıklığım*, translated by A. Demirhan. İstanbul: Klasik.

———. 2005. *Özgürlüğe kaçışım: zindandan notlar*, translated by H. T. Başoğlu. İstanbul: Klasik.

———. 2007. *İslam deklarasyonu ve İslami yeniden doğuşun sorunları*, translated by R. Ademi. İstanbul: Fide.

Karaarslan, F. 2013. 'Medeniyet tartışmalarına anti ütopyacı bir yaklaşım: Aliya İzzetbegoviç örneği'. In *Doğu ve batı arasında İslam birliği*, edited by M. A. Güvendi, pp. 25–33. İstanbul: İlmi Etüdler Derneği.

Meriç, C. 2002. *Umrandan uygarlığa.* İstanbul: İletişim.

Mestrovic, S. 2010. 'Doğu ve duygu ötesi bir batı arasında şekillenen Aliya İzzetbegoviç'in mirası'. In *Uluslararası Aliya İzzetbegoviç sempozyumu bildiriler kitabı*, pp. 138–50. İstanbul: Bağcılar Belediyesi.

Sorokin, P. A. 2008. *Bir bunalım çağında toplum felsefeleri*, translated by M. Tunçay. İstanbul: Salyangoz.

Spengler, O. 1997. *Batının çöküşü*, translated by G. Scognamillo and N. Sengelli. İstanbul: Dergah.

Sunar, L. 2010. 'Aliya'da doğu ve batı'. In *Uluslararası Aliya İzzetbegoviç sempozyumu bildiriler kitabı*, pp. 161–3. İstanbul: Bağcılar Belediyesi.

Toynbee, A. 1991. *Social and Cultural Dynamics*, (2nd ed.). New Brunswick: Transaction.

10 Debating Islam, Tradition, and Modernity in Contemporary Arab-Islamic Thought

Perspectives of Hassan Hanafi and Abdallah Laroui

Driss Habti

RETHINKING THE *TURATH*: AUTHENTICITY AND MODERNITY

The relation between the East and the West has always been that of a difference in power relations, historical confrontation, and ethnocentrism. Colonialism was only a historical culmination of long encounters and friction. The Arab-Islamic world has experienced two stages in the modernization process, that is, the introduction of Western modernity outside the West: (*a*) the colonial context with its colonial administration and economic exploitation and (*b*) the post-colonial context when the attempt at implementing the modernization project was voluntary, and despite the economic dependence of Muslim countries on the West, they were very meticulous in selecting the most suitable Western model to follow in their modernization project.

In spite of being in contact with the modernized and developed West since the eighteenth century, Arab-Muslims were in a state of backwardness and stagnation. The question that arose was 'How to catch up with the West?' This stage was characterized by defensiveness since the authorities sought a means by which they could protect and preserve Islamic values and identity and defend Islam from possible colonial intrusion. This historical context leant more towards defence than towards transformation and recognition of Western technological and scientific superiority. The second stage was an urge to modernize society along the lines of Western experience. Therefore, Arab-Muslims found themselves under the dominance and subordination of the foreign West. A state of defence was a political, cultural, economic, and religious challenge to them as imperialism menaced their political, religious, and cultural identity, and also their history (Esposito, Fasching, and Todd 2002, p. 185). The repercussions of Western rule and the modernization programme stirred up questions and challenged their beliefs and practices. Moreover, colonialism created a political crisis alongside a spiritual one because it was regarded as a menace to Islamic faith and identity (Esposito, Fasching, and Todd 2002). Their views and reactions, as a response to this new situation, ranged from rejection and confrontation to admiration and imitation.

The encounter between Islam and the West has crystallized an image of a materialistic developed West and a spiritualistic lethargic Arab-Muslim world. Studies reveal that the Orientalism of the West gave birth to an Occidentalism of stereotyping the utilitarianism and materialism of the West (Abu-Lughod 1963; Keddie 1968). This commenced in the nineteenth century with authors describing Western society as materialistic and one that lacked spirituality, despite its scientific, philosophical, and technological superiority. The West was rendered as a soulless, mechanistic 'other' to Islam, while the Islamic East was portrayed by Western Orientalism as an exotic, seductive, and untamed 'other' to the West. New meanings started to be constructed. Western images of exoticism in the East were met by a period of Occidentalism that comprised translations of literary works, reforms in accordance with Western models, and a re-reading of tradition (*turath*[1] in Arabic) from new perspectives (Habti, 2010).[2] The encounter between the two civilizations triggered an ongoing debate in the Arab-Muslim world on cultural identity, which has given much regard to the question of turath, authenticity, and modernity. The representation systems of the West and the Arab-Islamic world were partly influenced by the power relations existing between the two. The discourse of modernity and progress, then, came into being in concomitance with the discourse of cultural identity. The questions of modernity, authenticity, and self-identity have been at the heart of the debate between intellectuals and clerics, as they tried to find a way out of the complexities involved. Three trends of thought emerged in the nineteenth century: (*a*) a liberal current that undertook translations of Western works and sent students and scholars to Europe for learning and inspiration; (*b*) an Islamic *Salafi* current that burgeoned in Egypt and later spread in the Muslim world; and (*c*) a nationalist movement aspiring for democracy to counter despotic regimes. The reformist movement that burgeoned in the nineteenth century was called *al-Nahda* (renaissance), and it called for a 'return to the Islamic roots' of the *salaf* (predecessors). Their intellectual activities centred on political reform, cultural identity, and religious issues. Its pioneer reformist Muhammad Abduh (d. 1905) discussed the purification of Islam from 'un-Islamic' features and practices that had intruded in the preceding centuries of decadence. El-Messiri claims that the reformist intellectuals did not base their intellectual constructs on an exclusively Islamic world view, but that their ideas expressed universal ideals, and, thus, presented an inclusive world view. They found many positive things in Western modernity and attempted to reconcile Islam with Western modernity and the ways by which one could catch up with it (El-Messiri 2003, p. 5). Yet, this trend of thought often established a dichotomy between the Islamic world and the West, creating stereotypical representations of these poles that are still present. They foreshadowed a reaction that was to become a dominant response to Western civilization (Keddie 1968, p. 148) and that was mainly intellectual and spiritual in character (Rahman 1970, p. 317; Abu Rabiʾ 1995).

Throughout the twentieth century, similar debates and studies have covered the same questions: What went wrong? Why have we declined and the West developed? Intellectuals have embarked on looking at the question of modernity and the turath, Islam and the West, and identity and authenticity. Since the past provides a sense of selfhood and identity and an outlet from the present, the turath has been regarded as a shield from an *al-Ghazw al-Fikri* (intellectual invasion) of the West (Adonis 1983, p. 19). However, liberal secular thinkers see the turath negatively, rejecting it on the basis of it being a hindrance to modernization and development. Different ideological schools like Marxism, nationalism, and Islamism have grappled with the question of the constituents of the turath and their meanings, from their respective ideological positions. In the second half of the twentieth century, Arab-Islamic thought has been marked by the interplay between philosophy (mainly the philosophy of knowledge and phenomenology) and political ideology. The major aim is to construct a rational and 'authentic' method by which to define Arab-Islamic turath as a vehicle to rejuvenate the civilizational project of 'renaissance', and also to achieve modernity since the turath is the crucial element that shapes Arab-Islamic identity and civilization. Contemporary intellectuals adopt different perspectives in their analyses of these questions, especially in defining the epistemological limit of turath (see Abu Rabi' 1995, p. 41) and its importance to the present.

Landmark literature by prominent thinkers, clerics, and academics appeared on the subject in the late decades of the twentieth century to account for the failure in the modernization of the Arab world. Three broad intellectual trends have been classified in that period: (a) liberal thought, for instance, that of Marxists and generally secularized intellectuals (for example, Abdallah Laroui), which questions the efficiency of the turath in the face of contemporary cultural globalization, Westernization, and economic development; (b) Islamic (Islamist) thought, mainly conservative and traditionalist, which stress Islamic authenticity and identity (for example Rachid Ghannouchi and Hanafi); and (c) nationalist thought of advocates who preach a rapprochement between the Arab-Islamic turath and Western civilization (for example, Muhammad Abed Al-Jabri, Hichem Djait, and Muhammad Lahbabi). All these strands of thought probe important questions such as: To what extent can Arab-Islamic turath be relevant to the present and future of the Arab-Islamic world? Should we openly and uncritically embrace it, or should it be subjected to scrutiny, critical analysis, and interpretation? Is modernity a universal phenomenon manifested by a single experience as modernization theory claims, or can an authentic Arab-Islamic modernity, founded on a re-reading of the turath, be possible? Is modernity possible without turath and can Arab-Muslims take Europe as a model of modernity to copy from?

This chapter discusses the contributions of Hassan Hanafi and Abdallah Laroui, two prominent contemporary thinkers with different intellectual and ideological perspectives. They grappled with the issues of modernity and tradition in modern Arab-Islamic philosophy, taking one of the two as an alternative solution to the current Arab-Islamic 'problematique', and this within the contextual framework of the encounter between Islam and the West. The discussion here is restricted to these two intellectuals who (*a*) investigate the turath not solely from a perspective of religious foundation texts; (*b*) who look at the turath in the light of the present context and concerns in the Arab-Islamic world, and in relation to Western civilization; and (*c*) who are categorized as 'intellectuals' (academics) in these senses.

HASSAN HANAFI: AN ISLAMIC LEFTIST PERSPECTIVE

It is quite difficult to classify Hassan Hanafi ideologically, but he is regarded as an Islamist Leftist. He mentions, 'I have followed the intellectual path mapped out by Sayyid Qutb, whom I consider one of the early Islamist Leftists' (Sayed 2002, p. 2). He thinks 'revolution and religion blend very well, and together they have been at the core of my career as a university professor' (Sayed 2002). He studied at the Sorbonne University where he started building his philosophical consciousness, reading the history and development of modern European philosophy. He then quitted his idealism for an existence-oriented realism saying,

> The two moments of European consciousness: the *cogito* of the rationalist and the *Ego* of the existentialists during four centuries were represented in my life during eight years, rationalist idealism in 1956–1960, life reality and existence in 1961–1966. I kept the optimism of idealism and I left the pessimism of existentialism. I kept reason and its role in idealism and I abandoned the irrational in Existentialism. (Hanafi 1989, p. 241)

This shift was caused by the 1967 defeat, known as *nakba*, which shattered his dream of an Arab renaissance and drove him into deep intellectual and ideological thinking to construct a new Islamic methodology and theology. Hanafi's interest shifted to the question of Islamic turath, and this was the 'beginning of [his] political consciousness'. The critical intellectual became a political activist in the classic sense of involvement of intellectuals in the political arena. He became interested in his 'revolutionary religion' during his work at Philadelphia University (1971–5). After his return to Egypt, he started to develop his pivotal project of modernity and the renewal of turath. Throughout the next few years, he attempted to define an Islamic model of religion and revolution (Hanafi 1977b) and to provide both a comprehensive methodology and inclusive content for a new synthesis of the turath and modernity. Back in Cairo University, Hanafi commenced his work *al-Turath wa al-Tajdid* (Tradition and Renewal), so as to reconstruct the Arab-Islamic turath in the same way that Husserl had done for European philosophy (Hanafi 1989, p. 250). He published a five-volume magnum opus *Min al-'aqida ila al-Thawra: Muhawala li I'adat Bina' 'ilm Usul al-Din* (From Doctrine to Revolution: An Attempt at Reformulating Principles of Faith; 1988). This work was the first volume of his project on *al-Turath and Tajdid: mawqifuna mina Turath al-Qadim* (Tradition and Renewal: Our Attitude to Classical Heritage).

One of Hanafi's major goals is a radical reconstruction of religious thought (Shahrough 1997) using philosophy and phenomenology to develop a radical critique of the Arab–Islamic turath. His eclecticism–rationalism, phenomenology, social democracy, critical theory, and Sufism have put him at the forefront and have earned him prominence around the globe as a contemporary Arab-Muslim thinker and academic. He is controversially known for his *Muqaddima fi 'ilm al-Istighrab* (Introduction to Occidentalism, 1992), *Hiwar bayna al-Sharq wa al-Gharb* (Dialogue between the Orient and the Occident), and his theoretical works which attempt to liberate the turath from the 'hegemonic pretensions' of Western civilization. The first part of this chapter covers Hanafi's perspectives on the question of modernity and his project of the renewal of turath, and his thought on the West as an ideology, culture, and civilization through his Occidentalism.

Hanafi's Dialectic on Modernity, Authenticity, and the Renewal of Turath

Hanafi, in his dialectic analysis of tradition and modernity, sees renewal as modernity and argues that the study of the relationship between turath and new conditions is important in this age of

transformation and transition in which Muslims are living today. He
notes that religious movements lay more emphasis in their discourse
on 'authenticity' than on 'modernity', whereas the main intellectual
currents, essentially the secular, lean more towards 'modernity' than
'authenticity' (Hanafi 1981). He emphasizes that both are necessarily
interrelated and that 'authenticity without modernity' becomes an
unquestioning repetition of the old, while 'modernity without authenticity' becomes a premature radicalism that cannot be sustained. His
main goal is the historicization of turath by interpreting it in the light
of the present. For this purpose, he employs a phenomenological
method in his excavation of the turath. The latter encompasses the
past legacy termed as 'psychological storage'. His project explores this
'storehouse of consciousness' as its ideas keep guiding behaviour in
the present (Ismail 2003, p. 595). The travail undertaken in his analysis aims to identify the relation between the self and the 'other', and,
thus, to crystallize the scope of self-identity. The process of renewal
is then a process of finding the self, authenticating it, and liberating
it from foreign cultures, values, beliefs, and methods (Hanafi 1981).
According to Hanafi, there are two steps to take in this process: a
description of the behaviour, and its transformation to undertake a
social action. The aim of this description is to uncover the dynamics
of relations between the past and the present in consciousness, rather
than a simple citation of accumulated representations in history
(Hanafi 1981). The dynamism of the turath requires an analysis from
the historical context of its production and reproduction, with regard
to the social conditions of the present.

Hanafi thinks the renewal of the turath is the work of the revolutionary. He calls for a necessary revitalization of the turath through
the selection of the rational and revolutionary aspects of all traditional
Islamic sciences. However, efforts to authenticate the turath are not
theorized as an important methodological attitude for reconstructing
an Arab-Islamic framework of reference (as seen by Al-Jabri), but
rather as the outcome of considering two actual references: the facticity of Revelation (Qur'an) and the facticity of the actual social situation
in current Arab-Islamic societies. Hanafi thinks the two realities are
confluent in one single process since 'the basis of revelation is the
social reality' (Hanafi 1982, p. 94). Accordingly, he builds a phenomenological theory of 'Man in history' to attain the mutual fertilization

and final identification between being a Muslim and being a socially concerned citizen. This could be the ultimate outcome of his endeavour to authenticate the turath. Hanafi's aim is therefore to ground an interpretative authority on the historical facticity of Islam and the need to cope with the demands of the contemporary condition of the Arab world (Hanafi 1982).

Hanafi's trilogy of the 'three attitudes' centres on this dialectic between the 'self' (Arab-Islamic) and the 'other' (Western) in a specific historical reality (Hanafi 1992, p. 30). The first volume, *Our Attitude to Ancient Heritage*, puts the 'self' in its historical past and *al-Mawruth* (the inherited turath). The second volume, *Our Attitude to Western Heritage*, situates the 'self' in confrontation with the contemporary 'other' and *al-Waarid* (the Imported from Western civilization). The third volume, *Our Attitude to Reality: Theory of Exegesis*, places the 'self' in its highly factitive and lived reality, while taking the foundational texts, whether sacred or mundane, as part of the self's constitution. In his view, the first two 'confrontations' are civilizational and both are realities that Muslims are experiencing today, while the last one is a real facticity. He explains, in relation to this dialectic, that in each 'civilizational attitude' or confrontation, three variables interplay for its development: *al-Mawruth* (the inherited), *al-Waafid*, and the terrain of creativity wherein both of these interact. Moreover, he believes that the first two heritages are in fact *naql* (texts) from the past salaf or contemporary scholars, and both constitute turath; thus, contemporary Salafiyya movements take the naql as a basis for *al-'aql* (reason) (Hanafi 1992, p. 31).

Moreover, Hanafi re-appropriates the Arabic equivalent of 'fundamentalism' by endowing it with the politics of the last decades in Arab-Islamic world by using the term *sahwa* (awakening) or *nahda*. Hanafi believes the West mistakenly uses 'fundamentalism' for a covert opposition to modernity. In his view, if modernity is essentially a selective search for the authentication of turath, the notions of 'fundamentalism' and 'modernity' are in complementary distribution. Hence, Hanafi advances that Islamic fundamentalism rightly represents the modern time in the unfolding of Islamic civilization through a selective reconstruction of the turath that is preserved in the consciousness of the masses (Hanafi 1992, p. 34).

Hanafi clearly claims that to achieve Muslim aspirations, it is essential to take suitable aspects from the turath of the past and reinforce them with ideas and concepts which lie outside that turath. He strongly believes the masses will come to grasp his radical and esoteric reconstruction of the turath and then will be ready for mobilization, as other trends of thought and models have failed in the past century. Hanafi's dialectic of change is both abstract and diffuse, however, this is not true of his outline of action. His objective of the 'Islamic left', being rather utopian, is an awakening and revolution of Muslims through a scholarly critique of the turath (Hanafi 1988). However, when we look at the implementation of such a revolution, Hanafi appears to have taken from Marx's *Theses on Feuerbach*, saying that Islamic reformers have attempted to understand the world, whereas it is more important to change it (Hanafi 1988). In a rather idealistic way, Hanafi calls for the establishment of a revolutionary party, similar to Lenin's, for mass mobilization to raise consciousness and to liberate the populace from the shackles of dependency, colonialism, and underdevelopment (Hanafi 1988, pp. 387–8).

Like Al-Jabri, Hanafi believes Al-Ghazali's arguments have dominated Islamic thought, and hinder reform and change (Habti 2011). Al-Ghazali, in his view, is at 'the heart of the bulwark against the free and healthy use of reason' (Hanafi 1979, pp. 187–8). For Hanafi, the solution is to fight what he considers Al-Ghazali's attack on rational sciences, and philosophy. Moosa claims the stance of some Arab historiographers is inexplicable with regard to Al-Ghazali, who is accused of initiating the downfall of the complex construct called Arab-Islamic civilization (Moosa 2005, p. 25; see Laroui's analysis). Hanafi believes the turath is the kernel of contemporary awareness in society. For him, turath has no inherent value and its worth lies in it being the source of generating a scientific theory of action that can be used for the benefit of individuals. This tendency seems to appear secularist, but secularism's interest is more in human progress than in religious knowledge and experiences (Hanafi 1988).

Debating 'authenticity' and turath, Hanafi argues for an open and universalistic definition of what may constitute the Arab-Islamic turath. In his analysis, turath is not a fixed pattern of past behaviours and institutions. Esposito and Voll (1996, p. 81) state the word is used 'to represent a concept of evolving religious tradition prescribing norms but not necessarily reflecting words recorded in archives or practices ingrained in daily life: it is instantly under construction'.

Regarding hermeneutics, Hanafi sees the case of the Arab-Islamic world as a way of enlarging the scope of hermeneutic science to mean more than simply 'the science of interpretation' or the 'theory of understanding'. In sum, hermeneutics can be 'the science of the process of revelation from the letter to the reality or from logos to praxis, and also transformation of revelation from the divine mind to human life' (Esposito and Voll, 1996, p. 81). In the case of scriptural hermeneutics, Hanafi (1977a, pp. 1–2) believes 'Islamic' does not necessarily mean 'religious', but it means the most rigorous form of rationalization and the highest degree of 'axiomatisation'. The turath in this framework of analysis is not the inheritance of past practices. It is the axioms provided by Islamic Revelation that makes it possible to develop a 'general Islamic method' that would be a formulation of Islam for individual and social life' (Hanafi 1989, p. 228).

According to Hanafi, the method of interpreting the Qur'an explicates the direct relationship between turath and renewal. The rules of the method articulate that the interpreter who 'is looking for a solution to problems' is to create a synopsis of verses related to certain basic themes and subject them to linguistic analysis and examination of the 'factual situation' (Hanafi 1989). Then, the interpreter must make a comparison 'between the ideal and the real. After building the structure giving the qualitative theme and analysing the factual situation, the interpreter draws comparison between the ideal structure deduced by content-analysis from the text, and the factual situation induced by statistics and social sciences. The interpreter lives between text and reality'. The final step in the method is that the interpreter must take action and 'the complete realization of the Ideal and the Idealization of the real are natural processes of Reason and Nature' (Hanafi 1989). In this manner, turath and renewal come together through the actions of the interpreter of the turath acting in the reality of modernity. Hanafi concludes that 'the renewal of Islam is the solution'. He ardently criticizes scripturalists (or fundamentalists) who believe that the truth is in the Texts. In his view, meanings are not inherent in texts but are attributed to them by actual human beings (Hanafi 1988, p. 229).

Hanafi's main aim is to link contemporary values and concepts with those of the turath. However, despite his endeavours, he does not analyse historical evolution and crystallization of values and concepts in the past or present age. How have people come to endorse specific values in their consciousness in a historical time, be it past or present? Hanafi takes it for granted that certain values today had been absorbed in, and emanate from, earlier periods. He declares that his project attempts to unite 'the *Turath* and the renewal' and that 'the historical roots of the crises of the [present] age [are] in the old *Turath*, reading the past in the present and seeing the present in the past' (Hanafi 1988, p. 223). Hanafi advances that we find in our past the reasons for our current predicaments, and for the decline and breakdowns we have experienced. In his words, 'it is as though we choose from the old only what we want' (Hanafi 1981, p. 15). Hanafi then raises a transcendental consciousness that eliminates 'the historical imperatives of the present and the historicity of revelation' (Hanafi 1981). He says that when Muslims move back in time, they draw on their 'psychological storehouse' of values and symbols, based on their understanding of that turath. They move forward in time towards the present thanks to the appropriate elements of old *kalam* (discourse or arguments). At this level, in lieu of drawing on their 'psychological storehouse', they employ their perceptions and awareness of current problems in terms of the solutions that elements of turath can provide. He thinks that it is this supposedly dynamic process that will contribute to solving the current predicaments the Arab-Islamic world faces (Hanafi 1981).

Therefore, Hanafi attempts to show how human beings can 'renew' Islam and the turath through concrete interaction with their historical time, and also how this interaction materializes and with what results. However, Hanafi's contentions and method are weakly founded if we consider the question of 'democracy'. For Hanafi, the roots of democracy are to be found in the *shura*[3] of early Islam. Yet, he avoids demonstrating how the roots of democracy were developed in pristine Islam through a close historical analysis of groups, movements, and ideas. Hanafi needs to provide the specifics of the historical struggles that led to the understanding of shura in more than a divine scriptural context. Hanafi adds that his method avoids these problems and considers that early texts were written in historical time and place, which implies that understanding them necessitates an understanding of the incentives of their construction. Yet, he does not explain people's behaviour and ideas in concrete historical stages, and in connection with social, economic, and political groups, movements, and institutions. Thus, he has ironically fallen into the trap of the same ahistoricity for which he condemns the Islamists.

The most interesting aspect of Hanafi's theorizing is the extent to which the delimitation of the legitimacy of political authority through a theory of social revolution depends on the hermeneutics of the interpreter set up through a qualitative improvement of the traditional Islamic hermeneutics of the text (Hanafi 1981). Hanafi adheres to using reason and rationalism as clues for Muslims to overcome the impediments they encounter today. He believes the unit of analysis must be—not Islam—but Muslims living in concrete historical epochs. However, his method of seeing the past in the present and projecting from the present into the past appears to shrink the historically based analysis. Hanafi advances that in order to solve their current problems, Muslims can choose from the turath that suits them best. Yet, his phenomenological approach to the question of turath and modernity appears ahistorical. He does not really provide us with an analysis of how values of the past came to acquire specific meanings, in actual historical time and place, for the people of that time. Hanafi's project revolves around demonstrating the relevance of historical context for the significance of values. However, if he fails to demonstrate this for the past, then from where can these values derive? How can he justify their appropriateness for modern historical contexts?

Islam and Western Civilization: Hanafi's Occidentalism, or Reverse Orientalism

One of Hanafi's major concerns in his large reform project of the turath and the renewal is the study of Western civilization and analysing and interpreting Western society and intellectual traditions. He learned methods of phenomenology and religion that he believed would elucidate much about the West and its civilization and help him understand 'the difference between passion and reason, between faith and science' (Hanafi 1989, p. 245). In his second volume, *Mawqifuna mina al-Turath al-Gharbi* (Our Attitude to Western Tradition), he introduced a new science that he called 'Occidentalism' with the ultimate goal to study and understand the West. Hanafi's interest in Western history and its civilization underlay his need to understand the materials and to work on texts that were necessary for his tasks. The result was that he felt quite uneasy with what he called imperialism and 'Westernization'. Hence, Hanafi (2000a, p. 354) saw his study as liberation of the dominated from the shackles of the West, involving a complete cultural and intellectual liberation. Thus, the gist of his discourse is what he names a 'Self–Other continuous historical dialectic' wherein the dominated looks for a self-assertion of identity in relation with the dominant (Hanafi 1992, p. 24). Additionally, Hanafi (1989, p. 261) wants to draw attention to the vision of Westernization and wants people to know the 'realities' of Western society. He adds that the Arab liberal–modernist elite simply copy Western lifestyles and reject authentic endogenous traditions because they are non-Western (see discussion on Laroui later). Hence, he believes there is a tension between tradition and modernity that he builds from his *Tradition and Renewal* and *Muqaddima* (Introduction to Occidentalism) (Hanafi 2000a, p. 358).

Hanafi approaches his project from the perspective of *crisis theory* as a response to the 1967 defeat in the Egypt–Israeli war, representing a turning point in the contemporary history of the Arab world (Hanafi 1992, p. 1). He has tried to excavate the factors behind the defeat and failure of Arab nationalism and modernization. It is within this context that he constructed his reform project. In *Muqaddima fi 'ilm al-Istighrab*, he links his theories about the West, which he had tackled in his earlier writings. Here, Hanafi describes Arab-Islamic identity in light of what Jacques Lacan (1977, pp. 281–91) calls the 'mirror stage' by distinguishing the 'self' from the 'other'. However, Hanafi limits his discussion to the roots of these ideologies in the West and their consequences (Hanafi 1992, p. 2). He sees Westernization as an identity crisis because the aspects of this process 'threaten our civilizational autonomy' (Hanafi 1992). Hanafi adds that because of Westernization, a struggle for civilizational autonomy and identity recognition is necessary, and it is in the Islamist discourses and identity narratives of Occidentalism that this struggle is manifested (Hanafi 1992, p. 23). Hanafi considers the question of identity as a 'civilizational issue'. It is regarded as an extension to colonialism because they are seen as interrelated in the toil to 'obliterate the markers of Arab-Islamic identity' (Hanafi 1992, pp. 24–5). He adds that 'a considerable space of our contemporary culture has been turned into civilizational agencies [working] for the "other", and into an extension of Western paradigms'.

Hanafi argues that the outcome of the power relation between the colonizer and the colonized, and superiority and inferiority, is 'a historical complex in the conflict of civilizations' (Hanafi 1992, pp. 33–4). Occidentalism is then an 'urgent necessity' seeking neither domination nor hegemony, but rather equality (Hanafi 1992, p. 31). He considers that 'Occidentalism aims at debunking the myth that the West is representative of humanity ... [that] the world's history is the history of the West; humanity's history is the history of the West; the history of philosophy is that of Western philosophy' (Hanafi 1992, p. 42). Thus, Hanafi's Occidentalism is an avowal of the heterogeneity of global cultures and an assertion that 'world culture' is a myth created by the culture of the dominant to rule the dominated. To achieve complete decolonization, Hanafi thinks, Occidentalism can reverse that power relationship, so that the non-Western societies become the researcher and the West the object of research. Hanafi laments what he calls 'cultural holes', mentioning their role in spoiling Arab-Islamic culture by way of their manifestation in different spheres of life. This culminates in a gradual detachment from the self (Hanafi, 1992, p. 24). Occidentalism sees liberation as freeing the self from the control of the image imposed by the 'other' (Hanafi 2000b, pp. 355–6). Hanafi's argument is refutable since the emancipatory aims of the politics of identity may create, rather than restrain, the differences between the West and the Islamic 'other'.

Hanafi's project is criticized as lacking objectivity. Through his Occidentalism, he actually aspires to bend the West according to his own will to dominate it and hide the centrality that he himself has produced (Harb 1995, p. 50). Qansuwa (1997, p. 220) continues that Hanafi's goal is to enforce his 'racist' and religious Islamic centrality on all 'others' in the world. Hanafi tries to demonstrate that Islamic and Western civilizations are mutually exclusive. He insists that Western civilization does not have an *a priori* identity, and this deficiency has led historical methodologies to dominate Western thought, and hence its fascination with historicism, Marxism, and humanities. Contrary to this, Hanafi believes Islamic sciences (for example, Islamic jurisprudence, principles of Religion, Sufism and Philosophy) have one centre: the Revelation. They were creations of, and developed from, this centre (Hanafi 1992, pp. 16–17, 110–11). Al-Alim (1997, p. 26) claims that the difference between the two civilizations is that the Western civilization is historically minded yet lacking in structure, whereas the Islamic civilization is structurally founded without historical awareness, and this is argued by Laroui (discussed later). Hanafi sees European awareness as being the outcome of historical process, while Islamic awareness has an *a priori* identity. European identity possesses a structure that stems from formation and evolution, whereas Islamic identity has a permanent structure that precedes its formation and historical development. He also shows his extremism when he stresses a 'pure and permanent' Islamic identity, convinced that the 'self' is not historical but a crystallization of an a priori identity (Hattar 1986, p. 144).

While overlooking the objective and historical contexts and the dominant political and socio-cultural dimensions from and within which Islamic and Western civilizations were born, Al-Alim (1997, pp. 29–32) thinks Hanafi's stand tends to generalize when he states that Western civilization is diffuse and Islamic civilization is unifying. This evidences an absence of objectivity because both features can be spotted in either civilization. Furthermore, Hanafi's Occidentalism fails to distinguish ideologically between the imperialist and civilizational dimensions of the West, specifically in his emphasis on the mutually exclusive relationship between Western and Islamic civilizations in Arab-Islamic contemporary life. His book *Muqaddima* (as Hanafi suggests), in fact, ignores the objective understanding of the contemporary map of contradictions and conflicts (1997, pp. 33–6), and, thus, creates a sort of cultural wall between the 'self' and the 'other' (Harb 1995, p. 52). He fails to recognize the diversity of the cultural frames of reference that Arab-Islamic identity enjoys in the postcolonial period. Cultural or intellectual pluralism and exposure to the culture of the 'other' is possible as long as it is adjusted to cultural specificity (ideas) or environmental specificity (technology). Embracing Western technology and dismissing its cultural heritage is unfeasible, and Hanafi's rejection of cultural and intellectual pluralism itself is impractical, owing to the rapid process of globalization and the appearance of a kind of 'cultural transnationalism'. Indeed, 'westernization is a form of alienation' (Hanafi 1992, p. 25) when it enhances a modernity that rejects authenticity and specificity. Yet, his identity narrative and discourse is homogenizing and fails to demonstrate how his aspired version of Arab-Islamic identity can coexist with the imported cultural influences of the West, even if he believes that reflexivity—what he calls *inghilaq* (closure) from *al-Waarid* (the imported)—is a great danger (Hanafi 1992, pp. 25–6).

Hanafi argues that the West and its Orientalism facilitated its culture to dominate the Islamic culture and world view. Hanafi's Occidentalism strives to build an Arab-Islamic 'self' instead of imitating the Western 'other', by rendering the 'other' an object of knowledge for the Arab-Islamic 'self', rather than as a source of its knowledge (1981, p. 75; 1992, pp. 19–37). He also uses European Enlightenment concepts to rebel against the dominant Islamic system of reading that places too much emphasis on interpreting the Qur'an. Following Al-Jabri and Laroui, Hanafi (1981, p. 75) claims that Orientalists reduce Islam to politics, economics, and geography by applying methods of history, analysis, projection, and interaction. Al-Alim (1997, pp. 29–33) argues that Hanafi's focus on phenomenological interpretation in highlighting the importance of Revelation in Islamic civilization makes his approach lack historical objectivity. The historical approach isolates Islamic civilization from Revelation (the Qur'an and the Sunnah) by dealing with its historical foundations. The analytical method reduces the universality and comprehensiveness of Islamic civilization, two crucial features that stem from Revelation (Al-Alim, 1997, pp. 85–7). Hanafi lacks objectivity when he simply looks at the West as a religious civilization and a society of philosophers (Al-Alim, 1997, pp. 29–32). Yet, according to Harb (1995, p. 55), Hanafi's description of the process of *becoming*, of awareness, and of the structure of Western thought is the first perceptive Arab reading of Western philosophers.

For Al-Alim (1997, p. 29), Hanafi's *Introduction to Occidentalism* is not a scientific work as it does not set up its methodologies and principles. This is simply a claim that Hanafi's book is more of an ideological work rather than a scientific one. Harb (1995, p. 46) argues Hanafi's liberation from Western philosophical theories will lead to a liberation from Western domination. However, taking philosophy as an object of study does not mean enabling the Arab-Islamic world to dominate the West. Harb adds that Hanafi falls in the trap of 'reverse Orientalism' because he thinks studying Western thought will provide liberation from the West, preparing Islamic civilization to enter its 'third seven-centuries cycle'. Hanafi (1990, p. 458) claims that 'Western social science is not an innocent science free from bias but ideologically oriented and politically motivated'. His philosophy is more a philosophy of history and, thus, subjective in essence (Al-Alim, 1997, p. 29), while his ideology is based on Western philosophers whose theories are to be taken as a sign of the dynamic of Western civilization (Abd al-Hafiz, 1997, p. 184). Al-Alim claims that in the *postmodern* era, scientific studies have replaced Orientalism, whereas Abd al-Hafiz (1997, p. 29) views that Hanafi has re-established it in his *Muqaddima*.

Regardless of the incoherence and bias in his analysis, Hanafi has produced what he calls a 'new humanism' (Hanafi 1992, p. 56) which allows the underdeveloped world to assert itself, while making the West see its faults. However, Occidentalist (Islamist) modes of discourse are generally characterized by elements of subjectivity and otherness, and of resistance and defensiveness (see Laroui's debate discussed later). Despite their essentialism, they represent a counter-discourse that seeks the assertion of agency and the achievement of autonomy and recognition (Sadiki 2004, p. 131). Hanafi argues that under the banner of neutrality and objectivity, the European 'self' has camouflaged bias and subjectivity. However, Hanafi's leftist and revolutionary paradigm and his claim of Occidentalism's neutrality and objectivity are biased, because neutrality is hard to attain within value-laden and foundationalist knowledge practices. In the following section is a discussion of Abdallah Laroui's Marxist historicist perspective, as offered in his debate on the question of turath and modernity, Islam and Western civilization.

ABDALLAH LAROUI: A MARXIST HISTORICIST PERSPECTIVE

Like other contemporary Arab intellectuals, Abdallah Laroui has tried through his writings to develop and invigorate the socio-economic and cultural facets of post-independence Arab nations. He has looked to do this by transcending the historical horizons of his generation by way of his ideological overtones and the political commitment of his intellectual scholarship. His essay 'L'ideologie arabe contemporaine' (1967), which critics saw as 'simplistic, idealistic, or anti-Arab' (Choueiri 1989, p. 167), is an expression of his—and all Moroccans'—aspirations and apprehensions, as well as an embodiment of his own experiences (Laroui 1967, p. 3). He provides a critical reading of the condition of national culture in a post-independence time. His book *al-'arab wa al-Fikr al-Tarikhi* (The Arabs and Historical Thought) (1973) can be considered as a retort to critics of the first work as it reaffirms his ideological standpoint. The reason he tried to give for his aspired project was that of infusing the modernization project in the Arab world with a socio-historical methodology. He also examined Western works on Arab-Islamic historiography, providing evocative insights into its nature. He published an English translation of the latter work with new insights in 1976, showing the depth of his argumentative and critical analysis, as well as his *idée force* dwelling in the cultural and philosophical realms, more than the political. His unspoken goal is, however, a political transformation of Arab societies, despite his spoken goal being an objective criticism of the predicaments of the Arab world.

I think the importance of selecting Laroui in this chapter stems from his stance towards Arab-Islamic turath, which he rejects, advocating the adoption of Western culture to achieve the aspired modernity and development. Laroui as an intellectual has a hybrid philosophical and cultural background, which enabled him to interpret Europe to the Arab-Islamic world, and Arab culture to Europe. Laroui's reading of the Western scholarship on Islam and political development is subtle. He ventured into analysing problematic issues confronting the Arab world (Gallagher 2000) and profoundly reflected on the epistemological content and historical evolution of modern and contemporary Arab-Islamic thought. The Marxist tendencies of his early works changed into a strong criticism of the intelligentsia. He also detaches himself from Marxists and post-structuralists as he accuses the latter of adopting 'metaphysical' and 'mystical positions', which they levelled against traditional Western philosophy. In his later scholarship, he shifted from Marxism to Etatism, criticizing Arab intelligentsia for their failure to implement the changes needed for modernization and modernity, and meanwhile siding with the apparatus of the state in its social and political programme.

Being a historian and political analyst, Laroui categorizes three currents of ideology: the views of the religious cleric, the democratic liberal, and the nationalist technocrat. His critique of contemporary Arab ideology reveals his rejection of the three different interpretations of Arab authenticity for their methodological inadequacy, and according to him, 'the preceding developments all lead to one and the same conclusion: discard all objective knowledge of Arab society' (Laroui 1967, pp. 17–28, 45–9). He believes the only adequate method to explain and surpass the constant opposition between the call for authenticity and modernity is historical and dialectic. Laroui, in his cultural and historical critique, does not formulate a set of open confrontations between the 'self' and the 'other', or Islam and the West, as Hanafi does, though both embrace revolutionary ideology. His approach is based on a secular 'Westernized' perspective contained within a radical framework (Sharabi 1991, p. 23). He called for a historical approach to the study of Arab intellectual thought. His main thesis revolves around the concept of history as being marginal to the main currents in Arab-Islamic thought in modern and contemporary epochs, especially to two major rationales: the traditionalist and the eclectic. These two paradigms of thought are ahistorical, for the former signifies alienation in its past-oriented vision, and the latter connotes Westernization and an embrace of imported values. To his mind, the way out of this crisis resides in transcending the two rationales by adopting Marxist historicism (Laroui 1967). This section discusses the intellectual contribution of Laroui with a Marxist historicist perspective on the question of tradition, authenticity, and modernity, and the encounters of Islam and Western civilization.

In Search of the Self and Authenticity in the Modern

Laroui's works cover the condition of the 'epistemological map' of the Arab-Islamic world. The main problem and concern for Laroui is modernization, taking one sole form, that of the liberal state and society, and the rational scientism of Marxism. He (1967) argues that Arab-Muslims face a major hurdle, and in his view it is modernity, which is existentially Western though it has a universal destiny. He (1967, p. 6) assumes that the intellectual elite betrayed its historical mission of critical analysis of the pre-independence Arab world. His focus is to use the correct methodology to analyse the modern Arab world, with the main goal of accomplishing a re-reading of the past for a construction of the future. He believes that historicist analysis will sort out the weaknesses of Arab Reason and will help to create a novel intellectual map to rectify the predicaments faced in contemporary Arab-Islamic culture. At this point, an important question arises on the way the structure of modern Arab reason may be analysed. For Laroui, it is unnecessary to follow the same path of Al-Jabri in deconstructing Arab Reason and excavating the archive of the turath. He does not see the attainment of modernity as an easy goal to reach. He believes 'the desire for modernity, like the desire for tradition (*Turath*), is the insidious way in which domination works. Yet, there is no other path'. Laroui (1967, p. 4) claims that the 'Arab Self' has been deeply influenced by the encounter with the mono-lithic West. He sees Arab modernity as a space of disaster (Laroui 1967, p. 88)—a wound and defeat of the 'self' which excludes the possibility of regaining any lost authenticity, and of which any attempt to do so will do nothing but drive it further away.

Authenticity denotes the self, a collective self in contradistinction to the West as the 'other'. It means continuity with the past and its turath, which he laments as being one major obstacle that stands against rationalism and progress. He condemns the escape from the present as self-deceptive, an escape from the responsibilities of real-life into a delusional search for authenticity. Laroui (1967, p. 89) thinks contemporary Arab-Islamic culture is a *culture de la scission interieure* (culture of internal schism), where contemporary Arabs live in 'a hypnotic state', still unconscious of their loss (of the 'self'), but cannot free themselves from the past. Arab historical consciousness is at a stop and history is frozen in the 'unpresent' tense. While the past embodies turath, specificity, identity, and the cycle of life, its present is an interrupted continuity of its past that has no authentic-ity or particular disposition. The past and the future overshadow the present and make it transitory, and thus there exists a break between 'social reality and self-consciousness' (Laroui 1967, pp. 65–9). Thus, the present can recover its importance by hypothesizing its plausible ideological manifestations as an *objective evolution* (Laroui 1967, pp. 124–37). He (1987, p. 75) argues that aspects of modernity can be detected in the social, educational, political, and economic life of society, yet traditionalist intellectuals still carry the banner of authenticity against modernism, or spirituality against historical change.

Laroui's interest lies in the past or the present as a disrupted possibility or teleological process. Laroui suggests that universality (*raison universèlle*) is an alternative for authenticity because of the failure of the 'past' and the turath to satiate the demands of modernity. According to him, universality refers to a world view that allows Arabs to act and think in a rationalist way. Laroui's understanding of the dialectic method, the dynamic definition of authenticity, and the historical process permits him to untie the bond between authenticity and the turath. He strongly believes it is plausible to understand the present and to have social knowledge through a form of critical and dialectical analysis that avoids the downsides of different forms of 'positivistic dogmatism' and 'uses and abuses of history' (Laroui 1973, p. 30). He also delineates the notion of future 'ideologically', that is, intellectually and morally, since it should be part of the possibilities of the present. He preaches to do without authenticity and advocates universality and historicism instead: 'The European historical role—extending from the Renaissance to the Industrial Revolution—provides the only model for those revolutionary politics that aim to rid non-European countries of medieval conditions and lead them to modern ones' (Laroui 1984, p. 125). He believes in European history as a universal history by which one can achieve cultural revolution, political change, and liberalism, to the detriment of turath and the traditionalism and eclecticism of the Arab world.

Laroui (1967, pp. 139–55) finds it necessary to adopt this new 'homogenous and total model'. His use of historicist perspective seeks to analyse the past and to enlighten the route for modernity in the future (Laroui 1967, pp. 157–65). This methodology aims to reduce in time and space two historical movements and phases—liberalism and socialism—into one moment of a plan of action, and this was suggested under a remoulded Marxism fitting the Arab-Islamic contextual frame. As Choueiri (1989, p. 184) believes, Arab Marxism was conceived as an organic ideology that strengthens the disposition of specificity and decomposes authenticity in light of its false survival and nostalgia. Laroui's analysis of the three ideological trends (the views of the cleric, the liberal, and the technocrat) works as an alternative for the study of socio-economic structures that represent a shadow of an imposing reality. His overall aspiration is to transcend the slips of these trends to catch up with Western civilization, development, liberation of spirit from myth, and a national culture that is future-oriented, not backward looking. The Arab states found themselves amid the technical reason of the modern West and the totalistic vision of its turath. Laroui called for more political and cultural freedom for the intelligentsia so they could attain that authentic self-understanding and universalism needed for a leap to the future and modernity. However, his concept of *universality* is still elusive and his contention that the turath is to be opposed to reason is unfounded. He looks at the concept of reason with a Western philosophical frame of reference and thinks Western reason is the only expression of 'universal reason'.' He (1987, p. 80) believes the Arab world must opt for change, abiding by the conditions set by Western history and forces. Albert Hourani (1991, p. 445) thinks Laroui recommends 'a willingness to transcend the past, to take what was needed from it by a "radical criticism of culture, language and tradition", and use it to create a new future'. This position also resembles that taken by Hassan Hanafi in his revolutionary dialectic of turath and renewal.

Laroui (1967, p. 153) thinks objective Marxism is the most effective advanced system of social and economic analysis, and corresponds to an important leap in the modern history of Europe. It is the sum of the systematic methodology of modern Western history and thought. He used it to look at the future of the Arab-Islamic world by overlooking old values and traditionalism, and he even looked beyond Islam as a religion and an exclusive set of ideals (see also Berque 1964, p. 266). To overcome the present and look forward to a better future becomes a personal conviction. Intellectuals can rationalize their societies and make a new modernization programme that would provide 'a rational analysis of the past, the present, and the foreseeable future of the Arabs'. Laroui (1973, p. 35) stresses they must first accomplish 'hegemony' in the cultural arena as a *sine qua non* for the triumph of political struggle. Laroui (1973, p. 63) thinks Marxism to be the only intellectual system which provides 'the logic of contemporary era and modern science'. Yet, he views the omnipresence of traditionalism and its mentality that encompasses contemporary Arab-Islamic thought to be anachronistic and obsolete. He explains that the crisis of traditionalist intelligentsia is located in their mental enslavement to the past, which hinders historical consciousness and, thus, progress and emancipation. Laroui (1976, p. 154) finds the way to undermine this trend of thought by saying that the only way to do away with it 'consists in strict submission to the discipline of historical thought and acceptance of all its assumptions'.

On the basis of Laroui's argument, the major problem the contemporary Arab-Islamic world encounters is not Westernization, or cultural or historical alienation as Hanafi believes, but rather maintaining traditional categories of thought which are unable to address the current predicament of the Arab society. He critiques and expresses his disappointment with the scholarship of Arab intellectuals, their understanding of the turath and Islamic history, the West's history and thought, their role in developing Arab-Islamic thought, and their failure to meet the aspirations of the masses. He set out to deconstruct the discursive structural formations of Arab-Islamic thought in order to liberate Arabs from their adherence to the past and its turath. He thinks the reasons for backwardness are located in cultural and epistemological domains, rather than in economic or political ailments. In Laroui's eyes, the intellectuals seemed unable to detach themselves from deep-rooted patterns of intellectual practice. However, the question remains as to whether he implies that turath is antithetical to the aspirations of society and the product of a closed mental and theological system.

In his first oeuvre, Laroui (1967) raises questions pertaining to cultural and intellectual revolution that was needed to achieve modernization and modernity, the role of the intelligentsia in such a revolution, the causes of crisis and decadence in the Arab world, and the position the turath in the present. He maintains that Arab culture mirrors the inner alienation of contemporary Arab society from modern civilization. He calls for a total disengagement with turath as it merely carries dead weight from the past. This might seem a heavy charge against turath as it discards the sum of the historical continuities and cultural specificities of the Arab-Islamic world. Even though his aspiration is to surmount cultural and intellectual backwardness, the alternative he provides is simplistic. He suggests dismissing the past from the memory of Arab society and advocates a complete adoption of Westernization as a means of achieving progress and modernity. One way in which he examines this issue is through analysis of the encounters and relations between Islam and Western civilization.

Islam and Western Civilization: Between the 'Present Past' and the 'Future Perfect'

Laroui (1973, p. 7) sees the West as an epitome of universal development, but also as a universal domineering power guilty of 'economic exploitation, political domination' and of influencing conceptual systems and ethical practices. He argues that a Western national state is *inauthentic*, as well as bourgeois, since it represents Western history and experience. The culture and politics of the West are alien and bourgeois. He adds (1977b, pp. 3–5), 'Each day, we see more clearly the necessity of questioning the past concerning the two phenomena that haunt our political and intellectual life: our historical lag and its conscious compensation, that is, revolution.' Laroui argues (1977a) that culture, in its various religious forms and manifestations, reproduces the social structure at a higher level and acts as a unifying symbol. Its primary function in a society under European pressure made it an instrument of resistance and a quintessential element of national identity. As such, the past with its culture and traditions was resurrected as a defensive weapon against external aggression by a movement of a group of *ulama* (elite scholars) who appealed to the masses to safeguard their religion and ward off the devastating impacts of falling under European domination.

Arab subordination refers to form by which Arabs' identify with the 'other'. Laroui (1967, pp. 4–42) opines, 'It is in relation to the "Other" that Arabs define themselves. The "Other" is the West. Hence to describe the Arabs' quest for the "Self" means to present, at the same time, a history of the notion of the West.... Having started from the question, "who are we?" we are facing another question, "What is the West?".' Subordination is also manifested in the Arabs' strong attachment to the past—a *dead* past but still looked upon as a present element by the alienated 'self'. Thus, the West and the past speak from the vacuum of the Arab 'self', which results in a *retard culturel* (cultural retardation) and an obstruction of any flourishing growth of a modern 'self'. This is how Laroui sees the relation between the West and the Arab-Islamic world. The possibility of finding an authentic 'self' can only be realized through a critical reconsideration of our *outillage mental*. In the words of Laroui (1967, p. 6): 'Our world, social and mental, is steeped in influences.... Without undertaking a rigorous analysis of our mental tools, we can never be certain that we are actually talking about ourselves; and the testimony we sign as our own will require interpretation by others.'

For Laroui (1967, p. 84), alienation is the result of rejection—a rejection of traditionalist Arab-Muslims' interaction with the West. Discourses of identity and cultural authenticity such as Orientalism and nationalism disregard the long history of interaction and evolution between the Arab world and the West, and the oscillation of fixed identities. However, there is another kind of rejection that is more devastating and in which hegemony is concretized, and that is the dependence of the modern Arab forms of consciousness on those of the West. The history of change and interchange between the two would be rejected and would be ignored as long as the rejection was not rationalistically critiqued. The three paradigms of Arab modernity (religious, liberal, and technophile) all claim *authenticity* and originality, and are also indebted to a European model. Within the discursive terrain, intellectuals and thinkers express that 'it is always the Other that poses the terms of the question, draws the boundaries of the field of research, and it is within this frame that contemporary Arab-Islamic thought attempts to find its answers' (Laroui 1967, p. 33). These trends have simply debated why the West is developed, but not 'us', or, what is the cause of stagnation in the Arab-Muslim world that could have led 'us' to avoid the experience of colonialism.

Laroui (1967, pp. 33, 84) thinks that the three currents of thought and ideology have changed their methods and relationships in the independent state. The state inhibits universal Islam by co-opting a clerical elite and adopting official 'state' Islam, using it both as an ideological tool and as a connecting line between the rulers and masses. The liberals' presence has abated and technocrats constitute the basis of the new nation state. He maintains the process of change these intellectual trends have undergone reminds us of the three phases of European history and thought, although the point of convergence between these trends is the West. Laroui (1967, p. 44) claims that the religious cleric laments with a religious consciousness that the West has lost morality and human ethics. However, he holds a double attitude where he analyses society from a religious approach but the West as a liberal critic. Laroui (1973, p. 16) also admits that traditionalism (Salafiyya) still dominates as it has kept its old methods and perspectives, but he thinks that its proponents need to probe for a compromise with the West, despite their resistance against intellectual imperialism and their call for a defence of Islamic authenticity. Laroui maintains that Salafiyya's call for a return to early Islam denoted an effort to maintain the future by means of reinforcing traditional culture that continued to be the only common reference of society. Nationalism emerged from the specificity of the nation, and expresses a continuity of its past. It reaffirms the prevalence of the past over the present and is liable to reappear under various conditions and during certain events. Historicism resurges, but in lieu of mastering the future it legitimizes the past (see Al-Azmeh, 1985). This is deemed a state of reconciliation between the historian and the revolutionary, and, as Laroui claims (1977b, pp. 386–8), one yields to the past and the other frees himself of a retarded present. Laroui (1967, p. 32) believes that 'although it loses its dominant role, the religious thought (or consciousness) does not totally disappear in the liberal independent state.' However, he condemns them as advocators of insular authenticity and opponents of dialogue with the West. He adds that Arabs must benefit from the West as Western thought paves the way for Arab ideology to flourish beyond experience and real practice, and this is because Arabs are ideologically advanced but 'objectively' backward (Laroui 1967, p. 212).

Laroui's main argument surrounds the models' proponents who claim to be agents of modernity but who merely copy anachronistic forms of Western consciousness. He (1967, p. 34) thinks they just reproduce 'superseded forms of Western consciousness' that even the West does not recognize because it no longer conveys the real 'productive core of Western society'. Laroui mentions that 'in attempting to comprehend itself, the Orient acts as an archeologist in that it digs up the [intellectual and cultural] roles of the Western consciousness'. The West represents a means of instigating change in the Arab world, and contemporary Arab thought is indebted to the West. The various changes in Europe during the post-war and post–Cold War periods have shaped the Arab-Islamic world and its thinking (Laroui 1967, p. 37). The discourse of the three intellectual trends all centre around the thesis of *crisis*: crisis at the social, political, economic, and intellectual levels. The religious intellectual gropes for a way to address the question of faith in contemporary times, the politician to address liberalism and political modernization, and the technocrat to address scientific development and knowledge. Laroui states that 'historical distance' renders that recognition unlikely, and that 'contact between two societies can be inconsequential; for one society can simply *not see* the other' (Laroui 1967, p. 40). Time is an important element in Laroui's thought, and he depicts it as a rupture in the structure of consciousness and a 'falling out of synchrony'. Arab consciousness does not live in the present, but rather resides in a future—'a future already outlined elsewhere, which we are not free to reject':

> Our consciousness ... drifts between the determinations of the past and the call of the future. It dwells in the peculiar temporal category of an anterior future, which radically changes the meaning of all other temporal parameters: neither our present, nor our past, nor our future are real, and can be lived as such. (1967, p. 66)

Laroui (1967, p. 96) thinks the fate of the Arab world is determined in the West, and contemporary Arab-Islamic consciousness cannot fathom this because it resides in an 'unreal' or 'other' world constituted of a 'condensed image of the past', as a result of the shock of loss—'a self-defeat'. Laroui explains that Arab culture emanates from 'the solidified expression of a defunct society', of a regained 'folklore' that celebrates the vacuum of the Arab 'self', and that their reality is a totally modern European production. In a sense, he adds, there was never any existing Arab culture. Both the 'historical distance' between the Arab world and the West and between the critical historian and his society become 'incommensurable'. Laroui (1967, p. 175) believes a pure Arab authenticity might be difficult to achieve except through 'transcendental universality', because, as he sees it, Arab identity is intrinsically connected to Europe and an Arab self-understanding is also linked to the understanding of the Western 'other.' The present, for Laroui (1967, p. 167), denotes a subjectivity that Arabs do not possess, and they have to transcend their temporal dysfunction, their retard, if they do not wish to remain as 'parrots' of European modernity. To be modern is to own the present, to be emancipated from myth and from the 'past', to exclude voices of outsiders, and to have universal values such as cultural pluralism. Laroui calls for a resolution of all cultural ties, towards forging a novel universal identity—the only true route towards emancipation and agency for a reconciliation between the 'me' and the 'non-me': 'To recognize the universal is to become reconciled with oneself' (Laroui 1967). Referring to the historical relation of the Arab world with the West in terms of colonialism, religious expression, political thought, and technical creativity, Laroui provides two main grounds: (*a*) a cohesive cultural unity of Arab world and (*b*) colonialism as a break between medieval and modern Arab history and thought (Laroui 1967, p. 29).

Laroui considers that modern Arab ideology is a construct of a long interaction with the movement of Orientalism (see Habti 2010, pp. 54–84). He argues, in his analysis of Orientalist works, that political movements, economic structures, religious orders, and tribal communities are reduced to embodiments of cultural symbols and attitudes. Thus, the objects of study are tackled as concepts, and these Orientalists failed to grasp the history of north Africa and the overall Arab world, not because of their ideological contentions or the evaluation of their evidence, but rather, as Choueiri (1989, p. 172) claims, because of the lack of a 'full appreciation of the teleological movement of society, and the discovery of the substance which is concealed by deceptive forms of stasis and stagnation'. In fact, Laroui thinks that neither Western nor north African historians have succeeded in constructing the truth of a past that experienced a plethora of developments.

Towards an Arab Liberal Authenticity and Modernity

Laroui's narratives both touch on the present and look forward to the future, and are reformulations of a specific political programme. His Historicism entails continuous change at both ends of the spectrum. His approach liberates Arab identity into the tumultuous phase of *becoming*, while Orientalists practise 'de-historicization' in rigid fashion (Laroui 1977b, p. 328). Laroui condemns the authenticity of the nation as artificial blends that are aimed to freeze the present and annihilate the future, while at the same time saving its specificity as a practical polity. The course of the past is stripped of its feasibility and regarded as an oppressive present. It was no longer the time, in

Laroui's view, to look back towards the past or probe into Ibn Khaldun's vicious circles between nomadism and 'degenerate civilization', rather it was a time when the culture of the future had to be imbued 'with a national significance' (Laroui 1977b). Laroui (1967) suggests a complete dismissal of the turath from the memory of society and stresses the incompatibility of its basics with modernity. However, there is a wide gap between implementing modernity, and modernization in Arab society. For instance, although the Gulf countries have reached a high level of modernization, the prevailing thought and consciousness are traditional or conservative. Laroui questions: 'Is it possible to imagine a modern society without a modern ideology?' In this sense, new modern methodologies must be used, and a progressive thought structure needs to be constructed to achieve emancipation and progress.

This appears to be an Orientalist position since its thesis purports that the traditionalist mentality has features of reasoning founded on intellectual concepts that are no longer accepted. Importantly, Laroui believes that Marxism is the right method, ideology, and world view to be adopted as an alternative to solve the crisis of traditionalism. Al-Jabri, however, sees historical Marxism as a form of Western Orientalism (Sharabi 1991, p. 26). He strongly criticizes some Western authors for their empathic position to Islam and its culture for their failure to rid themselves of Western self-reference. He describes Marxism as another kind of Salafi reading of history, and believes that historical materialism leans towards the 'universality of European thought, to European history in general' (Sharabi 1991). Thus, the Marxist understanding of Arab-Islamic culture and history is externalist and, thus, similar to the Orientalist genre. Could it be that Al-Jabri implies that Laroui had possibly fallen into the trap of Eurocentrism and Orientalism?

The task of Laroui (1973, p. 174) is to dissipate 'the confusion between goals and aspirations', and to relate the Arab world future with that of humanity. Laroui (1973, p. 174) thinks contemporary Arab-Muslim intellectuals do not possess a highly developed historical consciousness in 'modern' thought. He reproaches them for their 'historical retardation' towards the liberal age and for their incapacity to fathom this important' historical stage and Marxist thought. However, this stance overlooks a number of debacles that incited modern Arab thought to grope for different currents with which to come to terms with the experience of lethargy and nakba in contemporary Arab consciousness. In his secularist and progressive philosophy, he aspires to change society from being backward and traditionalist to becoming modern, liberal, and progressive. He believes that to attain this goal religion as an ideology and a societal denominator must be abolished. Yet, no intellectual trend has been immune from discussing the question of Islam in modern and contemporary Arab-Islamic thought. Furthermore, Laroui argues that political Islam flourished before the ruling elite realized their faux pas and turned against its adherents. The question arises here whether Islamism (traditionalism) represents a deformed ideology in the current Arab world. Laroui does not seem to explain why Islamism has gained more assent and strength in late decades in the Arab-Muslim world. He looks at the question of religion from a critical Marxist perspective.

Laroui delves into critiques and analysis of the facets of Arab-Islamic culture, yet he asks the intelligentsia to renounce their legacies of thought, tradition, behaviour, and their world view. The question now is whether it is possible to analyse the contemporary condition of the Arab-Islamic world without considering the turath and by rejecting the past. He called intellectuals to uphold 'objective Marxism', but later recanted this world view. He turned against the intelligentsia, claiming they could not be pivotal in the reproduction of ideology in the contemporary Arab world, while still maintaining a crisis discourse, charging them with being in crisis themselves besides causing the crises of their own societies (Laroui 1987, p. 85). He does not think they can instigate a revolutionary action of mental change, or even transform themselves. Laroui (1987, p. 81) accuses them of failing to analyse and rectify the ailments of current Arab-Islamic society. The intelligentsia and the ruling elite have always had a hostile relationship with those who have been in favour of social mobilization, change, and development. He (1992, p. 159) later admitted that the state is the sole body that can enhance social development, civil society, and citizenry, and he reiterated the pivotal role of the state in implementing a modernization programme. For the modern state, the best way to attain economic success is through carrying the banner of public good (Laroui 1987, p. 43). However, many current Arab states suffer in their legitimacy as the populace is doubtful of its performance (Laroui 1983, p. 170). This shift reveals his turn towards elitism and etatism, thus, his project of 'epistemological liberation' seems to have been aborted, and he expresses his discontent with no salvaging alternatives as he alienates himself from intellectuals and the masses. Despite his erudite knowledge of the dynamics of modern Arab-Islamic thought, his critique of Arab-Islamic society has failed to provide a concrete solution to their main crisis. However, he made important contributions on Arab world history and contemporary Arab political thought.

***

Modern and contemporary Arab-Islamic thought, greatly influenced by Arab-Islamic culture and Western thought, tackles among other issues the question of the turath in relation to modernity and in the context of the socio-political changes undergone by Arab societies since the late nineteenth century. Contemporary Arab-Muslim intellectuals have grappled with the question of turath and modernity, and Islam and the West in their works in heuristic terms, hoping to find keys to the predicament their world finds itself in. According to the Orientalist paradigm, modern and contemporary Arab-Islamic thought is in an in-between phase in which Arabs must come to terms with modernity and change that supposedly originates from the West. Such an approach builds a dichotomy between turath and modernity, continuity and change, religiosity and secularity—presumptions born from Enlightenment thought (Brown 1996, p. 2). In this chapter, I have restricted discussion to contributions made by two prominent intellectuals who have been engrossed in these issues. By so doing, I have sought to introduce readers to this question from two different, and seemingly opposed, approaches and schools of thought.

The choice of the two thinkers emanates from my belief in the influences of an individual's ideas, rather than the general trends of thought he/she represents. This probably explains not only the choice of Hassan Hanafi who does not seem to represent any major trend of thought with his 'Islamic Leftism', but also the inclusion of Abdallah Laroui who introduced his historical approach to the question by way of what he calls 'Marxist historicism'. The main goal is to understand not only their works, but also the reactions and debates they have ignited in the last fifty years or more in Arab-Islamic and Western scholarship. Owing to the interdisciplinary nature of the thematic subject of tradition and modernity, it is deemed unavoidable not to discuss the encounter of Islam with Western civilization. This chapter leads off with the epistemological tendencies and intellectual ramifications of the two thinkers on the 'problematique' of modernity and turath from their intellectual (ideological) perspectives, as they aspired for reform, change, and development. The main question at the end is whether these have provided a solution to the problematique, if indeed it is to be defined as such. By and large, Arab-Islamic thought is today at an impasse, and friction exists between liberalist and Islamist advocates on the subject of turath, renewal, and modernity. Central to the intellectual discourses on the issue is a disagreement about what the Arab-Islamic turath stands for, and how and which of its components (religious or philosophical) are to be accorded relevance in socio-political discourse and life, its role in modern society, the function of Islam in society, and the essence of the Islamic political system in society.

This chapter has surveyed the positions and arguments of Hanafi and Laroui on these main questions. Yet, the nature of their scholarly pursuits has been tainted with political and ideological drivers. The obsession with the past is referred to as the question of turath, and so arises the question as to what it can furnish to solve the current predicament of the Arab-Islamic world. It has been debated in the context of two intellectual trends: Must they leave their past behind in order to leap forward to a better future (as Laroui has suggested) or should they cling to the past and their roots that are deeply embedded in the rich turath?—Or, should they invigorate the past with enriching values and norms of behavior so as to catch up with the train of modernity? They both seem to provide loophole antidotes, as does Hanafi's tenet to apply rationality of the turath and divest it of its mystic part, or Laroui's view to simply drop the turath and the past in an attempt to achieve modernization and modernity. Despite their differing perspectives, both viewpoints attempt to construct the historicity of the turath and its epistemic components to keep their ties with the past but not to be limited within its confines. Laroui believes the way to overcome the 'crisis' is through a mutual cross-cultural understanding with the West, an actualization of a true democracy in the Arab world, and by learning from the categories of the Western paradigm of modernity. The debates of both thinkers reveal the prevalence of two major tendencies in the Arab-Islamic world: the secularist and Islamist modes, both of which express the concerns of the population.

The contributions of both Hanafi and Laroui reveal the sense of angst they feel towards the question of tradition and modernity, along with an emerging debate on authenticity stemming from the encounters of the Muslim world with the West. Laroui adapted Western philosophy by using his Marxist critique to characterize Arab authenticity. He advocates a struggle against traditionalism, leaving the past, and instead opening dialogue with the West to reach a goal of Arab modernization and modernity. Hanafi, with his secular Marxist background, believes reform consists of 'taking from the old [turath] what you need and leaving what you do not'. More than that, the works of both thinkers show the difficulty they faced to address the issue of modernity and turath without delving into the question of secularism and Western civilization. They both try to reinterpret or reconstruct the turath, in the same way that the secularist tries to rid the Arab world of its 'burden' to attain modernity, while the Islamist tries to rejuvenate it by authenticating it to alleviate the predicament of the *ummah* (Islamic nation) and to come to terms with modernity and change. Hanafi looks back to the past to overcome the anomie he finds in the sacred authenticity of the present. Laroui advocates the realization of Arab authenticity within universalism as he finds an inauthentic nation state wherein the alien techne of the West and the *non-moi* contrasts with Arab-Islamic 'self'. As such, he seeks a universalist perspective that transcends local and regional authenticities. Though Hanafi and Laroui have different understandings and explanations of the Arab-Islamic tradition, they attempt to reach out for a full-fledged modernity. Understanding the past or other cultures entails a kind of rapprochement through what Hans-Georg Gadamer calls 'fusion of horizons, which is about self-awareness of difference, the recognition of the "Other" and their "alienness", instead of pretending to own what Richard Rorty calls "sky hooks", whereby they can swing clear of history' (Clarks 1997, pp. 13–14).

NOTES

1. Tradition (or *turath*) is constituted of Islam as monotheistic religion
   characterized by a metaphysical part of a transcendent God and a sacred
   text, the Qur'an. The Qur'an is complemented by the Sunnah, Prophet
   of Islam's traditions. The Sunnah is a concrete dimension made up of
   religious, social, cultural, and literary heritage of norms and practices.
   Both these components and the accumulated corpus of cleric interpretations around them have been in constant interaction. Besides, the cultural dimension of Islam is characterized by Arabic as a divine language
   through which the Islamic community conceives and expresses itself
   as a universal community of believers. Turath is the culmination of a
   long and complex socio-historical and religious background that brought
   about both conservation and expansion within its arena. The religious
   and historical construct of turath is what Wilfred C. Smith refers to as
   'cumulative tradition' that is 'diverse', 'fluid', 'it grows, it changes, it
   accumulates' (1963, p. 159). Muslims have instilled Hellenistic elements,
   mainly in philosophy and logic, into its corpus during the early epoch of
   Islam (see Corbin 1993).
2. Part of this chapter is based on a research thesis titled *Orientalism,
   Occidentalism and the Discourse of Modernity and Tradition in Contemporary
   Arab-Islamic Thought*, published by Lambert Academic Publishing, 2010.
   Saarbrucken. This work did not receive any funding.
3. 'Shura' literally means consultation, and theologically means consultative institution in Islam. In modern times, it might refer to a council of
   ministers and the parliament.

BIBLIOGRAPHY

Abd al-Hafiz, M. 1997. 'Dirasa Naqdiyya li Kitab 'ilm al-Istighrab' [Critical
   Readings of Occidentalism]. In *Qira'at Naqdiyya fi Fikr Hassan Hanafi:
   Jadal al-Ana wa al-Akhar [Critical Readings of Hassan Hanafi's Thought:
   Dialectic of the Self and the Other]*, edited by Atiyya, Ahmad Abd Al-Halim,
   pp. 109–14. Cairo: Maktabat Madbuli al-Saghir.
Abu-Lughod, I. 1963. *Arab Rediscovery of Europe: Study in Cultural Encounters*,
   part of the Princeton Oriental Studies, no. 22, pp. x, 188. Princeton, NJ:
   Princeton University Press.
Abu Rabi', I. 1995. *Intellectual Origins of Islamic Resurgence in the Modern Arab
   World*. New York: State University of New York Press.
Adonis. 1983. *Al-Thabit wa al-Mutahawal* [The Endogenous and the Renewed],
   Vol. 1. Beirut: Dar al-'Awda.

Al-Alim, M. A. 1997. *Mawaqif Naqdiya min al-Turath* [Critical Views on Turath]. Cairo: Dar Qadaya Fikriyya.

Al-Azmeh, A. 1985. 'Bayn al-Marksiyya al-Mawdu'iyya wa saqf al-Tarikh' [Between Objective Marxism and Historicism]. *Dirasat 'Arabiyya* 21(3): 3–27.

Al-Jabri, M. A. 1991. *Al-Turath wa al-Hadaatha: Dirasaat wa munaqashaat* [Tradition and Modernity: Studies and Discussions]. Beirut: Markaz Dirasaat Wahda al-Arabi'a.

Berque, J. 1964. *The Arabs: Their History and Future*. London: Faber and Faber.

Binder, L. 1988. *Islamic Liberalism: A Critique of Development Ideologies*. Chicago and London: University of Chicago Press.

Brown, D. 1996. *Rethinking Tradition in Modern Islamic Thought*. Cambridge: Cambridge University Press.

Choueiri, Y. M. 1989. *Arab History and the Nation-State: A Study in Modern Arab Historiography 1820–1980*. London and New York: Routledge.

Clarke, J. J. 1997. *Oriental Enlightenment*. London and New York: Routledge.

Corbin, H. 1993. *History of Islamic Philosophy*. London: Kegan Paul.

El-Messiri, A. W. 2003, July 17. 'Towards a New Islamic Discourse'. *On Islam*. Retrieved from http://www.onislam.net/english/reading-islam/research-studies/islamic-thought/414456.html, accessed 20 February 2006.

Esposito, J., D. J. Fasching, and L. Todd. 2002. *World Religions Today*. New York: Oxford University Press.

Esposito, J. and J. Voll. 1996. *Islam and Democracy*. New York and Oxford: Oxford University Press.

Gallagher, N. 2000. 'The Life and Time of a Moroccan Historian: An Interview'. In *Autour de la pensee de Abdallah Laroui*, edited by B. al-Kurdi, pp. 75–95. Casablanca: Le centre Culturel Arabe.

Habti, D. 2010. 'Modernity as an Orientalist Discourse'. In *Orientalism, Occidentalism and the Discourse of Modernity and Tradition in Contemporary Arab-Islamic Thought*, edited by D. Habti, pp. 54–84. Saarbrücken, Germany: Lambert Academic Publishing.

———. 2011. 'Reason and Revelation for an Averroist Pursuit of *Convivencia* and Intercultural Dialogue'. *Policy Futures in Education* 9(1): 81–7.

Hanafi, H. 1977a. 'Hermeneutics as Axiomatics: An Islamic Model'. In *Religious Dialogue and Revolution: Essays on Judaism, Christianity and Islam*, edited by H. Hanafi. Cairo: Anglo-Egyptian Bookshop.

———. 1977b. *Religious Dialogue and Revolution: Essays on Judaism, Christianity and Islam*. Cairo: Anglo-Egyptian Bookshop.

———. 1979. 'Al-Juzur al-Ta'rikhiyya li Azmat al-Hurriya wa al-Dimoqratiya fi wujdaanunaa al-Mu'aasir' ['The Historical Roots of the Impasse Regarding

Freedom and Democracy in Our Zeitgeist']. *Al-Mustaqbal al-Arabi* [Arabic Future] 5: 130–9.

Hanafi, H. 1981. al-Turath wa al-Tajdid [Turath And Renewal]. Cairo: Al markaz al-Arabi.

———. 1982. 'The Relevance of the Islamic Alternative in Egypt'. *Arab Studies Quarterly* 4(1–2): 54–74.

———. 1988. *Mina al-'Aqida ila al-Thawra* [From Doctrine to Revolution] (vol. 1). Cairo: Maktabat Madbuli.

———. 1989. *Al-Din wa al-Thawra fi Masr, 1952–1981* [Religion and Revolution in Egypt, 1952–1981] (vol. 6). Cairo: Maktabat Madhbuli.

———. 1990. 'New Social Science'. *Islam* 2: 447–71.

———. 1992. *Muqaddima fi 'ilm al-Istighrab* [Introduction to Occidentalism], second edition. Cairo: al-Mu'assasa al-Jaami'iyya.

———. 2000a. 'From Orientalism to Occidentalism'. In *Islam in the Modern World* (vol. 2), edited by H. Hanafi, pp. 395–409. Cairo: Dar Kebaa.

———. 2000b. *Islam in the Modern World* (vol. 2). Cairo: Dar Kebaa.

Harb, A. 1995. *Naqd al-nass* [Textual Criticism], second edition. Beirut and Casablanca: Markaz al-Thaqafi at-'Arabi.

Hattar, N. 1986. *Al-Turath, al-Gharb, al-Thawra: Bahth hawl al-Asala wa al-Mu'aasara fi Fikr Hasan Hanafi* [Turath, the West, Revolution: Study on Authenticity and Contemporaneity in Hassan Hanafi's Thought]. Amman: Shaqir wa Akasha li Tibaa'a wa Nashr wa al-Tawzi'.

Hourani, A. 1991. *A History of the Arab People*. Cambridge, MA: Harvard University Press.

Ismail, S. 2003. Islamic Political Thought. In *The Cambridge History of the Twentieth-Century Political Thought*, edited by T. Ball and R. Bellamy, pp. 579–601. Cambridge: Cambridge University Press.

Keddie, N. 1968. *An Islamic Response to Imperialism*. Berkeley and LA: University of California Press.

Laroui, A. 1967. *L'ideologie arabe contemporaine: Essai Critique* [Contemporary Arab Ideology: Critical Essay]. Paris: Maspero.

———. 1973. *Al-'arab wa al-Fikr al-Tarikhi* [The Arabs and Historical Thought]. Beirut and Casablanca: al-Markaz al-Thaqafi al-'arabi.

———. 1976. *The Crisis of the Arab Intellectual: Traditionalism or Historicism?* Berkeley, CA: University of California Press.

———. 1977a. *Les origines sociales et culturelles du nationalisme marocain 1830–1912* [Social and Cultural Origins of Moroccan Nationalism]. Paris: Maspero.

———. 1977b. *The History of the Maghrib*. Princeton: Princeton University Press.

———. 1983. *Mafhum al-Dawla* [The Concept of State]. Beirut: Dar al-tanwir.

Laroui, A. 1984. *Mafhum al-Idyuluujiyya* [The Concept of Ideology]. Casablanca: Arab Cultural Center.

———. 1987. *Islam et modernité* [Islam and modernity]. Paris: La Decouverte.

———. March–April, 1992. Al-Tahdith wa al-dimuqratiyya [Interview: Modernization and Democracy]. *Aafaq: Majallat Ittihad Kutab al-Maghrib* [Perspectives: Magazine of Moroccan Intellectuals Society], 3–4.

———. 1997. 'Western Orientalism and Liberal Islam'. *Middle East Studies Association Bulletin*, 31(1): 3–10.

Moosa, E., ed. 2005. *Ghazali and the Poetics of Imagination*. North Carolina: University of North Carolina Press.

Qansuwa, S. 1997. 'Qiraa'a Mukhtalifa li 'ilm al-Istighrab' [A different reading of occidentalism]. In *Qira'a naqdiya fi fikr Hssan Hanafi: Jadal al-Ana wa al-Akhar*, edited by A.A. Atiyya. Cairo: Madbuli al-Saghir.

Rahman, F. 1970. 'Islamic Modernism: Its Scope, Method and Alternatives'. *International Journal of Middle East Studies* 1(4): 317–33.

Sadiki, L. 2004. *The Search for Arab Democracy: Discourses and Counter-discourses*. New York: Columbia University Press.

Sayed, N. 2002, February 13. 'Hassan Hanafi: Consolations of Philosophy'. *Al-Ahram Weekly*, 572. Retrieved from http://weekly.ahram.org.eg/2002/572/profile.htm, accessed 2 March 2006.

Shahrough, A. 1997. 'The Dialectic in Contemporary Egyptian Social Thought'. *The International Journal of Middle East Studies* 29(3): 377–401.

Sharabi, H. 1991. *Theory, Politics and the Arab World: Critical Responses*. New York: Routledge.

Smith, W. C. 1963. *The Meaning and End of Religion: A New Approach to the Religious Traditions of Mankind*. New York: Macmillan.

Part III

Modernization, Globalization, and the Future of the Civilization Debate

11 Erring Modernization and Development in the Muslim World

Syed Farid Alatas

This chapter looks at the various critiques of modern society in the context of the phenomenon of erring modernization. It is argued that various diagnoses of the problems and shortcomings of modern civilization contribute to our understanding of the origins and nature of erring modernization. Although this chapter reflects on the Muslim world, it does not take the view that the Muslim world is a homogenous entity and is characterized by problems that do not exist elsewhere. The aim of this chapter is to reflect on certain common problems to be found in the Muslim world and how they have been thought about by Muslims themselves.

This, then, leads to the question of what intellectual resources we may make use of in order to reflect on the state and nature of modernity. The dominant ideas of our age belong to the Western tradition. The dominance of these ideas, even in the various non-Western societies, can be explained in terms of the prevalence of Eurocentric orientations in the humanities and social sciences. Here, a distinction should be made between the old and new Eurocentrism. The old Eurocentrism was characterized by the familiar dichotomies of progressive–backward, rational–irrational, or civilized–uncivilized, which correspond to the Occident–Orient divide. Various, mainly negative, stereotypes informed these dichotomies and were the subject of analysis and critique by scholars such as Anouar Abdel-Malek, A. L. Tibawi, Syed Hussein Alatas, and Edward Said in the 1960s and 1970s (Abdel-Malek 1963; Alatas 1977; Said 1979; Tibawi 1963, 1979). By the post–World War II period, the various disciplines of the social sciences and the area studies had expunged these dichotomies from their theories and research outputs. The Eurocentrism so characteristic of the nineteenth and earlier centuries had been transcended. There remains one feature of Eurocentrism, however, that continues to define social sciences and humanities today. This is the marginalization, and even neglect, of non-Western ideas, concepts, and theories. Although non-Western societies are studied, concepts and perspectives that are indigenous to these societies are rarely deployed in the theoretical frameworks applied. For example, while Ibn Khaldun has been recognized as the founder of scientific history and sociology, a Khaldunian theory of society has rarely been applied in empirical studies of history and contemporary societies. The pre-modern ideas of Ibn Khaldun are merely one resource.

Among contemporary resources, we can cite Malik Bennabi, Ali Shariati, Said Nursi, Mohammed Abed al-Jabri, Roger Garaudy, Syed Hussein Alatas, Syed Muhammad Naquib Al-Attas, and others. These thinkers reflected on and theorized about the conditions of modernity with original ideas rooted in their own religious and philosophical traditions. At the same time, they were more than familiar with Western discourses in their respective fields and did not fail to engage with the pivotal ideas of the time.

From the nineteenth century on, social thinkers and theorists paid attention to the big problems of modernity. Scholars such as Marx, Weber, Durkheim, and Martineau brought attention to the manner in which modernity failed to make good on the promises of the Enlightenment. They highlighted how modern humans remained inhibited in a variety of ways. For Marx, humans were not free to fully realize their potential as human beings and were alienated. Weber theorized that humans imprisoned themselves in an 'iron cage' of rationality, while Durkheim understood humans as having been enslaved by desire and fallen into a state of anomie. While their views continue to be relevant, it is unfortunate that much of the teaching and writing in this area is focused almost exclusively on Western and male thinkers, as if no woman, Asian, or African of the nineteenth century reflected on the conditions of modern civilization.

This attitude of the neglect of non-Western thinkers has continued into the twenty-first century. For example, the Muslim thinkers mentioned previously are rarely discussed in books and courses about the nature and problems of modern civilization. This is a result or symptom of what was referred to earlier as the new Eurocentrism. There is a need, therefore, to pay more attention to the thinkers of the Muslim world who addressed the problems of modern civilization. The spirit that informs this reaction to the new Eurocentrism is necessarily a critical one because of its attitude against dominant and official perspectives.

An example of this critical attitude can be seen in the work of the late Roger Garaudy on the 'holocaust'. Garaudy never denied the mass murder of Jews in Europe. However, he provided a critical assessment of terms such as 'genocide' and 'holocaust' and the claim that Hitler had intended to exterminate the Jews as a whole. His critique was based on the compatibility of claims and empirical reality. What he understood as possible or impossible was based on the consideration of the reality of things; or as Ibn Khaldun said, *haqa'iq al-ashya*. An example that Garaudy furnishes is the question of the use of gas chambers in the 'extermination' of Jews during the Nazi regime. The gas that was allegedly used was Zyklon B. According to an expert account cited by Garaudy, the use of Zyklon B requires several conditions such as airtight chambers, door joints made from asbestos, neoprene or Tefla, a separate drainage system, an appropriate ventilation system, and other features. The alleged gas chamber sites at Auschwitz, Birkenan, and Majdanek did not have these features. Had these sites been functioning as gas chambers, they would have done so at the great peril of the life of the operators and those nearby (Garaudy 1996).

The purpose of this chapter is to suggest the direction that a social theory of modern Muslim societies may take. The focus is on the critique of modernization and the aim is to suggest a perspective that is both critical and which transcends Eurocentrism.

THE CRITIQUE OF MODERNIZATION

Modernization refers to a process that involves the introduction of modern science and technology.

Modernization, at present has been associated with a number of traits of developed societies, such as secularization, industrialization, commercialization, increased social mobility, increased material standard of living, and increased education and literacy. The list of traits can be further increased as to include such things as the high consumption of inanimate energy, the smaller agricultural population compared to the industrial, and the widespread social security network. (Alatas 1996, pp. 70–1)

These can be said to be among the essential characteristics of modernization. The essence of modernization should not be confused with those aspects that accompanied or were consequences of the process that took place in the West but which can properly be considered as accidental properties of modernization. These include the form of economic and political arrangements that began in the West and various aspects of modernity such as individualism, modern art, the conception of the family, and so on. Here, the failure is to distinguish the universal process of modernization from the particular form it took in the West (Alatas 1996, p. 2).

The process of modernization began in the West with the rise of capitalism. The early critique of modernization took place in the context of the explanation and assessment of capitalism among scholars in the nineteenth century. One such critic was Max Weber.

Capitalism as an economic system requires an attitude that Weber called 'the spirit of capitalism'. This attitude obtained its content from Protestantism. For Weber the 'question of the motive forces in the explanation of modern capitalism is not in the first instance a question of the origin of the capital sums which were available for capitalistic uses, but, above all, of the development of the spirit of capitalism' (Weber 1958, p. 68). Weber says, 'Where it [spirit of capitalism] appears and is able to work itself out, it produces its own capital and monetary supplies as the means to its own ends, but the reverse is not true' (Weber 1958, pp. 68–9). In other words, the spirit of capitalism creates the institutions but not the reverse.

The spirit of capitalism is a unique phenomenon that existed in a certain historical period in Europe. It has specific traits and characteristics whereby the acquisition of money was combined with the avoidance of spontaneous enjoyment of life. In other words, acquisition of money is not for the satisfaction of material needs. It is for a higher reason, as is evident from a quote from the Bible: 'Seest thou a man diligent in business? He shall stand before kings' (Weber 1958, p. 53).

The attitude in pre-capitalist times was one of traditionalism—man does not wish to earn more and more money but wants to live as he is accustomed to living and to earn as much as is necessary for that purpose (Weber 1958, p. 60). From a capitalistic point of view, this is the backwardness of traditionalism. On the other hand, in the spirit of capitalism both labourer and entrepreneur regard work as an end in itself, as if it were a religious calling (Weber 1958, p. 63). Therefore, the chances of overcoming traditionalism were greatest where there was religious upbringing. There was something about Protestantism that instilled an attitude in people that was very capitalistic in nature. It is opposed to traditionalism, which is expressed, for example, in Catholicism—'activity directed to acquisition [of capital] for its own sake ... was to be tolerated only because of the unalterable necessities of life in this world' (Weber 1958, p. 73).

Capitalism requires an outlook on life that makes acquisition of capital a religious calling. Only then can it become a systematic way of life. This is the effect Protestantism had. Weber never claimed that capitalism could not exist outside the Occident. Rather, he claimed that the spirit of capitalism, an attitude of commercial gain and profit based on rational calculation, could originate only in the West and was a result of certain characteristics peculiar to the worldly asceticism of Puritanism, a Protestant movement in the sixteenth and seventeenth centuries, derived in part from the doctrines of Calvin.

Puritanism is not against activity in this world. It is not even against wealth acquisition. The moral objection to wealth is the 'relaxation in the security of possession, the enjoyment of wealth with the consequence of idleness and the temptations of the flesh, and above all distraction from the pursuit of a righteous life' (Weber 1958, p. 157). For Weber, modern capitalism was the result of the melding of capitalist enterprise with ascetic Protestantism, above all, the Calvinistic version (Weber 1958, p. 128). Economic activity as the pursuit of profit is seen as a spiritual end. The spirit of modern capitalism was influenced directly by Calvinism in which worldly asceticism was a means of salvation. The effect of this Protestant ethic was psychological—it freed the acquisition of wealth from the inhibitions of traditionalistic ethics (Weber 1958, p. 171). It also drove its adherents to hard work, discipline, and frugality since the attainment of wealth as a fruit of labour in a calling was a sign of God's blessing. The practical result of all this was an ascetic compulsion to work hard, to save, and to avoid spontaneous enjoyment. This attitude towards life is what Weber calls 'the spirit of capitalism'.

Third World consumption of Weber has been such that the discourse assumes that for Weber capitalism was an advanced, progressive economic system, and, thus, something 'good and desirable' and, following from this, that Western society was superior in this respect. But, Weber was also conscious of the ill-effects of modern capitalism. He was critical of the kind of order that capitalism, industrialization, and bureaucratization created. Modern humans are born into an order based on technical and economic conditions of machine production and factory life. The capitalist order created a highly efficient system for the management of capitalism. This is based on the bureaucratic division of labour. But there is a tension between the need for technical efficiency in administration and the human values of freedom and autonomy. Weber referred to this phenomenon as us being trapped in the iron cage of rationality:

> The Puritan wanted to work in a calling; we are forced to do so. For when asceticism was carried out of monastic cells into everyday life, and began to dominate worldly morality, it did its part in building the tremendous cosmos of the modern economic order. This order is now bound to the technical and economic conditions of machine production which today determine the lives of all the individuals who are born into this mechanism, not only those directly concerned with economic acquisition, with irresistible force. Perhaps it will so determine them until the last ton of fossilized coal is burnt. In Baxter's view the care for external goods should only lie on the shoulders of the 'saint like a light cloak, which can be thrown aside at any moment'. But fate decreed that the cloak should become an iron cage. (Weber 1958, p. 181)

In modern capitalist society, people are no longer governed by a religious ethic but by bureaucratic norms of efficiency and calculability. We have developed bureaucracies to cover almost all areas of life. Bureaucracies have many virtues but they can become vices.

For example, overspecialization is often a problem. Job fragmentation is universal. It involves limited activities and requires the use of little of our total abilities. On top of that, there is little variation in performance and no scope for initiative. Due to this dehumanization, there is not much enthusiasm for work, which can eventually affect productivity.

Another problem is that of hierarchy. It is good because it concentrates authority and gives direction and enables coordination. But excessive hierarchy leads to irresponsibility. At each level of the hierarchy there is a fixed jurisdiction. Everyone is concerned with their own area of jurisdiction and careful not to invade another's territory.

Yet another problem is that of the impersonal nature of work. Impersonality is good because it means impartiality. But it can be carried too far, especially when it reduces humans to cases, cards, files, and numbers. Anonymity and impartiality reinforce among employees the fear of victimization or of unkind treatment from impersonal bureaucrats. In other words, bureaucracy can be irrational and dehumanizing when it pervades all spheres of life.

Weber also refers to this formal rationalization of life in terms of the problem of disenchantment. In his famous essay 'Science as a Vocation', he writes, 'The fate of our times is characterized by rationalization and intellectualization and, above all, by the "disenchantment of the world"' (Weber 1946, p. 155).

Syed Muhammad Naquib Al-Attas' critique of modern civilization is centred around the problem of a similar phenomenon, that of secularization, that is, the freeing of humans from the religious and metaphysical control over his reason (Al-Attas 1978, p. 15). This liberation of humans is a process that entails the disenchantment of nature, and ultimately the removal of the divine from the scheme of things (Al-Attas 1978, pp. 15–16).

Also significant was Bediuzzaman Said Nursi's critique of modern civilization, which is worth considering at some length here. Nursi is not merely critiquing the materialist outlook on life, but also the deceptive nature of this outlook. At the same time, Nursi recognized that there was an emerging awareness in the West about destructive philosophy. He says:

> Because of the extreme tyranny and despotism of this last World War and its merciless destruction, and hundreds of innocents being scattered and ruined on account of a single enemy, and the awesome despair of the defeated, and the fearsome alarm of the victors and their ghastly pangs of conscience arising from the supremacy they are

unable to maintain and the destruction they are unable to repair, and the utter transitoriness and ephemerality of the life of this world and the deceptive, opiate nature of the fantasies of civilization becoming apparent to all, and the exalted abilities lodged in human nature and the human essence being wounded in a universal and awesome manner, and heedlessness and misguidance and deaf, lifeless nature being smashed by the diamond sword of the Qur'an, and the exceedingly ugly, exceedingly cruel true face of world politics becoming apparent, which is the widest and most suffocating and deceptive cover for heedlessness and misguidance, most certainly and without any shadow of a doubt, since the life of this world—which is the metaphorical beloved of mankind—is thus ugly and transient, man's true nature will search with all its strength for eternal life, which it truly loves and yearns for, just as there are signs of this occurring in the North, the West, and in America. (Nursi 2004, p. 167)

Nursi's summary of the problem of European civilization is presented in the collection of aphorisms entitled 'Seeds of Reality'. Here Nursi states that modern civilization is founded on five negative principles:

1. Its point of support is force, the mark of which is aggression.
2. Its aim and goal is benefit, the mark of which is jostling and tussling.
3. Its principle in life is conflict, the mark of which is strife.
4. The bond between the masses is racialism and negative nationalism, which is nourished through devouring others; its mark is collision.
5. Its enticing service is inciting lust and passion and the gratification of desires. However, lust transforms man into a beast. (Nursi 2001b, p. 548)

How can one conceptualize Nursi's statement of the central problem of modern civilization? I propose that at the heart of Nursi's claim is the marginalization of God from humanity's concerns, or what we may refer to as the phenomenon of desacralization. This follows logically from Nursi's criticism of the dominance of naturalism in modern civilization, a philosophy according to which everything is explained in terms of natural causes. As a result, 'minds become strangers' to non-material explanations. Throughout Nursi's writings, it is possible to identify various problems discussed or touched upon that are manifestations of the desacralization of life. These include problems such as alienation and anomie. However, a more general problem that subsumes those of alienation and anomie is that of nihilism.

I am not suggesting here that Nursi directly addressed the problem of nihilism or that he was consciously engaging the philosophy of nihilism that had already developed in his time, particularly in Europe and Russia. I would say, however, that Nursi was acutely aware of the problem of meaninglessness in life and that he related this meaninglessness to the expunging of spiritual matters from the concerns of modern humans. By nihilism, I refer to both moral nihilism in the sense of the idea of the removal of moral restrictions on behaviour, as well as existential nihilism, which has to do with the idea of the purposelessness or meaninglessness of life.[1] Nursi has hinted at the problem of meaninglessness on various occasions. The aphorism 'If there is no imagined goal, or if it is forgotten or pretended to be forgotten, thoughts perpetually revolve around the "I"' refers to the meaninglessness of life (Nursi 2001b, p. 546).

The five negative principles that form the basis of modern civilization are related to the problem of nihilism. To the extent that moral restrictions on behaviour are removed and to the extent that life is seen as purposeless and meaningless, people will live by the five principles, particularly principles one, two, three, and five. What Nursi was referring to here are principles such as self-interest, the gratification of desires, and the use of force to realize these interests and desires. While these characteristics and traits are to be found in all civilizations in all times, Nursi is saying that they are principles of modern civilization. To better appreciate the connection between Nursi's negative principles of modern civilization and the philosophy of nihilism, it is necessary to briefly introduce nihilism. This will be done by way of reference to Fyodor Dostoevsky's *The Brothers Karamazov*. It tells the story of existentialist, nihilist rebellion.

Dostoevsky's *The Brothers Karamazov* tells the story of what in Nursi's terms would be the negative principles of Russian society. Through the characters Ivan Karamazov and Zosima the Monk, Dostoevsky discusses how the influence of Enlightenment ideas paradoxically leads to authoritarianism, individualism, despair, and the loss of values, all of which are disguised in a Roman Catholic reform orientation espoused by the Westernized Russian elite, and the response to this from the supporters of Russian orthodoxy. The context is nineteenth-century Russia in the midst of the breakdown of the feudal system and the influx of Western Enlightenment ideas.

Ivan Karamazov is unable to reconcile Christ-like love for men with the presence of evil on earth. He considers Christ-like love for men to be a miracle on earth, impossible to realize. Ivan's alternative is revealed through the character of the Grand Inquisitor, a character in a poem of Ivan himself. Ivan confronts God over the presence of evil and the meaninglessness of suffering, through the Grand Inquisitor. The story told in Ivan's poem is set in Seville, Spain, during the time of the Spanish Inquisition, which was notorious for its public judging and burning of heretics. God takes human form once again and visits Seville a day before a hundred heretics are burnt by the cardinal, the Grand Inquisitor. He is surrounded by people whom He blesses, His love and compassion radiating towards the crowd that gathers around him. He performs miracles, restoring the sight of an old blind man and bringing to life a dead young girl. At some point, somewhere by the steps of the Seville Cathedral, He is noticed by the Grand Inquisitor who has Him taken away by guards to a gloomy, vaulted prison. Then begins the monologue in which the Grand Inquisitor does all the talking while He is silent. The Inquisitor informs Him that he has no right to speak or to add anything to what He had said centuries earlier when He had first appeared. The Grand Inquisitor chastises Him for promising to make man free, and for burdening man with responsibilities he could not fulfil. Freedom has not enabled man to provide for himself, and he cries, 'Feed us, for those who have promised us fire from heaven haven't given it' (Dostoevsky 1993, p. 26.). Recognizing that freedom and bread are inconceivable together, people said to the Inquisitor, 'Make us your slaves, but feed us' (Dostoevsky 1993, p. 26.). So, he feeds them, using God's name. God gave them freedom, but they prefer peace and sustenance. In Ivan's story, God is aloof, allows suffering, and allows fifteen centuries to pass since he promised to return. But, with the rise of the new German heresy [a reference to Protestantism], Christ came down before the time He promised to return, and Himself became subject to the Grand Inquisition. It is declared that He is the worst of heretics and that He will be condemned to burn at the stake.

This is because the freedom He bestowed upon man unleashed dispute and conflict over who should be rightfully worshipped. People are seduced by freedom but it causes suffering. In that way, God laid the foundation for the destruction of His own kingdom. Man is unable to deal with his God-given freedom as he is rebellious in nature, and creating strife and anarchy, he eventually says, 'He who created them rebels must have meant to mock at them' (Dostoevsky 1993, p. 29). So, the Grand Inquisitor tells Him, he has worked with Satan to correct His work. The silence and imprisonment of God, His aloofness and inaction mean that, as Ivan says, 'Everything is lawful' (Dostoevsky 1993, p. 37).

At the same time, the promises of science to liberate man, as noted by Zosima the Monk, are false. Science's denial of spirituality and the proclamation of the reign of freedom only resulted in the multiplication of desire, envy, isolation, and even suicide. The problem is with the elite who want to base justice on reason alone and dispense with Christ. Rationalists like Ivan no longer have faith in God because God failed to live up to His promise of saving humanity. Instead, He allowed suffering and misery on earth to run its course. If God were truly just, He would allow for perfection on earth by ordering the world in such a manner to eliminate suffering and provide comfort for all. Furthermore, since God is unjust there is no morality, since morality can only come from a good God. Ivan, therefore, advocates the leading of immoral lives founded on self-interest, worldly desires, and the rejection of God. This is his nihilistic outlook. From Nursi's point of view, self-interest, the pursuit of worldly desires, excessive faith in reason, and egoism would be among the traits that make up the negative principles of Russian society.

Nursi's critique of modern civilization was not one-sided and biased. He did not reserve moral critique for the West alone. Nursi did not deny that Muslim societies were also adopting the negative principles of modern civilization. At the same time, he believed that there were other problems that beset Muslim societies, which accounted for the material backwardness of the Muslim world in comparison to Europe. He referred to these collectively as the six dire sicknesses of Muslim nations (Nursi 2001a, pp. 26–7). They are (*a*) the rise in despair and hopelessness; (*b*) the decline of truthfulness in social and political life; (*c*) the growth of enmity; (*d*) ignorance of the luminous bonds that bind the believers to one another; (e) despotism; and (f) restricting effort to what is personally beneficial.

Nursi's reference to the pervasiveness of despair is very instructive. Despair is an important theme in social theory, particularly since the nineteenth century, and continues to be an important phenomenon today. In European thought, despair is often treated under the category of anomie. Anomie refers to a state in which society fails to exercise sufficient regulation or constraints over the desires of individuals so that they are tormented at not being able to satisfy these desires. The unlimited desires and their insatiability due to the nature of things constantly renew the torture of individuals, finally resulting in despair. This is the condition of the anomie discussed by Durkheim (Durkheim 1989, pp. 241–8). It is interesting to inquire how despair (*al-ya's*) in Nursi differs from the same in Durkheim. Despair and related concepts such as anomie are important themes in Western thought and have spawned important theories and empirical research. Although despair and anomie are important phenomena in the Muslim world, they are under-researched. Nursi's identification of the phenomenon should result in serious conceptual and empirical attention being directed towards the problem.

Another significant critique of modernization comes from the traditionalistic orientation. Traditionalism refers to the orientation that regards tradition, defined as belief and practice handed down from generation to generation, as having been lost to the West during the second half of the second millennium AD. Traditionalists believe that the West is in crisis due to the failure of this tradition to be transmitted (Sedgwick 2004, p. 24). The most well-known proponent of traditionalism to have come from Iran is Seyyed Hossein Nasr. Nasr's notion of knowledge from a traditionalist perspective is best captured by the expression *scientia sacra* or sacred knowledge. This refers to knowledge that 'lies at the heart of every revelation and is the center of that circle which encompasses and defines tradition' (Nasr 1981, p. 130). The eclipse of sacred knowledge in the modern world, beginning with the desacralization of knowledge in the Occident among the ancient Greeks (Nasr 1981, p. 34), indicates that there is a need for a science that can 'relate the various levels of knowledge once again to the sacred' (Nasr 1993, p. 173). The problem with modern science is that its rejection of several facets of a particular reality and its reduction of symbols to facts is partly responsible for the desacralization of knowledge and existence which is so characteristic of the modern world (Nasr 1981, p. 212).

For Nasr, there is an added emphasis on methodology. The definition of knowledge in Islam does not differ from the corresponding term in Latin, *scientia*. The Islamic sciences include the natural sciences (*al-`ulum al-tabi`iyya*), the mathematical sciences (*al-`ulum al-riyadhiyya*), and the occult sciences (*al-`ulum al-khafiyya*) (Nasr 1980, p. 4). What distinguishes the Islamic sciences from modern knowledge, which are for the most part based on observation and experimentation, is the fact that the former employs various methods 'in accordance with the nature of the subject in question and modes of understanding that subject' (Nasr 1980, p. 7). What defines the Islamic sciences as *Islamic* is its 'paradigm', which is based on the Islamic world view. The world or universe that was the object of study for the early Muslim scientist was taken to be an Islamic cosmos. Furthermore, the mind and eyes of the scientists were Muslim minds and eyes transformed by the spirit and form of the Qur'an (Nasr 1980, p. 8.). The Islamic theory of knowledge is based on a hierarchy of the means of access to knowledge, ranging from revelation and illumination to ratiocination as well as empirical and sensual knowledge (Nasr 1980, pp. 8–9). An important principle of Islamic science is that Islam defines a particular method or sets of methods for each discipline, whether it is jurisprudence, physics, or *tasawwuf* (mysticism). These methods are not seen to be contradictory but complementary. The multiplicity of the various methods and sciences are integrated in Islam into a totality in accordance with the doctrine of unity (*tawhid*) (Nasr 1980, pp. 8–9).[2]

There is more to traditionalism than the above, however. Traditionalism has to do with the goal of the restoration of the traditional sciences in society. At the personal and devotional level, it involves initiation into a traditionalistic community. Nasr, himself, had joined the Maryamiyya[3] (Sedgwick 2004, p. 154). According to Nasr:

> But the opposition of tradition to modernism, which is total and complete as far as principles are concerned, does not derive from the observation of facts and phenomena or the diagnosis of the symptoms of the malady. It is based upon a study of the causes which have brought

about the illness. Tradition is opposed to modernism because it considers the premises upon which modernism is based to be wrong and false in principle. (Nasr 1981, p. 84)

The traditionalistic orientation can be seen as an inverse form of Orientalism. Sedgwick was correct to note that both are dualistic systems that are textualist in approach and downplay observation. In the traditionalist dichotomy, however, the Middle East is characterized by tradition, spirituality, and wisdom and this is contrasted with a West characterized by modernity, materialism, and technical skill, a portrayal not more accurate than that of classical Orientalism (Sedgwick 2004, p. 266).

RESACRALIZING THE WORLD: THE FAILURE
OF ISLAMIC ECONOMICS

Much of the critique of modernization and modernity was directed at the problem of the desacralization of the world. An attempt to resacralize society came from the proponents of Islamic economics. Generally speaking, economists have sought to maintain a rigorous separation between positive and normative economics. In the Muslim world, however, concerted attempts have been made to relate moral conduct to economic institutions and practices. This is a result of dissatisfaction with both modernization and Marxist-inspired theories that are understood by Islamic economists as being located within the orbit of a modernist discourse and wedded to the principles of nineteenth-century liberal philosophy. In the Muslim world, demands for an alternative discourse to both modernization and Marxist theories had led to the rise of Islamic economics.

The notion of Islamic economics did not arise from within the classical tradition of Islamic thought. In the classical Islamic tradition, there were discussions and works on economic institutions and practices in the Muslim world, but the notion of an Islamic science of economics and a specifically Islamic economy did not exist. Islamic economics, therefore, is a modern creation. It emerged as a result of dissatisfaction with capitalist and socialist models and theories of development in the 1950s (Rauf 1984; Sadr 1982; Shariati 1980).

But the Islamic critique of development studies is not directed solely at modernization theory, but generally at the corpus of development of thought encompassing the entire spectrum of perspectives from the left to the right that is seen to be located within the discourse of modernism. For the Islamic economists, the philosophical foundations of development from the Islamic point of view can be understood in terms of four concepts (Ahmad 1980; Ghazali 1990, pp. 22–3). Tawhid, or the principle of the unity of God, establishes the nature of the relationship between God and man, as well as that between men. *Rububiyyah* refers to the belief that it is God who determines the sustenance and nourishment of man and it is He who will guide believers to success. It follows that successful development is a result of man's work as well as the workings of the divine order. *Khilafah* is the concept of man as God's vicegerent on earth. This defines man as a trustee of God's resources on earth. *Tazkiyyah* refers to the growth and purification of man in terms of his relationship with God, his fellow men, and with the natural environment. The putting into practice of these principles results in *falah*, that is, prosperity in this world as well as the Hereafter (Ahmad 1980, p. 179).

Islamic economics suffers from a number of problems, some of which have been dealt with by others.[4] The following remarks on Islamic economics, however, are centred around the distinction between ethical and empirical forms of theory.

Ethical theories express preference or distaste about reality in accordance with certain standards of evaluation. In addition to this, they specify the ideal goal towards which changes should be made. Empirical theories, on the other hand, are generalizations about observable reality and require the process of abstraction and conceptualization.

Islamic economics presents an ideal of development that is based on an Islamic philosophy of life. Arising from this alternative vision of development, various policy options have been suggested, such as the introduction of interest-free banking and *zakah* (poor tax) (Aímad 1987; Ariff 1982; Iqbal and Mirakhor 1987; Karsten 1982; Khan 1986; Khan and Mirakhor 1987; Uzair 1976). What is presented as Islamic economics, in fact, comprises ethical theories of production, distribution, price, and so on. When Islamic economists discuss the traditional categories of economics such as income, consumption, government expenditure, investment, and savings, they do so in terms of ethical statements and not in terms of analyses and empirical theory. Contrary to what is claimed, it would be difficult to refer to an Islamic science of economics, although we do have the scientific study of economies in Muslim countries, as well as the study of Muslim economic institutions and commercial techniques.

When Islamic economists are doing empirical theory, what is presented as Islamic economics turns out not to be an alternative to modernist discourse as far as empirical theory is concerned. The foci and method that have been selected by Muslim economists for economic analyses is essentially that of Keynesian and neo-classical economics. The foci are the traditional questions that come under the purview of theories of price, production, distribution, trade cycle, growth, and welfare economics with Islamic themes and topics involved, such as zakah, interest-free banking, and profit-sharing. There are a few problems associated with this.

First of all, the techniques of analysis that have been selected, that is, the building up of abstract models of the economic system, have generally not been translated by Islamic economists into empirical work. For example, works on interest tend to construct models of how an interest-free economy would work. There is no empirical work on existing economic systems and the nature, functions, and effects of interest in these systems.

Second, these attempts at Islamic economics have sought to ground the discourse in a theory of wealth and distribution in very much the same manner as that of Western economic science, as a glance at some of their works will reveal (Mannan, 1982; F. Khan 1984; M. Khan 1986; Siddiqui and Zaman 1989; Zarqa 1983). When they are engaged in the sort of discourse that one could understand as constituting empirical theory, they are not doing so from a specifically Islamic scientific approach. The point here is that attempts to create a 'faithful' economic science have not yielded policy options for the problems that are being addressed, because what 'Islamic economics' amounts to is neo-classical economics dressed and made up in Islamic terminology.

In the 1930s, 1940s, and 1950s economists in Latin America, Europe, and the United States began to pay attention to underdeveloped areas. The dominant school of thought used to explain development in advanced capitalist countries was neo-classical economics, according to which the operation of free market forces can maximize aggregate economic welfare, and the growth of output under full employment will continue as long as there is a positive propensity to save and invest in excess of what is needed to maintain capital equipment. Islamic economics is very much embedded in that tradition of neo-classical economics in terms of its near exclusive concern with technical factors such as growth, interest, tax, profits, and so on. A host of issues relating to political economy such as uneven development, unequal exchange, bureaucratic capitalism, corruption, and the role of the state that have been addressed by structuralist, neo-Marxist, dependency, and new institutional economic theorists are not dealt with at the theoretical and empirical levels by Islamic economists. This is not to suggest that Islamic economists should uncritically adopt these other perspectives to replace neo-classical economics. The successful indigenization of development economics and the claim to scientific status depend on the degree to which indigenization efforts retain what is of utility in neo-classical and other theories of development.

The main problem is that under the guise of 'Islamic economics', the policies generated in industrialized capitalist centres are implemented in the Muslim world and are legitimized, thereby undermining the very project that Islamic economics is committed to. In attempting to ground itself in a theory of rational man and a hypothetical-deductive methodology, it has merely substituted Islamic terms for neo-classical ones, retaining the latter's assumptions, procedures, and modes of analysis. As such, it has failed to engage in the analysis and critique of a highly unequal world economic order in which the gaps are ever widening. That this supposedly anti-Western economics was co-opted and made to serve those very trends that it outwardly opposes must be considered. Not being very different from neo-classical economics, it extends a technical–economic rationality over a wide range of problems which presupposes viewing different ends as comparable outcomes, which, in turn, entails the elimination of cultural hindrances to the comparability of outcomes.

ERRING MODERNIZATION

The previous critiques of modern civilization dealt with modernity in terms of its religious and metaphysical foundations. Syed Hussein Alatas' critique of modernization, however, is not directed at its

religious or metaphysical foundations but at the process of modernization itself and the role of intellectuals in that process. This requires
an understanding of Alatas' concepts of the captive mind and erring
modernization.

Alatas originated and developed the concept of the captive mind
to conceptualize the nature of scholarship in the developing world,
particularly in relation to Western dominance in the social sciences
and humanities. The captive mind is defined as an 'uncritical and
imitative mind dominated by an external source, whose thinking is
deflected from an independent perspective' (Alatas 1974, p. 692). The
external source is Western social science and humanities, and the
uncritical imitation influences all the constituents of scientific activity
such as problem-selection, conceptualization, analysis, generalization, description, explanation, and interpretation (Alatas 1972, p. 11).
Among the characteristics of the captive mind are the inability to be
creative and raise original problems, the inability to devise original
analytical methods, and alienation from the main issues of indigenous
society. The captive mind is trained almost entirely in the Western
sciences, reads the works of Western authors, and is taught predominantly by Western teachers, whether in the West itself or through
their works available in local centres of education. Mental captivity is
also found in the suggestion of solutions and policies. Furthermore,
it reveals itself at the levels of theoretical as well as empirical work.

Alatas (1972, 1974) elaborated the concept in two papers published
in the early 1970s, but had raised the problem in the 1950s by referring to the 'wholesale importation of ideas from the Western world to
eastern societies' without due consideration of their socio-historical
context as a fundamental problem of colonialism (Alatas 1956). He
had also suggested that the mode of thinking of colonized peoples
paralleled political and economic imperialism. Hence, the expression
'academic imperialism' (Alatas 1969, 2000), the context within which
the captive mind appears.

Since the latter part of the nineteenth century, scholars in the non-
Western areas such as India, Southeast Asia, and the Middle East,
noting that the humanities and social sciences originated in the West,
raised the issue of the relevance of these fields of knowledge to the
needs and problems of their own societies. From the 1950s onwards,
there was a strong recognition of the academic dependence of the

Third World on the West as far the social sciences were concerned. This dependence was seen in terms of both the structures of academic dependency as well as the ideas derived from alien settings whose relevance was in question. The former can be gauged from the relative availability of First World funding for research, the prestige attached to publishing in American and British journals, the high premium placed on a Western university education, the design of curricula, and the adoption of textbooks in non-Western universities, as well as several other indicators (S. F. Alatas 2006; Altbach 1977; Weeks 1990, p. 236.). The latter problem of dependence on ideas can be illustrated by a survey of concepts and theories that are in vogue across a range of disciplines in the developing world. The captive mind exists within this context of dependency.

Alatas begins his conceptualization of the captive mind with a parallel idea, the demonstration effect in connection with consumer behaviour, developed by James Duesenberry. According to the idea of the demonstration effect, rising income would result in higher levels of consumption as consumers attempt to match the consumption patterns of those whose lifestyles they wish to imitate (Duesenberry 1949). Alatas suggests that the thinking of Third World social scientists can be understood in terms of the demonstration effect. According to this interpretation, the consumption of social science knowledge from the West arises from the belief in the superiority of such knowledge. Among the traits of this consumption that parallel the economic demonstration effect are (*a*) the frequency of contact with Western knowledge; (*b*) the weakening or erosion of local or indigenous knowledge; (*c*) the prestige attached to imported knowledge; and (*d*) that such consumption is not necessarily rational and utilitarian (S. H. Alatas 1972, pp. 10–11).

Alatas provides illustrations of the workings of the captive mind from development studies. The dangerous consequences of the captive mind lie in the weaknesses of the thought pattern in, for example, development studies in the West that is being imitated elsewhere. These cover various areas of scientific activity such as abstraction, generalization, conceptualization, problem-setting, explanation, and the understanding and mastery of data (S. H. Alatas 1972, p. 12). For instance, in the area of abstraction and generalization, Alatas discusses the work of Tinbergen (1967) on development planning as being marred by general and abstract propositions that are redundant (S. H. Alatas 1972, pp. 12–13). In another illustration, this time from the work of Kuznets, Alatas criticizes some of the propositions for being so general that they lack any utility for meaningful analysis. This problem could have been avoided had the work attempted to derive propositions and conclusions directly from historical and comparative data (S. H. Alatas 1972, p. 14). Another problem in development studies discussed by Alatas is that of erroneous judgement as a result of unfamiliarity with data or ignorance of the context. The example given is Hagen's view that digging with the Southeast Asian hoe is an 'awkward process', but the spade, which is a better instrument, can only be of limited use in low-income societies to the extent that shoes are not widely used (Hagen, 1962, pp. 31–2; Alatas 1972, p. 15). Alatas suggests that Hagen did not comprehend the function of the hoe in its proper context. In the Southeast Asian context, the hoe is actually the more efficient instrument because of terrace cultivation on mountain slopes. Hagen's failure to judge the efficiency and utility of the hoe by reference to its context is a violation of an important anthropological principle (Alatas 1972, p. 15).

It is problems such as these in development studies, as well as the social sciences in general, that are imitated and assimilated by the captive mind and resulting in ill-conceived development plans. Dominated by Western thought in a mimetic and uncritical way, the captive mind lacks creativity and the ability to raise original problems, is characterized by a fragmented outlook, is alienated both from major societal issues as well as its own national tradition, and is a consequence of Western dominance over the rest of the world (Alatas 1974, p. 691).

The consequence of the domination of the captive mind is erring modernization. According to Alatas, the phenomenon which directly challenges much of the developing world is erring modernization. Its characteristics, as listed by Alatas, are as follows:

(a) The mere introduction of science and technology without the necessary related elements such as scientific reasoning, research, and the proper concept of relevance. (b) The gearing of science and technology towards aims which violated the values of modernization such as increased standard of living, social justice, human wellbeing and the respect for the individual personality. (c) Negative imitation in the planning of development projects. (d) Acceptance of perpetual dependence on foreign knowledge and skill beyond that dictated by the need of the moment. (e) The isolation of the modernization process from a philosophy collectively and consciously upheld by the elites constructed with reference to modern scientific knowledge. (f) The prevalence of a fragmented outlook on the function of science. (g) The acceptance of disintegrative practices such as corruption and maladministration. (h) Indifference towards the rule of law. (i) The presence, side by side with science and technology, of archaic modes of thought and beliefs to a degree which stifles the growth of a scientific outlook. (Alatas 1975)

It is the pervasiveness of these traits that explains the erring nature of modernization in many Muslim and other developing societies.

***

It was during the nineteenth century that Muslims across Asia and Africa became aware of the changing nature of the society and political economy of the times. The process of modernization that had taken off in Europe earlier had already been spreading in the Muslim world and presented opportunities and challenges to people there. Among the problems identified by Muslim thinkers from the nineteenth century on ward are those that can be placed under the category of Westernization. But many Muslim critics of Westernization were not xenophobic. They were critical of certain aspects of Western, European, or modern civilization. Their criticisms of European civilization can be divided into structural and cultural criticism. Many of the problems they identified in Western and, therefore, modern civilization, remain valid for today and can be captured under the concept of erring modernization. Erring modernization is a term that emerged in the 1970s amidst concern with the problem of modernization having gone wrong in the Third World.

This chapter has suggested that the problems of modern society in the Muslim world do not only lie at the metaphysical or spiritual level. Even if Muslim societies were able to sacralize their economies and polities, this does not mean that the problem of erring modernization would be addressed. The example of Islamic economics discussed earlier has shown how the policies generated in the industrialized centres are reproduced in Muslim economies while being legitimized by the field of Islamic economics. This is because Islamic economics tend to be as conservative as its mentors, neo-classical and Keynesian economics, and unaware of the problems addressed by the theory of erring modernization.

Discussions on development in the Muslim world tend to be preoccupied more with economic growth and less with other issues that have implications for long-term development. Many Muslim economies grow as a reflection of economic expansion of advanced industrialized countries. There is, therefore, the problem of economic dependency. This dependency is manifested in the areas of trade, debt, technology, and foreign investment. These problems are not going to disappear in the near future. Attention to the problem of erring modernization is necessary if development in the Muslim world is to be self-directed and comprehensive.

NOTES

1. In this connection, see Özdemir (2009).
2. Nasr's ideas and the interpretive methods of *tafsir* and *ta'wil* are discussed by Bakar (1984).
3. Tariqa Maryamiyya is a modern Sufi order, founded by Sidi Isa Nur, it was mostly known by his Swiss-German name Frithjof Schuon. It is a branch of Shâdhilîyyah lineage. Schuon believed that the Virgin Mary appeared to him and gave him a universal mission. For more information, see Sedgwick (2004, pp. 147–60).
4. For example, see Kuran (1983, 1986, 1989); Fazlur Rahman (1964, 1974).

BIBLIOGRAPHY

Abdel-Malek, A. 1963. 'Orientalism in Crisis'. *Diogenes* 44: 103–40.

Ahmad, K. 1980. Economic Development in an Islamic Framework. In *Studies in Islamic Development*, edited by K. Ahmad, pp. 178–9. Jeddah: ICRIE.

Aímad, Z. 1987. 'Interest-Free Banking in Pakistan'. *Journal of Islamic Banking and Finance* 4: 8–30.

Alatas, S. F. 2006a. *Alternative Discourses in Asian Social Science: Responses to Eurocentrism*. New Delhi: SAGE.

———. 2006b. Islam and the Science of Economics. In *The Blackwell Companion to Contemporary Islamic Thought*, edited by I. Abū-Rabi', pp. 587–606. Blackwell Publishing.

Alatas, S. H. 1956, November. 'Some Fundamental Problems of Colonialism'. *Eastern World*, 10: 9–10.

Alatas, S. H. 1969, September. 'Academic Imperialism'. Paper presented at the meeting of the History Society University of Singapore, Singapore.

———. 1972. 'The Captive Mind in Development Studies'. *International Social Science Journal* 24(1): 9–25.

———. 1974. 'The Captive Mind and Creative Development'. *International Social Science Journal* 26(4): 691–700.

———. 1975. 'Erring Modernization: The Dilemma of Developing Societies'. Paper presented at the meeting of the Asian Institute for Economic Development and Planning on the Symposium Developmental Aims and Socio-cultural Values in Asian Society, Bangkok.

———. 1977. *The Myth of the Lazy Native: A Study of the Image of the Malays, Filipinos, and Javanese from the Sixteenth to the Twentieth Century and Its Functions in the Ideology of Colonial Capitalism*. London: Frank Cass.

———. 1996. 'Erring Modernization: The Dilemma of Developing Societies'. Paper presented at the Symposium on the Developmental Aims, pp. 70–1.

———. 2000. Intellectual Imperialism: Definition, Traits and Problems. *Southeast Asian Journal of Social Science* 28(1): 23–45.

Al-Attas, S. M. N. 1978. *Islam and Secularism*. Kuala Lumpur: Angkatan Belia Islam Malaysia (ABIM).

Altbach, G. P. 1977. 'Servitude of the Mind? Education, Dependency, and Neocolonialism'. *Teachers College Record* 79(2): 187–204.

Ariff, M., ed. 1982. *Money and Banking in Islam*. Jeddah: ICRIE.

Bakar, O. 1984. The Question of Methodology in Islamic Science. In *Quest for New Science*, edited by R. Ahmad and S. N. Ahmad, pp. 91–109. Aligarh: Centre for Studies on Science.

Dostoevsky, F. 1993. *The Grand Inquisitor—With Related Chapters from* The Brothers Karamazov. Indianapolis: Hacket Publishing.

Duesenberry, J. S. 1949. *Income, Saving and the Theory of Consumer Behavior*. Cambridge, MA: Harvard University Press.

Durkheim, E. 1989. İntihar, translated by Ö. Ozankaya. İstanbul: Cem Yayınevi.

Garaudy, R. 1996. 'The Founding Myths of Israeli Politics'. Retrieved from http://vho.org/aaargh/fran/livres/RGfounding.pdf, accessed 1 June 2016.

Ghazali, A. 1990. *Development: An Islamic perspective*. Petaling Jaya: Pelanduk Publications.

Hagen, E. E. 1962. *On the Theory of Social Change: How Economic Growth Begins*. Homewood: Dorsey Press.

Iqbal, Z. and A. Mirakhor. 1987. 'Islamic Banking'. *Occasional Paper*, no. 49. Washington, DC: International Monetary Fund.

Kahf, M. K. 1982. 'Savings and Investment Functions in a Two-sector Islamic Economy'. In *Monetary and Fiscal Economics of Islam*, edited by M. Ariff, pp. 107–23. Jeddah: ICRIE.

Karsten, I. 1982. 'Islam and Financial Intermediation'. IMF Staff Papers 29(1): 108–42.

Khan, F. 1984. 'A Macro Consumption Function in an Islamic Framework'. *Journal of Research in Islamic Economics* 1(2): 1–24.

Khan, S. M. 1986. 'Islamic Interest-Free Banking: A Theoretical Analysis'. *IMF Staff Papers* 33(1): 1–27.

Khan, S. M. and A. Mirakhor, eds. 1987. *Theoretical Studies in Islamic Banking and Finance*. Houston: Institute for Research and Islamic Studies.

Kuran, T. 1983. 'Behavioral Norms in the Islamic Doctrine of Economics: A Critique'. *Journal of Economic Behavior and Organization* 4: 353–79.

———. 1986. 'The Economic System in Contemporary Islamic Thought'. *International Journal of Middle East Studies* 18(2): 135–64.

———. 1989. 'On the Notion of Economic Justice in Contemporary Islamic Thought'. *International Journal of Middle East Studies* 21(2): 171–91.

Mannan, M. A. 1982. 'Allocative Efficiency, Decision and Welfare Criteria in an Interest-free Islamic Economy: A Comparative Policy Approach'. In *Monetary and Fiscal Economics of Islam*, edited by M. Ariff, pp. 43–62. Jeddah: ICRIE.

Nasr, S. H. 1980. 'Reflections on Methodology in the Islamic Sciences'. *Hamdard Islamicus* 3(3): 3–13.

———. 1981. *Knowledge and the Sacred: The Gifford Lectures*. Edinburgh: Edinburgh University Press.

———. 1993. *The Need for a Sacred Science*. Surrey: Curzon Press.

Nursi, B. Z. S. 2001a. *The Damascus Sermon*. Istanbul: Sözler Publications

———. 2001b. 'Seeds of Reality'. In *Letters: 1928–1932*, edited by B. Z. S. Nursi, pp. 541–54. Istanbul: Sözler Publications.

———. 2004. *The Words: On the Nature and Purposes of Man, Life and All Things*. Istanbul: Sözler Publications.

Özdemir, I. 2009. *Existence and Man: A Study of the Views of Said Nursi and J. P. Sartre* [Blog post.]. Retrieved from http://iozdemirr.blogspot. com/2009/12/said-nursi-and-j-p-sartre.html, accessed 1 June 2016..

Rahman, Fazlur. 1964. 'Riba and Interest'. *Islamic Studies* 3: 1–4.

———. 1974. 'Islam and the Problem of Economic Justice'. *Pakistan Economist* 14: 14–39.

Rauf, Abdul. 1984. *A Muslim's Reflections on Democratic Capitalism*. Washington, DC: American Enterprise Institute.

Sadr, S. M. B. 1982. *An Introduction to Principles of Islamic Banking*. Tehran: Bonyad Be'that.

Said, E. 1979. *Orientalism*. New York: Vintage Books.

Sedgwick, M. 2004. *Against the Modern World: Traditionalism and the Secret Intellectual History of the Modern World*. New York: Oxford University Press.

Shari'ati, A. 1980. *Marxism and Other Western Fallacies: An Islamic Critique.* Berkeley: Mizan Press.

Siddiqui, S. A. and A. Zaman. 1989. 'Investment and Income Distribution Pattern under Musharka Finance: A Certainty Case'. *Pakistan Journal of Applied Economics* 8(1): 1–30.

Sinha-Kerkhoff, K. and S. F. Alatas, eds. 2010. *Academic Dependency in the Social Sciences: Structural Reality and Intellectual Challenges.* Delhi: Manohar.

Sunar, L. 2014. *Marx and Weber on Oriental Societies: In the Shadow of Western Modernity.* Farnham: Ashgate.

Tibawi, A. L. 1963. 'English Speaking Orientalists'. *Muslim World,* 53, vol. 1: 185–204; vol. 2: 298–313.

———. 1979. 'Second Critique of English-Speaking Orientalists and Their Approach to the Islam and the Arabs'. *Islamic Quarterly,* 23(1): 3–54.

Tinbergen, J. 1967. *Development Planning.* London: Weidenfeld and Nicholson.

Uzair, M. 1976. 'Some Conceptual and Practical Aspects of Interest-Free Banking'. *Islamic Studies,* 15/4: 247–69.

Weber, M. 1946. *From Max Weber: Essays in Sociology,* edited and translated by H. H. Gerth and W. C. Mills. New York: Oxford University Press.

———. 1958. *The Protestant Ethic and the Spirit of Capitalism,* translated by T. Parsons. New York: Charles Scribner's Sons.

Weeks, P. 1990. 'Post-Colonial Challenges to Grand Theory'. *Human Organization* 49(3): 236–44.

Zarqa, M. A. 1983. 'Stability in an Interest-Free Islamic Economy: A Note'. *Pakistan Journal of Applied Economics* 2: 181–8.

12 Civilizations in an Era of Globalization

The Implications of Globalization for the Clash of Civilizations Debate

Yunus Kaya

Samuel P. Huntington's (1993, 1996) 'clash of civilizations' thesis created a firestorm of controversy and debate, both in the public sphere and academia in the 1990s, which still goes on today, although apparently with less fervour. Huntington's pessimistic vision of the post–Cold War world entailed scenarios of conflict among what he called civilizations, which he loosely based on culture, especially religious adherence, and geography. Huntington (1996) argued that new fault lines in world politics would emerge across cultural and religious boundaries, and the competing world views of different civilizations would inevitably lead to conflict, especially between the Western and the Islamic civilizations. He argued that 'culture and cultural identities, which at the broadest level are civilizational identities, are shaping the patterns of cohesion, disintegration, and conflict in the post-Cold War world' (Huntington 1996, p. 20).

However, the period following the collapse of the communist bloc also saw increasing levels of economic, political, and institutional integration and an ever-increasing flow of capital, goods and services, people, and information across national borders. This process, which is labelled as globalization, has become one of the most widely debated phenomena among scholars, politicians, bureaucrats, activists, and pundits of the public debate. Many have embraced it as the new reality of human existence, while others condemned it for various reasons or questioned its very existence.

The ever-expanding debate on globalization and evidence that has been accumulated, though contradictory at times, can shed some light on the clash of civilizations debate; and linking these two debates can improve our understanding of the contemporary world. Unfortunately, there have been relatively few attempts to connect these two debates. Huntington (1996) himself only indirectly engaged the globalization literature, which, to be fair, was in its infancy at the time. In his book, he implied that increasing integration of the world elevated people's consciousness about civilizations, both about the differences among them and similarities within them (Huntington, 1996). He also alluded that increasing integration has separated people from local identities; and religious identities, which have become increasingly deterritorialized, started filling this gap.

This chapter aims to bridge these two debates and discuss the implications of globalization for the debate on Huntington's 'clash of civilizations' thesis. In the process, it will discuss the impact of the globalization on cultures and identities around the world, and will present the results of a case study on the impact of globalization on attitudes towards immigrants.

A review of globalization literature reveals two contradictory accounts pertaining to the impact of globalization on local cultures and identities, and the relations among the people with different cultural affinities and identities. On the one hand, there are scholars and intellectuals who see globalization as a positive force bringing societies and peoples together through increasing economic and cultural exchanges and by improving their lives in the process. On the other, there are scholars and intellectuals who perceive globalization as a destructive force that threatens local cultures and economies, and endangers the livelihood of most people around the world.

Overall, this chapter will argue that globalization has been an uneven and contradictory process that has integrated economies and societies around the world while pitting them against each other and creating potentials for conflict. As globalization has created winners and losers both among and within nations, promoted transnational identities, and threatened and roused national and tribal ones, it has opened doors for conflict at various levels and on various issues. However, these conflicts have not been among relatively well-defined and unified civilizational blocs. The following section includes a brief overview of the debate on globalization. The subsequent sections discuss the impact of globalization on cultures and identities, and detail the two contradictory accounts on the impact of globalization.

THE GLOBALIZATION DEBATE

Globalization emerged as a compelling concept in the early 1990s in social sciences and popular discourse. The term 'globalization' was not widely used in academic and public debate until the early 1990s (Robertson 1992). By the end of the 1990s, however, there were countless articles and books on globalization. Although it has many dimensions and the theories of globalization project long historical trajectories, the locus of thinking on globalization has been the changes in the world economy during the last two or three decades. One major issue in the globalization literature has been the uniqueness of the current level of integration in the world economy, compared to earlier periods in human history (see Kaya 2010).

In one extreme of the globalization debate, we see some intellectuals, journalists, and business thinkers—often writing for a general audience—who claim that the world economy is experiencing a historically unprecedented integration. As the concept of globalization gained popularity in the second half of the 1990s, business thinkers such as Ohmae (1999) and Greider (1997), whose ideas are labelled as 'hyperglobalist' by Held and colleagues (1999), enthusiastically claimed that globalization created a borderless world where nation states and their borders did not mean much. In a more recent example, *New York Times* columnist Thomas Friedman (2006) published a widely popular book on globalization with the striking title *The World Is Flat*. In the book, he argued that the new digital economy created a world where geographic distances and borders do not matter and made optimistic connections between economic globalization and democracy, prosperity, and modernization.

The sceptics of globalization, however, rejected the idea that the current era is fundamentally different from earlier periods in world history, especially the late nineteenth century (for example, Bairoch 1996; Hirst and Thompson 1996; Obstfeld and Taylor 2003). Hirst and Thompson (1996) claimed that developments labelled as globalization are not historically unprecedented. They argued that the integration and interdependence among countries was higher in the late nineteenth century, with higher trade to national output ratios and more liberal trade and foreign investment policies, and more intense migration. In a similar fashion, Obstfeld and Taylor (2003) claimed that foreign capital is now discouraged by poor countries more than it was a century ago, and the ratio of investment to the size of the world economy was higher in earlier periods. Hirst and Thompson (1996) also argued that most of the transnational corporations (TNCs) depend on the sales or production in their home markets and labelled them as multinational corporations (MNCs) instead of TNCs.

From a different angle, world systems and dependency scholars have also been sceptical about the idea of globalization. For example, Wallerstein (2000) argued that the discourse on globalization is a misreading of the current reality. According to him, 'globalization' is something imposed on us by powerful groups. He claimed that there is not an independent process called globalization, but the transition of the entire capitalist world system to something else. Similarly, Chase-Dunn and colleagues (2000) contended that globalization of world trade was through cyclical processes, not with a take-off after 1970. In a well-known study, McMichael (1996) also labelled globalization as a project enacted by the same actors that shaped earlier periods of the world economy.

Against these critics, many globalization scholars rallied to identify and emphasize the distinctiveness of the integration in the current era. For example, Baldwin and Martin (1999, p. 4) claimed that the late nineteenth century and the current era 'have superficial similarities, but are fundamentally different'. They argued that the current period is different because of the dramatic reduction in transportation and communication costs, and greater heterogeneity of the world (Baldwin and Martin 1999). Held and colleagues (1999) claimed that the current period is different with its extensiveness, real time and round-the-clock economic transactions, and the diverse set of financial products. Dicken (2011) argued that unlike the 'shallow integration' of the earlier periods, the current global economy (post–World War II) is characterized by the 'functional integration' of economic activities. He stated that the global networks of firms, cross-cutting national boundaries, replaced the 'arm's length' trade between countries. In a clever account, Levinson (2006) showed how the mass utilization of shipping containers, starting in the 1960s, decreased the cost of transportation, especially reducing the cost of handling products at the ports. The global reorganization of manufacturing, which is sometimes labelled as the new international division of labour, has also been seen as one of the defining characteristics of the latest wave of globalization (Fröbel, Heinrichs, and Kreye 1980). Scholars observed that manufacturing is now organized through complex networks of firms, where leading firms, mainly from developed countries, engage in complex sets of relations with firms from less developed countries through investment and subcontracting (for example, Dicken 2011; Gereffi 2005). They argue that the single-site complexes that were one of the defining characteristics of early industrialization have been replaced by global manufacturing networks (Dicken 2011).

Following Robertson (1992), Held and colleagues (1999), Dicken (2011), and others, this chapter perceives globalization as a long historical process. Thus, it accepts that the latest wave of globalization has similarities to the earlier periods in world history, while maintaining that this wave has some distinct properties. This chapter also maintains that the globalization process went beyond a mere integration on national economies and has changed, transformed, and challenged cultures and identities worldwide. The following section discusses the impact of globalization on culture, and asks whether a global culture is in the making, and if certain cultures dominate it.

GLOBALIZATION OF CULTURE

Appadurai argues that 'the central problem of today's global interaction is the tension between cultural homogenization and cultural heterogenization' (Appadurai, 1990, p. 295). Although it may seem like an overstatement to some, this accurately points out one of the key issues in the debate on the globalization of culture, an issue that has been contentious among scholars, intellectuals, politicians, and activists worldwide.

When analysing the contemporary world, many scholars argue that the economic, political, and military hegemony of the West, particularly the US, also translates into a cultural hegemony. According to this perspective, an emerging global culture, dominated by the American culture, is asserting itself and eliminating cultural diversity by eradicating local cultures around the world. This perspective has its roots in the cultural imperialism thesis in the postcolonial theory (Tomlinson 1991). According to cultural imperialism thesis, the Western culture spread outside the West accompanying the military and economic expansion. In the process, it destroyed many local cultures while significantly transforming many others. The Western culture positioned itself as superior and more 'civilized', while non-Western cultures were seen as inferior and backward, a position shared by both the majority of people in the West and the Westernized local elites in non-Western societies (Said 1993; Spivak 1988).

In the globalization literature, many scholars point out to the control of global media, movie, and music industries by Western, and especially American, corporations (for example, Thussu 2007). They draw attention to the power and global reach of American corporations and cultural icons such as Coca-Cola and McDonald's (for example, Hamelink 1983; Watson 1997). For example, Watson (1997) describes how the opening of McDonald's restaurants in Hong Kong changed the fundamentals of daily diet and introduced new 'traditions' such as the celebration of birthdays and, of course, the birthday parties, although he acknowledges that McDonald's slightly altered its menu to accommodate local taste.

Many scholars, however, reject the notion of cultural homogenization and argue that globalization may have the opposite effect. They argue that globalization has created a backlash and has led many people around the world to emphasize differences rather than commonalities (for example, Appadurai 1990; Barber 1995). Huntington (1996) himself dismisses the adoption of certain aspects of Western culture outside the West as superficial and for having no significant and long-lasting effect.

Despite tacitly accepting the emergence of a global culture, many, arguably as a middle ground, perceive a hybridization of cultures instead of the domination of the Western or American culture and the assimilation of local cultures to a single global culture (for example, Kraidy 2005; Wang and Yeh 2005). For example, Wang and Yeh (2005) show how global entertainment companies Disney and Sony adapted the Chinese folk story 'Mulan', written by Robert D. San Souci, and a novel by Chinese writer Wang Dulu, *Crouching Tiger, Hidden Dragon*, and turned them into globally popular movies. Ritzer's (2008) well-known study on 'McDonaldization' also exemplifies this line of thinking. Ritzer defines McDonaldization as 'the process by which the principles of the fast-food restaurant are coming to dominate more and more sectors of American society, as well as the rest of the world' (Ritzer 2008, p. 1). He postulates that the four dimensions of McDonaldization (efficiency, calculability, predictability, and control) are shaping every industry and aspect of life in contemporary societies. Although, he asserts the universality of this form, he points out to a willingness to adapt to local cultures and tastes. He gives the example of the changing menu of McDonald's from one country to another, although most of the menu and the overall organizational form are kept the same. He also argues that local tastes can become global by adapting the four dimensions of McDonaldization. The transition of many local dishes originating from outside the West, such as sushi, into a globally sought and available product and the increasing number of establishments serving so-called ethnic food in the US and European countries can exemplify this (Bestor 2000).

Although the hybridization thesis provides a convincing argument, the asymmetry between the actors involved in the globalization process should be noted. For example, the expansion of local cuisines originating from the developing countries have been limited and dependent on immigrants from these countries moving to other countries. However, American corporations such as McDonald's and Starbucks have been expanding the reach of their products much faster without such limitations.

Robertson (1992) argues that what we see today is not globalization but a globalization process, which he defines as 'the globalization of the local and the localization of the global'. According to this perspective, globalization is a dual process of universalizing and particularizing tendencies. Thus, globalization emerges as a force that challenges and transforms the local cultures, but, at the same time, opens up avenues of expansion in front of them, which were not available before. Overall, the interplay between the local versus the global and the universal versus the particular is very important, since it reveals the complex and contradictory effects of the globalization process, which is especially important when discussing its implications for the debate on civilizations.

GLOBALIZATION AND THE DEBATE ON CIVILIZATIONS

When discussing the implications of globalization for the debate on civilizations, two questions stand out. First, is it possible to draw boundaries based on culture in an increasingly integrated world? Second, does increasing integration of economies and societies make people, who belong to different cultures, more hostile or receptive towards each other?

Huntington (1993, 1996) is neither clear nor convincing when it comes to defining civilizations. He is not very clear about how one can separate civilizations from one another. He uses culture, particularly religion, and geography haphazardly to define civilizational boundaries without providing a clear theoretical or methodological basis. For example, he lumps relatively geographically dispersed majority-Muslim countries into a single civilization, but he does not always employ a similar approach when it comes to other religions. In his typology of civilizations, most of the countries with Christian majority populations are categorized into four separate civilizations: Western, Latin American, Orthodox, and sub-Saharan. In a more empirically based effort, Inglehart and Baker (2000) categorized countries in terms of expression of traditional versus secular-rational and survival versus self-expression values into cultural blocs, using Huntington's thesis as guide. However, the fluidity of boundaries among these groups, exemplified by many countries that they had struggled to fit into a category did not provide any significant support for Huntington's conceptualization.

An underlying assumption in Huntington's (1993, 1996) theory is that the people in these civilizational blocs share an underlying cultural orientation, which unifies them and separates from people in other civilizations. Although Huntington (1996) acknowledges the heterogeneity within these civilizational blocs, he seems to be downplaying its importance. For example, Islamic civilization shows immense regional and ethnic diversity; and the divide between Sunni and Shia Islam has behind it a history of conflict and competition that goes back over a thousand years. The same problem surfaces for other civilizations he defines as well.

As stated above, Huntington (1996) postulates a heightening of people's consciousness about civilizations with the increasing integration of the world. He assumes that increasing integration of the world will lead people to emphasize the differences between them and the people belonging to other civilizations, and the commonalities within their own civilization. He also seems to have subscribed to the deterritorialization thesis, which claims that identities are increasingly less tied to territory or geography and more to culture.[1] In his book, he argues that people are increasingly separated from local identities (Huntington 1996).

However, as mentioned previously, evidence accumulated in the globalization literature points to a dual process of concurrent universalization and particularization. For example, unlike Huntington's views, a broader literature on transnational political communities views globalization as a powerful force challenging and changing local, regional, and national identities. Many argue that relatively well-defined and stable identities that had been tied to geography, culture and/or ethnic and racial groups became more fluid and increasingly mixed with other sources of identity that transcend these boundaries (for example, Featherstone 1995; Tomlinson 2003). Some even claimed that new forms identity, such as the ones pertaining to virtual communities, emerged with the recent wave of global integration and expansion of communication technologies (for example, Rheingold 1993). On the other hand, however, some argue that as increasing integration of the world can spark reactionary nationalist movements and Balkanization among the masses, and this will promote transnational identities and transnational solidarity among elites (Barber 1995; Karim 2012).

Referring to globalization's contradictory and asymmetrical effects within and across nations, some linked globalization to the rise of a transnational capitalist class or global ruling elite (for example, Carroll 2010; Robinson 2004). According to this account, since the 1970s the owners and managers of leading MNCs and private financial institutions have become increasingly aligned in their strategies and interests, forging ties and allegiances that surpass national boundaries (Robinson and Harris 2000). With the spread and development of global production networks, this class of 'corporate executives, globalizing bureaucrats, and politicians, professionals, and consumerist elites' (Sklair 2001, p. 4) has grown increasingly transnational and unified in character. Proponents of the transnational capitalist class thesis point to steady increases in foreign direct investment (FDI) and capital flows, off-shoring and the reach of global production networks, and cross-border mergers and business alliances as evidence (Robinson 2004). Among the world's largest corporations, they argue, there has been a significant increase in the number of interlocking directorates; and the improvements in information technology and the rise of a 'networked world' further consolidated control over the global economy (Harris 2001; Kentor and Jang 2004). Studies of specific industries or individual countries reveal a proliferation of cross-border ties and feelings of global solidarity among managers and professions (for example, Kennedy 2004; Sener 2008). Overall, the transnational capitalist class thesis predicts that globalization provides the conditions for the rise of a new global elite united by a shared class consciousness. This consciousness surpasses national or cultural boundaries and links small groups of elites in each society to each other. Therefore, according to this account, the real division is between this transnational capitalist class and the masses they exploit in each country, who are less likely to have a feeling of solidarity or shared interest with the masses in other countries although they share a similar faith (see Kaya 2008).

A closer review of literature reveals two accounts regarding the effect of globalization on various ethnic, racial, national, and religious identities and the relations among the people who subscribe to them. On the one hand, there are intellectuals and scholars who perceive globalization as a positive force bringing peoples and cultures together by facilitating a better understanding of one another and improving the well-being of everybody (for example, Bhagwati 2004; Friedman 2006; McGrew 1997). On the other hand, there are many intellectuals and scholars who see globalization as a destructive force, one that worsens the economic and social conditions of the masses, polarizes the social structures, and pits societies and cultures against one another (for example, Appadurai 1998; Barber 1995; Chomsky 1998).

The more positive outlook regarding the impact of globalization builds on the idea that the increasing economic welfare and exposure to democratic ideas and foreign cultures through globalization will help societies to embrace openness and prevent radicalism and violence. Although many proponents of this approach can be found in popular literature (for example, Friedman 2006; McGrew 1999), many scholars also project a positive influence of globalization. In the globalization literature, many scholars imply that the most recent wave of globalization has been a positive influence, improving economies and social structures. In one of the boldest defences of globalization, Bhagwati (2004) argued that the recent wave of globalization improved living conditions of the people, helped women, and increased democratic participation in countries all around the world. Similarly, Bhalla (2002) claimed that globalization increased the well-being of people overall and caused significant reduction in poverty and inequality. In popular literature, Friedman (2006) made very optimistic observations and predictions about the impact of increasing integration to global economy on economic well-being, social modernization, and democracy. In an earlier book, he had famously argued that 'no two countries where both had a McDonald's, had fought a war against each other since each got its own McDonald's' (Friedman 1999, p. 195). International institutions such as the IMF and the World Bank use similar arguments when advocating economic liberalization and openness, especially in the developing world. They present a positive picture of globalization where economic, ideological, and cultural benefits of globalization are realized together. Overall, according to this approach, globalization introduces previously alien cultures to one another, increasing social interaction across different cultures, hence enhancing tolerance towards people unlike themselves.

In contrast to this optimistic account, many argue that the economic conditions and political climate created during the latest wave of globalization is a ripe environment for conflict and intolerance towards others. Many people around the world attribute their declining fortunes to the increasing integration of economies and societies. For example, Scheve and Slaughter (2001) showed that American workers perceive globalization, measured by international trade, investment, and migration, as a primary source of their economic troubles. Swank and Betz (2003) found that increasing international flows of trade and investment contribute to the electoral success of right-wing parties in Western European countries. As mentioned earlier, Appadurai (1998) argued that globalization sharpens and threatens identities and creates reactionary backlash all around the world, often leading to violent ethnically based disputes. Barber (1995) also contended that as globalization demands the integration of national economies, it pits cultures against each other and people against people. He predicted a dual process of globalization and Balkanization, through a way in which strengthening global forces trigger a backlash and an embracing of national/tribal identities. Similarly, Kaldor (2004) claimed that globalization inflated 'new nationalism' and politics of identity, both by threatening ethnic and religious identities and opening new avenues for expressing them. Reflecting partly on the war in ex-Yugoslav republics in the 1990s, Meštrović (1996) observed a Balkanization of social identity and breaking of collective consciousness. He also argued that an increasing flow of information did not lead to increasing consciousness about the suffering of others and collective action. He stated that 'despite extensive knowledge about the genocide in Bosnia, cancer, pollution, and other phenomena, most persons seem confused about the appropriate actions to take with regard to the social problems they represent. The various "spins" put on all this knowledge by competing groups serve to Balkanize societies and to make individuals feel isolated from neighboring communities' (Meštrović 1996, pp. 94–5).

To assess these contradictory perspectives empirically, Ekrem Karakoc of Binghamton University and I analysed the impact of globalization on anti-immigrant attitudes in sixty-seven countries (Kaya and Karakoc 2012). The results of this analysis are presented in the following section.

ASYMMETRICAL AND CONTRADICTORY EFFECTS OF GLOBALIZATION: THE CASE OF RISING PREJUDICE

Reflecting on the debate presented earlier and linking it to the debate on prejudicial attitudes in sociology, my colleague and I discerned and tested two contradictory accounts of the impact of globalization on anti-immigrant prejudice. There has been a long line of research on prejudice in social sciences. A dominant line of thinking in the study of prejudice has been the 'group-threat' and 'competition' theories, which argue that the size of the minority groups, economic conditions, and competition over resources shape the prejudice against them (Blalock, 1957; Blumer 1958). In contrast, the 'contact theory' contended that an increase in the size of minority groups or immigrants creates opportunities for sustained and personal contact between the members of dominant and minority groups, thus reducing prejudice (Allport 1954; Hewstone and Brown 1986).

Our reading of globalization literature revealed two seemingly contradictory accounts, one which echoed the contact, and the other the group threat and competition theories in the prejudice literature. On the one hand we observed the intellectuals and scholars who perceived globalization as a force for connecting people all around the world to one another and enhancing economic growth and social welfare (for example, Bhagwati 2004; Friedman 1999, 2006; McGrew 1999). Partly following Guillen's (2001) and Lizardo's (2006) conceptualization, we called this approach the 'civilizing/integrative globalization' thesis. On the other, there were many intellectuals and scholars who saw globalization as a destructive force, which had worsened the economic and social conditions of the masses, polarized the social structures, and caused protest and backlash (for example, Appadurai 1998; Chomsky 1998; Swank and Betz 2003). Again following Guillen (2001) and Lizardo (2006), we labelled this approach the 'destructive globalization/globalization as a threat' thesis. We postulated that if the 'civilizing/integrative globalization' account was correct, globalization would help to create sustained and equal contact between immigrants and native populations, and prevent the perception of increased threat by spreading economic gains to everybody. However, if the 'destructive globalization/globalization as a threat' thesis account is correct, inequalities and economic troubles caused by globalization would increase anti-immigrant prejudice by intensifying competition over dwindling resources and by causing the native populations to perceive increasing immigrant populations as a threat. The Syrian refugee crisis and the Great Britain's exit from the European Union, which is closely tied to immigration fears, are two recent examples of this.

For our multi-level analyses of the impact of globalization on anti-immigrant attitudes, we included over 150,000 individuals from sixty-seven countries, both developed and developing, and used data from the World Values Surveys (WVS). The dependent variable in our analyses was derived from the WVS question of whether or not respondents would like to have 'immigrants/foreign workers' as their neighbours.[2] The independent variables comprised both individual and country-level variables. At the individual level, we assessed the impact of income, education, age, and gender. At the country level, we operationalized globalization through the international flows of goods and services, capital, and people. Our globalization variables were trade openness (exports as a percentage of GDP + imports as a percentage of GDP), inward foreign direct investment (FDI) stock, and international migrant stock (the percentage of migrants in the total population in a country).

In our sample, our analyses revealed that among the country-level variables, trade openness significantly increased anti-immigrant prejudice. There was also some evidence that existence of a larger immigrant population relative to domestic population, with the existence of high unemployment in a country, triggered anti-immigrant prejudice. By contrast, FDI had a weak effect. Overall, our analyses revealed some support for 'destructive globalization/globalization as a threat' thesis indicating that insecurities created by increasing integration of nations and their economies led to the fear of 'others' and a backlash towards them.

However, our study also emphasized the multi-dimensional and multi-faceted character of globalization, which results in varying effects of globalization across and within societies. First, different dimensions of globalization did not have a uniform effect in our analyses. Second, high-income countries, which arguably benefited more from globalization, had significantly less prejudice although they attracted the majority of immigrants. Third, within societies, individuals with higher income and education had significantly less prejudice across our models. Finally, the negative impact of the size of the immigrant population was conditional on the presence of a high level of unemployment. Therefore, although globalization has to be an integral part of any conceptualization of the contemporary world, it is critical to take into account its asymmetrical and often contradictory impact among and within societies.

***

This chapter attempted to link the debate on Huntington's (1993, 1996) clash of civilizations thesis to the globalization debate. Since the end of the twentieth century, our world experienced increasing economic, social, and political integration although there have been periods of hiatus such as the Great Depression and two world wars. Although there is an ongoing debate about how unprecedented this has been, there is a growing consensus that the world we live in today is more integrated than at any time in human history, as a result of globalization.

Many in the globalization literature predict a proliferation of trans-national identities and increasing cooperation and mutual under-standing among nations and peoples with globalization. In contrast, many others argue that globalization has created a fertile ground for conflict by threatening the identities and livelihoods of people around the world. In an empirical analysis of the impact of globalization on anti-immigrant prejudice, Karakoc and I found evidence suggesting that globalization can lead to fear of others and backlash towards them, especially when facing economic hardship (Kaya and Karakoc 2012). Therefore, we added to growing evidence in the literature per-taining to the detrimental effects of globalization on peoples around the world and the relations among them.

However, although the scholars and intellectuals who have a more pessimistic outlook on globalization argue that conflict will inherently arise with increasing integration of economies and societies under globalization, they do not proclaim that it will be among relatively well-defined civilizational blocs. Huntington claims that in today's world 'the most pervasive, important, and dangerous conflicts will not be between social classes, rich and poor, or other economically defined groups, but between peoples belonging to different cultural entities' (Huntington 1996, p. 28). However, the evidence these schol-ars accumulated points to a world that is fractured at many different levels. In this world, a wide variety of identities, local, national, and global, compete and coexist at the same time. Inequality, both within and between the nations, shapes the lives of billions of people around the world. While some in each society are positioned to gain from increasing integration of the world and have even become the main force behind it, others who stand to lose from it are increasingly turning against it (Brady and Denniston 2006; Carroll 2010; Fernandez-Kelley 1983; Lee 1998; Robinson 2004). The research on globalization strongly suggests that societies today are integrated and divided at the same time, not clustered around shared cultural affinities.

Overall, globalization has emerged as a contradictory process, which can bring people who had previously been separated by geography and borders together while carrying the potential to pit them against each other. It reveals both universalizing and particularizing tendencies, which leads to proliferation of supranational identities and galvanization of local and tribal ones at the same time. However, whether it reveals a proliferation of global identities and increasing cooperation among cultures or a resurgence of various local and national identities, and inherent conflict that are tied to them, the evidence accumulated in globalization literature does not support Huntington's clash of civilizations thesis. Huntington's thesis provides a convenient and seductive simplification of the contemporary world, which pays little attention to empirical evidence and the reality on the ground. A comprehensive and grounded understanding of the current human condition can only be possible by accounting for the complex ways that the societies and peoples are integrated and connected under globalization, and their diverse effects within each nation, society, or region.

NOTES

1. Roy (2004) makes somewhat similar observations regarding deterritorialization, but it somehow seems to apply mostly to Muslims in his conceptualization.
2. The question in the WVS questionnaire was the following: 'On this list are various groups of people. Could you please sort out any that you would not like to have as neighbors?' Then respondents were asked if they would prefer 'immigrants/foreign workers' alongside other groups. It was translated into local languages by the teams that conducted the survey in different countries.

BIBLIOGRAPHY

Allport, G. W. 1954. *The Nature of Prejudice*. Reading: Addison-Wesley.

Appadurai, A. 1990. 'Disjuncture and Difference in the Global Cultural Economy'. *Theory and Society* 7: 295–310.

———. 1998. 'Dead Certainty: Ethnic Violence in the Era of Globalization'. *Public Culture* 10(2): 225–47.

Bairoch, P. 1996. 'Globalization Myths and Realities: One Century of External Trade and Foreign Investment'. In *States against Markets: The Limits of Globalization*, edited by R. Boyer and D. Drache, pp. 173–92. New York: Routledge.

Baldwin, R. E. and Philippe Martin. 1999. 'Two Waves of Globalization: Superficial Similarities, Fundamental Differences'. In *Globalization and Labor*, edited by H. Siebert, pp. 3–58. Institutut fur Welwirtschaft an der Univesitat Kiel.

Barber, B. R. 1995. *Jihad vs. McWorld*. New York: Times Books.

Bestor, T. C. 2000. 'How Sushi Went Global'. *Foreign Policy* 121: 54–63.

Bhagwati, J. 2004. *In Defense of Globalization*. New York: Oxford University Press.

Bhalla, S. S. 2002. *Imagine There's No Country: Poverty, Inequality, and Growth in the Era of Globalization*. Washington: Peterson Institute.

Blalock, H. M. 1957. 'Percent Non-white and Discrimination in the South'. *American Sociological Review* 22(6): 677–82.

Blumer, H. 1958. 'Race Prejudice as a Sense of Group Position'. *Pacific Sociological Review* 1(1): 3–7.

Brady, D. and R. Denniston. 2006. 'Economic Globalization, Industrialization and Deindustrialization in Affluent Democracies, 1960–2001'. *Social Forces* 85(1): 297–329.

Carroll, W. K. 2010. *The Making of a Transnational Capitalist Class: Corporate Power in the 21st Century*. New York: Zed Books.

Chase-Dunn, C., Y. Kawano, and B. D. Brewer. 2000. 'Trade Globalization since 1795: Waves of Integration in the World-System'. *American Sociological Review* 65(1): 77–95.

Chomsky, N. 1998. *Profit over People: Neoliberalism and Global Order*. New York: Seven Stories Press.

Dicken, P. 2011. *Global Shift: Mapping the Changing Contours of the World Economy*, sixth edition. New York: Guilford Press.

Featherstone, M. 1995. *Undoing Culture: Globalization, Postmodernism and Identity*. Thousand Oaks: SAGE.

Fernandez-Kelley, P. 1983. *For We Are Sold, I and My People*. Albany: State University of New York Press.

Friedman, T. L. 1999. *The Lexus and the Olive Tree: Understanding Globalization*. New York: Farrar, Straus and Giroux.

———. 2006. *The World Is Flat: A Short History of the Twenty-First Century*. New York: Farrar, Straus and Giroux.

Fröbel, F., J. Heinrichs, and O. Kreye. 1980. *The New International Division of Labour: Structural Unemployment in Industrialised Countries and Industrialisation in Developing Countries.* Cambridge: Cambridge University Press.

Gereffi, G. 2005. 'The International Economy and Economic Development'. In *The Handbook of Economic Sociology*, edited by N. J. Smelser and R. Swedberg. Princeton: Princeton University Press.

Greider, W. 1997. *One World, Ready or Not: The Manic Logic of Global Capitalism.* New York, NY: Simon and Schuster.

Guillen, M. F. 2001. 'Is Globalization Civilizing, Destructive or Feeble? A Critique of Five Key Debates in the Social Science Literature'. *Annual Review of Sociology* 27: 235–60.

Hamelink, C. J. 1983. *Cultural Autonomy in Global Communications: Planning National Information Policy.* New York: Longman.

Harris, J. 2001. 'Information Technology and the Global Ruling Class'. *Race & Class* 42(4): 35–56.

Held, D., A. G. McGrew, D. Goldblatt, and J. Perraton. 1999. *Global Transformations.* Stanford, CA: Stanford University Press.

Hewstone, M. and R. Brown, eds. 1986. *Contact and Conflict in Intergroup Encounters.* Oxford: Blackwell.

Hirst, P. and G. Thompson.1996. *Globalization in Question.* Cambridge: Polity Press.

Huntington, S. P. 1993. 'The Clash of Civilizations?' *Foreign Affairs* 72: 22–49.

———. 1996. *The Clash of Civilizations and the Remaking of World Order.* New York: Simon and Schuster.

Inglehart, R. and W. E. Baker. 2000. 'Modernization, Cultural Change, and the Persistence of Traditional Values'. *American Sociological Review* 65: 19–51.

Kaldor, M. 2004. 'Nationalism and Globalisation'. *Nations and Nationalism* 10(1/2): 161–77.

Karim, S. 2012. 'The Co-existence of Globalism and Tribalism: A Review of the Literature'. *Journal of Research in International Education*, 11(2): 137–51.

Kaya, Y. 2008. 'Proletarianization with Polarization: Industrialization, Globalization and Social Class in Turkey, 1980-2005." *Research in Social Stratification and Mobility* 26(2): 161–81.

———. 2010. 'Globalization and Industrialization in 64 Developing Countries, 1980–2003'. *Social Forces* 88(3): 1153–82.

Kaya, Y. and E. Karakoc. 2012. 'Civilizing vs. Destructive Globalization? A Multi-Level of Analysis of Anti-immigrant Prejudice'. *International Journal of Comparative Sociology* 53(1): 23–44.

Kennedy, P. 2004. 'Making Global Society: Friendship Networks among Transnational Professionals in the Building Design Industry'. *Global Networks* 4(2): 157–79.

Kentor, J. and Y. S. Jang. 2004. 'Yes, There Is a (Growing) Transnational Business Community: A Study of Global Interlocking Directorates 1983–98'. *International Sociology*, 19(3): 355–68.

Kraidy, M. M. 2005. *Hybridity, or the Cultural Logic of Globalization.* Philadelphia: Temple University Press.

Lee, C. K. 1998. *Gender and the South China Miracle.* Berkeley, CA: University of California Press.

Levinson, M. 2006. *The Box: How the Shipping Container Made the World Smaller and the World Economy Bigger.* Princeton, NJ: Princeton University Press.

Lizardo, O. 2006. 'The Effect of Economic and Cultural Globalization on Anti-US Transnational Terrorism, 1971–2000'. *Journal of World Systems Research*, 12(1): 149–86.

McGrew, A. 1997. 'Democracy beyond Borders? Globalization and the Reconstruction of Democratic Theory and Practice'. In *The Transformation of Democracy? Globalization and Territorial Democracy*, edited by A. McGrew, pp. 231–65. Cambridge: Polity Press.

McMichael, P. 1996. *Development and Social Change: A Global Perspective.* Thousand Oaks: Pine Forge Press.

Meštrović, S. G. 1996. *Postemotional Society.* London: SAGE.

Obstfeld, M. and A. M. Taylor. 2003. 'Globalization and Capital Markets'. In *Globalization in Historical Perspective*, edited by M. D. Bordo, A. M. Taylor and J. G. Williamson, pp. 121–89. Chicago: University of Chicago Press.

Ohmae, K. 1999. *The Borderless World: Power and Strategy in the Interlinked Economy.* New York: HarperCollins Publishers.

Rheingold, H. 1993. *The Virtual Community: Homesteading on the Electronic Frontier.* Reading, MA: Addison-Wesley.

Ritzer, G. 2008. *The McDonaldization of Society 5.* Thousand Oaks, CA: Pine Forge Press.

Robertson, R. 1992. *Globalization: Social Theory and Global Culture.* London, UK: SAGE Publications.

Robinson, W. I. 2004. *A Theory of Global Capitalism: Production, Class, and State in a Transnational World.* Baltimore: Johns Hopkins University Press.

Robinson, W. I. and J. Harris. 2000. 'Towards a Global Ruling Class? Globalization and the Transnational Capitalist Class'. *Science and Society* 64(1): 11–54.

Roy, O. 2004. *Globalized Islam: The Search for a New Ummah.* New York: Columbia University Press.

Said, E. W. 1993. *Culture and Imperialism.* London: Chatto and Windus.

Scheve, K. and M. Slaughter. 2001. *Globalization and Perception of American Workers.* Washington, DC: Institute for International Economics.

Sener, M. Y. 2008. 'Turkish Managers as a Part of Transnational Capitalist Class'. *Journal of World-Systems Research* 13(2): 119–41.

Sklair, L. 2001. *The Transnational Capitalist Class*. Oxford: Blackwell.

Spivak, G. C. 1988. 'Can the Subaltern Speak?' In *Marxism and the Interpretation of Culture*, edited by C. Nelson and L. Grossberg, pp. 271–314. Urbana: University of Illinois Press.

Swank, D. and H. G. Betz. 2003. 'Globalization, the Welfare State and Right-Wing Populism in Western Europe'. *Socio-Economic Review* 1(2): 215–45.

Thussu, D. K. 2007. *Media on the Move: Global Flow and Contra-flow*. London: Routledge.

Tomlinson, J. 1991. *Cultural Imperialism: A Critical Introduction*. London: Pinter.

———. 2003. 'Globalization and Cultural Identity'. In *Global Transformations Reader*, edited by D. Held and A. McGrew, pp. 269–77. Malden: Blackwell.

Wallerstein, I. 2000. 'Globalization or the Age of Transition? A Long-Term View of the Trajectory of the World-System'. *International Sociology* 15(2): 249–65.

Wang, G. and E. Yueh-yu Yeh. 2005. 'Globalization and Hybridization in Cultural Products: The Cases of Mulan and Crouching Tiger, Hidden Dragon'. *International Journal of Cultural Studies* 8(2): 175–93.

Watson, J. L. 1997. *Golden Arches East: McDonald's in East Asia*. Stanford: Stanford University Press.

13 Conceptualizing Civilization between Othering and Multiculturalism

Murat Çemrek

> By that battered, single-fanged monster you call 'civilization'?
> —Mehmet Akif [Ersoy] at the Independence March

> We shall elevate our national culture above the level of contemporary civilization.
> —Mustafa Kemal [Atatürk] in his address on the tenth anniversary of the republic)[1]

The self ontologically requires the 'other' to define itself as a constitutive being, though the other denotes divergence from any given self and its normative stand. However, neither the self nor the other is constant, but the self uses its power to draw boundaries for the other to make and keep it constant as an absolute challenger against whom it can wage war eternally. Thus, othering can be intrinsically practised with any religious, sectarian, racial, ethnic, or even geographical basis. Within the boundaries of this chapter, our focus will be on civilization. Othering becomes the first step of the domination–subordination relation of politics as no self pays attention to the other as superior, so the dichotomy of self–other is naturally power-dependent and could be based on anything to ensure superiority for domination.

For example, othering in modern cartography has resulted in misrepresentation of genuine locations and distances on maps, as in the example of British cartographers centring Britain and drawing it larger than it really is. Thus, the creation of other is a fiction, an invention, and a construction on the basis of the self through attributing negative connotations to the other, since the self sets itself as the norm. This is also how hierarchy is established between the self and the other. It is noteworthy to cite Edward Said and his pivotal work *Orientalism* (2003), which opened the path to cast a critical eye on the huge quantity of literature on Orient in which the other 'East' is created through the literary works of the West. According to Said, the Orient is depicted and represented through the lenses of the Occident in these studies. Moreover, feminist literature challenges the normality of men in patriarchal culture as it creates woman as its other. In this context the 'other' and 'othering' have become crucial concepts in social sciences through multiculturalism created via rising globalization where the nation states try to cope not only with the rising number of immigrants, but also with the already settled citizens' demands in the name of identity. That is how multiculturalism has become a hotspot in daily politics alongside academic literature.

The vast literature on multiculturalism gets inflated through the multidisciplinary approaches, focusing on different times and spaces in contrasting ways. Multiculturalism is not only popular but is also a buzzword that has puzzled analysts and has been deeply disputed within the disciplines of social sciences, from anthropology to international relations, since the term has become a 'conceptual grab bag' (Mills 2007, p. 89), especially after the 9/11 attacks that triggered the escalation of subaltern and postcolonial studies. Thus, one can not only trace the roots of multiculturalism in the public policy practices of the Western world, but can also meet 'colonial seeds of multiculturalism', as defined by Sneja Gunew (2004, p. 33), in response to the possibility of sincere recognition and dialogue with marginalized groups. That is why recognition through multicultural education is not only for the recognition of group culture, especially in arts and literature, but also in conjunction with the history of group subordination and its concurrent involvement (Gooding-Williams 1998).

Historically, multiculturalism became the basis of mainstream public policy after World War II stimulated the end of the European colonial system and institutionalized racism, which had reached its peak in Nazi Germany. Multiculturalism emerged since toleration of group differences in the Western liberal societies had fallen short of treating minority group members as equal citizens. Thus positive accommodation of group differences came forth through Will Kymlicka's 'group-differentiated rights' (1995) such as exemptions from generally applicable laws in virtue of their religious beliefs. In this context, multiculturalism as an umbrella term illustrates the political claims of a wide range of disadvantaged groups, from women to disabled people, although the main tenet of multiculturalism focuses on immigrants who are members of ethnic and religious minorities such as Muslims in Western Europe, minority groups such as Kurds in several Middle Eastern states, and indigenous peoples like Indians in North America. Multiculturalism then has been equated with protecting minority rights and providing the minorities with full access to 'equal opportunities' guaranteed by liberalism for the sake of keeping society intact.

According to C. James Trotman, multiculturalism is precious as it 'promotes respect for the dignity of the lives and voices of the forgotten ... and tries to restore a sense of wholeness in a postmodern era that fragments human life and thought' (2002, pp. 9–10). In the same vein, multiculturalists argue that different cultures can enrich society, so multiculturalism is possible when there is a mutual acceptance between the host society and the immigrants, with each accepting the culture of the other. According to multiculturalists, multiculturalism makes a more tolerant society possible with the ability to be more practical and adapt better to social issues; the more culture changes the more the world changes. Thus, multiculturalism has the potential to be practised and institutionalized as cultural diversity becomes the norm and governmental policies are ready to promote it through institutions, from schools to military barracks.

Multiculturalism essentially responds to cultural differences, including religious, gender, or sexual dimensions, and that is why it is used to define disadvantaged groups, from women to disabled people, as well as immigrants, and it is associated with identity politics (Young 1990; Taylor 1992). The recognition of diversified cultures within the mostly homogeneous educational system of the nation state through multicultural education has become the hot topic, since education triggers bureaucracy, and indeed the government, to be more adoptive towards the others and their cultures besides the national one.

Will Kymlicka, the most persuasive theorist of multiculturalism, argues that culture is instrumentally valuable to individuals as it ensures self-respect and makes one feel secure, and it also enables individual autonomy providing milieus of choice. Thus, Kymlicka believes in 'a liberal egalitarian theory ... which emphasizes the importance of rectifying unchosen inequalities' (1995, p. 109) to justify group rights. In this context, immigrants are viewed as voluntary economic migrants who chose to relinquish access to their native culture by migrating. However, Bhikhu Parekh, arguing that liberal theory cannot postulate an impartial framework of relations between different cultural communities, believes that the challenges faced by the minorities when 'demanding special rights' are nothing but 'thinly veiled racis[m]' and goes on further to argue that multiculturalism is in fact 'not about minorities' but 'about the proper terms of relationship between different cultural communities' (2002, p. 13). Although multiculturalism is culturalist in essence, it is quite political in the sense that it removes the barriers of discrimination, and also economic, since power needs economic backing to overcome the problems that the multiculturalists' requests raise.

Although the metaphor of the 'salad bowl' of multiculturalism challenges the 'melting pot' of assimilation, multiculturalism is also heavily criticized for eroding national identity. The liberal critics argued that multiculturalism challenges the very essence of a liberal society in which one can do whatever s/he wants, but when there is such group affirmative action then immigrants or women are thought to be homogeneous blocks, detrimental to the essence of the individual and his/her willingness to volunteer to be part of the society. Although multiculturalism has been the basis of public policies in the Western world since the 1970s, it does not mean that it is widely accepted at the social level since we still talk about 'skinheads', affirmative policies for the immigrants, xenophobia, and Islamophobia.

A major criticism of multiculturalism is related to the ideas of freedom of association and conscience, necessitating the defence of the individual's right to form and leave associations anytime with no special protections for groups. Chandran Kukathas argues that the state should surpass its role of protecting civility while promoting 'cultural integration' of minority groups (2003, p. 15). Another critique is based on the requirements of equality, which, as Brian Barry contends, is that religious and cultural minorities should be responsible for the consequences of their own beliefs and practices, since justice safeguards a reasonable array of equal opportunities but does not ensure equal access to any particular choice of religion (2001, p. 37).

If we follow the culturalist perspective of multiculturalism in response to civilization, then how can politics be shaped in any nation state while politics underlines itself as the roots of civilization? How could identity and its politics be formed in such a context? This study is devoted to questioning the identity form, shaped through the imposition of national identity on the intellectual schemes of the masses as the single unique identity formed principally through national education with the help of the national media—this is also valid for the perception of civilization being moulded in the same way. Does civilization force a single identity upon us? Does singularization of identity originate from the nature of civilization or is its existence due to the relation of civilization with politics? Does power essentially impose a single civilization identity on individuals? In short, is this condition ontological or extrinsic? Is it possible to transform this singularity into plurality if we conceptualize civilization within the social and/or civilian context but not the political? Could we be members of only one civilization and should we really be? Or could we belong to several civilizations simultaneously? Then, how could we bring this plurality into being in a healthy manner? This list of questions could certainly be lengthened to understand the nature of civilization within the identity context.

WHAT TO DO WITH CIVILIZATION?

Civilization is among the meta-concepts that I call 'unfortunate concepts'; culture and globalization come to mind initially. The misfortune of these concepts is that they fall into the trap of explaining nothing while they are thought to cover and explain everything. Thus, the concept of civilization resembles a warehouse, including anything that one throws into it. That is why it is necessary to indicate civilization's references to the Arabic roots of 'urban' and Latin roots of 'construction' while mentioning civilization in a prudential way.

Every civilization in its teaching, praxis, imagination, invention, art, and even fiction characterizes other civilizations besides itself as barbarous through its compact vision, encompassing political, economic, social, cultural, and other dimensions. This essentialist rhetoric of barbarity is intrinsic to the nature of civilization, while the concomitant manner of deriving enjoyment by inflicting accusation and humiliation grants every civilization the possibility of construct-ing its own identity through 'the other'. Barbarity, in this context, keeps its seat as an ever-ready counter-concept, providing civilization with instrumental (methodological) functions of bringing itself into existence (ontological) and describing (epistemological) the universe. In this setup, civilization paradoxically joins with barbarity, its enemy (or at least its 'other', if not enemy), while progressing through its solidarity dialectically. Civilization, organizing identity dimensions as 'we' and 'they', carries this difference into the field of rhetoric at every opportunity and does not hesitate to bring it into the field of war when conditions are ripe enough. Civilization, though sounding like a 'perpetual state of peace', constantly opens the path for con-flict, since civilization is always on alert to prevent barbarity and it is already implied within its definition that civilization will wage war against barbarity in order to defeat it.

For any civilization, the last utopian resort is to reach a state of such unity/singularity where all the differences in the world have been terminated. However, every civilization is quite aware that real-ization of this utopia is not that easy. Even while stepping towards this singularization/unification ideal, parties, factions, cliques, and fractions end up accusing each other of otherness and harbor feelings of enmity towards each other within the context of same civilization. Every division names itself as the 'party of salvation' (*fırka-i-naciye*) on the path of grace (*sırat-ı-müstakim*), anchoring its reference point to the rhetoric of a nostalgic as well as an anachronistic imagined golden age (*asr-ı-saadet*). Even in this identity construction, the 'we's' within the same civilization do not abstain from labelling each other as 'barbarian', a term appropriate for the 'other' when division comes forth and is observed clearly. Thus, every civilization employs a tran-scendental and epic language to keep its existence intact, and to be easily noticed by their followers. That is why every civilization accred-iting itself with a transcendental singularity claims to be in a state of perpetual war with barbarity, as it could never affirm that it is waging a war against another civilization since inherently every civilization regards itself as 'the civilization'.

Every civilization, through the legitimacy of its own production, is naturally 'the absolute goodness' in essence, however, despite being a representative unit of perpetual peace, it finds itself at war with barbarity, 'the absolute evil'. According to the necessity of the ancient moral principle about the war between good and evil, when this unending war ends, and I am aware of the paradoxes of the wording game, it is considered certain that absolute goodness will win the war. Just as every civilization attributes to itself unity, singularity, and even uniqueness, it also labels itself as the *sui generis* universality. Every civilization by implication defines itself as 'the end of history' and does not refrain from preaching that any deviation from the point it has reached will result in a catastrophe for all humanity, not only for its followers. On the other hand, every civilization could possibly form 'conjectural' alliances and unions with barbarians against other barbarians in the case of necessity, since the discourse employed is that such tactical and strategic manoeuvres do not harm the essence of civilizations, and any civilization will present this development as the method employed to eradicate barbarity via the hand of barbarians themselves. Moreover, every civilization propounds this generous overview of itself as an operation to win over the hearts of barbarians, in order to extend an invitation to them for gaining salvation and also to leave the door of unity ajar for this objective.

As humans we do not really recognize all our activities connected to our identity or belief as a part of culture or civilization, we simply perform the activities in the ways we want to. Thus, we do not think of ourselves as breaking off our civilization, indeed, we actually think we are reviving it. As an example, tying shoddies to trees is extension of paganism, when it is combined with doom visits; by indulging in such activities, we revive our civilization, but because we are members of civilization based on monotheist religions, we simultaneously encourage barbarity. We also adapt the earlier practices of our civilization into daily conditions to energize our civilization. For example, Omar's (the second Rashidun Caliph after the Prophet Muhammad, peace upon Him) refusal to keep donating a share from the alms to non-Muslims to gain their hearts for Islam is correlated with no further need of Islamic civilization which could signal the end of Keynesian politics and/or decline of the welfare state to be described as the dynamism of liberalism. What I mean is that the already strong practices or even the tenets of any civilization could be given up and this act of relinquishing could even be legitimized for the sake of the civilization itself.

Every civilization continues absorbing followers of other civilizations and their rituals to maximum capacity—though still defining them as barbarians—and presents this in the form of 'official tolerance' as a public relations exercise and as public diplomacy practice. In fact, such tolerance is othering-orientated, exclusionary, and even humiliating with regard to the concept of civilization. When any civilization starts to lose ground by showing official tolerance towards the followers of different civilizations who are inherently potential enemies, it produces 'Armenian offspring' from the loyal nation (*millet-i-sadıka*), the dirty ones having stabbed us from behind, the Arabs without whom we could not exist, Islamophobia and/or immigrant problems from the guest workers (Gasterbeiter) who are welcomed in to improve Western economies and the ones brought in to endow society with *bon pour l'Orient* (good for the East) diplomas, as they start to move towards the centre from the peripheries. The same situation is also valid for the heterodox/deviant/revisionist minority masses such as the Hanafi school members in Iran and the Alawites in Turkey. This is the price of being 'different' and is to be paid back when someone is not part of the civilization s/he lives in.

In fact, if observed with a careful eye, one could question the paradox of this study since the given examples have been gathered from the ones examining religious, sectarian, and nation state dimensions. That is exactly what I would like to underline: no civilization is one-dimensional but is composed of several layers, like an onion; furthermore, different dimensions of colours and tastes generate a civilization. Civilization reaches a state of further complexity with space and time emerging as new dimensions. For example, when we talk about Islamic civilization, less than forty years following the conquest of Constantinople in 1453 and its transformation into Istanbul, the fall of Granada in 1492 resulted in contrary perceptions of Islam being formed within two different geographies. In this context, singularization is a crime against civilization as it is nothing but reductionism, and perhaps even robs its essence. In the same vein, our social roles provide us with identities, although they contradict each other sometimes; the civilization that we have membership of is one of the roles among all at the last instance, by which I mean we could belong to several civilizations on the one hand, and on the other civilizational identity is one of the identities we have.

THE NEW BATTLE OF GLOBALIZATION WITH THE NATION STATE ON CIVILIZATION

The nation state's effort to impose on us a collective political identity through shaping us into a singular form led to the confinement of our religious, sectarian, ethnical, and gender identities within a box. Our social roles are shadowed under the primary one but they are looking for an opportunity to come forth, our identities follow the same track to reach the surface, following any rupture towards freedom. For example, the identities already swept under the carpet amidst security anxieties during the Cold War have surfaced following the collapse of the Soviet Union, and this has become a milestone for the discipline of International Relations (IR). Thus, religious, sectarian, ethnic, and gender identities that were thought to have been dead in the name of the invention of *homo Sovieticus* rose again in the form of fifteen different nation states. Yugoslavia's example has followed its Soviet counterpart, and one can also identify the struggle of different identities to surface, following the incidents of Iraqi occupation and the Arab Spring.

Globalization, on the other hand, has brought us closer to cosmopolitanism, introducing the idea of 'world citizenship', dating back to Stoicists in Ancient Greece, while keeping our different identities intact. However, one must refrain from equating globalization with Hollywood-style Americanization or American imperialism in its purest sense. At the very least, we have realized that globalization is far more complex and entangled, as observed through our experiences in the last twenty years. Globalization, through liberalization of the market at the global level, is democratizing our world by carrying participation from economy to politics. As much as this development increases the presentation of products into the market, the colours of the market vary rather than taking on the green of American currency. As globalization creates different modernities and makes different modernity readings with their practices possible, the monopoly of the white man on development is broken. This, in a subtle way, introduces the possibility of—or even necessity for—new conceptualizations rather than 'Westernizing' or 'developing' countries. Moreover, civilization is not a constant point and is apt to change through time and space as a human product, and it also has the ability to change in relation to its surroundings. Just as we need to ask 'which century?' or 'which geography?' when we talk about Islamic civilization, we also need to question either socialist or capitalist variation when we talk about Western civilization.

Where am I going with all of this? The process of globalization has made it clear that civilizations are in conflict with each other and they also have their domestic factionary battles. The ecological movements and especially the empowerment of animal rights as well as the rise of women's rights within human rights activities could be cited as examples. Thus, we all belong to one civilization of humanity and the plurality of civilizations originates from the necessity to make this plurality survive within unity. Our belonging to all civilizations simulates the rivers of the human civilization. Our simultaneous roles, like our multi-identity existence, are fostered through being multicultural and multi-civilizational. Even if we want to name ourselves as part of a single civilization, it is impossible to do that since civilizations contain different layers of connections to each other through their historical interactive relations, having waged wars with each other in the name of ending barbarity. The common words, as well as common behaviours and symbols, signify this fact. For example, the framework of the Silk Road has orientated different civilizations towards peaceful cooperation, while the Crusades have offered the warring counterparts of the Christian West and the Muslim East the chance to teach other. So, the civilizations have not only fought with each other but have also developed peaceful exchanges during ceasefires.

The two epigraphs at the beginning of this text are the two well-known phrases every Turkish citizen gets used to hearing and internalizing from the early days of their official national education, just like in other nation states citizens are forced to learn by heart similar oaths and heroic phrases as they pass through the national education system.

The harm done by the nation states to their citizens has such a dimension that they have to live through suppressing such contradictions to the point where it is dangerous to vocalize them when they notice them. For example, it is difficult to find two dicta such as these summarizing the foundational philosophy of the Turkish Republic very succinctly, and yet contradicting each other. One could develop such analysis to pass over, remove, or explicate this paradox: the 'Independence March' is a poem presented to a contest of reward by a Muslim Ottoman citizen—Islamist in his own political vision and Albanian in ethnicity—when the Ottoman state was under occupation and the Grand National Assembly was established in Ankara to fight against this occupation, a fight that later came to be called the Independence War. On 12 March 1921, Mehmet Akif's poem won the contest and it was accepted as the Independence March, the national anthem. When one pays attention to the dates and the context of this poem, it can be seen that it starts with the address 'To Our Heroic Army', presenting moral support to the national army that is at the stage of establishment from different groups with artilleries vis-à-vis the European/Western powers. Thus, regarding the concept of 'civilization' in the Independence March, the poet criticizes the relentless secular European civilization, but it is certain that he is not against the concept of civilization when one pays attention to the whole poem. However, the other epigraph is part of the address propounded at the ceremony for the tenth anniversary of the Turkish Republic by its founder and the first president, Mustafa Kemal. The address at the tenth anniversary of the republic includes praise: 'We have succeeded a lot and have done great things in a short time. The greatest among them is the Turkish Republic based on Turkish heroism and high Turkish culture'. The founding fathers of the Republic were very eager to reach their target to catch up and even surpass the European/Western civilization, and they showed their eagerness in the very first ten years through reforms they accomplished. Moreover, these two statements not only belong to two different people but there is also a time span of more than ten years between them. However, this is not a satisfactory explanation for the schizophrenic journey that involves everyone internalizing these two contradicting statements through the [law on] Unity of Education (Tevhid-i-Tedrisat) of the Republic framing the national education monopoly by the Ministry of National Education in Turkey.

DO CIVILIZATIONS REALLY NEED TO CLASH?

Civilization in general, and Western civilization in particular, is not independent from politics and its nucleus of power. Janus-facedness and/or double standards have shaped the intellectual schemes of every civilization and their followers, as well as politics, since the ancient times. Any civilization to which we attribute membership has reached its current point not through bloody occupations, but through glorious conquests of our beliefs. Perhaps following along these lines, the critique that 'both of them are not the same' emerges in our minds. Of course, both of them are not the same and, in order to protect our mental health, we need to stay away from them since we neither like to blame the civilization to which we swear allegiance, nor do we want to get our hands bloodied, as we recall the bloody occupations that we have already memorized as glorious conquests. For example:

> The Nazis under the leadership of Hitler looted French works of art. The French under the leadership of Napoleon looted the Italian works of art. The Russians under the leadership of Stalin looted the German works of art. The Crusaders looted the Byzantines; they razed the Byzantine capital to the ground and even carried the famous horse-shaped sculptures to Italy. The Crusaders demolished everything in Anatolia via their cruelty labelled as 'cannibalism' by their authors. The Spanish were not contented with only looting the artworks of the continent of the Americas but they also transported thousands of tons of gold and silver to their motherland. Today many Western museums particularly the British Museum and Louvre are full of exhibits from Turkey, Egypt, Greece and Italy. Today many art objects of Anatolian origin are imprisoned in twelve different countries. (Özatik, n.d.)

In this extract the author, despite mentioning the lootings of the Western civilization within itself and the rest of the world, skips over the others. In order to avoid deepening the schizophrenia exposed to us through national identity and in order to preserve our mental health to whatever extent possible, suppression of these facts and transference to the subconscious is a necessity. For example, the swords of the Prophet Muhammad and his subsequent four Rashidun Caliphs are kept as Holy Relics (Kutsal Emanetler) in the Topkapı Palace in Istanbul.

While Ahmet Davutoğlu depicts the egocentric nature of civilization as 'egocentric illusion' with reference to Toynbee's figuring of

Western civilization's historical understanding, Samuel P. Huntington, from the same perspective, presents Turkey as '[the] most obvious and prototypical country' torn apart between Islamic and Western civilizations in his famous 'Clash of Civilizations?' (1993, p. 42).[2] The common approach of Davutoğlu, Toynbee, and Huntington is to take civilization as the unit of analysis while comprehending the past, present, and even the future. Huntington's thesis divides the earth into nine different civilizations: Western, Orthodox, Latin, Islamic, African, Indian, Buddhist, Japanese, and Chinese. Huntington has preached that civilizations with deeper historical roots will replace ideologies as the determining factor for alliances and contradictions in the international system, following the end of the Cold War after the collapse of the Soviet Union. Accordingly, starting with the twenty-first century, clashes among civilizations are inevitable. In this context, Huntington's thesis is a deterministic approach summarizing the main reason of the micro-nationalist and sectarian conflicts in the New World Order, as well as the forthcoming wars, as civilizations maintaining enmity towards each other on historical and religious grounds. Huntington claims that the conflict between Islam and the West especially is inevitable and will shape the future of the world. However, he views the First and Second World Wars as 'civil wars' of the Western civilization. Likewise, when we look at the Iran–Iraq War through the lenses of Islamic history, we observe that it has cost more than one million lives within a span of eight years between two Muslim-populated countries. Huntington, moreover, negates the founding proto-nation trait of the primary ethnicity at the base of the nation states while missing out the inner worlds of the civilizations, labelling them as 'big camps'. For example, Huntington's denomination of Orthodox civilization is of no use without the Catholic equivalent, additionally it is not easy to intellectually digest the notion of keeping Russian Orthodoxy and the Armenian Orthodoxy at the same level. However, in order to prevent his thesis from being manipulated after the 9/11 attacks, Huntington has retreated: 'In fact, it is Osama bin Laden's target to turn the war declared by a terrorist organization towards a civilized nation as the clash of civilization between Islam and the West. It would be a disaster if he could succeed [at] it' (Samuel P. Huntington'un Ardından 2009).

In contrast to Huntington, I want to suggest that if the manifestation of contradiction among layers is high in the multi-layered structure of 'the civilization', and if fault lines are activated often, the aforementioned situation of being torn apart, as in the example of Turkey, is quite crystallized. In this context, Israel and Greece (where the tension between religious and secular is deep), as well as Huntington's examples of Mexico, Russia, and Australia, could be named as torn countries. In Israel the ones fostered from the Enlightenment tradition, such as leftist political parties and their supporters especially, are quite unhappy with the ample use of religious symbols for political purposes as well as the exemption of the clergy from military service. The reference to Orthodoxy for Greek citizenship is also worrisome to some Greeks. These two examples serve to illustrate the fact that there is a deep tension between secular policies and religion in other countries as well.

Even regarding discussions on abortion in the United States, one could easily mention elements of society being torn apart. In short, every individual, community association, and state could experience being torn in different modes and in different times with reference to being exposed to activation of fault lines within their civilizations. In fact, I do not present this reality as something negative and I even affirm that the dynamism of civilizations is fostered by such inner contradictions.

It is not meaningful to denote civilization as Adam Smith's 'invisible hand' metaphor in the light of what is mentioned previously. It is better to underline the interactive relation between civilization and politics, since neither civilization nor politics could (re)produce itself without the other. In fact, as power does not accept its counter equivalent in principle, it is natural for any civilization to put itself forward as 'the civilization' while singularizing and even particularizing itself. As this process transforms the identity of any civilization to be singular and particular, conflict arising out of the effort to construct a single national identity is quite possible. For example, in Turkey, there has always been a tension with the Republic and the Ottoman state since the founding fathers of the Republic have tried their best to render the Ottoman past forgotten by passing reforms, adopting the Latin alphabet, or through the annulment of the Sultanate and the Caliphate. However, the Ottoman state has been animated through symbols with the rightist governments especially after 1999, the seventh anniversary of its establishment, bringing to the fore the dichotomy of either being an 'Ottoman grandchild' or a 'Republican child'. The conflict of national identity with supranational and/or subnational identities, such as religion, sect, and ethnicity, has either been that of othering or of assimilation by the national identity's approach towards the other identities.

Civilization is a dynamic phenomenon and even when we talk about the ancient civilizations, we latently mention the dynamism of them at their peak points. Likewise, when we mention Western or Islamic civilization, it is quite clear that we do not include single typology covering all time and space. In Benedict Anderson's *Imagined Communities: Reflections on the Origin and Spread of Nationalism*, first the nationalist intellectuals and afterwards the readers of dailies and novels imagine, mount, construct, and sanctify the nation and lynch the ones who are against their product. That is how our relation with civilization develops. We reconstruct civilization every day, again and again. However, during this process we shadow the dynamism of civilization by imprisoning it inside a golden c/age. When we mention Islamic civilization, we imagine the harmony attributed only to the era of the Prophet Muhammad (peace be upon Him), which has never been broken in the succeeding periods of the Rashidun Caliphs, the Umayyads, the Abbasids, and so forth. However, if any conflict in any age did not terminate the structure on its own, it has served to strengthen it, following Nietzsche's famous dictum 'That which does not kill us makes us stronger'. Such a holistic vision is also valid in our reaction against other civilizations, the fact that we prefer to call them barbarous. When we recall Western or Islamic civilization, we produce a ghost that even its followers would perceive as a monolithic structure. Likewise, when Islam is the issue, especially following the then US President George W. Bush's conceptualizations of occupations of Afghanistan and Iraq as 'Crusades' in response to the 9/11 attacks, reactions to Islamic civilization blatantly turns into Islamophobia. However, we come across the fact that Western civilization is composed of contradicting colours, and their tones range from fascism to liberalism, which is also valid for its Islamic equivalent and so forth.

Such a zero-sum approach turns out to be an analytical methodology worth abstaining from if we are to evaluate civilization. In fact, any civilization could simultaneously include architectural and engineering masterpieces for the progress of humanity, as well as technological instruments or ideas against humanity. For example, Rome, among ancient civilizations, can still inspire modern architecture with its arenas and coliseums into which enslaved humans were thrown as food for lions while excited spectators watched them. There is a need to question the labelling of such activities as barbarity by ones who are themselves used to watching wars on live television programmes in which high-tech rockets kill civilians with unerring accuracy.

Our definition of civilization, based on development indices in parallel with Western civilization, is an extension of the progressive theory of history and even Social Darwinism. That is why civilized societies can maintain their historical walk as they battle against and defeat barbarity, so the remaining victor is always civilization. Such a progressive/developmentalist approach inevitably transforms the competition to be leaders in the fields of science, art, and technology into a war, which clarifies the barbaric nature of civilization. Any war is the peak point of barbarity, as the formation of collective insanity, and civilizations try to defeat and even exterminate each other through wars. Civilizations are in perpetual need of producing a scapegoat that they can characterize as barbaric, and in the process legalize their own existence, as witnessed in the enslavement and labelling of the Aztec and Mayan civilizations by the West. Civilizations prove their superiority over each other not only through annihilation, but also transformation. Probably the history of Hagia Sophia is the best example of such a transformation. First constructed as a Christian temple, the remarkable monument was transformed into a mosque after the capture of the city by Muslims, and then it was turned into a museum since the political authority of the early Turkish Republic wanted to see itself as a part of a different civilization rather than Islam. Whether a temple or a museum, no one before the sublimity of Hagia Sophia would hesitate to admit that it is part of the common civilization of humanity.

Through the need for the *madinah* (المدين, city) and for the *madani-yyah* (الحضارة, civilization), we will observe what kind of transformation escalating urbanization will bring about in relation to modernization, as the process called globalization transforms our earth into a global village. In the same vein, to disassociate civilization from culture and reduce it to technical hardware is of no use besides robbing the concept of its essence. Likening or differentiating the German 'Kultur' and French 'Civilization' is not enough to solve our problems other than for the purpose of etymological richness. Just as different cultures can cohabit within the same civilization, a culture can belong to different civilizations within the context of time and space (or not). This notion has been quite effective until the replacement of compulsory national identity policies by multicultural policies of the nation state.

***

Having started with literature on multiculturalism, we can conclude with the multi-civilizationalist approach to overcome the deficiencies being stuck into a single civilization and adopting its civilizationist dictum. The vital question is, 'Can any human be only uni-cultural?' If we liken German 'Kultur' to French 'Civilization', then we could ask whether anyone can be uni-civilizational. The answer could easily be 'yes' if we were to live in very narrow communities having no interaction with others. However, thanks to globalization as a process binding all humanity through a complex network, it is not easy anymore to say that we are mono-cultural or mono-civilizational beings. Then, briefly, the literature on multiculturalism endows us with the ability to track our multiple dimensions to apply it to civilization. When one follows this path, the clash of civilizations ceases to make sense ontologically and epistemologically, since all humans benefit from each others' civilization, as civilization has different branches despite keeping itself intact and unique for the whole humanity.

Consequently, this research offers an interpretation of all civilizations—though they accuse each other of barbarity—as branches of human civilization, while reading civilization itself as the civilization of humanity. Thus, both alliances and conflicts among civilizations happen within the larger civilization of humanity. We can protect ourselves from humiliation even if we become dispersed, lose ground, and deviate in our every action as long as we can conceptualize the unity of civilizations despite their abundance. The national identity imposed by the nation state in its aim to attribute the single identity of civilization to one and all, results in conflict of several identities.

The power manifests itself in daily events and, from the Foucauldian perspective, as we experience such identity conflicts in our daily routines these conflicts become part of our identities. Thus, to keep our sanity, we need to declare ourselves as the single authority in order to make the appropriate decisions and to decide how we will revive our identities, in the process refusing to sacrifice our identities for the sake of a national identity. Likewise, the need to determine our membership of a certain civilization/s as an act of civilization fostered by civic courage is quite clear. It is essential, but not eclectic, to denominate that we are part of the entire civilization of humanity more than the synthesis 'I am from the Turkish nation, Islamic ummah, and Western civilization' that has prevailed since the time of Ziya Gökalp, one of the prominent ideological fathers of Turkish nationalism (1977, p. 45).

Last but not least, as the literature on multiculturalism underlines, the group rights need to be protected when the nation state is less eager to do that; this would ensure that essentially we can enjoy being members of the civilizations that we are born into, but there is more to enjoy as we come across and differentiate our knowledge in conjunction with different civilizations. It seems the right time to challenge the idea of being univocal about civilization and taste the eclectic conjectural memberships of all civilizations as branches of the civilization of humanity.

NOTES

1. Since Mustafa Kemal and Mehmet Akif received 'Atatürk' and 'Ersoy' consecutively following the Law on Surname in 1934, the brackets are employed.
2. Huntington (1993) replied to the critics of his famous article first at *Foreign Affairs* and then collected his other articles and the concomitant criticisms in *The Clash of Civilizations? The Debate* (Huntington 1996a). He then enlarged his article into a book of *The Clash of Civilizations and the Remaking of World Order* (Huntington 1996b).

BIBLIOGRAPHY

Anderson, B. 2011. *Hayali cemaatler: milliyetçiliğin kökenleri ve yayılması,* translated by İ. Savaşır. İstanbul: Metis.

Barry, B. 2001. *Culture and Equality: An Egalitarian Critique of Multiculturalism.* Cambridge, MA: Harvard University Press.

Çevre ve Şehircilik Bakanlığı. 2013, 17 Ocak. *Temiz çevre için 1,5 milyarlık yatırım.* Retrieved from http://www.csb.gov.tr/turkce/index. php?Sayfa=faaliyetdetay&Id=454, accessed 30 January 2013.

Davutoğlu, A. 1997. Medeniyetlerin ben-idraki. *Divan* 1(1): 1–53.

Gökalp, Z. 1977. *Türkçülüğün esasları.* İstanbul: Kadro Yayınları.

Gooding-Williams, R. 1998. 'Race, Multiculturalism and Democracy'. *Constellations,* 5(1): 18–41.

Gunew, S. 2004. *Haunted Nations: The Colonial Dimension of Multiculturalisms.* New York: Routledge.

Huntington, S. P. 1992. The Clash of Civilizations? *Foreign Affairs* 72(3): 22–49.

———. 1993. 'If Not Civilizations, What?: Paradigms of the Post-Cold War'. *Foreign Affairs* 72(5): 186–94.

———. 1996a. *The Clash of Civilization? The Debate.* New York: Foreign Affairs

———. 1996b. *The Clash of Civilizations and the Remaking of World Order.* New York: Simon and Schuster.

Huntington'un Ardından, Samuel P. 2009. 'Medeniyetler Çatışması', translated by M. Tüzel. *Frankfurter Allgemeine Zeitung.* Available at http://tr.qantara.de/wcsite.php?wc_c=14965, accessed on January, 2013.

Kukathas, C. 2003. *The Liberal Archipelago: A Theory of Diversity and Freedom.* Oxford: Oxford University Press.

Kymlicka, W. 1995. *Multicultural Citizenship: A Liberal Theory of Minority Rights.* Oxford: Oxford University Press.

Mills, C. W. 2007. Multiculturalism as/and/or Anti-racism? In *Multiculturalism and Political Theory,* edited by A. S. Laden and D. Owen, pp. 89–114. New York: Cambridge University Press.

Özatik, N. n.d. *Medeniyet yoluyla barbarlaşma!* Retrieved from http://mekam. org/mekam/medeniyet-yoluyla-barbarlasma, accessed 30 January 2013.

Parekh, B. 2002. *Rethinking Multiculturalism: Cultural Diversity and Political Theory.* Boston: Harvard University Press.

Said, E. 2003. *Orientalism.* London: Penguin.

Seyyar, A. 2012, September 30. 'Mustafa Kemal Paşa, muasır medeniyet kavramını ilk kez ne zaman kullanmıştır?' *Milat Gazetesi.* İstanbul.

Taylor, C. 1992. 'The Politics of Recognition'. In *Multiculturalism: Examining the Politics of Recognition,* edited by A. Gutmann, pp. 98–131. Princeton: Princeton University Press.

Trotman, C. J. 2002. Introduction. In *Multiculturalism: Roots and Realities,* edited by C. J. Trotman, pp. ix–xvi. Indiana: Indiana University Press.

Williams, M. 1998. *Voice, Trust, and Memory: Marginalized Groups and the Failings of Liberal Representation.* Princeton: Princeton University Press.
Young, I. M. 1990. *Justice and the Politics of Difference.* Princeton, NJ: Princeton University Press.

14 An Epistemological Base for a Dynamic Conception of Civilizations and Intercultural Relations

Khosrow Bagheri Noaparast

> 'O mankind! We created you from a single (pair) of a male and a female,
> and made you into nations and tribes, that ye may know each other
> (not that ye may despise each other).'
>
> —Qur'an (49: 13)

There have been two static conceptions of civilization and relationship among cultures. One conception might be called universalistic: it attempts to introduce some basic principles and truths that are taken to be common among different human civilizations and cultures. At best, this conception attempts to show that principles and truths are rooted in the universe and human realities, so that all differences among human civilizations and cultures are superficial or phenomenal and they can be considered as different manifestations of the same principles and truths. At worst, the universalistic conception is a masked particularistic view in which a certain civilization and culture is taken to be basic, and other civilizations and cultures are reduced one way or another to the basic one. A case in point is the idea that the contemporary Western civilization and the Islamic civilization in the middle ages are just extensions or deformed versions of the ancient Greek civilization.

The other static conception is opposite to the first one, and might be called particularistic or relativistic. According to this view, civilizations and cultures are profoundly different. This conception has also two versions. In its most radical version, this view takes different civilizations as incommensurable, each being closed in a particular universe without any common or interchangeable language. A less radical or weak version holds that different civilizations can somehow be compatible. A famous or infamous recent view in the latter version is Samuel P. Huntington's theory on the clash of civilizations. While Huntington holds that there is an incommensurable relation among civilizations, he talks about the commonalities among them that can be reduced by the threat of a clash between them. However, this appeal to commonalities is an attempt to not only subsume other civilizations, namely Islamic and Sinic, but also to overwhelmingly elevate another one, namely the Western civilization, as explained further.

This chapter poses challenges to these two static conceptions, arguing that they are epistemologically flawed. The first conception underestimates differences. In its best version, this conception takes knowledge at the most abstract level without considering contexts of different cultures seriously. In its worst version, it underestimates differences in terms of a predominant civilization. The second conception, in its radical version, ignores the commonalities among human civilizations and cultures, and wrongly holds that knowledge or basic ideas of different civilizations are encapsulated units without any relationship to other civilizations whatsoever. The weak version of the second conception takes commonalities into account, but in a superficial and instrumental way, which makes it vulnerable. This chapter argues first that both abstract and contextual aspects of knowledge need to be taken into account to provide a sound account of knowledge, and second that the abstract ideas need not be restricted to just some allegedly privileged civilizations and cultures. In effect, a dynamic conception needs to be held according to which knowledge, both in its theoretical and practical versions, exists in the form of a give-and-take relationship among different civilizations and cultures. Thus, while different civilizations and cultures borrow from each other, each one adds value to the received heritage.

What follows is first a conceptual clarification of civilization in relation to culture. Second, the relativistic or incommensurability conception is critiqued. Third, the universalistic view is examined in order to reveal the importance of particularities in human knowledge. Finally, by means of analysing the dynamic characteristic of cultures, a middle way is suggested according to which concrete and abstract aspects of human knowledge are taken as compatible and even complementary.

CULTURE, CIVILIZATION, AND RELATIONS
AMONG CIVILIZATIONS

The word 'civilization' is taken from the Latin 'civitas', which is equal to the Greek 'poleis'. 'Civitas' for ancient Romans was associated with a superior way of life in a city that had political institutions and particular laws for social relations. This complex structure of a city which brings with itself a superior way of life is contrasted with less systematized ways of life which the ancient Greeks referred to as barbarian.

The question concerning the basis of human civilizations is answered differently by different scholars. In a very broad classification, there are two viewpoints in this regard: one taking material values and the other non-material values as the basis of formation and development of human civilizations. According to the first viewpoint, it is the material condition of a society that determines its culture. The most important proponent of this viewpoint was Karl Marx who held that according to every stage of material development, be it primitive communal, slave-owning, feudal, capitalist, or socialist, there will be a relevant culture. In all these stages of development, culture remains dependent on material conditions of life.

However, the second viewpoint places the emphasis on non-material values, even though there are discrepancies among the supporters of this viewpoint as to what is the most important non-material value. Albert Schweitzer (1949), for instance, holds that philosophy is the cornerstone of a civilization so the decline of a civilization can be traced to a decline in its underlining philosophy. Others, such as Mashhad Al-Allaf (2003), challenged the view that held philosophy as the basis, and have taken law as the foundation of a civilization, in particular Islamic civilization, arguing that what can control and systematize human impulses and orient them towards a civilized order is law. Law, according to him, has the advantage of dealing with day-to-day human behaviours that are tangible and their changes are observable. In the same vein, Tosi holds that the defining feature of a civilization is the state and government. He suggests that the perspective that civilization equals state can give us a proper understanding of civilization where the 'state refers to any complex form of institutionalized government that allows the coexistence of different groups within a single political system' (Tosi 1998, p. 21). Thus, according to the second perspective, social laws, which are associated with institutionalized governments, are the pivotal point of civilization.

Still others, such as Huntington (1996), regard the central position of culture as the defining characteristic of civilization. Referring to the post–Cold War world, he holds that 'culture and cultural identities, which at the broadest level are civilizational identities, are shaping the patterns of cohesion, disintegration, and conflict' (Huntington 1996, p. 20). In other words, according to Huntington, even though a civilization has different components, such as customs, political institutions, language, and culture, what can be taken as the defining feature of a civilization is its culture. Not only this, Huntington goes further and holds that, at least in the post–Cold War world, the defining feature of culture is religion, as he holds that the future clashes will be between the Islamic and Confucian cultures on the one hand, and the Christian West on the other. This is in line with the views of Arnold Toynbee who also holds that the defining feature of civilization is culture, and the defining feature of culture is religion. Toynbee (1956) relates history to some divine plan and regards people like Moses, Jesus, Muhammad, and Peter the Great as the creative personalities who were the turning points of human cultures and civilizations.

The relationship between culture and civilization is a complicated matter that cannot be pursued here. It suffices to mention that there are two styles in determining their relationship (Botz-Bornstein, 2012). The first one is the English style, exemplified in Edward B. Tylor's definition in which civilization and culture are taken in a holistic way without a clear distinction between them. The second is the German style, and to some extent the French style, in which culture is different from civilization so that culture refers to the more inward and abstract characteristics manifested in art and philosophy, while civilization refers to more outward aspects of society, such as techniques and customs. That is why in France culture was used to refer to education to show the particularities of a people, while civilization was used at an international level. As Botz-Bornstein pointed out, Huntington relies mainly on the Tylorian way of integrating civilization and culture. Undermining the German style of dealing with culture, Huntington holds that 'the efforts to distinguish culture and civilization ... have not caught on, and, outside Germany, there is overwhelming agreement ... that it is delusory to wish in the German way to separate culture from its foundation civilization' (Huntington 1996, p. 41).

Seen from Huntington's view, the three stances regarding the foundation of civilizations are not incompatible, given his integrated conception of civilization and culture in which philosophy and law are included too. As for the relation between philosophy and law, it cannot be denied that any law has an implicit philosophy beneath the manifest feature of its concrete rules. What make different law systems different are not merely the concrete rules, as these rules embody abstract conceptions concerning the nature of humans, the characteristics of a desired human being, ways in which the existent human can be transformed to the desired one, and so on and so forth. Thus, culture, taken in a broad sense, can include both philosophy and a law system. When Huntington (1996, p. 305) refers to cultural and political aspects of Western civilization, he mentions components that include philosophy and law: 'Historically, American national identity has been defined culturally by the heritage of Western civilization and politically by the principle of the American Creed on which Americans overwhelmingly agree: liberty, democracy, individualism, equality before the law, constitutionalism, private property.' Among these components, philosophy and law are included implicitly or explicitly. Thus, culture in its broad sense can be taken as the defining characteristic of civilization as Huntington suggests. However, the German style of defining culture by referring to more abstract dimensions, which are different from civilization, seems to be more instructive since it can account for the existence of a culture without civilization. This is the case in contemporary Muslim countries where there is an Islamic culture, while they are simultaneously living under the modern civilization settings. Ibrahim Abu-Rabi claims that since the Muslim world does not have its own civilization in the modern time, we can say that 'the Muslim world has culture but lacks civilization' (Abu-Rabi 2004, p. 189, cited by Botz-Bornstein 2012, p. 16). This is an acceptable claim. Thus, in the present article, culture and civilization will be differentiated in this way.

A further point concerns the defining feature of culture itself. In this regard, Toynbee and Huntington alike hold that religion is the defining feature of culture. This position can also be challenged because there is no logical or factual problem in having a pagan or materialistic culture and, *a fortiori*, civilization. In fact, the modern secular civilization serves as a counterexample to any view that holds religion as the defining feature of a civilization.

When it comes to the relation among different civilizations and cultures, Huntington's view on the clash of civilizations becomes less evident and controversial points arise. Here, again, there is an agreement between Huntington and Toynbee on the idea of a clash among civilizations and cultures in recent times, as was first suggested by Arnold Toynbee in his *Civilization on Trial* in 1948. In this book, he warns that if a revolt occurs in the future against Western civilization, it will be led by Islam. The last long paragraph of the tenth chapter of his book is worth quoting:

> Pan-Islamism is dormant, yet we have to reckon with the possibility that the sleeper may awake if ever the cosmopolitan proletariat of a 'Westernized' world revolts against Western domination and cries out for anti-Western leadership. That call might have incalculable psychological effects in evoking the militant spirit of Islam—even if it had slumbered as long as the Seven Sleepers—because it might awaken echoes of a heroic age. On two historic occasions in the past, Islam has been the sign in which an Oriental society has risen up victoriously against an Occidental intruder. Under the first successors of the Prophet, Islam liberated Syria and Egypt from a Hellenic domination which had weighed on them for nearly a thousand years. Under Zangi and Nur-ad-Din and Saladin and the Mamelukes, Islam held the fort against the assaults of Crusaders and Mongols. If the present situation of mankind were to precipitate a 'race war', Islam might be moved to play her historic role once again. *Absit omen*. (Toynbee 1948, chapter 10)

In the same spirit, Huntington talks about the clash of civilizations in general, and those of Islamic and Western civilizations, in particular. As Jeff Haynes pointed out, the importance of Huntington's thesis was not so much its correctness, as for fitting in with the end-of-the-Cold War zeitgeist in relation to globalization, as well as the need for a new enemy before the West. Referring to Huntington's thesis, Haynes states:

> It is almost irrelevant that his focal point: the impossibility of the West—read the USA—and 'Islam'—read 'Islamic fundamentalism'/'extremism'—living together in harmony was laughingly over-simplified, redolent of the paranoia of someone experiencing the shattering of a stable, safe, and unchanging world suddenly and demonstrably confronted with the scenario of the post–World War II paradigm smashed to smithereens. (Haynes 2013)

The idea of a clash among civilizations, is contrasted with a rival idea called 'dialogue among civilizations'. In 1998, Seyyed Mohammad Khatami, the then president of Iran, in a speech made at the United Nations' annual Heads of States summit stated the following:

> I would like to propose in the name of the Islamic Republic of Iran, that the United Nations, as a first step, designate the year 2001 as the 'Year of Dialogue Among Civilizations', with the earnest hope that through such a dialogue the realization of universal justice and liberty be initiated. Among the wealthiest achievements of this century is the acceptance of the necessity and significance of dialogue and rejection of force, promotion of understanding of the foundations of liberty, justice and human rights. (Khatami 1998)

Even though the phrase 'universal justice and liberty', to refer to the consequence of the dialogue, is used here somewhat ambiguously, one interpretation of this universality presupposes that different civilizations and cultures have the same spirit. This interpretation puts forward the universalistic view of the nature of culture in contrast to the particularistic view that leads to the idea of a clash among civilizations.

The crucial point is that the nature of culture as the defining characteristic of civilization is not properly captured, neither in universalistic nor in particularistic views. As far as the relativistic view is concerned, cultures are regarded as unified and coherent monads without overlapping areas. As for the universalistic view, unique aspects of cultures are undermined and underestimated. This chapter is going to argue that we need a more dynamic conception of culture, and, for that matter, of civilization, according to which cultures are open to each other and are in the process of give and take. This picture can not only reveal the autonomous characteristic of cultures, but can also provide a better ground for cooperation and coexistence of cultures instead of the clash of civilizations.

PRACTICAL KNOWLEDGE AND THE STATIC CONCEPTION OF CULTURE

In the debate concerning the general versus the particular aspects of human knowledge, the advocates of relativism stress particular characteristics of knowledge. This view, also called nominalism, has a long history in the realm of philosophy. According to this view, general concepts do not refer to real entities in the world and, instead, are taken merely as names with functions, such as providing us with a summary of a large number of cases. For instance, when we use an abstract concept, such as human, the concept does not refer to an entity, it is not a Platonic idea, but functions as a summary of a large number of particular concepts each referring to a particular person.

Advocates of the particular as opposed to the general in the realm of epistemology, attempt to reduce all sorts of theoretical knowledge to practical knowledge, which is contextual, and thereby deny any kind of universal criteria for truth. In supporting practical knowledge, Wilfred Carr, among others, states that 'there are no impersonal standards of rationality, no universal criteria of truth, no rigorous philosophical methods that are wholly independent of philosophy's own historically contingent language, culture and practice' (Hirst and Carr 2005, p. 623). Carr calls his preferred position 'postfoundationalism'. While foundationalism is associated with universal criteria of truth, postfoundationalism would mean going beyond absolute truth and, thus, would be associated with relativism. This epistemological position is vastly critiqued in the realm of philosophy. Harvey Siegel (1998, p. 30) holds that postfoundationalist arguments are self-defeating, since postfoundationalists presuppose what they want to reject. This is because this school of thought rejects the possibility of objective knowledge but at the same time holds that some claims are valid in all situations, such as the statement that any proclaimed truth is constrained by its cultural situation, which is the main claim of postfoundationalism. Responding to Siegel, Carr (2006, p. 151) says, 'But of course postfoundationalism is not an epistemological thesis that "rejects the possibility of objective knowledge" but an explanatory thesis about how objective knowledge emerges.' This reply, however, does not rescue postfoundationalism from relativism, since the explanation that Carr refers to is intended to be objective, along with a validity that goes beyond the horizon of the postfoundationalist, so that it can convince a foundationalist as well.

The relativistic position in the realm of civilization and culture is taken by Huntington (1969) among others. He holds a mainly incommensurable relationship among cultures and civilizations. This position presupposes a conception of cultures as unified monads that are internally coherent and externally distinct from each other in a mutually exclusive way. Huntington might from time to time talk about some shared concepts among cultures, but holds that they are interpreted in a way that nothing remains from the commonalities presupposed. He gives the example of prohibition of taking innocent life. However, the question of who is an innocent might be a matter of interpretation, which leads to opposed decisions with regard to saving a person's life. The monadic conception can be observed where Huntington refers to multiculturalism as a real threat to a 'common American culture':

> In the late twentieth century both components of American identity have come under concentrated and sustained onslaught from a small but influential number of intellectuals and publicists. In the name of multiculturalism they have attacked the identification of the United States with Western civilization, denied the existence of a common American culture, and promoted racial, ethnic, and other subnational cultural identities and groupings. (Huntington 1996, p. 305)

This unified monadic conception of culture can also be seen in Huntington's treatment of Islamic culture. Huntington has attempted to offer a unified conception of Islamic culture in an antagonistic sphere with regard to the Western civilization.

As Milani and Gibbons (2001) state, Huntington gives a monolithic view of Islamic culture in terms of violence and brutality, while the history of Islam includes both tolerance and intolerance towards the people of other religions, as well as Muslims themselves. According to Milani and Gibbons, Huntington does not care about the following

facts: that at some periods of the history of Islam there was a positive relationship between Islam and the West when, for instance, in
the eighth century BC, Muslim scholars provided the movement of
translation of Greek philosophical and scientific books into Arabic;
that a large number of Islamic scholars view *jihad* or the holy war as
a defensive rather than an offensive strategy; and that recent Muslim
thinkers have different positions with regard to Western civilization
and culture including absorption, rejection, and purification. Having
these clear facts in mind, the question arises as to why Huntington
does not take them into account. This is because Huntington's
presupposition concerning incommensurability of human cultures
has provided him with a bias that prevents him from noticing the
mentioned facts. However, it is not deniable that these facts indicate
that Islamic civilization and culture, like any other civilization and
culture including the Western one, has a multifaceted character that
undermines any unified conception in this regard. It is true that the
phrases such as 'Islamic culture' and 'the Western culture' will be
meaningless without a sort of unification, but the point is that this
unification does not necessarily need to be so strong that it does not
tolerate any kind of plurality.

UNIVERSAL KNOWLEDGE AND THE STATIC
CONCEPTION OF CULTURE

The advocates of universal knowledge take the first side of the controversy concerning general versus particular aspects of human knowledge. According to this position, the universal truths are not only
general but also fundamental, and it follows that particular features
of knowledge are short of revealing the real nature of truth and might
even be misleading by trapping people in the deviant equation of general with particular. This conception of knowledge goes back to Plato.
He took the general and abstract ideas as keys to truths while their
particular cases in the physical world are deviant features of the ideas.

Aristotle is a bit different in giving more force to the particular
cases. Referring to justice and the changing features of what are
regarded as just in different places, Aristotle says, 'Some people think
that all rules of justice are merely conventional, because whereas a
law of nature is immutable and has the same validity everywhere, as

fire burns both here and in Iran, rules of justice are seen to vary. That rules of justice vary is not absolutely true, but only with qualifications' (Aristotle 1996, p. 127). While, according to Aristotle, in a sense justice is not the same in different places, it is the same everywhere. In other words, the principle of justice as a general value is stable but in terms of particularities in different contexts, it differs from place to place.

Given the important differences among the particular cases, it follows that an attempt to introduce the universal truth without taking the differences seriously into account would lead to an inadequate general concept which would fall short of covering all its cases. On the other hand, the worst version of the universalist view is that which masks a particular position. This is because in this version some but not all available cases are accounted for, and this can be misleading. That is to say, the abstract that is drawn from some cases might not be a just candidate for showing the general character of the cases that are not taken into account. Referring to this sort of shortage in providing a real universal in the realm of jurisprudence, Twining states the following:

> Nearly all Western modern normative jurisprudence is either secular or explicitly Christian. Post-Enlightenment secularism has deep historical roots in the intellectual traditions of Western Christianity. Even those theories that claim universality have proceeded with only tangential reference to, and in almost complete ignorance of, the religious and moral beliefs and traditions of the rest of humankind. When differing cultural values are discussed, even the agenda of issues tends to have a stereotypically Western bias. (Twining 2001, p. 5)

This stereotypical bias clearly prevents us from providing a genuine universal standpoint. Taking such a standpoint requires that all available cultures are empathically studied as far as it is possible.

A DYNAMIC CONCEPTION OF CULTURE

So far, the two static conceptions of culture, namely the relativist and the universal views, have been critiqued. The shortcomings of these views are what exactly drive us towards a third candidate that can more adequately capture the real nature of human civilization and culture. These shortcomings have led different scholars to take a middle position between the strong universalist and the radical relativist stances. Susan Haack (1993), for instance, attempted to open a way between foundationalism and coherentism. Foundationalism looks for stable and eternal truths, while coherentism denies a stable position for any part of a system of belief and looks for truth in the coherence that can be achieved in the entire system as a whole Haack introduces the concept of 'foundherentism' in order to escape from the both positions and pave the ground for a middle way.

In the same vein, Joseph Raz supports universalism on the one hand, and takes the importance of particular cases into account on the other. According to him, we should not realize the universal and the particular in an antagonistic way, they should rather be taken as complementary. Raz introduces a good interpretation of multiculturalism. While multiculturalism is usually associated with relativism, Raz holds that multiculturalism can be taken as compatible with the universalistic position. This can be done in the way that any and every culture can be viewed as a manifestation of the universal value or truth. Thus, he states, 'At the heart of multiculturalism lies the recognition that universal values are realised in a variety of different ways in different cultures and that they are all worthy of respect' (Raz 1998, p. 204).

While Raz talks about the different ways of realization of universal values in different cultures, the crucial point is the kind of relationship between universal values and truths on the one hand, and the different cultures on the other. One might approach this relationship in exactly the same way as one approaches the relationship between an abstract concept and its particular manifestations. In the latter relationship, every case is a full substantiation of the abstract concept. Thus, the relationship of every case to the abstract concept is exactly the same as any other case to that abstract concept. For instance, one might mention ten characteristics for the abstract concept of culture, but one might also hold that every particular case of culture should have all the ten characteristics. In this model, the main dominance is for the universal value or truth, while the particulars are under the full government of the universal idea. This is the model that was established by Plato's philosophy.

There is a rival model to which Wittgenstein (1953) refers as 'family resemblance'. Using this phrase, he has introduced another sort of relationship between a general concept and its particular cases. This model seems to be helpful here for providing us not only with a better understanding of the relations between particular cultures and the general concept of culture but also of the relations that the particular cultures have with each other. First, let us take note of what Wittgenstein means by family resemblance. The resemblance among the members of a family does not require that the members have an exact similarity; rather from say ten characteristics in a family, one member might possess eight, another six, and a third one five. An example Wittgenstein provides relates to games. While we refer to different sorts of games by the general concept of 'game', there are significant differences among them. In dealing with the question of what characteristics constitute a game, there is no fixed answer. If, for instance, we hold that playfulness is one of the defining characteristics of games, it is clear that some games that are painful would not fall under this category. Thus, Wittgenstein suggests that we should look for such fixed characteristics for games that any kind of game can possess. Rather, what we find is that from the whole number of characteristics of games, some belong to a particular game while some others belong to another set of games even though there are overlaps between the two.

Now, if we want to extend this analogy to the realm of civilization and culture, we can expect better results. First, as far as the relation between the abstract concept of culture and its particular cases is concerned, there will not be a similar condition that will apply to every particular case of culture. That is to say, while one particular case of culture might possess certain characteristics from among the number of characteristics attributed to the general concept of culture, another particular case might possess a different sum from among the same number of the characteristics.

When it comes to the relationship that particular cases of cultures have with each other, it is instructive to realize that the differences among them are much more complicated than what is the case in the Platonic model. While in the latter, differences among particular cultures are related to manifestation, in the Wittgensteinian model differences are related to substantiation. That is to say, in the Platonic model, substantiation is full in all cases but manifestation of them are different from case to case; whereas in the Wittgensteinian model, substantiation is not necessarily complete in each case, but rather one case substantiates some characteristics and another case substantiates some other characteristics, with less or more overlaps between the two.

The relationship in terms of family resemblance is more convincing in the case of human civilizations and cultures since it can capture the rich experiences of human cultures in a better way. This model provides us with the unification needed in phrases such as 'Islamic civilization and culture' or 'the Western civilization and culture' without ignoring the differences between the cases. When the particular cases can be different not merely in manifestation but in substantiation, then the doors would be open for a richer give-and-take relationship among particular cultures as there will be a place for differences as well. This is because a culture, in addition to commonalities with other cultures, would possess what another culture lacks, and vice versa, and this paves the way for a dynamic relationship among different cultures. Thus, for instance, Islamic civilization takes rational thinking from Western civilization, if we can consider Ancient Greece as the source of Western civilization. Islamic civilization, in turn, develops the experimental sort of thinking. In a later period of Western civilization after the Renaissance, the West takes experimental thinking from Islamic civilization and develops it further along the lines that lead to the modern world. Robin Cook, as the UK Foreign Secretary, referred to the mutual misunderstanding between the West and Islam that needed to be removed, as well as to the fact of their intertwined civilizations, and said:

> We see each other too much through the dangerous prism of stereotype. Islam sees the West as materialistic, lacking respect for the spiritual, anti-Islamic and determined to use our liberal values as a way of undermining their societies.... The West owes much to Islam. Islam laid the intellectual foundations for large portions of Western civilization. From our numbers to our understanding of the stars, much of the basis of our civilization is rooted in Islamic learning. One of the biggest errors the West could make would be to think that Islamic culture is something alien.... Our cultures are intertwined throughout history. They intertwined today, and they must continue to do so. (Cook 1998)

The dynamic relationship among civilizations is not limited to the complementary give-and-take relationship. In addition to that, the differences among the civilizations can give rise to tensions among them. For instance, the new Western civilization initiated secularism but this characteristic led to challenges for the Muslim world and also for Christianity, which is part of the Western world itself. This shows that the dynamism of culture is very complicated, since not only can there be intra-cultural tensions, but also intercultural tensions. The crucial point here is how to interpret these tensions. Clash or war is neither the sole nor the best way of interpretation while dealing with the differences and tensions.

A trilogy can be suggested with regard to the differences and tensions. First, the differences that appear as tensions might be superficial and illusory. A proper and truth-seeking dialogue among civilizations can remove the illusions and provide a better understanding. A case in point is the misunderstandings between the West and Islam to which Cook referred to in the extract quoted earlier. For instance, the view that most Muslims hold regarding the alleged materialistic Western civilization is but a misunderstanding that can be removed by relevant evidence. Take, for instance, Toynbee and Huntington as two recent thinkers. Both of them have strong religious inclinations. Toynbee has given a divine account of human history in which religion has a crucial role to play, not only in the past but also in the future of human history. Huntington (2004), in turn, in *Who Are We?* holds that the American culture is basically religious. By appealing to the phrase written on US dollars, namely *In God We Trust*, and many other cases in American culture, Huntington concludes that religion, namely Protestantism, has deep roots in this culture. There is much more evidence to show that the West is not materialistic, but what is mentioned is enough to falsify the misunderstanding. It is noteworthy though that the same sphere of Huntington's previous book (1996) is present in *Who Are We?*; but while in the former, Islamic culture was considered as a threat to American culture, in the latter it is the threat of Latinos, and particularly Mexican immigrants, that Huntington is concerned about. He warns that the American culture is going to be divided by Hispanic and other immigrants into two cultures because they are not assimilated into American Anglo-Protestant culture.

On the other hand, the stereotype of terrorism and Muslims and Islamic religion, is but a misunderstanding on the Western side of the conflict. Islamic view does not support terrorism even though it puts strong emphasis on resistance against oppression. The Qur'an states that 'if any one slew a person—unless it be for murder or for spreading mischief in the land—it would be as if he slew the whole people: and if any one saved a life, it would be as if he saved the life of the whole people' (Qur'an, 5: 32). This is a statement that shows an extraordinary support of human life. At the same time, the Western thinkers should not forget the reactionary nature of the terroristic attacks which have roots in colonialism as bad treatment of the West by Muslim countries. Even though this is not to say that terrorism is justified on those grounds, it is an invitation for the Western thinkers to be fair in their judgements.

Second, differences can be instructive. Some differences that might lead to tensions are due to shortcomings on either or both sides of a conflict. Thus, a dialogue can lead to a completion on one or both sides. A case in point is the challenge posed by secularism in modern Western civilization. This challenge has been both intra-cultural and intercultural; the former with regard to the Western civilization itself, and the latter with regard to the relation between Islam and the West. This challenge has been instructive on both sides. Jurgen Habermas (2010) coined the phrase of 'post-secularism' regarding this challenge and its instructive character. As far as secularism is concerned, post-secularism indicates, according to Habermas, that secularists were too fast in withdrawing religion from the public realm and limiting it to the private realm. Religion has shown in recent times that it has social roles to play in human life and that attempts to marginalize it and jettison it to the private realm have not been successful. Religion is alive today not only in societies, but also at the international level in global conflicts, such as current events in the Middle East. Even if it is true that warmongers use religion as a pretext for their benefits, it should be admitted that religion holds social significance for people.

Criticizing secular reason in terms of social significance, Habermas states:

> Secular morality is not inherently embedded in communal practices. Religious consciousness, by contrast, preserves an essential connection to the ongoing practice of life within a community and, in the case of the major world religions, to the observances of united global communities of all of the faithful. The religious consciousness of the individual can derive stronger impulses towards action in solidarity,

even from a purely moral point of view, from this universalistic communitarianism. (Habermas 2012, p. 75)

On the other hand, according to Habermas, the challenge of secularism has posed a problem for religious institutions regarding the relation between religion and rationality and has led them to take rationality more seriously into account. Habermas concludes that as a consequence of this challenge, we have learnt that both secularism and religious thinking need to be made compatible after the separation that occurred between them in the modern time. This learning process, however, has taken a big toll.

> At any rate, it throws a different light on that reciprocal learning process in which the political reason of the liberal state and religion are already involved. This touches on conflicts which are currently being triggered around the world by the unexpected spiritual renewal and by the unsettling political role of religious communities. Apart from Hindu nationalism, Islam and Christianity are the main sources of this disturbance. (Habermas 2010, p. 19)

A good and timely dialogue can prevent us from paying a price as big as that being paid in the current conflicts.

Third, differences among civilizations and cultures can persist and prove to be irremovable, at least in the short run. This sort of difference can be important in imparting uniqueness to civilizations and cultures. It is not deniable that people live in different situations with different requirements. As a matter of creativity, this leads to different lifestyles and there is no need to expect that human civilizations and cultures will be similar to each other in all aspects. As there can be different solutions to the same problem, people have created different cultures and civilizations from the basic human needs within different contexts. This rationale can help us to tolerate this sort of difference in the dialogue among civilizations. Contrary to what Habermas (1974) refers to as consensus or as the resultant point of a dialogue that is conducted in the 'ideal speech situation', a good dialogue should also prepare a place for what cannot be led to a consensus and should treat it by means of tolerance. Even though this does not pre-empt the possibility of achieving a consensus concerning the third type of difference, the irremovable one, in the long run, a safe position should be allocated for this type of difference.

Lyotard (1986) aptly critiqued Habermasian consensus as a view that is contaminated by the Enlightenment tendency towards metanarratives that leave no room for plurality of views. No doubt, this type of difference can be a pretext for warmongers to provide civilizations with a reason to be at war with each other, but this is more due to political tricks than cultural differences, as a cultural difference per se does not give rise to a war.

The dynamic conception reveals a relationship among civilizations and cultures that appears to be more complicated when compared to the idea of mere conflict that undermines commonalities and the idea of mere cooperation which does not take differences into account. The model of family resemblance is, then, more capable in providing a proper relationship among civilizations than the Platonic model of a pyramid in which a top point encompasses all the points at the base as its equal manifestations, and the model of distinct islands of the particularistic or nominalistic view.

Let us end with quoting a verse from the Qur'an in which both commonality and difference are taken into account:

> O mankind! We created you from a single (pair) of a male and a female, and made you into nations and tribes, that ye may know each other (not that ye may despise each other). Verily the most honored of you in the sight of Allah is (he who is) the most righteous of you. And Allah has full knowledge and is well acquainted (with all things). (Qur'an, 49: 13)

This verse interestingly alludes to the fact that commonality and difference are both necessary conditions for mutual understanding between humans. First, it is mentioned that all humans are of the same origin. Not only is it the case that all humans belong to the same species, but also that they have the same origin. This simple point is easily forgotten by those people who hold that there is a contrastive relationship among human cultures and civilizations. If humans are of the same species and origin, how would it be possible to have no overlaps in their cultures and civilizations? On the other hand, it is alluded in the above-mentioned verse that difference is also needed in understanding each other. Belonging to different nations and tribes, people will have differences that will pave the way for differentiation as another condition for understanding. Without any differentiation, two things cannot be 'two'. Of vital value here is that the differences of colour, race, and so on per se do not provide any superiority to any nation or tribe. If there is a criterion for superiority, it is only a moral character and righteousness.

***

Two ideas concerning the relationship among civilizations and cultures are examined: relativist and universalist views. On the one hand, Huntington, among others, holds that competing civilizations are incommensurable. On the other, there is a universalistic view according to which local aspects that refer to particularities are not tenable, and at stake are the principles that are common among different views. The irony is that most of the universalistic viewpoints have, in fact, local identities one way or another, but their manifest language is general. It is argued that the epistemological basis of relativism is shaky, since its own objectivity and validity is undermined by its claim. On the other hand, the universalist view does not take differences among cultures seriously. The two positions are alike in offering a static view about the human cultures.

Inspired by Wittgenstein's family resemblance, a model is suggested for providing a better understanding of the relation among cultures. This model changes the relation between the general concept of culture and its particular cases as well as the relation among particular cultures themselves. In the vertical relation, according to the suggested model, a particular case possesses some characteristics of the general concept of culture, while another particular case possesses some other characteristics with an overlap between them. In the horizontal relation among the particular cases, substantiation is different and not merely the manifestation. One case substantiates some characteristics and another case substantiates some other characteristics. This leads to a richer difference among particular cases, which in turn leads to a more dynamic relation among cultures in terms of give and take. The trilogy of differences among civilizations and cultures consists of, first, superficial and illusory differences and tensions that can and should be removed by a proper dialogue; second, real differences that are due to incompleteness in one or both sides and are, no doubt, removable and instructive for one or both sides; and third, real differences that are not removable, at least in the short term, and should be tolerated and respected.

BIBLIOGRAPHY

Abu-Rabi, I. M. 2004. *Contemporary Arab Thought: Studies in Post-1967 Arab Intellectual History*. London: Pluto Press.

Al-Allaf, M. 2003. *Mirror of Realization*. St. Louis: IIC Classic Series.

Aristotle. 1996. *The Nicomachean Ethics*, translated by H. Rackham. London: Wordsworth Classics of World Literature.

Botz-Bornstein, T. 2012. 'What Is the Difference between Culture and Civilization? Two Hundred Fifty Years of Confusion'. *Comparative Civilizations Review* 66 (Spring): 10–28.

Carr, W. 2006. 'Education without Theory'. *British Journal of Educational Studies* 54(2): 136–59.

Cook, R. 1998, October. *Speech at the Ismailia Centre in London*. London, UK.

Haack, S. 1993. *Evidence and Inquiry: Towards Reconstruction in Epistemology*. Oxford: Blackwell.

Habermas, J. 1974). *Theory and Practice*, translated by J. Viertel. London: Heinemann.

———. 2010. *An Awareness of What Is Missing: Faith and Reason in a Post-secular Age*, translated by C. Cronin. Cambridge: Polity Press.

Haynes, J. 2013, February 10. *Twenty Years after Huntington's Clash of Civilizations*. Retrieved from http://www.e-ir.info/2013/02/10/twenty-years-after-huntingtons-clash-of-civilisations/.

Hirst, P. and W. Carr. 2005. 'Philosophy and Education: A Symposium'. *Journal of Philosophy and Education* 39(4): 615–32.

Huntington, S. 1996. *The Clash of Civilizations and the Remaking of World Order*. London: Simon and Schuster.

———. 2004. *Who Are We? The Challenges to America's National Identity*. London: Simon and Schuster Inc.

Khatami, S.M. 1998. *Speech at the United Nations' Annual Heads of State Summit*.

Lyotard, F. 1986. *The Postmodern Condition*. Manchester: Manchester University Press.

Milani, M. M. and M. Gibbons. 2001. 'Huntington's Dangerous Paradigm'. *Global Dialogue* 3(1):1–15.

Quran, translated by Abdullah Yusuf Ali.

Raz, J. 1998. 'Multiculturalism'. *Ratio Juris* 11(3): 193–205.

Schweitzer, A. 1949. *Philosophy of Civilization*. New York: Macmillan.

Siegel, H. 1998. 'Knowledge, Truth and Education'. In *Education, Knowledge and Truth: Beyond the Postmodern Impasse*, edited by D. Carr, pp. 19–36. London: Routledge.

Tosi, M. 1998. 'Cultural Diversities and the Origin of the Earliest Civilizations'. In *The Nature of Dialogue of Civilizations: Proceedings*, pp. 19–22. Tehran: Sazmane Madareke Farhangi Enghelabe Islami.

Toynbee, A. 1948. *Civilization on Trial*. New York: Oxford University Press.

———. 1956. *A Historian's Approach to Religion*. London: Oxford University Press.

Twining, W. 2001. *Normative Jurisprudence and Cultural Relativism*. Tilburg-Warwick Lectures: General Jurisprudence.

Tylor, Edward B. 1920. *Primitive Culture: Researches into the Development of Mythology, Philosophy, Religion, Language, Art, and Custom*, 2nd ed, 2 vols. London: John Murray.

Wittgenstein, L. 1953. *Philosophical Investigations*, translated by G. E. Anscombe. Oxford: Blackwell.

Notes on Editor and Contributors

EDITOR

Lutfi Sunar is an associate professor at the Department of Sociology in Istanbul University, Turkey. His major research interests include classical sociological theory, orientalism, modernization, social change, and political economy. He has published various articles in international journals around this field. Among his recent books are *Marx and Weber on Oriental Societies* (2014), *Türkiye'de Toplumsal Değişim* (as editor, 2014), and *Eurocentrism at the Margins: Encounters, Critics and Going Beyond* (as editor, 2016).

CONTRIBUTORS

Mahmut Hakkı Akın is an associate professor in the Department of Sociology at the Necmettin Erbakan University, Turkey. His areas of study are political socialization, political behaviour, and sociology of culture. His recent publications are *Siyasallığın Toplumsal İnşası: Siyasal Toplumsallaşma* (2013), *Toplumsallaşma Sözlüğü* (2011), and *Aliya İzzetbegoviç: Özgürlük Mücadelecisi ve İslam Düşünürü* (with Faruk Karaarslan, 2014).

Syed Farid Alatas is an associate professor at the National University of Singapore. His areas of interest are historical sociology, sociology of social science, sociology of religion, and inter-religious dialogue. Among his recent books are: *Alternative Discourse in Asian Social*

Science: Responses to Eurocenticsm (2006), *Ibn Khaldun* (2013), and *Applying Ibn Khaldun: The Recovery of a Lost Tradition in Sociology* (2014).

Cemil Aydın is an associate professor in the Department of History at the University of North Carolina-Chapel Hills, US. He studies Japanese and Turkish modernization and Asian thought, and teaches courses on international/global history. His recent and important publications are *The Politics of Anti-Westernism in Asia: Visions of World Order in Pan-Islamic and Pan-Asian Thought* (2007) and 'The Question of Orientalism in Pan-Islamic Thought: The Origins, Content and Legacy of Transnational Muslim Identities' (2009).

Murat Çemrek is an associate professor in the Department of International Relations at the Necmettin Erbakan University. His areas of specialization are globalization, multiculturalism, and the politics of Central Asia. His publications include 'How Could the Rights to Education and Representation Challenge National Security?' (2004), 'The Impact of EU Enlargement on the US: The New Transatlantic Relations' (2004), and 'The Family in Turkey: The Battleground of the Modern and the Traditional' (with Dilek Cindoglu, Sule Toktas, and Gizem Zencirci, 2008).

Mustafa Demirci is currently a professor in the Department of History at the Selcuk University, Turkey. He studies on Seljuk History, history of education, medieval history. His recent publications are 'The Role Sabaeans of Harran in Translation of Helenic Science and Philosophy to the Islamic World' (2006), *Selçuklu'dan Osmanlı'ya Bilim, Düşünce ve Sanat* (as editor 2008), *İslam'ın Dört Çağı: Bir Dönemlendirme Denemesi* (2011).

Necmettin Doğan is an associate professor in the Department of Sociology at the Istanbul Commerce University, Turkey. He studies Turkish modernization, classical sociology, and German thought. Some of his publications include *Kültür Sosyolojisi* (as editor with Köksal Alver, 2007); *The Origins of Liberalism and Islamism in the Ottoman Empire (1908–14)* (2007); *Alman Sosyoloji Geleneği: Meta-Teorik Bir Bakış* (2012).

Driss Habti is a researcher at Karelian Institute, University of Eastern Finland. His main research focus is on international highly skilled migration and mobility, Muslims in Europe, cultural diversity and ethnicity, career research, cultural encounters, and contemporary Arab-Islamic thought. Some of his publications include 'The One-way Mobility of North-African Highly Skilled to Nordic Countries: Facts, Constraints and Aspirations' (with Muhammed Sabour, 2010) and 'The Religious Aspects of Diasporic Experience of Muslims in Europe within the Crisis of Multiculturalism' (2014).

Vahdettin Işık is the secretary general in Fatih Sultan Mehmet Waqf University Alliance of Civilizations Institute, Turkey. His area of interests are Turkish politics and thought in the modernization era, philosophical and institutional transformation of education, issues of modern Islamic thought, and Islamism. He is the editor of *Şair ve Düşünür Sezai Karakoç* (2008) and *Vefatının 75. Yılında Mehmed Akif* (2011) and the author of *Kültürel Yabancılaşma: II. Meşrutiyetten Günümüze* (2012).

Yunus Kaya is an associate professor in the Department of Political Science and International Relations at the Istanbul University, Turkey. His areas of specialization are globalization and development, economic sociology, political sociology, social inequality and comparative/historical sociology. His recent publications include 'A Cross-National Analysis of Physical Intimate Partner Violence Against Women' (with Kimberly J. Cook, 2010), 'Globalization and Industrialization in 64 Developing Countries, 1980–2003 (2010), 'Civilizing vs Destructive Globalization? A Multi-Level Analysis of Anti-Immigrant Prejudice' (with Ekrem Karakoc 2012).

Seyed Javad Miri is a professor in the Institute for Humanities and Cultural Studies as well as University of Sharif in Tehran, Iran. He has taught in China, Russia, and Singapore on Islamic thought and contemporary philosophy. He is the editor of *The Islamic Perspective Journal*. His recent publications are *Reflections on the Social Thought of Allama M. T. Jafari* (2010), *Alternative Sociology: Probing into the Sociological Thought of Allama M. T. Jafari* (2012), and *East and West: Allama Jafari on Bertnard Russell* (with Dustin Byrd 2013).

Khosrow Bagheri Noaparast is a professor of philosophy of education at the University of Tehran, Iran. He has made significant contributions to philosophy of education, religion, and personal construct psychology. His interests also include action theory, deconstruction, hermeneutics, and Islamic philosophy of education. Some of his recent works include *The Idea of a Religious Social Science* (2009), 'Deconstructive Religious Education' (with Khosravi, Zohreh 2011), and 'Al-Attas Revisited on the Islamic Understanding of Education' (2012).

Anthony Pagden is a distinguished professor in the Departments of Political Science and History at the University of California, Los Angeles. His main area of research has been the prolonged contact of Europe with the non-European world. He has also written on the history of law, anthropology, and of modern Spanish America, and about the history of ideas. He has published several books, which have been translated into several European and Asian languages. His most recent works include *Worlds at War: The 2,500-Year Struggle between East and West* (2009) and *The Enlightenment—And Why It Still Matters* (2013).

Halil Ibrahim Yenigun is a fellow of Europe in the Middle East—the Middle East in Europe (EUME) at the Forum Transregionale Studien, Berlin. His research focuses on Muslim political thought, Islamism, peace activism, and Turkish democracy. Some of his recent publications include 'The Political and Theological Boundaries of Islamist Moderation after the Arab Spring' (2016) and 'Siyaset Teorisinde Yeni Ontolojik ve Teolojik Tahayyüller ve Demokrasi' (2013).

Index

Davutoglu, Ahmed 79, 81, 99, 105,
110–11, 188, 381–2
Dayton Agreement 265
de Tocqueville, Alexis 200, 221n17
decolonization 144, 154–5, 162, 166,
298
democracy 71, 186, 195, 196, 201,
228, 232, 287, 290, 295, 317, 352,
360, 394
democratic ideas 20, 360
democratic institutions 220
democratization 111
dependency 110, 214, 293, 341, 343,
346, 353
despot 71, 72
despotic regimes 287
despotic societies 69
despotism 9, 10, 11, 59, 60, 61, 62,
67, 68, 71, 72, 181, 200, 201, 217,
331, 336
determinism 29, 153, 258, 276
deterritorialization 358, 365n1
developing countries 356
developing economies 111,
developing societies 345
developing world 342, 343, 344, 360
development projects 345
development theories 56
dialectic materialism 74
dialogue 96, 149, 150, 197, 200, 202,
216, 218–19, 226, 230, 239, 259,
290, 310, 317, 371, 396, 404–6,
408
dichotomies 200, 236, 249, 325–6
divine law 8
division of labour 54–5
Dostoevsky, Fyodor 2, 333–5
dualism 269, 273–5, 281
Durkheim, Emile 74, 326, 336, 252

Eastern Asia 104

Eastern bloc 5
Eastern civilization(s) 94, 149, 155,
158
Eastern Europe 106
Eastern identity(ies) 152, 162,
164n15
Eastern people 158
Eastern societies 62, 67, 70, 84, 342
Eastern world 71
Easterners 141, 204–5, 222n18
Eastern–Islamic civilization 160
ecclesiastic eras 173
eclecticism 19, 21, 290, 305
economic: dependency 346;
development 288; imperialism
342; liberalization 360; rationality
341; recession 102, 104;
structure(s) 97, 100, 109, 183,
305, 312; system(s) 183, 190, 244,
247, 249, 340, 256, 328, 330, 340
Egypt 67, 103, 107, 109, 120, 147,
150, 157, 210, 221–2n18, 279,
287, 290, 297, 381, 395
Elias, Norbert 1, 118, 172, 195
el-Messiri, Abdel-Wahab 287
emancipation 233, 307, 312, 313
emancipatory revolution 207
empires 71, 83, 88, 91–2, 94, 102–7,
112, 148–9, 156, 187
Encyclopédie 50
enlightened despotism 181
enlightened thinkers 228
Enlightenment: 3, 7–8, 12, 16, 21,
31–2, 35, 47–51, 62, 65, 74, 81,
156, 173, 199, 215–16, 255, 263,
269, 270, 272, 326, 407; concepts
of 300, ideas of 333–4, 383;
ideals of 222n24, intellectuals
of 64; period of 11, 56–7, 72,
74; philosophy of 83; political
thought of 78; secularism of 400;

Ibn Khaldun 12, 13, 57, 105, 117,
119–40, 198, 204, 213, 220, 313,
326–7
Ibn Rushd 100–1
Imam Mawardi 121, 141
imperial expansion 148, 162. *See*
European imperial expansion
imperial liberalism 77
imperial world 152, 157
imperialism 1, 11–12, 14, 91, 107–9,
118, 145–7, 150, 152–3, 158,
161, 172, 185, 190, 205–6, 214,
222n20, 230, 242, 286, 297, 310,
342, 355, 378
imperialist discourse 180
imperialist expansion 14
imperialist legacy 159
imperialist thought 160
imperialist West 156
imperialist world 158
India 14, 17, 48, 67, 69, 70–1, 129,
146, 149, 151, 153, 157, 160, 172,
222n20, 342
Indian civilizations 215
Indian Muslims 160
Indian religions 57
Indians 205, 372
Indus Basin 100
industrial civilization 222
Industrial Revolution 81, 263, 305
industrial society 41, 55
intellectualization 331
inter-civilizational dialogue 200, 226,
230, 239, 259
inter-civilizational perspective 227,
234
inter-civilizational relations 20
interdependence 40, 353
inter-societal relations 20
intra-civilizational violence 212
intra-cultural tensions 404

Iqbal, Muhammad 6, 16, 18, 259,
264, 339
Iran, 93, 96, 100, 103, 107, 110, 122,
129, 155, 186, 226–8, 230–3, 241,
244, 250, 255, 266, 279, 336, 377,
382, 396; economic system of
249; traditional society of 231;
Muslims of 150; nationalism of
251; regime of 228; culture of 96;
intellectuals of 230, 231–2
Iranian thinkers 230
Iranians 85, 88, 155, 232
Iraq 100, 129, 382, 384
Islam 1, 10, 16–18, 22n5, 70, 80,
83–112, 122, 133, 150–3, 174–8,
180, 183–7, 189–91, 195–6, 202,
204, 206–9, 212, 215, 221n17,
226–8, 231–2, 234, 237, 239–40,
246–51, 254, 256–7, 264-6, 269,
273, 279–81, 283, 286–7, 289,
292, 294, 296, 300, 302–3, 306,
308, 310, 314–16, 318n1, 337,
358, 377, 382, 384–5, 395–6,
398–9, 403–6
Islamic: activism 158; age 98, 103,
104; art 187; authenticity 209,
228–9, 260, 310; awareness
299; civilization(s) 4, 6, 10–11,
15–17, 22, 79–81, 86, 89, 91–2,
94, 96, 102, 105–6, 112, 149,
151, 160, 172–3, 181–5, 188,
191, 196–8, 203–4, 206, 211–14,
218–19, 221n17, 266, 279–80,
283, 292–3, 299–301, 350, 358,
377, 379, 384, 390, 392, 399, 403;
community(ies) 110, 135, 318n1;
concepts 203; consciousness 311;
critique 338; cultural area 99;
culture 18, 86, 97, 104, 279–80,
282–3, 298, 300, 304, 313–15,
394, 398–9, 403–4; democracy